Students in network-based classrooms converse in writing through the use of communications software on local-area computer networks. Through the electronic medium they are immersed in a writing community – one that supports new forms of collaboration, authentic purposes for writing, writing across the curriculum, and new social relations in the classroom. The potential for collaborative and participatory learning in these classrooms is enormous.

This book examines an important type of network-based classroom known as ENFI (Electronic Networks For Interaction). Teachers have set up ENFI or similar classrooms in elementary and secondary schools and at more than 100 colleges and universities. In these settings, teaching and learning have been dramatically transformed, but the new technology has brought with it difficulties and surprises. The process of creating such a classroom raises important questions about the meaning and the realities of educational change.

Network-based classrooms

Network-based classrooms
Promises and realities

Edited by

BERTRAM C. BRUCE
University of Illinois at Urbana-Champaign

JOY KREEFT PEYTON
Center for Applied Linguistics, Washington, DC

TRENT BATSON
Gallaudet University, Washington, DC

CAMBRIDGE
UNIVERSITY PRESS

Published by the Press Syndicate of the University of Cambridge
The Pitt Building, Trumpington Street, Cambridge CB2 1RP
40 West 20th Street, New York, NY 10011-4211, USA
10 Stamford Road, Oakleigh, Victoria 3166, Australia

First published 1993

Printed in the United States of America

Library of Congress Cataloging-in-Publication Data
Bruce, Bertram C.
Network-based classrooms : promises and realities / Bertram Bruce,
Joy Kreeft Peyton, Trent Batson.
p.   cm.
Includes bibliographical references.
ISBN 0-521-41636-1 (hc)
1. English language – Composition and exercises – Study and
teaching – Computer-assisted instruction.   2. English language –
Rhetoric – Computer-assisted instruction.   3. English language –
Study and teaching – Computer-assisted instruction.   I. Peyton, Joy
Kreeft.   II. Batson, Trent W.   III. Title.
LB1576.7.B79   1993
808'.042'0285–dc20   92-31680
                                                              CIP

A catalog record for this book is available from the British Library

ISBN 0-521-41636-1 hardback
ISBN 0-521-45702-5 paperback

Contents

Contributors

David Bartholomae
English Department
University of Pittsburgh
Pittsburgh, PA

Trent Batson
Gallaudet University
Washington, DC

Bertram Bruce
College of Education
University of Illinois at Urbana-
  Champaign
Champaign, IL

Cynthia Cochran
English Department
Carnegie Mellon University
Pittsburgh, PA

Mary Fowles
Educational Testing Service
Princeton, NJ

Terilyn Gillespie
English Department
Carnegie Mellon University
Pittsburgh, PA

Thomas Hajduk
English Department
Carnegie Mellon University
Pittsburgh, PA

Karen Hartman
English Department
Carnegie Mellon University
Pittsburgh, PA

Fred Kemp
English Department
Texas Tech University
Lubbock, TX

Marshall Kremers
English Department
New York Institute of Technology
Old Westbury, NY

J. Douglas Miller
English Department
Gallaudet University
Washington, DC

Christine M. Neuwirth
English Department
Carnegie Mellon University
Pittsburgh, PA

Michael Palmquist
English Department
Colorado State University
Fort Collins, CO

Joy Kreeft Peyton
Center for Applied Linguistics
Washington, DC

Thomas Reynolds
General College
University of Minnesota
Minneapolis, MN

Geoffrey Sirc
General College
University of Minnesota
Minneapolis, MN

Michael Spitzer
School of Arts and Sciences
SUNY Institute of Technology at Utica/
  Rome
Utica, NY

Diane Thompson
Northern Virginia Community College
Woodbridge, VA

Acknowledgments

Emerging collaborative technologies make palpable the idea that knowledge is socially constructed. This is evident in the collaborative technique called ENFI (Electronic Networks for Interaction) in which everyone "talks" at once. We have become accustomed to classrooms where everyone is generating messages on their keyboards and sharing them with the group. The computer network then transforms this cacophony of concurrent multivocality into a coherent conversation. This experience leads away from the traditional notion of identifying one name – or even three – with the work of many and toward a new tradition of acknowledging group process. In the ENFI lab, the old claim that teachers learn as much from the students as the students learn from them ceases to be an empty platitude.

Therefore, we want to acknowledge first the many teachers and students who have helped us understand their interpretations and adaptations of ENFI. In addition to the ENFI teachers writing in this book, Laurie George, Tony DiMatteo, R. Toby Widdicombe, Susan Suchman, and Sylvia Broffman at NYIT; Harry Markowicz and Steve Lombardo at Gallaudet; Cathy Simpson at NVCC; Maggie McCaffrey and Diane Langston at CMU; Terry Collins at Minnesota; and Wayne Butler and Paul Taylor at the University of Texas talked to us for long hours, made conference presentations, and wrote papers, all of which contributed to our understanding of ENFI. Terry Collins was also a co–principal investigator for the ENFI project.

The members of the ENFI Advisory Board supported and challenged the ENFI developments for 3 years, and gave helpful feedback to our early conceptions of the book: Sarah Freedman, Nancy Frishberg, Dixie Goswami, John R. Hayes, Shirley Brice Heath, Sarah Michaels, Dawn Rodrigues, and Helen Schwartz. Sarah Michaels chaired the meetings and contributed to our work way beyond the call of duty.

Steve Ehrmann, the project officer at the Annenberg/Corporation for Public Broadcasting (CPB) Project, responded enthusiastically to the vision for ENFI and helped shape it. Later, Scott Roberts joined him to continue as project officer until the end of the ENFI Project. With Rebecca Oxford (also at Annenberg/CPB during the time of our project) and Peter Dirr, they

ix

challenged the initial conceptions of the research and pushed us to try to pull together the many threads.

John Scully, Nancy Creighton, and Kavita Pipalia at Gallaudet, Valerie Smith at Bolt Beranek and Newman, and Myrna Craig at the University of Illinois helped to see that this book finally took publishable form. Lizanne DeStefano, Colleen Gilrane, Genell Harris, Julia Hough, Andee Rubin, and an anonymous reviewer made valuable comments and suggestions on the manuscript. Colleen Gilrane gave us special help by preparing the index.

Portions of Chapters 1 and 2 have been adapted from B. C. Bruce and A. D. Rubin (1993), *Electronic Quills: A situated evaluation of using computers for writing in classrooms,* Hillsdale, NJ: Lawrence Erlbaum Associates. Reprinted by permission of the publisher. Andee Rubin deserves special thanks for her contributions to developing the theory of situated evaluation. Chapter 3 was adapted from B. Bruce and J. K. Peyton (1990), "A new writing environment and an old culture: A situated evaluation of computer networking to teach writing," *Interactive Learning Environments,* *1,* 171–191. Reprinted with the permission of Ablex Publishing Corporation.

As is probably clear throughout the book, the ENFI Project has sparked our imaginations, driven us crazy, and pushed us to think harder about things we thought we knew. The best part of it all has been the friendships we've formed with all of these people, which extend far beyond the project and these pages.

Introduction

Network-based classrooms are appearing for all age and grade levels of students, for all subject areas, and in all sorts of educational institutions. They hold the promise of transforming the traditional classroom by engaging students in more direct participation in their own learning. Their appearance raises exciting possibilities for education, but also important questions about how changes in education occur.

This book discusses an important class of network-based classrooms, those in which students use communications software on computer networks to converse in writing. The book explores how new technologies and new pedagogies transform and are transformed by existing institutions.

Electronic networks for interaction

We focus on an approach known as ENFI (Electronic Networks For Interaction), which was developed in 1985 at Gallaudet University, a well-known school for the deaf in Washington, DC. Trent Batson and Joy Kreeft Peyton, two of the editors of this book, were also developers of this approach to network-based classrooms.

Students at Gallaudet used communications software on a local-area computer network to converse in writing. Through the electronic medium they improved their abilities to write, read, and engage in collaborative problem solving. Since the development at Gallaudet, ENFI and similar approaches have spread to basic writing classes for hearing students and deaf students, classes for English as a second language, and advanced rhetoric classes, first through a small consortium of colleges and universities,* and later to at least 100 other institutions. Precollege versions are also in use.

ENFI, like hypertext, is a concept, not a particular software program. Several different types of software were used for ENFI work at the various consortium sites. The original software used at Gallaudet was the CB Utility,

---

* The consortium included Gallaudet University, Carnegie Mellon University, University of Minnesota, New York Institute of Technology, and Northern Virginia Community College. It was funded in part by the Annenberg/CPB Project.

1

which was bundled with a local-area network called 10-Net, then sold by Fox, now by DCA. Later, Realtime Learning Systems of Washington, DC, developed Realtime Writer (RTW) to support ENFI. Shortly after RTW appeared, the Daedalus Group of Austin, Texas, started marketing Interchange as part of the Daedalus Instructional System to support ENFI-like activities in college classrooms. On many campuses, people don't talk about ENFI, but about "interchange," the lower case recognizing its arrival as a generic descriptor. At about the same time, Carnegie Mellon University (CMU) developed CECE Talk, a program that works within CMU's Andrew system. Contributors to this book all describe their ENFI experiences, but variously refer to RTW, Interchange, or CECE Talk.

Network-based classrooms at Gallaudet

With RTW, used at Gallaudet and three other sites, students and the teacher each sit at computer terminals and compose messages in a private window at the bottom of their computer screens. When they press a key, their message is immediately transmitted to all of the screens in the class. As users type and send messages, their messages scroll up the screen in a continuous dialogue tagged with the name of the sender (or whatever name the sender logged on with), as in the script of a play. While individuals are composing, the messages of the other class members continue to scroll visibly up the screen. Participants can scroll back to read previous messages they might have missed, but new messages continue to be received at the same time.

The computer stores the entire discussion, which can be reviewed at any point during the class session or printed out in its entirety at the end. Discussions occur on different network channels, each of which can include from two participants to the entire class. Using a video switch the teacher can at any time view the writing of an individual student or of a group of students on a channel, or can display the writing of one student to the entire class.

Figure I–1 shows a sample student screen, with a student's privately visible message in the bottom window (" 'The Dead' was one of the deadest stories I have ever read.") and publicly visible teacher and student messages in the upper window.

This particular use of a local-area computer network was developed at Gallaudet to give deaf students opportunities to use written English in ways they would otherwise not have. The problems that deaf people have reading and writing in English are well documented (e.g., see Quigley & Paul, 1984), and at least part of this difficulty can be attributed to lack of opportunities to interact in English (Charrow, 1981). With a computer network and software that allows for interactive writing, deaf students can use written English not simply to complete grammar exercises or to produce compositions to be evaluated, but also to spontaneously communicate ideas that are meaningful

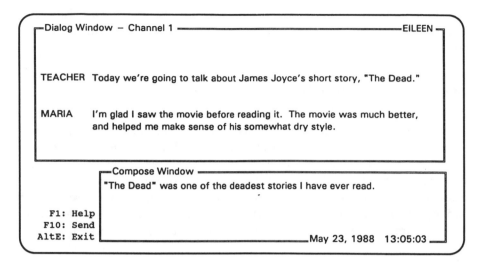

Figure I-1. ENFI computer screen at Gallaudet (from Bruce & Peyton, 1990)

to them with a community of other writers who are interested not in evaluating, but rather in understanding what they are saying. Written English can be used to joke and play with language, to discuss literature or serious social issues, to brainstorm ideas or collaboratively produce a draft for a paper, and to critique writing in progress. In short, written English can be used in many of the ways that oral English is used by hearing people, as well as for extended text production and critique. When a competent English user (such as the teacher) is writing on the network as well, correct forms and structures can be modeled immediately, in the context of genuine communication (see Peyton & Batson, 1986, for discussion).

As information about the Gallaudet project was disseminated, other colleges and universities became interested in the potential of real-time interactive writing for hearing students. A consortium of five colleges and universities was formed to implement and study network-based classrooms for both deaf and hearing students. As schools across the country set up these classrooms, the original technology assumed new forms. New software configurations were developed within the consortium; distance networking as well as local was implemented at one of the sites; and parallel efforts (such as Daedalus Interchange at the University of Texas at Austin) were begun.

A vision – New forms of writing in the classroom

Developers of ENFI clearly expressed their vision for how a "total immersion method" of teaching writing to college students (Batson, 1987, p. 4) would transform and revolutionize the traditional writing classroom. This vision and its history are elaborated in Chapter 5. We discuss five major threads of the vision here.

New social dimensions in the classroom

An important premise of the original ENFI Project was that writing on a computer network would blur social distinctions in the classroom. This would result in "entirely new pedagogical dynamics" (Batson, 1988a, p. 32) and changing roles for both teachers and students. The role of the teacher would shift from lecturer and director of discussion to collaborator in writing, and student participation would be more equally distributed. In short, it was hoped and hypothesized that traditional classroom interaction patterns would be radically altered when classes began to communicate on a network, in writing.

Writing for authentic purposes

Whereas students previously wrote to a single audience – the teacher – now they would participate in a full-fledged writing community that included their peers. Whereas before their sole purpose in writing was to be evaluated, it would now include all the purposes of speech: "to inform and persuade, to entertain and enlighten, to develop social relationships, to explain experience (as much to ourselves as to others), and to create and develop ideas" (Batson, 1988a, p. 15). All communication would take place in writing – greetings and closings, procedural details, and requests for elaboration or clarification, as well as formal lessons and composition-related activities. Students would make and negotiate meanings through writing, and their classroom person-alities and roles would be established in writing. Writing would therefore come alive for students; they would use writing for their own purposes and see it as an important means of lively communication, not simply as an eval-uated performance for others (Peyton & Batson, 1986). In this context, writing would become less formal and more conversational, and students would move easily in writing from one type of communication to another. Conversation and composed text would merge (Langston & Batson, 1990).

Immersion in a writing community

Another goal was to immerse students in writing – their own, the teacher's, and other students'; the classroom would become a writing community. It was hoped that this immersion in writing would change the nature of the writing class in a number of ways. Students would have many more oppor-tunities to write than they do in other types of classes. Writing would be done for a present audience, and students would receive immediate feedback on their ideas. The writing process would be made visible to students; they would see their own writing mingled with that of the other students, the teacher could demonstrate various aspects of the writing process for students, and students and teachers could watch and comment on each others' writing while it was being produced. Teachers would encourage freedom and variety in writing. As in speaking, students would "adopt different accents, throw in slang, include personal elements, think aloud, talk ... through tasks, and work out new ways of saying things" (Langston & Batson, 1990, pp. 13–14).

Collaboration in writing

The creation of a writing community can lead to new approaches to writing, especially increased collaboration in the act of writing:

Most collaborative learning classes stop short of actual group writing. They may think together and plan together and then, after they write individually, critique their writing together, but they probably won't write together. They don't observe each other's writing process. ENFI makes this last step possible. (Batson, 1987, p. 26)

Writing across the curriculum

Although ENFI was first implemented in English classes, it was hoped that writing would be used to accomplish a range of purposes in other subject areas like mathematics, science, and history. Thus the vision included that ENFI would promote writing across the curriculum. Of the five threads, this was the one least realized in practice; the ENFI sites have so far involved only English classrooms.

Realizations of the vision

The five threads of the ENFI vision (new social dimensions in the classroom, writing for authentic purposes, immersion in a writing community, collaboration in writing, writing across the curriculum) point to a powerful context for writing, one that reflects much of current theory about writing pedagogy and development. A question naturally arises: To what extent were these visions for ENFI realized in the classrooms? In addressing this question, we came to see how the idealized version of ENFI was realized in different ways in different settings. It soon became clear that to understand ENFI it was necessary to look in detail at the writing practices within the different classroom discourse communities. Moreover, we needed a framework for analyzing these practices and the ways ENFI, as an innovation for change, was incorporated into them.

The framework we adopted is situated evaluation, a detailed examination of the different ways the ENFI vision was re-created through use. Through stories of individual classrooms we see that adopting an innovation is a creative process involving critical analysis of the institutional context, student needs, and pedagogical goals. This process of re-creation of innovations is not only unavoidable, but a vital part of the process of educational change. Although the book focuses on one educational innovation, we believe that the processes, stories, and general patterns we report are applicable to educational innovations in general, and that they have important implications for program evaluators, teacher educators, curriculum developers, and teachers.

In Part I we present a view of innovation and change flexible enough to do justice to the wide varieties of realizations of ENFI. We discuss there general themes and issues of the ENFI experiences. In Part II we present the ENFI theory and technology, or the idealization. We also explore specific stories of how network-based classrooms developed in different settings. Part III complements the situated evaluation with summative analyses of students' writing. The analyses of the writing samples serve to characterize more fully the ENFI realizations. At the same time, the site-based reports in Part II provide a basis for interpreting the analyses of writing samples in Part III.

Part I

Studying the re-creation of innovations

As we began to examine the writing practices associated with ENFI use in diverse settings, a key definitional problem arose: What was ENFI? The variety of practices we observed suggested that the concept was too broad to be viewed as a single innovation, yet not broad enough to be equated with the educational use of electronic networks in general.

One way to resolve the definitional problem was to return to the ENFI source documents, such as the Annenberg/CPB (Corporation for Public Broadcasting) Proposal and various articles about ENFI, or to the ENFI developers themselves to articulate a criterial definition. Following this path we would then identify archetypical ENFI practices to focus on, attaching labels such as *semi-ENFI, part ENFI, similar to ENFI,* or *non-ENFI* to other practices that nevertheless used the ENFI name.

The difficulty with this approach was that from the beginning, people doing ENFI had valued experimentation and diversity in teaching approaches. There seemed to be no precise definition of ENFI in terms of technological tools and little value attached to promoting or fixing on a single piece of software or hardware. Nor was there a precise set of pedagogical goals and activities beyond the threads we outlined in the Introduction. Thus, devising some ex post facto criterial definition was arbitrary and not reflective of actual ENFI practice. Moreover, it would serve only to exclude some of the ongoing ENFI activities that were valued highly by the ENFI community.

An alternative approach was to view ENFI quite broadly, such as "using electronic networks to enhance education." The difficulty with this approach was immediately apparent: The range of educational uses of electronic networks was much broader than that exhibited within the ENFI community. People within the community had a shared sense of "ENFI" that had a strong shape, if not sharp boundaries.

That shared sense of purpose and community posed a quandary. Newcomers to the ENFI community, such as the outside evaluators Bruce, Bartholomae, and Fowles, and even those within the community who might attempt to take an outsider perspective, such as Peyton and Batson, saw a community of teachers and researchers who viewed themselves as implementing

ENFI in the classroom, doing ENFI research, and participating in the ENFI community. Yet defining ENFI independent of the community seemed problematic.

We are accustomed to thinking of innovations, particularly those built on new information technologies, as having rather solid and precise definitions or specifications. But in this case, the meaning of ENFI seemed not only to be fluid, but to be defined more by a community of practice than by some specific tools or tenets. We were thus in the position that Michelle Rosaldo describes in her book, *Knowledge and Passion* (1980). She finds that the Ilongot people in the Philippines use the term *liget* to describe activities ranging from gardening to killing other people in war. How can this one term have such a range of meanings, without losing all meaning for those in the community? Rosaldo realizes that no lexicon will provide the answer. It is only by immersing herself in the set of practices associated with the use of *liget* that she can begin to uncover its meaning for the Ilongot.

As we studied the set of practices associated with the use of ENFI, we came to see that the community-of-practice definition of meaning for the innovation resolved the quandary of defining ENFI. Moreover, we began to see that this situation was not unique, but rather exemplifies a general pattern. Comparisons to other innovations (e.g., Quill, as reported in Bruce & Rubin, 1993; Rubin & Bruce, 1990) show that practice-based conceptions of innovations are needed.

Part I develops the practice-based conception of innovations. In Chapter 1 we explore different notions of innovation and social change, progressing toward a model that integrates ideas about communities of practice with the specifics of the technologies employed. In Chapter 2 we discuss the implications of this view of innovation for evaluation and, in particular, the various approaches we took to the evaluation of ENFI. We present *situated evaluation* as a type of evaluation that takes into account the varieties of ways that innovations are realized in practice. In Chapter 3 we examine multiple realizations of the ENFI vision and in Chapter 4 the common threads among these realizations.

1   Innovation and Social Change

Bertram C. Bruce

When educators attempt to implement an innovation, they typically face a complex challenge of meshing new ideas with well-established beliefs and practices. As a result, they often realize the innovation in a way that reflects situation-specific compromises between the old and the new ways of doing things (Bruce & Peyton, 1990; Bruce & Rubin, 1993; Rubin & Bruce, 1990). A major goal of this book is to explore this process of realizing innovations and to consider the implications for models of educational change, for the evaluation of innovations (Cronbach, 1982), for the role of teachers in implementing innovations (Hord, Rutherford, Huling-Austin, & Hall, 1987), and even for the basic notion of what an innovation is.

The linking of new technologies to a vision of transformed pedagogy is a distinguishing feature in many proposed innovations in education. It is rare that the developer of an innovation would adopt the goal of simply facilitating current practices with a new technology. The reification of the developers' pedagogical theories is viewed as vital to achieving their pedagogical goals, and the argument is made that the expense of adopting new methods and tools is justified by the major improvements that will occur. Conversely, proposals to transform teaching practices often incorporate new technologies, which might include new media, computers, curricula, kits of manipulatives, or step-by-step procedures for teaching or learning.

Thus, new technologies are commonly linked to visions of educational change. Sometimes the new technology is viewed as sufficient unto itself to effect the desired changes. In that case, we succumb to technocentrism (Papert, 1987), the tendency to conceive technology independent of its contexts of use. With this mindset, we assume that if only teachers and students had access to the power of the new technology, all aspects of the wonderful vision would be realized.

Studies of the process of educational change (e.g., Fullon, 1982) show that access to new information, procedures, or tools alone rarely leads to change. One reason is that the *same technology* has different meanings in different settings. The already functioning social system and traditional practices in which the technology is placed shape the ways the technology is understood

9

and used. In fact, those who do adopt innovations are typically faced with a challenging task of resolving conflicts between old practices that derive from powerful situational constraints and imperatives of the new technology. As these conflicts are resolved by different people in different settings, the original technology takes on multiple forms; the *it* becomes *them*.

In this book we examine the process by which ENFI was realized in many classrooms. But the general form of the process recurs for the introduction of any innovation, whatever the domain. The parameters, constraints, and issues related to change are in large part the same across settings; accordingly, the examples in this chapter come from a variety of fields. Many of the examples pertain to innovations that incorporate new technologies, but the essential points apply to all innovations, even those built around older technologies such as books, paper and pencil, or the blackboard.

We view an innovation as the manifestation of a set of beliefs and values about change. Thus when we refer to the innovation, we include not only pieces of software or hardware, but also all of those documents and practices that define and support its intended uses. At a minimum these include user's guides, documented examples of previous use, training for users, and texts describing the innovation. But in the final analysis, we see an innovation as a process – the meeting ground of various interests and practices. What we need to investigate is the meaning of this broader sense of the innovation for the social systems in which the innovation is used.

This view raises some broad questions: Under what circumstances will a social system change, resist change, or change in unexpected ways? What is the role of innovations in producing change? What institutional factors promote or inhibit change? How can we best analyze the process of change when it does occur? What are the implications of these issues for the evaluation of innovations?

Discourses on social change

Discourse is a useful construct for describing differing approaches to the study of innovation and social change. For the purposes here, we conceive a *discourse* as a socially, culturally, and historically defined set of social relations, manifested in large part, though not exclusively, through language use (Gee, 1990).

We begin this chapter by looking at two conflicting discourses on innovation and social change. One is *innovation focused;* it talks of changes in social systems brought about by an innovation. Within this discourse, these changes are seen as significant and positive. The second discourse is *social system focused;* it emphasizes underlying social, cultural, economic, or political processes that undermine innovations, resulting in negative outcomes or, more often, precluding any change at all.

For example, Lepper and Gurtner (1989) describe both the "dream" and the "nightmare" visions of the use of computers in education. The dream is characterized by accounts of how using computers will lead to restructuring of classrooms, student control of learning, greater engagement, more challenging activities, development of thinking skills, and deeper understanding of subject matter. The nightmare sees few positive changes as it looks at existing social practices, power relationships, surrounding contexts, conflicting goals, and cultural values. It usually concludes that technological factors are of little consequence. Similarly, Hawisher and Selfe (1990) contrast the "rhetoric" and the "realities" of technology.

The differences between the two discourses are thus great and difficult to reconcile. We argue that neither discourse alone accounts for important aspects of technological and social change; rather, an integrated model is needed. From this integrated perspective we discuss six major ways that change occurs when innovations are introduced into social systems.

Innovation-focused discourse

The two discourses focus on different issues; they also criticize each other for not sharing that focus. From an innovation focus, therefore, we read that social scientists give little heed to the workings of technological innovations. Writing about change in an article introducing a special issue of *Scientific American* on the mechanization of work, Ginzberg (1982) adopts an innovation focus. He sees economics as impoverished by its lack of acknowledgment of the importance of technology: "Most economists – free market, Marxist, or otherwise – have failed to give technology its due" (p. 69). Classical theories assume static technologies as they explicate "with ever greater subtlety how demand, supply, and price interact in competitive markets to establish or reestablish equilibrium" (p. 69).

Similarly, within anthropology Bernard and Pelto (1987) see other anthropologists as neglectful of the importance of technological innovation:

The study of technological innovation and its effects on social and cultural systems remains one of the most neglected areas in anthropological research. Very few anthropological studies have concentrated on the analysis of particular technological innovations or changes, even though field workers are constantly reminded, in the course of research, of the penetrations of roads, dams, air travel facilities, new types of vehicles, medical systems, new cultivation techniques, and other technical modifications into previously "untouched" areas. (p. 1)

Innovation-focused discourse tends in practice to highlight improvement in conditions – for work, communication, transportation, learning, health, or whatever area the innovation addresses. These improvements are generally seen as entailing significant change and are often unabashedly described as "revolutions." Not surprisingly, innovation-focused discourse tends to include mostly references to the future. When it does refer to the past, it points to long-term trends, rather than to underlying forces that resist change. Because the changes are positively valued, the tone is generally optimistic. For example, as Ginzberg (1982) says,

The easing of human labor by technology, a process that began in prehistory, is entering a new stage. The acceleration in the pace of technological innovation inaugurated by the Industrial Revolution has until recently resulted mainly in the displacement of human muscle power from the tasks of production. The current revolution in computer technology is causing an equally momentous social change: the expansion of information gathering and information processing as computers extend the reach of the human brain. (p. 67)

Innovation-focused discourse assumes not only that change is possible and that it does occur, but that the goal of discussion is to articulate the path to that change. Thus its stance is essentially that of the engineer. Goals are identified and contrasted with existing practices. Technology is described in terms of what it *can* do in achieving these goals, and only incidentally in terms of what it is actually used for. There are frequent references to efficiency, productivity, and new ways of thinking. More often than not, positive examples are highlighted. Problems are presented as remaining obstacles to overcome, not as reasons for ultimate failure. The tone is often visionary, rejecting detailed analyses of current practice as being too conservative.[1]

An extreme innovation focus assumes that the innovation directly changes social practices. The social system is seen as an arena in which the innovation does its work. Variations in use are attributed to improper implementation. This assumption underlies the dominant theories of evaluation today and shapes many analyses of social change, as well as the design of innovations. Papert (1987) relates this extreme innovation focus on the technological object to a child's early focus on the self:

Egocentrism for Piaget does not, of course, mean "selfishness" – it means that the child has difficulty understanding anything independently of the self. Technocentrism refers to the tendency to give a similar centrality to a technical object – for example computers or Logo. This tendency shows up in questions like "What is THE effect of THE computer on cognitive development?" or "Does Logo work?" (p. 23)

Social system–focused discourse

The discourse focused on social relations and organizations has a complementary complaint. It sees discussions of technologies as too often isolated

---

[1] Staudenmaier (1985) provides an in-depth discussion of these issues in a history of the first twenty years of the journal *Technology and Culture*. There is a gradual move from innovation-focused discourse toward more "contextual" discourse that considers the settings in which technologies are used.

from an understanding of the settings in which the technologies are used. For instance, in a discussion of the role of technologies in education, Michael Apple argues that too much attention is paid to technical issues and too little to the political context in which technologies are employed. The current political context highlights issues such as accountability, management, and control. From the perspective of social system–focused discourse, technical concerns are seen as superficial, political concerns as central: "At the very core of the debate, are the ideological and ethical issues concerning what schools should be about and whose interests they should serve" (Apple, 1986, p. 153). Focusing on the technical aspects of the innovation is seen as failing to address crucial ideological and ethical issues.

In contrast to the generally optimistic tone of innovation-focused discourse, system-focused discourse tends in practice to be pessimistic; it typically finds little real improvement, and what change there is is incremental and slow. Rather than revolution, it finds reemergence or reinforcement of established patterns that are often negatively valued. For example, writing about the minimal positive effect that mechanization has had on women's work, Scott (1982) said,

In certain essential respects, however, the work that women do has changed little since before the Industrial Revolution. . . . A decade of historical investigation has led to a major revision of the notion that technology is inherently revolutionary, at least as the notion applies to women. The available evidence suggests that on the contrary mechanization has served to reinforce the traditional position of women both in the labor market and in the home. (p. 167)

System-focused discourse thus has a stance complementary to the engineering stance of innovation-focused discourse. It takes on the role of the critic. It places little faith in visionary goals, or in the methods for reaching those goals. Instead of looking to the future by articulating a plan for change, system-focused discourse looks at actual use and asks whether anything has changed. It is less concerned with what the technologies could in principle do and more with what they are actually used for in ordinary contexts. Problems are seen not as obstacles to overcome, but as indicators of underlying systemic processes that the innovators have not even addressed. It is skeptical of claims about the impact of innovations and assumes that, absent strong evidence to the contrary, everything is likely to continue to be "the same."

Although social system–focused discourse may not attend to the specifics of a given technology, it is noteworthy that it tends to use the plural form, *technologies,* whereas innovation-focused discourse often refers to *technology* in general. The multiple forms and meanings of technologies are thereby emphasized and subjected to criticism, rather than accepted as a monolithic force (Bijker, Hughes, & Pinch, 1987; Staudenmaier, 1985).

Integrating analyses of change

Conflicting discourses arise naturally when the issues are complex and diverse, militating against a single, coherent perspective. More importantly, different agendas invoke different ways of talking about social change. The designer of an innovation naturally focuses on technical details, just as the social critic focuses on social processes. But the maintenance of separate and parallel perspectives hampers our ability to understand social change and to design better innovations.

Suchman (1988) describes the two discourses as "separate spheres":

By and large, we are taught to view the political and the technological as separate spheres, the former having to do with values, ideology, power, and the like, the latter having to do with physical artifacts exempt from such vagaries of social life. (p. 174)

The maintenance of these separate spheres makes it difficult to see how changes to a social system occur through other than simple, one-directional causation. This impedes both the development of successful innovations and the understanding of social change.

Latour (1986) makes a similar point in his discussion of an example of mapmaking. He tells how the French explorer La Perouse journeyed to the island of Sakhalin. While there he drew a map of the island, based on information provided by people who lived there, people who had themselves never made or seen a map on paper. He then returned with the map to the court in Versailles. In order to understand such things as why La Perouse undertook such a long journey (and to Sakhalin in particular), why it was so important for him to produce such a map, why the map needed to be on paper, how he was able to find his way there, why it was not important to the Sakhalin residents to have such a map, and so on, one must understand intricate technological and sociopolitical details; but more importantly, one must understand the way social relations are mediated by technical artifacts. As Latour says,

Commercial interests, capitalist spirit, imperialism, thirst for knowledge, are empty terms as long as one does not take into account Mercator's projection, marine clocks and their markers, copper engraving of maps, rutters, the keeping of "log books," and the many printed editions of Cook's voyages that La Perouse carries with him. . . . But, on the other hand, no innovation in the way longitude and latitude are calculated, clocks are built, log books are compiled, copper plates are printed, would make any difference whatsoever if they did not help to muster, align, and win over new and unexpected allies, far away, in Versailles. The practices I am interested in [inscribing information in permanent, but mobile forms] would be pointless if they did not bear on certain controversies and force dissenters into believing new facts and behaving in new ways. (p. 6)

Thus neither an innovation focus nor a system focus is sufficient to understand this or many other historical events. Latour's notion of "inscription,"
in which technology is used to produce "immutable mobiles," is one construct
useful for integrated analyses. Another is the idea that the design of an artifact
is mediated by social relations. Akrich (1992) shows how "technical objects
and people are brought into being in a process of reciprocal definition" (p.
222). Design of technology is a process that represents the intersection of the
physical apparatus aspect of technology with its social relations aspect.

For example, she describes the design of a photoelectric lighting kit for use
in less-developed countries. One design goal was that the kit should work in
spite of any environmental (or user) interference. It had a watertight battery
for anticipated use in exposed environments. It was designed without a switch
and with nonstandard plugs to prevent tampering by unsophisticated local
electricians. This physical design expressed the French designers' assumptions
about the knowledge and capabilities of the users in another country. The
effort to produce an interference-proof kit reflected other aspects of the social
relations between designers and users as well. It is clear, for instance, that
the prevention of interference was not simply a convenience for the user, but
an effort at control from afar.

Functional specifications cannot be separated from a complex of social
relations. A consequence in this case was that the lighting kits could not be
used successfully for long. True, the lights could not be modified by local
technicians, but they could not be repaired either. The special watertight
battery was not available in local markets. Clearly, understanding the usefulness of the kits requires an understanding of both technical and social
systems.

The design of any technology must be understood not simply as the construction of a physical artifact to meet a functional specification, but as a
process in which relations among people are realized. By observing the use
of the lighting kits, we begin to see how these relations are embodied in the
technology. Akrich (1987) points out that we cannot even *see* the structure
of the kit without seeing it in use:

Before leaving Paris for Africa, the potential significance of nonstandard
plugs, direct current, or waterproof batteries had not occurred to me. It was
only in the confrontation between the real user and the projected user that
the importance of such items as the plugs for the difference between the two
came to light. The materialization and implementation of this technical object,
like others, was a long process in which both technical and social elements
were simultaneously brought into being—a process that moved far beyond
the frontiers of the laboratory or the workshop. (p. 210)

An earlier work with an affinity for Akrich's notion of the simultaneous
fabrication of technical and social elements is that of Victor Papanek (1973).
A successful and prolific designer, who like Akrich is concerned with design

for the third world, Papanek argues for design teams that include representatives of the people who will use the design. This is one element in his idea
of "integrated design." He presents many examples of designs that could lead
to safe, inexpensive, and useful innovations, contrasting those with other
designs that are dangerous, expensive, and of little inherent value. His central
conclusion is that an integration of technical and social issues is necessary:
"The main trouble with design schools seems to be that they teach too much
design and not enough about the social, economic, and political environment
in which design takes place" (Papanek, 1973, p. 193).

Rethinking the realization process

Examples such as those given by Akrich make it difficult to maintain a view
of innovations as fixed objects that get applied to produce changes in social
systems. Instead, they lead us to see innovations as processes, ongoing man-
ifestations of social relations. This calls for a historical perspective in which
we follow social changes over time, including those changes related to the
development of the innovations. In contrast to an innovation focus or a system
focus, we need to conceive of the adoption of an innovation as a process in
which innovations are incorporated into a dynamic social system that may
lead to changes in the innovation, acceleration of change in the social system,
or no effect at all.

An important distinction to make is that between what the developers of
an innovation intend and what happens when the innovation is realized in a
particular social setting. The developers may intend that the innovation modify the social system so that certain desirable characteristics are achieved.
They see the innovation set into an idealized context and used in an idealized
way. Their vision of the changed social system is thus an *idealization*. What
happens in practice is that the social system may or may not change at all,
and if it does change, it may not do so in accord with the developers' goals.
Each resulting social system is a *realization*. The distinction between ideal
and real suggests a process, the *realization process*, whereby the innovation
leads to practices potentially different from those intended by the developers.

It is possible to view a realization as a distortion of the innovation, just as
Plato saw every actual circle with "particular qualities" as an imperfect manifestation of the real circle (Hamilton & Cairns, 1961, 7.343a–c). This view
is represented in Figure 1–1. The solid circle on the left represents the effect
of the innovation in an ideal world, the lens represents the realization process,
which distorts the ideal form, and the dotted shape on the right represents a
particular realization.

The widespread prevalence of "distortions" of innovations is a clue that
the conventional model of implementation is inadequate. It fails to account

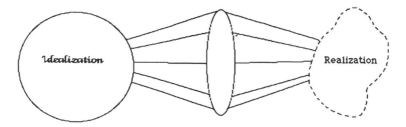

Figure 1-1. A Platonic view of the realization process

for the fact that existing goals and practices of institutions and individuals determine what happens with an innovation more than features of the innovation itself (Bruce & Rubin, 1993; Cohen, 1988; Cronbach, 1982; Cuban, 1986; Hawkins, 1987a; Kling, 1980; Kling & Scacchi, 1982; Rubin & Bruce, 1990). In reality, the innovation is but one small addition to a complex social system. Instead of seeing it as the primary instrument of change, it is better to see it as a tool that is incorporated into ongoing processes of change.

We are thus led to a different model for implementation of innovations. In this model, the active agents are not innovations, but the participants in the setting in which the innovation is placed. Participants interpret the innovation and then re-create it as they adapt it to fit with institutional and physical constraints, and with their own goals and practices. The Platonic view is thus inadequate; social practices related to the use of an innovation are not imperfect attempts to mimic some ideal form, but are rather the thing itself. Whereas we may contrast the use of an innovation with its idealization, we do not assume that users are imperfectly following preset rules. The situation instead is more akin to Wittgenstein's (1953) language games:

In philosophy we often *compare* the use of words with games and calculi which have fixed rules, but cannot say that someone who is using language *must* be playing such a game. – But if you say that our languages only *approximate* to such calculi you are standing on the brink of a misunderstanding. For then it may look as if what we were talking about were an *ideal* language. (¶ 81)

Wittgenstein goes on to show how language *use*, not some rigid set of rules, determines meaning. Nevertheless, many continue to search for the vacuum bottle ideal for language: "We think it [the ideal] must be in reality; for we think we already see it there" (¶ 101).

In a similar way, we cannot specify the pure, or ideal, case for the *use* of

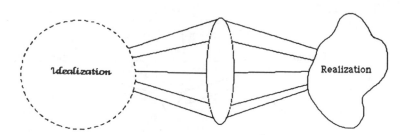

Figure 1-2. A Wittgensteinian view of the realization process

an innovation, only its idealization in the minds of the developers. Users inevitably interpret an innovation in distinctive ways, apply it idiosyncratically in their own contexts, and even re-create it to satisfy their own needs. We say that the innovation that is not prepared for this reshaping is poorly designed, not that it is maligned by the user.

Again, Wittgenstein's discussion of games is apropos:

We can easily imagine people amusing themselves in a field by playing with a ball so as to start various existing games, but playing many without finishing them and in between throwing the ball aimlessly into the air, chasing one another with the ball and bombarding one another for a joke and so on. And now someone says: The whole time they were playing a ball-game and following definite rules at every throw.

And is there not also the case where we play and – make up the rules as we go along? And there is even one where we alter them – as we go along. (¶ 83)

The innovation-in-use, like the actions of people playing with a ball, is the phenomenon we want to understand. A better view of the realization process is that shown in Figure 1–2, in which the solid shape on the right represents a specific and quite tangible set of social practices that emerge after the introduction of an innovation. Its characteristics reflect a history of interacting social processes, of which the innovation is only a latecomer, and one whose effects are shaped by layers and layers of previous events. The dotted circle on the left is the idealized form of the innovation, an imagined system, whose correspondence to the given realization depends as much upon the developers' understanding of the context of use as upon the inherent power of the innovation to effect change. In other words, its similarity to the realization depends upon the developers' assessment of the underlying social processes in the context of use.

The diversity of the realization process is revealed as we examine what happens when an innovation is introduced into various settings. As social relations and structures vary across settings, one idealization spawns an in-

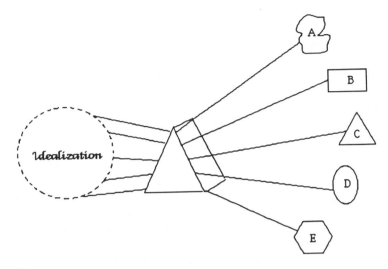

Figure 1-3. Alternate realizations of an innovation

definite number of realizations. Continuing our optics metaphor, we might say that instead of the realization process being a lens, it is a prism that produces a wide spectrum of different realizations (Figure 1–3). As an innovation comes into being in real settings, it acquires new and unexpected shapes. It is not only used differently, it is re-created to conform with the goals and norms of the people who use it.

How innovations develop

Because innovations come into being through use it is difficult to predict the eventual patterns of use for an innovation. In some cases developers or social critics overestimate the likely acceptance of and need for the innovation. Thus the video or picture telephone now seems unlikely to be a commonplace device by the year 2001, belying Stanley Kubrick's portrayal of it in *2001: A Space Odyssey*. Yet long before that film was produced, AT&T (American Telephone & Telegraph) had introduced its Picturephone system at the 1964 New York World's Fair. Many people then considered the picture telephone to be an obvious and inevitable next step in the telephone's evolution. In the ensuing 27 years, however, the cost, quality, and usefulness of the device never crossed the necessary threshold into widespread consumer use. AT&T offered a consumer video telephone for the first time in 1992.

There are endless examples of other potentially useful technologies that have not been adopted widely by the consumer – videodiscs (for home use), central vacuum cleaners, and so on – each touted as imminent by some people at one time. The adoption of these technologies must be understood in terms of the social contexts of potential use, not just in terms of the speed, efficiency, or polish of the new innovation per se (Bijker, Hughes, & Pinch, 1987; MacKenzie & Wajcman, 1985).

In other cases people underestimate the growth of an innovation. The xerographic process is a notable example. Thought of first as a novelty or a specialized tool, copy machines have transformed offices everywhere and are now being marketed as standard home appliances. Other technologies that we view as ordinary, even necessary, today were likewise exotic in their beginnings. Telephones, televisions, faxes, computers, and automobiles are examples of technologies that have radically reshaped our lives in ways few predicted. These underestimated technologies satisfied hidden needs or created new ones. Viewing their impact in quantitative terms alone (a car as moving four times as fast as a horse, for example) would only obscure the complex ways in which the technology transformed the social world and was in turn transformed by it.

One reason it is difficult to assess the impact of an innovation is that change can occur through diverse processes. The innovation can be re-created along many different paths. At the simplest level, the social system may assimilate the innovation and exhibit incremental change. More generally, one change in the system may trigger other changes, so that there is a cascade of connected changes. Typically these changes occur independent of or even counter to anyone's overt plan. Sometimes the new social practices called for by the innovation are dissonant with existing social values. Ultimately this can lead to a change in values. In other cases dissonance can lead to nonstandard uses, or to resistance to the innovation expressed through token use or nonuse.

Finally, change may occur because of a modification of the innovation by either developers or users. People make up the rules or alter them as they go along. These types of changes are often slighted in discussions of technology and social change, perhaps because the analyst sees the technology as something fixed and imposed from the outside. In fact, innovations are by nature experimental and typically die if they do not allow re-creation. Higher-order changes may come through the re-creation process as well. Often, in fact, we see a cascade of changes to both the innovation and the context of use, each triggering changes in the other.

Thus in practice it may be difficult to say exactly which type of change is occurring, and any real example is likely to involve a mixture of these types. Moreover, the judgment that a particular type of change has occurred is an interpretation from within a discourse. For example, "consonant change" and "cascades of changes," as defined in the following text, are most often cited in innovation-focused discourse, and "change due to dissonance" is more often noted in system-focused discourse. With these caveats in place, it is still useful to make some abstractions of the realization process as we look briefly at several important types of change. Figure 1–4 shows some of the major

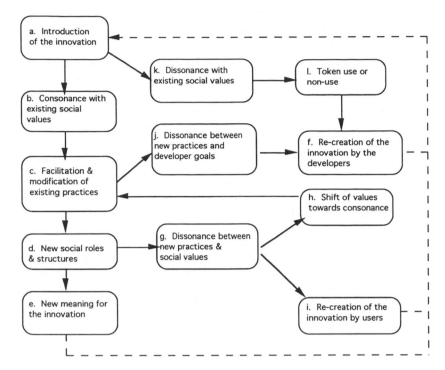

Figure 1-4. Idealized model of paths of social change

paths of change in an idealized form. It is meant to be only a sketch of some of the possible forms of change that take place as an innovation is realized.

Consonant change. The simplest sort of social change following the introduction of an innovation is that in which the innovation is *consonant* with the values of the social system, in which case it facilitates, extends, or perpetuates existing social practices. These practices change exactly enough to assimilate the innovation. Typically the innovation promises greater productivity for existing functions. Pure consonant change does not exist, but aspects of it are common when an innovation is introduced, especially in early stages of use. This is the type of change usually assumed in innovation-focused discourse.

The process for consonant change is relatively simple. An innovation is introduced. If it is consonant with existing social values, it is adopted easily. Existing social practices are facilitated and may change somewhat as the innovation is used. Schematically, then, the pattern for simple consonant change is the ⟨a-b-c⟩ path in Figure 1–4. In some cases, the process could be viewed as stopping after some modification of existing practices.

For example, many discussions of office automation begin by describing how documents can be produced, stored, or exchanged more quickly and cheaply – basically a substitution of new processes for old. The change in processes may also lead to higher quality products. Moreover, there can be changes in the time and place dependence of work. Further analysis includes some social change issues such as the extension of managerial control or changes in office organization (Evans & Bernard, 1987). But often, these discussions assume no change in the fundamental purposes for documents or the social roles of office workers; the emphasis is on technical capabilities, economic factors, and user acceptance.

Examples of discourse assuming consonant change can be found in a book addressed to managers making decisions about electronic mail for the office (Caswell, 1988). The book details the history of the technology, explicates technical details, and lays out options for the managers. It lauds electronic mail as a technology that "adds regularity" to existing processes:

Electronic mail, however, has a long-term impact that is far broader. Because electronic mail adds regularity to our telecommunications network, it makes a critical contribution to our evolving system of global communications, which is a necessary component for the evolution of mankind. In this context, developing electronic mail systems is a noble pursuit. (p. xiii)

The text continues with the claim that the impact on people of this new technology is quite straightforward, despite the technical complexities:

Although the networks and the technologies that create them are quite complex, the implications are very simple. Advanced information networks will magnify the ability of people to store, gather, prepare, and communicate important information. (p. 1)

Thus the central issue for managers is simply to determine how to ensure that the new technology gets used:

The challenge, which extends to both top executives and mid-level managers, is to cut through the complexity of the myriad technologies on the market and mold them into a unified, integrated network that serves the people who use them. (p. 1)

The assumption here is that there is no significant difference between the sense of "communication" embodied in existing office practices and that embodied in electronic mail, and thus that the types of change described therein would be consonant. But there are good reasons to doubt this assumption. New technologies such as electronic mail provide new arenas for sorting out social relations; the uses of the technology are never straightforward extensions of existing practices. Nevertheless, the assumption of consonant change and the corresponding focus on the innovation is representative of the writing typically found as an innovation is being introduced or promoted.

Dissonant change. Change attributable to an innovation is often not smooth; in fact, it may be disruptive in ways that have little to do with the innovation's purported function. People may resist the innovation or use it in ways never intended, or social systems may be profoundly disturbed by its presence. A model for one aspect of dissonant change has been proposed by Bernard and Pelto (1987). In their model the introduction of new technology calls for new practices, but not immediately for new ways of thinking. These new practices may conflict with established cultural ideas. The dissonance thereby produced can lead to a shift in values:

A key mechanism for bringing about behavioral (social) change is the drive to reduce cognitive dissonance – the tendency to change values (e.g., in response to new technology) when new behaviors (in response to new technologies) are no longer consonant with previously held values. This mechanism is presumed to operate, for example, when a farmer changes his economic activities, especially if those economic activities no longer produce sufficient income to maintain the standard of living that his family has come to value. (Bernard & Pelto, 1987, p. 362)

A classic example of this is the story of the introduction of the steel axe to the Yir Yoront people living on the west coast of Cape York in Australia. Sharp (1952) tells how the Yir Yoront accepted this modern tool, but only as a substitute for the stone axe, not as the multifaceted tool it was in other settings. Thus there was initially a consonant change without notable positive effects or any cascade of positive changes (discussed in a later section):

Among the Yir Yoront the new axe never acquired all the uses it had on mission or cattle stations (carpentry work, pounding tent pegs, use as a hammer, and so on); and, indeed, it was used for little more than the stone axe had been, so that it had no practical effect in improving the native standard of living. It did some jobs better, and could be used longer without breakage; and these factors were sufficient to make it of value to the native. (p. 82)

But the adoption of the steel axe did lead to many other changes. Stone axes were more than tools for cutting wood; they served symbolic functions as well. Stone axes signified power in the hands of the older men, who were the only ones allowed to possess them. Steel axes were, in contrast, plentiful; they were given to women and to younger men by missionaries and other outsiders:

A result was that older men no longer had a complete monopoly of all the axes in the bush community. Indeed, an old man might have only a stone axe, while his wives and sons had steel axes which they considered their own and which he might even desire to borrow. All this led to a revolutionary confusion of sex, age, and kinship roles, with a major gain in independence and loss of subordination on the part of those able now to acquire steel axes when they had been unable to possess stone axes before. (p. 84)

These were changes to the basic social structure of the community. But as dramatic as they were, other effects of the presence of the steel axe may have been more profound. The most disturbing changes emerged "in the realm of traditional ideas, sentiments, and values" (p. 85). There was a need to account for this new and now important element within the community, but the steel axe was neither "always there" nor created by a known clan. It was first associated with the Corpse clan, as were all other things pertaining to the white man. This posed a conceptual dilemma because the stone axe is a totem of the Sunlit Cloud Iguana clan and the steel axe seems to belong there as well:

Moreover, the steel axe, like most European goods, has no distinctive origin myth, nor are mythical ancestors associated with it. Can anyone, sitting of an afternoon in the shade of a ti tree, create a myth to resolve this confusion? No one has, and the horrid suspicion arises that perhaps the origin myths are wrong, which took into account so little of this vast new universe of the white man. The steel axe, shifting hopelessly between one clan and the other, is not only replacing the stone axe physically, but is hacking at the supports of the entire cultural system. (p. 88)

Sharp concludes that an eventual consequence of the introduction of the steel axe was the collapse of a system of ideas and, subsequently, "cultural disintegration" and "demoralization of the individual" (p. 89). Thus, dissonance between values embodied in the new practices associated with the innovation and those of the social system led to dramatic cognitive and social turmoil little evident in the technical artifacts. This in turn led to a shift of values for those affected by the innovation.

In the terms of Figure 1–4, the first part of the process was the same as that for consonant change. People adopted the innovation and changed their practices accordingly because it was consonant with some existing social values. The changed practices, though, were dissonant with other social values. Values then shifted to reduce the dissonance. Schematically, it looks like the path ⟨a-b-c-d-g-h⟩ in Figure 1–4. The key is step g, the point at which dissonance emerges between new practices and existing social values.[2]

Thus when changes in a community occur following the introduction of an innovation, the types of change reflect the match between the values manifested in the innovation and those in the social context of use. When the match is *dissonant* there can be rejection of the innovation (discussed in the section to follow), radical changes in its modes of use (i), re-creation of the innovation (f), or shifts in values for both users and developers of the innovation (h) (as in the stone axe example). Any study of the adoption of an

---

[2] It is important to notice that this dissonance is between the practices and the ideas of the users of the technology, not between their practices and the ideas of the technology's developers. The latter case is discussed in the section titled "Redesign of the innovation."

innovation must therefore take into account existing values and beliefs, the ways they affect its adoption, and the ways they are themselves changed in the process.

Resistance to change. Often, no change occurs at all. Innovations too often succeed in pilot tests and then fail to have any lasting impact on the system as a whole. The nonuse of many patented inventions and the failure of technologically innovative products and companies attest to this fact. A model for this response of the social system to an innovation looks like the path ⟨a-k-l⟩ in Figure 1–4.

In the realm of education, one reason for resistance to change is that there are conflicting functions for schools, as democratizing institutions and as institutions for sorting people into jobs and status within society (Bowles & Gintis, 1976). Another is that instruction is typically organized in a way that modifies an innovation to fit or rejects the innovation if it cannot be modified. Cohen (1988) makes this point based on a historical analysis of a variety of new curricula:

So, while the new curricula were used, they were used within the extant organization of instruction. In a minority of cases this meant they were used intelligently and sympathetically, but even in these cases the new content did not bring radical change in the ways that classes were conducted, that teachers taught, or that students learned. But in most cases, the new curricula were assimilated to an inherited and rather rigid organization of subject matter, teaching, and learning. In either case, it seems fair to say that the new materials seem [not] to have changed the organization of instruction in any dramatic way. More often than not, the extant organization changed the materials. (p. 237)

A similar point is made by Cuban (1986). New technologies are incorporated only if they facilitate existing practices:

Thus, those technologies incorporated into routine teacher practice responded to daily classroom needs without undercutting the teacher's control of the class. . . . Teachers *have* altered their practice when a technological innovation helped them do a better job of what they already decided had to be done and matched their view of daily classroom realities. (pp. 65–66)

In some cases users may do the opposite of what is intended. One reason this occurs is that there are contradictions within the innovation's design that become apparent only with use. More precisely, aspects of the design *become* contradictions when realized in certain contexts. For example, the use of word processing in classrooms for the teaching of writing has often been linked with a deemphasis on formal aspects of language in favor of an emphasis on meaning (Bruce, 1991). Printed output, which is neater and easier to read than handwritten copy, is seen as a way to encourage students to think more about their audience and meaningful purposes. But, paradoxically, because printed output reveals mistakes and looks more finished, it has led in some classrooms to an increased focus on spelling and punctuation.

Similarly, visions for the computer in the classroom may include the idea of a writer turning to the computer to make changes as the need for them naturally arises during the thinking/writing process (Bruce & Rubin, 1992). This model assumes that the writer can spend time at the computer pondering the text and making complicated edits. In many school situations, however, there is limited computer access. This resource limitation becomes relevant when teachers attempt to ensure equity of use. Most teachers ensure equity of use by giving each student a fixed period of time per week, say 30 minutes, to use the computer. The result is that students cannot go to the computer to make changes to their texts as the need arises. Nor can they afford to use their limited time allotment to sit and think about their text. Instead, they have to use the time for pressing keys. This means that copyediting is often the only reasonable way to use the time effectively. Thus in a context in which there is limited computer access and the allocation of fixed, equal portions of time to each student, the dimensions of equity and meaning-centered revision come into conflict.

An important type of resistance to change is that which occurs when an innovation attempts to alter existing forms of distribution in society. Addressing inequities in classrooms has been a major goal of many innovations that are based on new technologies. As Foucault (1972) says, however, "We well know that in [education's] distribution, in what it permits, and in what it prevents, it follows the well-trodden battle-lines of social-conflict" (p. 227). These innovations do little to change underlying inequities.

The most pernicious effects may occur when innovations are used well, for differential access may compound the inequalities in education that already exist between rich and poor, black and white, male and female. Such a compounding is evident with computer use (Hawkins, 1987b; Russell, Mokros, & Foster, 1984). Wealthier schools have greater access to new technologies. Moreover, students in wealthier schools more often use computers for open-ended learning activities, such as writing, Logo programming, and science simulations, whereas students in inner-city schools use them for drill and practice on basic skills (Boruta et al., 1983; Shavelson et al, 1984). Even within a single classroom there is evidence that the distribution of access and information "follows the well-trodden battle-lines of social-conflict." Students already marginalized in special programs become more so when they miss the introduction to the computer because of being pulled out of class (Michaels, Cazden, & Bruce, 1985).

Cascades of changes. Changes beget other changes. In the appropriate context, an innovation may have unanticipated secondary and tertiary effects.

As Burke (1978) suggests, there can be a "trigger effect." When conditions are right, a new innovation can set in motion a "continuing sequence of connected events" (p. 12). For example, in discussing early Egyptian society, he refers to the scratch plow as the "trigger of civilization":

At about the same time as these first attempts at irrigation, the digging stick changed its shape; it became a simple scratch plough, with a forward-curving wooden blade for cutting the soil, and a backward-curving pair of handles with which the farmer could direct the oxen. . . . This simple implement may arguably be called the most fundamental invention in the history of man, and the innovation that brought civilization into being, because it was the instrument of surplus. . . . It is not until [a community] can produce food which is surplus to requirements, and is therefore capable of supporting those who are not food producers, that it will flourish. This development was made possible by the plough, and it caused a radical transformation of Egyptian society.

With these tools the Egyptians administered an empire whose power and influence was unparalleled in the ancient world. . . . The first man-made harvest freed mankind from total and passive dependence on the vagaries of nature, and at the same time tied him forever to the very tools that set him free. The modern world in which we live is the product of that original achievement, because just as the plough served to trigger change in the community in which it appeared, each change that followed led to further change in a continuing sequence of connected events. (pp. 9, 10, 12)

This example is basically technocentric – "the digging stick changed its shape," "the innovation that brought civilization into being," "the modern world is the product of that achievement" – which is no surprise considering that it comes from a book (and television series) whose thesis is that connections among innovations – their genealogy – account for significant aspects of historical development. Even so, this and similar examples in the book reveal, in spite of its thesis, that the changes described are not simple effects of technology. The beginning of a surplus economy depended upon the social conditions for change being appropriate, not just on the scratch plow. Just as the Aztecs used the wheel for toys and not for commerce, the Egyptians could have used the scratch plow in ways that did not trigger great social changes. Moreover, the second- and third-order changes developed from a complex interplay of institutional, political, cultural, social, and technological forces.

Malone and Rockart (1991) discuss analogous changes in society in terms of the higher order effects of new transportation technologies:

A first-order effect of transportation technology was simply the substitution of new transportation technologies for the old. People began to ride in trains and automobiles rather than on horses and in horse-drawn carriages.

As transportation technology continued to improve . . . a second-order effect emerged: people began to travel more. They commuted further to work each day. . . .

Then, as people used more and more transportation, a third-order effect eventually occurred: the emergence of new "transportation-intensive" social and economic structures. These structures, such as suburbs and shopping malls, would not have been possible without the wide availability of cheap and convenient transportation. (p. 128)

They suggest that a similar sequence of effects may occur with new information and communication technologies. In the beginning, people will simply substitute new technologies, such as electronic mail, for the old, such as postal mail. Later, they will communicate more, as communication becomes cheaper and more convenient. Finally, organizational structures will become more communication intensive, in their estimation, more flexible and less hierarchical.

The pattern for cascaded change is similar to that for consonant change, except that here the modification of existing practices (step c in Figure 1–4) leads to more fundamental social change, such as new organizations or changed social roles. When this happens, the early period of implementation in a particular setting results in a new social context that, in turn, influences later realizations of the innovation. In the changed context, the original innovation takes on a new meaning, becoming effectively a new innovation. Thus we get a cycle of changes, the ⟨a-b-c-d-e(-a)⟩ path in Figure 1–4.

One limitation of the cascaded change model as presented is that it assumes inadvertent change. The innovation is introduced, it gets used, and later we observe social change. This may be appropriate when we consider many types of innovation (for example, dams, hybrid seeds, or snowmobiles), for in those cases, the innovation is not designed primarily to bring about social change, even though it typically does so. In contrast, the primary purpose of some innovations is *precisely* to change social relations. This is especially true of educational innovations like ENFI.

Redesign of the innovation. Innovations influence social practices when they are seen as consonant with existing values, whereas dissonance in the match of an innovation to the social context can lead to nonuse or to unforeseen changes. These are the principal forms of change described in many studies of social change. In each case the innovation is a given, often one imposed by a colonizer, a government agency, or a large corporation. What is studied is the adaptation of the culture to the innovation, or the assignment of meaning to the innovation within the culture.

But innovations themselves are never fixed; they are active elements in the organization of relationships among people. As such, they are continually interpreted and evaluated with respect to the way they express these relationships. Whenever the expression is not appropriate as, for example, when the relationships change, there is a tension that must be resolved. Sometimes this tension results in further discordant social change. At other times, and to varying degrees, people can and do change the innovation.

Generally what happens is this: People try out an innovation, find that some aspects of it are worthwhile, some are not, and others need to be changed. When they have the power to modify the innovation they do so. This process of interpretation, evaluation, selection, and modification is effectively a re-creation of the innovation by the users. Whether users do in fact re-create an innovation depends in part on their technical skills and their ability to select or modify elements of the innovation, but more importantly on their having the social power to do so. There is of course great variation in the degree to which users are allowed to shape the technology they use (Bjerknes, Ehn, & Kyng, 1987; Hawkins, 1987a; Papanek, 1973; Suchman, 1988).

The user redesign process follows the path ⟨a-b-c-d-g-i⟩ in Figure 1–4. Notice that the dissonance in step g is between the new practices and the social values of the users. One especially interesting case of user re-creation is that of open-ended innovations in education, such as ENFI. On the one hand, many such innovations call for the active participation of users (teachers and students) in the ongoing development of the innovation. Thus the definition of the innovation is explicitly dynamic: Developers intend that users will re-create the innovation. A key assumption behind this intention is that the social values of the users and the developers will be similar. Ironically, what often happens is that these open-ended innovations are in fact used because they are flexible enough to be re-created in the image of the traditional classroom they were intended to supplant (Cohen, 1988; Cuban, 1986).[3]

Finally, we cannot omit the role played by the developers in the development process. They look at the use of their innovation in different contexts, and choose to modify it to respond to perceived problems with its use. Upon seeing that the innovation is realized in unforeseen ways, they may learn things that guide a revision of the innovation. Thus development becomes a cycle in which innovations are repeatedly evaluated and re-created.[4]

---

[3] The resistance-to-change model described earlier could be considered a special case of users re-creating the innovation. In that case users anticipate that use of the innovation will be dissonant with their values; accordingly, they refuse to use it or adopt it in a token fashion. Thus the resistance response, which might be termed an "unfaithful use" in traditional evaluation discourse, is in our terms a re-creation of the innovation by the users.

[4] This distinction between changes initiated by users of the innovation, as they mold the innovation to fit their needs and abilities, and those initiated by its developers need not be absolute. In fact, many of the problems that arise with the introduction of innovations can be attributed to separation of and conflict between users and developers (Akrich, 1987; Noble, 1984; Papanek, 1973; Staudenmaier, 1985; Suchman, 1988). Successful innovations require collaborative development. Our abstraction here of separate processes reflects the realities of most innovation development today.

The model for developer redesign includes dissonance between the new practices and the idealized practices envisioned by the designers – between their goals and the realities of use. The innovation is thus realized in unexpected, and often undesired, ways. Many times the story ends there; but the innovation can usually be changed. In response to the dissonance, developers may re-create the innovation so that desired effects are better achieved. This process is represented by the cycles ⟨a-b-c-j-f⟩ and ⟨a-k-l-f⟩ in Figure 1–4.

Implications for the study of innovations

The variety of paths that the realization process of a given innovation may follow show that the effects of an innovation on a social system are not properties of the innovation or of the social system alone. Moreover, the very boundaries and character of the innovation must be seen as a process shaped by users and developers. The most significant indications of an innovation's characteristics are revealed only through a careful study of the properties that emerge as it comes to be used in different settings.

When television became available, for example, many people predicted the demise of radio. Yet radio has survived and prospered as a communications medium, even in situations in which television programming and receivers are widely available. There are several reasons for this. Radio does not require the user to focus attention on the communications device itself as television does. A radio listener is free to drive a car, work, or read a book and still benefit from a radio program. The apparent limitations of radio can also be advantages. Many people find that the video portion of the television signal distracts them when they listen to music, or constrains their imagination in a dramatic presentation. Moreover, the mere possibility of video has been transformed into a necessity – television demands good video, to the point that programming, even news, is structured to highlight interesting visual material, excluding that which cannot be made visual (Mander, 1978). Thus radio offers a balance of content different from that of television. Finally, although television technology has become simpler and less expensive, it is still much easier to set up a radio station than a television station. It is also easier for the consumer to install a radio than a television. Most homes may have one or two televisions, but radios are ubiquitous. They are found in cars, small boats, shower stalls, and swimming pools; they are attached to clocks, telephones, headbands, and exercise machines. This general availability and easy use of radios has thus allowed the older medium to survive in the face of apparently superior technology.

A forecast for the radio and television industries in 1950 might have focused primarily on technical characteristics, perhaps comparing the two media in terms of information transfer rate or on the ability to represent different categories of information. Such a forecast might have included reports of experimental studies of people's reactions to the relative power of the different communication channels. Alternatively, a commentator might have dismissed the features of the two technologies and focused entirely on existing social needs and practices. Neither of these approaches would have provided an adequate accounting for the ways in which these technologies came to be used, how they changed, and how differences in their actual use emerged.

It is difficult to assess relative technical strengths and weaknesses of different technologies; therefore, it is difficult to forecast their growth. The radio/TV example illustrates an additional problem: The modes of use as well as the technology itself change over time. Thus, although the prevalence of radio has actually increased, the uses of radio have changed dramatically since the introduction of television. People no longer gather around the radio for an evening's entertainment as they once did. Radio drama has almost disappeared, existing primarily in some children's programs or in novelty revivals. These changes can be understood only by a careful analysis of the social contexts of use.

What happened with radio over the last four decades was a rich interaction of social contexts with the technology. The technology was adapted to fit new social needs; in turn, it catalyzed changes in social relationships. This complex and iterative interaction between the innovation and the social context – each modifying the other in a dynamic system of interrelationships – is one reason it is so difficult to analyze the "effect" of an innovation.

Rather than thinking of interactions between a fixed innovation and a static social context, we should view the process of innovation as a *transaction* (Dewey & Bentley, 1949; Rosenblatt, 1978) among ideas, cultural values, sentiments, institutional structures, social practices, and the structure of the innovation. An appreciation of the nature of this process leads to new perspectives on innovation and social change, new questions to ask about the effects of innovations, and a new approach to evaluation.

The shift in perspective from the view that realizations are distortions of an ideal to one in which realizations are creations that result from active problem solving has implications for the evaluation of educational innovations. In a method of evaluation known as *situated evaluation* (defined more fully in Chapter 2), the social context in which the educational innovation is used becomes central. In this method, questions such as the following must be considered:

- How do *the overall goals, practices, and gateposts in the institution* shape, constrain, or direct the use of the innovation?
- How do *teachers' pedagogical theories, personalities, and practices* relate to the way they incorporate the innovation into their class-

rooms, the kinds of activities they engage in, and their evaluations of its success?

- How do *student characteristics and expectations* affect the implementation of the innovation and their evaluations of its success?
- How do *features of the technology* – hardware, software, room location and layout – affect the innovation's use?
- How do *available resources* – funding, technical assistance, teacher time – affect the innovation's use?

These elements of the educational setting – the institution, the teacher, the students, the technology, and the resources – contribute to the different realizations of the innovation and the degree to which it will be successful. In order to understand the implementation process and to evaluate the outcomes of the introduction of the innovation, we need to identify and characterize realizations of the innovation. In the chapters to follow we discuss the diverse paths taken in the realizations of network-based classrooms.

2   A Situated evaluation of ENFI

Bertram C. Bruce and Joy Kreeft Peyton

Implementing an innovation means introducing something new into an existing system. If the innovation is significant, it will trigger changes in the system, some of which may be easily predictable and others of which may be surprising. People involved with the system naturally want to know what those changes may be and what they mean. The notion of change that is implied by an innovation thus calls for an evaluation. Such was the case for ENFI, an approach to the teaching of writing using computer networks.

As with any program evaluation, we had two initial questions when we began our evaluation of ENFI: How well does it work (summative evaluation) and how can it be improved (formative evaluation)? As we studied the practices associated with ENFI, we came to see the importance of a third question: What influences the re-creation of the innovation in each setting? Addressing this question led us to call for a new type of evaluation, *situated evaluation*. In this chapter we discuss how we tried to answer these questions and the process that led to the writing of this book.

Purposes of evaluation

In this section we briefly describe the summative and formative evaluations of ENFI, identifying some of their limitations. These limitations reflect some methodological and ontological assumptions underlying both formative and summative evaluations as they are usually carried out. A variety of alternative methods of evaluation have been proposed to address these concerns. After discussing a few of these alternatives, we turn to *situated evaluation*, a fundamentally different type of evaluation built upon different assumptions about the purpose and object of evaluation.

Summative evaluation of ENFI

A summative evaluation of an innovation typically focuses on the impact of its use. The evaluation might, for example, report a substantial increase in the writing scores of students who learned using a new curriculum. Evaluators often compare one or more experimental groups who used the innovation with control groups who did not (or used only parts of it). This information is generally used in making decisions regarding the innovation and may lead to changes in the innovation or in the ways it is used. Summative evaluations frequently involve any of a wide range of quantitative methods, but they are not limited to these, and can involve qualitative measures with quantitative results (as in Fowles's study, Chapter 14) or descriptions of outcomes (as in Bartholomae's study, Chapter 13).

In the ENFI Project we were interested in whether interactive writing on a computer network, as one substantial activity in a writing class, would have an impact on other writing that students would do in their classes. As stated in the proposal to the Annenberg/CPB Project, we wondered whether "the learning theory behind ENFI can be translated into more effective practice in writing classrooms at all levels of undergraduate and graduate work" (Batson, 1987, p. 9). To investigate this question, we carried out two types of summative evaluation in the form of assessments of the quality of students' compositions. One yielded a description of specific qualities of students' writing, and one a quantitative comparison.

Although descriptive in nature, Bartholomae's study of student writing at three consortium sites constitutes one type of summative evaluation, with the focus being the impact of ENFI on students' compositions. Bartholomae examined over 800 essays collected from the beginning, middle, and end of the year in ENFI and non-ENFI classes. The texts were drawn from actual classroom work and (in ENFI classes) closely tied to ENFI activities. In some cases, he had the printed transcripts of those activities as well.

He found differences between the ENFI and non-ENFI texts. Although not always the case, the ENFI essays *tended* to be less formal, more conversational and idiomatic, less predictable, more focused on the writer as author and the writer's own experiences, and more likely to address an audience directly. The non-ENFI essays tended to look more like traditional compositions, with the writers carefully following standard formats (a thesis with four or five supporting paragraphs and a conclusion) and attempting to achieve a dispassionate, "academic" voice. It appears that the conversational nature of the network writing promoted a conversational style in compositions.

Because this study did not use a uniform writing prompt and scoring rubric, it provides a close look at what actually occurred in the classrooms involved and affords a qualitative understanding of the effects that ENFI activities can have on students' other writing. It also allows us to see how those effects are shaped by classroom dynamics and teacher and student goals. With this approach we trade uniformity of conditions for rich description and fidelity to actual classroom practices. This kind of information can easily be given back to the students and teachers and used to reshape their practices.

Mary Fowles of Educational Testing Service (ETS) carried out a second type of summative evaluation. A sample of ENFI and non-ENFI students was selected from four consortium sites, and site representatives met to select appropriate writing prompts and scoring guidelines. At the beginning and end of one semester the students wrote about a personal experience, the students and teachers provided information about other writing activities in the class, and background information on the students was collected. The essays were scored using a 6-point scale, and the results were compared for the ENFI and non-ENFI groups.

The scores showed no significant difference between the two groups. Both ENFI and non-ENFI groups at every site showed small score gains during the semester. The greatest differences among students seemed linked to writing ability, with the students who began the semester with the highest scores making the greatest gains and those who began with the lowest scores making the least. This could be interpreted as showing no benefit for the effort put into ENFI, or more positively, as evidence that ENFI students, who were learning new forms of writing, could still perform as well as others on a conventional writing assessment.

In Chapter 14, Fowles describes in detail the design and results of this study and discusses the difficult issues that a study of this type raises. On the one hand, there is the desire for controlled, systematic information across a number of contexts in order to say something about the general impact of the innovation. On the other hand, the diversity evident throughout this book makes collecting and interpreting that information very difficult. Not only did software, hardware, student backgrounds and abilities, and ENFI activities vary considerably from site to site and from class to class, but the teachers had different goals for their students' learning, and had difficulty even agreeing on an appropriate writing prompt for the study. The results – essay scores that must necessarily be merged to provide adequate numbers – mask this diversity. Even when she looked more carefully at features of the writing itself, Fowles could not find any differences among papers beyond individual student styles. It appears that the uniformity of the task itself masked individual classroom differences. In her chapter, Fowles discusses ways that a summative writing assessment could be made more sensitive to diversity among classes.

Formative evaluation of ENFI

Formative evaluation is a second major approach to the study of innovations. Here the audience may include the end user, but is often the developers of the innovation. Evaluators introduce the innovation into a suitable context or a small number of such contexts. They then monitor its use to determine how different features work, with the goal being to make appropriate modifications to the innovation. They might detail comments from users and list changes to be made to the materials used. The methods are typically observations and interviews.

For example, suppose the developers observe that one student has difficulty deciphering a particular screen display. In the formative evaluation process this would probably be taken as a sign that the display should be examined and possibly modified. Because the developers are still engaged in shaping the innovation, they cannot afford to ignore any indicators of how the innovation functions, even without a formal statistical analysis. In contrast, in a summative evaluation the point is to assess how the innovation as a whole achieves its goals. One takes the innovation as fixed, ignores the details that are not believed to make an overall difference, and looks for general effects. A single student's difficulty in understanding the screen may not be taken into consideration in a summative evaluation.

In the ENFI Project, the formative evaluation was carried on at individual sites as they set up their network and implemented network activities, and across the sites in consortium meetings. At Gallaudet, for example, extensive evaluation of the network hardware and software had occurred before the wider consortium formed. Members of the English department met over many months and considered various software and hardware options to identify the optimal number of windows, speed of scrolling, and method of recording the interaction. Once software was selected, researchers observed classes and interviewed teachers, and then proposed changes that would meet needs for various student groupings, network security, and ease of entry into the program. Various classroom layouts were also tried.

When the consortium formed, the observations, interviews, and conversations continued, this time with a broader basis for sharing and making comparisons. Based on observations of pair work at CMU and interviews with students after a paired network session, for example, we discovered that groups of three worked better than pairs for particular activities, because two students sometimes got stuck on a point and needed a third to move them along. Likewise, after discussions of student groupings at consortium meetings, members with large classes began grouping their students on separate channels rather than having them work as an entire class. In consortium meetings and electronic mail discussions among consortium members, we discovered that student flaming was common in almost all classes and discussed ways to channel it in more productive directions.

As occurred in the ENFI Consortium, formative evaluation typically proceeds as a trial-and-error process in which the innovation is repeatedly revised in response to experiences with its use. The emphasis on experience with use and the concern for modifying details of the innovation mean that formative evaluation usually reveals more about the process of use than does summative evaluation. But because the focus in formative evaluation is on improving the innovation, there is little attention paid to variations in use; nor is there a concern with long-term changes in the social context of use or in the ways the innovation is assimilated by institutions, teachers, and students. These issues cannot be ignored if we want to understand how an innovation is realized in a given context.

Concerns about summative and formative evaluation

As they are often conceived, both summative and formative evaluation operate as if the innovation were a fixed and clearly defined thing. In summative evaluation we measure *its* impact; in formative evaluation we study how to improve *it*. In neither case is there an explicit provision for examining the interaction of the innovation with the situation in which the innovation is used. This makes it difficult to attend to the situated process of change, and consequently to many of the concerns people have about innovations.

R. M. Wolf (1990) describes three key limitations that follow from the conception of the innovation as an object. First, without a direct consideration of the contexts of use, evaluations often do not identify the reasons for the observed phenomena. They do not say *how* the innovation can be improved or what aspect of it produced the measured effects. Second, not being able to account for why changes occur means that it is questionable to generalize to other settings in which the innovation might be used. Third, the development process often continues after the evaluation, so that most evaluations are effectively of innovations that no longer exist. Again, without knowing more about the situation and process of use, one cannot say whether initial results are still valid for the changed innovation.

A related point is that in order to assess before-and-after changes in performance the evaluator needs to know the measure at the beginning of the evaluation period. But many of the most intriguing effects of an innovation are not anticipated, and thus not measured in advance. Consider the case of a computer program called Quill, which was used to foster elementary school students' writing (Bruce & Rubin, 1993). The associated curriculum emphasized revision, and it was assumed that the presence within Quill of a word processor would facilitate the mechanical act of revising a text. Revision did occur in Quill classrooms, but in some this occurred because the computer's presence catalyzed changes in the social organization of writing, not because revision was now easier. For example, students milled around the computer waiting for a turn and thus had greater opportunities to read each others' work (Bruce, Michaels, & Watson-Gegeo, 1985). This milling around was not a planned feature of the project, yet may have been a significant element in the realized curriculum. Thus evaluations may gloss over the details of the complex processes that lead to observed changes.

Alternative methods of evaluation

Various alternative methods of evaluation have been proposed to address these limitations. For example, *adversary evaluation* (Clyne, 1990) and *judicial evaluation* (R. L. Wolf, 1990) entail that the audience for summative evaluation is not only the user, but other evaluators presenting an opposing viewpoint. *Decision-oriented evaluation* (Borich, 1990), *goal-free evaluation* (Stecher, 1990), and *illuminative evaluation* (Parlett, 1990) vary the purpose for the evaluation, from responding to the potential user's stated criteria to revealing whatever one can find about the innovation. *Naturalistic evaluation* (Dorr-Bremme, 1990) and *case study methods* (Stenhouse, 1990) allow for a greater variability of settings. Other methods similarly vary the types of results produced, the time of assessment, or the measurement tools.

Another approach has been to emphasize formative over summative evaluation. The argument is that traditional summative evaluation provides a summary of effects, but is removed from the way the innovation is actually used. Formative evaluation, on the other hand, is more concerned with the details of actual use because it needs to detail changes to the innovation based on problems with its use. Thus it is more pertinent to the question of how to effect educational change. Recognizing this, some researchers have argued that one should do formative evaluation whenever possible, both to improve the innovation and as an alternative to standard summative evaluation. But to the extent that the innovation is viewed as a thing separate from its use, this approach still obscures the way innovations actually function.

Others have argued for broadening the range of measurement tools used for summative evaluation specifically to include qualitative measures and results. Miles and Huberman (1984), for example, present a variety of qualitative methods for use in summative evaluation. These methods include interviews, observations, surveys, and self-reports. They typically result in verbal descriptions of effects of the innovation, or sometimes visual displays such as networks to show causal relationships between factors in the situation and the implementation of the innovation, or diagrams that show variations in use along two dimensions. With these methods both the measures and the results can be qualitative.

Nevertheless, for many qualitative researchers the commonalities across cases or settings are of primary interest, as they are for standard summative evaluation (Miles & Huberman, 1984):

More and more qualitative researchers are using multisite, multicase designs, often with multiple methods. The aim is to increase generalizability, reassuring oneself that the events and processes in one well-described setting are not wholly idiosyncratic. . . . The researcher uses multiple comparison groups to find out the kinds of social structures to which a theory or subtheory may be applicable. Having multiple sites increases the scope of the study and, thereby, the degrees of freedom. By comparing sites or cases, one can establish the range of generality of a finding or explanation, and, at the same time, pin down the conditions under which that finding will occur. (p. 151)

The overall goal is the same as for strictly quantitative summative evaluations: to assess the usefulness of the innovation. These qualitative approaches maintain the standard summative evaluation goals, audience, and overall methodology. There is still an emphasis on generalizations rather than on contrasts, on "effects" of the innovation rather than on identifying its realizations, and a minimal concern for the details of the innovation.

Another alternative method is *responsive evaluation*,[1] a method that attempts to achieve a better understanding of the process of change by being more sensitive to the perspective of the users of the innovation (Stake, 1990):

Responsive evaluation is an approach to the evaluation of educational and other programs. Compared to most other approaches it is oriented more to the activity, the uniqueness, and the social plurality of the program.

The essential feature of the approach is a responsiveness to key issues, especially those held by people at the site. It requires a delay and continuing adaptation of evaluation goal setting and data gathering while the people responsible for the evaluation become acquainted with the program and the evaluation context.

Issues are suggested as conceptual organizers for the evaluation study, rather than hypotheses, objectives, or regression equations. The reason for this is that the term "issues" draws thinking toward the complexity, particularity, and subjective valuing already felt by persons associated with the program. (p. 76)

Responsive evaluation is thus particularly sensitive to the interests and values of the variety of participants involved with the innovation. Formative evaluation, for example, can be done in a way that brings the users of the innovation into the development process. Their issues can then be made central to the activity of (re)designing the innovation. Similarly, summative evaluations can be made more responsive by focusing on desired educational results identified by the users of the innovation. Chapters 6–12 in this book represent an example of a responsive evaluation method in that they are written by the participants involved in the innovation.

Case studies (Stake & Easley, 1978; Stenhouse, 1990) are widely used in evaluations for attending to differences across settings. One reason for the case study approach is that variations among settings can be greater than variations among innovations. Thus, an insightful evaluation must include a wide variety of situations of use. The need to look at variations in situations is made by Dukes (1965) in a famous article ("$N = 1$") on the value of psychological experiments with only one subject. Dukes argues that since

[1] A related method is *ecological evaluation* (Lucas, 1988a, 1988b), which seeks evaluation procedures that directly improve, rather than hamper, instruction.

situations vary greatly, a researcher may learn as much or more by observing one subject in many situations as by observing many subjects in one situation. In effect, representative sampling is applied to problems or situations rather than to subjects: "In fact, proper sampling of situations and problems may in the end be more important than proper sampling of subjects, considering the fact that individuals are probably on the whole more alike than are situations among one another." (Brunswik, 1956, p. 39).

These and other alternative methods of evaluation have been used successfully in the study of innovations and change. They respond to the criticism that standard evaluations do not show why changes occur, how changes are different across settings, or how they relate to changes in the innovation. Alternative methods of evaluation address these problems to a certain extent, but may inherit the same limitations. For example, a set of case studies done within the summative framework entails the need to express conclusions in terms of a summary statement about the effects of using the innovation. Much of the richness of the case studies is lost as users are categorized and aggregate statements are formulated. As long as the focus is on the innovation, it is difficult to circumvent this problem.

It is noteworthy that even though there is considerable disagreement among alternative methods over *how to evaluate* an innovation, there is a general consensus about *what is to be evaluated* – namely, that the evaluation should be of the innovation, and that *innovation* is a meaningful, well-defined term. This presupposes that the setting in which the innovation is used is passive and is thus essentially technocentric. A consequence is that the process of change is conceptualized as a function of the innovation alone, or else it is effectively ignored. What is needed is a different focus entirely for the evaluation process, one which we call *situated evaluation*.

Situated evaluation of educational innovations

This book reports on a *situated evaluation* (Bruce & Rubin, 1993) that analyzes the varieties of use of ENFI. The evaluation is focused on the innovation-in-use, and its primary purpose is to understand the different ways in which the innovation is realized. We use the term *situated evaluation* to emphasize the unique characteristics of each situation in which the innovation is used. Our guiding assumption is that the innovation comes into being through use. The object of interest is not the idealized form in the developer's head, but rather the realization through use. Situated evaluation seeks to characterize alternate realizations of the innovation and to identify new variables. It assumes that measuring predetermined variables is insufficient, no matter how well those measurements are made.

Purposes of situated evaluation

A situated evaluation examines the various *realizations* of an innovation in different settings. Its concern is with the characteristics of contexts that give rise to different realizations. The careful articulation of the process whereby an innovation becomes realized in different ways can be useful in several ways:

- *Explain why the innovation was used the way it was.* A situated evaluation can help explain what happened, as opposed to just describing effects.
- *Predict the results of using the innovation.* This explanation can in turn provide the basis for predicting the realization of the innovation in similar contexts, providing the new context is well-understood.
- *Identify dimensions of similarity and difference among settings.* Examination of a realization of an innovation can reveal characteristics of a setting, such as a teacher's underlying pedagogical philosophy, that might be less visible otherwise.
- *Improve the use of the innovation.* Users of the innovation can refer to the situated evaluation as they work on improving the use of the innovation. They might find a realization whose setting has similar aspects to their own and specifically adopt practices of that setting.
- *Improve the technology.* Developers, likewise, can refer to the situated evaluation as they try to improve the innovation in terms of its interaction with different contexts. In this way, situated evaluation serves as a sort of formative evaluation.
- *Identify variables for later evaluation.* Finally, a situated evaluation can help structure future observations of an innovation's use. One way it does this is by focusing attention on the most salient dimensions of the innovation with respect to particular contexts. This can be used to guide a complementary summative evaluation.

Aspects of situated evaluation

Situated evaluation cannot be proceduralized; it is a process of discovering relationships. Nevertheless, within this process we can identify analysis of three crucial elements: the idealization of the innovation, the settings in which it appears, and the realizations within each setting. Whereas we may discuss these elements as discrete entities, no situated evaluation would proceed by stepwise analysis of them any more than a writer would move mechanically through predetermined stages of writing.

   In what follows we elaborate upon these aspects of situated evaluation. The process is iterative – the implication of the result of doing part of a situated evaluation may be to reanalyze other aspects in light of the new findings.

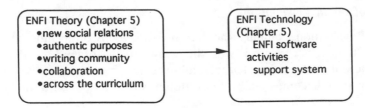

Figure 2-1. Analysis of ENFI, the innovation

1. The idealization of the innovation. A thorough analysis of the elements of the innovation independent of its use within real settings is part of a situated evaluation because it serves to characterize how participants in the setting of use might have perceived the innovation. It is also an index of the intentions of the developers, who participate not only in the initial creation of the innovation, but also in its re-creation in context.

In contrast to the priorities for summative evaluation, the idealized version of the innovation is not privileged over any of its realizations; similarity to the idealization does not count as more successful use, and nonuse can be as important to consider as "faithful" use. Moreover, the innovation is not seen as an agent that acts upon the users or the setting, but rather as one more element added to a complex and dynamic system. It would be more correct to say that *the users act upon the innovation,* shaping it to fit their beliefs, values, goals, and current practices. Of course, in that process they may themselves change, and their changes as well as those to the innovation need to be understood as part of the system.

There are several aspects of the innovation that need to be analyzed critically (see Figure 2–1). First, each innovation emerges from a theory, articulated to varying degrees in documents about the innovation. Any educational innovation has a theory of both learning and teaching. For ENFI this is presented in the Introduction, in Chapter 5, and in various articles about ENFI (Batson, 1987; Langston & Batson, 1990; Peyton & Batson, 1986; Peyton & Mackinson, 1989). The learning theory incorporated ideas about communication and its relation to education and community. The teaching theory had specific commitments to pedagogical principles such as collaboration and purposeful writing.

The idealization of an innovation also includes new technologies, if only in the form of texts that imply changes in practices. We conceive of the technology broadly. It includes various tools, artifacts, or apparatus, and in the case of ENFI, a new software system. Moreover, it includes prescriptions for use of the new tools, in this case, the activities as articulated in various articles and guidebooks (Beil, 1989; Neuwirth, Palmquist, & Gillespie, 1988; Neuwirth, Gillespie, & Palmquist, 1988). Finally, there is a support system for users, for those who are to carry out the new procedures or activities. Obviously, the elaboration of these elements varies greatly among technologies.

2. *The settings in which the innovation appears.* The shift in perspective from the view that realizations are distortions of an ideal to one in which realizations are creations that result from active problem solving has implications for the sorts of questions researchers need to ask in evaluating innovations. With this perspective, the social context in which the innovation is used becomes central. Questions relating to cultural, institutional, and pedagogical contexts need to be addressed. To answer these questions in full is a formidable task, but focusing on a few specific aspects may go far in providing what is needed for a situated evaluation. In the ENFI study we found that cultural, institutional, and pedagogical contexts were all critical in shaping realizations. Of these, the pedagogical context was probably the most important.

Characteristics of a social setting, including the goals and expectations of students and teachers, the institutional practices, constraints, and resources, and the classroom instructional environment contribute to the different realizations of an innovation. In order to understand these realizations, we need to understand these settings in detail. In the ENFI study we collected information on the settings through observations, interviews, and written reports by teachers. The information we gathered augmented the subsequent interpretations we made of ENFI's use. Analyses of ENFI's use in turn led us to rethink our initial understandings of the settings.

3. *The realizations of the innovation.* The third aspect of a situated evaluation is to study the realizations of the innovation in different settings. The study of the realizations should attend to the three limitations of evaluations described earlier. First, one should examine the ways the innovation was used and search for the reasons that changes occurred. This step includes examining whether the idealization was consonant or dissonant with existing social practices (as described in Chapter 1). It also includes analyzing how the innovation's use led to new social organizations. Second, one should look at the variety of uses across settings, treating each of these as an independent re-creation of the innovation, rather than as a data point for an aggregate statement about the innovation. Third, one should examine changes in the design of the innovation brought about by its use and the ways these changes relate to new practices.

Understanding the reasons for change. Extreme variations among realizations may lead one to feel that no valid generalizations about the innovation are possible. But the variations in use are actually beneficial for a situated evaluation. The reason is that our goal is not context-free summaries, but rather hypotheses about how and why the innovation was realized in different ways in different contexts, in other words, the beginnings of understanding the reasons for change. Thus situated evaluation seeks to identify new relevant variables to study. Through this process the evaluators may reach a deeper understanding of the idealization, elements of the settings, or the realizations, thereby obtaining successively more refined analyses of the use of the innovation.

Differences across settings. As we look for the reasons for change, we describe, then compare and contrast each of the realizations. The purpose is not to rank the effectiveness of the innovation across settings, nor is it to identify problem cases that must be discarded or analyzed separately, as they would need to be in the standard framework. Instead, the variations become the objects of study. The variations in use lead us to characterize the effect of the innovation as a function of elements of the setting in which it is used.

In some cases one can identify an entire set of classroom practices as a separate realization. This makes sense when the practices are significantly different from other classrooms on several dimensions, as when, for example, a change in topic is consistently associated with a change in student collaboration patterns, a new role for the teacher, and new goals for a writing activity. Different realizations of ENFI use were not confined to different sites, but occurred in different classrooms and class sessions within sites as well. As we reviewed the classroom practices we observed, we applied five heuristics to decide whether to designate a given practice as a separate realization:

First, the practice differed substantially from other activities on *more than one dimension.* Thus, if nothing more than the topic of the discussion differed, we did not conclude that we had found a new realization. But if the difference in topic was accompanied by different purposes for the activity, different participant roles, or a different amount or type of teacher involvement, we were more likely to consider the activity a different realization. In our observations of ENFI classrooms, we noted substantial variation along several dimensions, including:

- Room layout
- Hardware and software features
- Physical proximity of participants, varying literally from different campuses to shared chairs
- Group size
- Degree and manner of teacher involvement
- Roles of participants in the interactions
- Degree and nature of network interaction
- Degree of face-to-face interaction (oral or signed) accompanying the network interaction
- Purpose for the network activity
- Discussion topics

- Formality of the discourse
- Relation of network discourse to other activities and texts

Second, it was *coherent with identifiable elements within the setting of use.* In other words, when a practice made sense in terms of characteristics of the institutional setting, the teacher's goals and practices, or the student population, there was more reason to think of it as a separate realization than when there were no independent reasons for its existence.

Third, it was neither a characterization of desirable practices nor a mere logical possibility; *it really happened.* Evidence for the existence of a realization could be found not only in the occurrence of a particular activity, but also in other observational and interview data such as the physical layout of the room, course descriptions, and the discourse of students and teachers.

Fourth, it *persisted through many class sessions.* Activities that occurred only once were not considered a separate realization.

Finally, it *differed enough from all previously identified realizations* that it was less plausible to include it within a previously identified realization than to place it in a new category.

These heuristics served as a rough guide to identifying realizations. Even though no two classrooms were alike in every way, we did not think of every classroom or every class period as a distinct realization or as only one realization. One setting could give rise to more than one realization, and one realization could occur in several settings.

The characterizations produced by these analyses can be used in various ways. For the user, they give some indication of what to expect from the innovation given knowledge of the context. They also suggest what to change in the context in order to achieve particular results. For the developers, the characterization can be used in a formative way to revise the innovation, perhaps by including more explicit ways to alter the context, or to make the innovation more adaptable to different contexts.

Changes in the innovation. A situated evaluation should make it easier to describe not only differences across settings, but differences across time as the innovation changes. We have seen such changes in ENFI. Change is a normal part of the process of implementation, a process described as a mutual adaptation between an innovation and its social setting (Berman & McLaughlin, 1975). The adaptation can be to any aspect of the innovation – its technological apparatus, the procedures for its use, or the support system. Even the underlying theory may be revised.

Part of this analysis is to examine how new users conceptualize the innovation. Such an examination bears some resemblance to formative evaluation, but in situated evaluation there would be no assumption that a particular setting of use was typical. Thus the purpose would be to understand the varieties of actual use, not to identify a list of changes to the innovation.

Table 2-1. *Comparisons among three types of evaluation*

	Summative	Formative	Situated
Focus	Effects of the innovation	Innovation as tool	Social practices in contexts in which the innovation is used
Audience	User	Developer	Developer and user
Purpose	Decide whether to adopt innovation	Improve the innovation	Learn how the innovation is used
Variability	Controlled by balanced design or random sampling of settings	Minimized to highlight technology	Attended to for contrastive analysis
Measurement tools	Outcome measures	Observation/ interview/survey	Observation/ interview/survey
Time of assessment	After initial development	During development	During and after development
Results	Table of measures of contrasting groups	List of needed changes to the technology	Ethnographic description

Comparison with summative and formative evaluations

The paradigm underlying situated evaluation sees the innovation as coming into being through actual use. It does not focus on the innovation as idealization or on its effects, but rather on the social practices within the settings in which the innovation is re-created. This shift in focus has implications for the audience of the evaluation, the role of variability across settings, the tools for evaluation, the time of assessment, and the presentation of results.

We can now summarize the discussion of situated evaluation by comparing it with summative and formative evaluations as they are frequently practiced, as shown in Table 2–1.

Focus. Summative evaluations are usually concerned with the effects of using an innovation. Thus a summative evaluation assesses changes in, say, students' learning of a new concept, with less concern for the technical details of the innovation. In contrast, formative evaluations tend to focus on the innovation as a set of new technologies to be debugged. Although the ultimate goal may be to bring about some change in the users or the setting of use, the immediate focus is on the technology. In both cases there is usually an operative assumption that a single entity is being evaluated. As Walberg and Haertel (1990) say:

The term *evaluation* refers to a careful, rigorous examination of an educational curriculum, program, institution, organizational variable, or policy. The primary purpose of this examination is to learn about the particular entity studied, although more generalizable knowledge may also be obtained. The focus is on understanding and improving the thing evaluated (formative evaluation), on summarizing, describing, or judging its planned and unplanned outcomes (summative evaluation), or both. (p. xvii)

In contrast, situated evaluation examines the way the innovation becomes diverse social practices. The focus in situated evaluation is on the setting, as a complex, historically and culturally defined system, in which the innovation is one element. Thus, differences in versions of the innovation do not shape the design of the evaluation, but simply provide more variation to study. As a result, it is more feasible to compare and contrast cases of classrooms that use prototype versions of the innovation with those that use advanced versions, than it would be with summative evaluation, which is built upon assumptions of a single entity being evaluated.

Audience. Summative evaluation results are often published so that any of a large number of potential users can make informed decisions about the innovation. In contrast, formative evaluation is done for (and by) the developers so that they can make improvements to the innovation. They typically make changes as needed and do not report the results outside of a small community. Situated evaluation results can be used by both users and developers. Users can make decisions not only about whether to use the innovation, but how to use it in their particular context. Developers can learn how to revise the innovation taking into account the variations in use.

Purpose. Evaluations are done for some purpose, usually one that includes a specific action with respect to the innovation. This action is of course dependent upon the audience for the evaluation. For summative evaluation the action – whether to adopt the innovation – rests with the audience of potential users. In the case of formative evaluation, the audience of developers takes action to improve the innovation based on experiments with its use. For situated evaluation the audience is broad, as are the actions. The results could lead to developers changing the innovation, to users changing their practices, to adoption of only parts of the innovation, or to deeper understanding of the process of use.

Variability of settings. While doing a summative evaluation, one focuses on the value of the innovation. Thus one looks for controlled variation in the settings in which the innovation is implemented. If the settings are not all the same, there is nevertheless a preference for, say, a balance (e.g., among rural, urban, and suburban settings). One needs to assume that variations in use can either be attributed to fairly well understood causal factors, or that random variation will be of no consequence with a sufficiently large sample size. The study is structured to constrain the effects of context in order to say more about the effects of the innovation itself.

In a formative evaluation, there is a similar concern for controlled variation. Because the primary concern is to improve the innovation, one wants contexts that are typical, representative, or that at least reveal meaningful strengths and weaknesses of the innovation, contexts in which the innovation is used as intended by the developers. "Nonstandard" uses are not particularly informative at this stage, and could even induce changes that are inappropriate for the majority of users.

The central concern for situated evaluation is with characterizing the way an innovation comes into being in different contexts. Because the audience for the evaluation wants to know how to improve the use of the innovation, it is important to have a variety of contexts that they can compare to their own setting or to ones they might create. Thus differences across settings are not only acceptable; they are welcomed as resources to enrich the description of the possible realizations of the innovation.[2] This is one reason why situated evaluation is not equivalent to qualitative evaluation, although they may use similar methods. Often, qualitative research is applied to emphasize common patterns and to dismiss idiosyncratic results. Situated evaluation seeks to capture the idiosyncrasies and to understand their origins.

Measurement tools. A variety of tools can be employed for any type of evaluation, so it is simplistic to imply that there is a one-to-one correspondence between measurement tools and evaluation types. Nevertheless, certain tools are typically associated with particular types of evaluation. Because summative evaluations often seek quantitative, statistically significant results, they are usually conducted within a formal experimental design using predefined outcome measures such as writing sample scores. In contrast, formative evaluation does not often call for quantitative results. Instead, the personal reactions elicited by interviews and observations are usually the most useful tools. The emphasis in situated evaluation on differences across contexts implies the use of qualitative tools, including observations and interviews that are structured to elicit information about recurring social practices in settings and to draw out differences among realizations.

Time of assessment. The evaluation types can also be distinguished by their time of application. Summative evaluation is performed after the development

---

[2]   This is not to say that divergent settings are *necessary* for a situated evaluation. Instead, what appears as a problem within one paradigm appears as a useful feature in the other. This shift of status in something as fundamental as the nature of difference is one indication that we are talking about distinct paradigms.

has reached a stopping point, whereas formative evaluation, by definition, is carried out during development. Once the innovation is developed enough to be placed in a classroom, situated evaluation can start, in contrast to formative evaluation, which might begin earlier. Situated evaluation can continue well after the developers have finished.

Results. Summative evaluations typically yield quantitative results with quantitative bounds on the possible "error of measurement." These results can be stated concisely, and are often represented by a table or graph. Formative evaluations typically produce qualitative results, such as a list of changes to be made to the innovation.

Because a situated evaluation seeks to characterize alternate realizations and the changes in practices, it requires multiple, detailed descriptions of specific uses. Changes need to be described using appropriate quantitative or qualitative representations, but more importantly, the reasons for changes need to be discussed and linked to characteristics of the settings of use. The process of change, including changes in the innovation, in the users, and in the setting, becomes paramount. For these reasons, narrative accounts of diverse uses are most useful. Chapters 5–12 are such narrative accounts – stories of the ENFI experiences in different classrooms, with different students and teachers.

3   Understanding the multiple threads of network-based classrooms

Joy Kreeft Peyton and Bertram C. Bruce

An innovation is often viewed as a thing, which has a name – ENFI, Logo, Quill, cooperative learning, and so on. Even when it evolves in different contexts to the point where it is nearly unrecognizable from its original form, it retains the name. Therefore, everyone involved in the ENFI Consortium (teachers, researchers, administrators, students, funders, evaluators, and advisory board members) described consortium members' activity as "doing ENFI," whether they were engaged in whole-class written discussions of a text or issue within a class and across distance, or were sending composed and orally negotiated paragraphs to other groups in the class; whether they were using CECE Talk, Realtime Writer, or Interchange. ENFI was what brought consortium members together, challenged them to reflect on theories and practices, and provided the impetus for our evaluation. The term itself was key for establishing and maintaining a community of like-minded people. Our challenge in this process was not to arbitrarily and prematurely limit the use of the term, but to understand what it was that people were doing when they said they were using ENFI. We saw that to do justice to the diversity we observed, we needed the perspective of the ENFI users. We asked them to describe, explain, interpret, and evaluate their own practices, as they have done in Chapters 5–12.

Defining ENFI

Early in our evaluation of ENFI we essentially attempted to describe its "effects" in spite of the immediately evident diversity. But we soon encountered definitional problems. In the first instance, we found that we could not identify ENFI with a single technology. Within the consortium alone two different hardware and four different software systems were in use:

- Realtime Writer, from Realtime Learning Systems, Washington, DC, running on 10-Net and Novell networks with IBM PCs (The realizations of ENFI described in Chapters 6, 7, 11, and 12 involve the use of Realtime Writer.)
- CECE Talk, at Carnegie Mellon (CMU), running on the Andrew

50

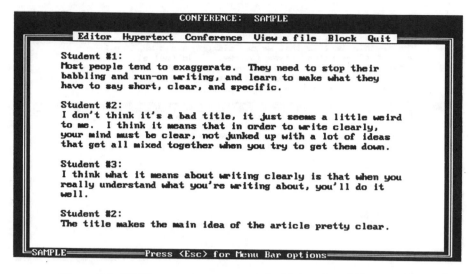

Figure 3-1. ENFI computer screen at the University of Texas, without the composing window

system in a Unix environment using high-function workstations (See Chapter 10.)
- The CB Utility included with the 10-Net local-area network from DCA running on IBM PCs (See Chapter 8.)
- Daedalus Interchange, one component of the Daedalus Instructional System, developed by the Daedalus Group of Austin, TX (See Chapter 9.)

One of the schools switched during the project from the CB Utility to Realtime Writer, and in the interim used yet another system, CT System 3, also from Realtime Learning Systems.

Realtime Writer was described in the Introduction. At the University of Texas, Fred Kemp and his colleagues used a program called Interchange. It is similar to Realtime Writer in that there is a private composing window and a group dialogue window. However, with this software the composing window is only visible when the writer calls it up. Figures 3–1 and 3–2 show the Interchange screen without and then with the composing window, respectively. Thus, the writer temporarily leaves the dialogue to compose a message and only reenters it after the send key is hit and the comment is "published." There is no limit to the length of the message, and a full-screen editor with limited word-processing capabilities allows for easy revision and editing before a message is sent.

Both Realtime Writer and Interchange convert multiple messages from the group into a single sequence, ordered by the time of transmission. However, they differ in that with Realtime Writer the public window continuously

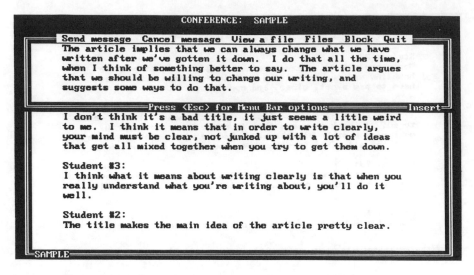

Figure 3-2. ENFI computer screen at the University of Texas, with the composing window

scrolls. Many users report that this feature makes them feel at the leading edge of the sequence, as in spoken conversation. Interchange may be used in this way but also has an option that allows a participant to "hang back" and read messages that might be several minutes "old." Some participants sensed this as being more akin to an electronic mail system than a spoken conversation.

On CECE Talk at CMU, each participant in a discussion has his or her own composing window, which is visible to all members of the discussion at all times. Because of the multiple windows, CECE Talk works best on large-screen monitors. Students can write messages of any length, which scroll within that window. Figure 3–3 shows the screen for this system. Larry has initiated a discussion with Wilma about a paper he is writing about problems with the food service. In practice, the multiwindow approach is workable only with small groups, generally no larger than four. The advantage of this approach is that it is completely in real time – the keystrokes appear on all screens at the same instant. None of the other programs is as quick.

There were also many different applications of the networks besides real-time interaction within a class, including real-time distance interaction between two campuses and non-real-time uses such as electronic mail and bulletin boards.

The physical layout of networked classes also varied greatly. At Gallaudet computers were arranged in a circle facing the center of the room, with the teacher's station in the circle, at the front. At Northern Virginia Community

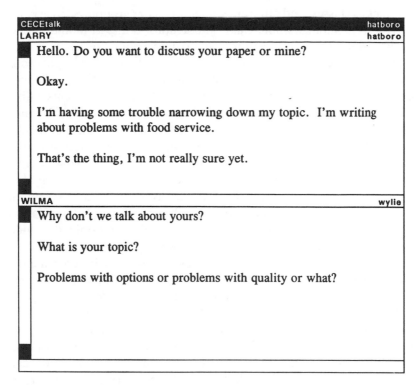

Figure 3-3. ENFI computer screen at Carnegie Mellon University (from Bruce & Peyton, 1990)

College (NVCC), the computers were arranged around the outside of the room facing the walls, and the teacher had no special station. At Minnesota, the students worked in separate carrels, similar to the style of a language lab, and could not see each other. At CMU, New York Institute of Technology (NYIT), and the University of Texas the computers were in the traditional arrangement of rows facing the front of the room. But even within this structure there were significant variations. At Texas the teacher's computer was at the back of the room, barely distinguishable from the students' computers, whereas at NYIT the teacher's station was highly visible at the front, on a large raised platform.

Knowing that we could not describe ENFI simply as a technology, we considered describing it as a theoretical orientation – the development of writing in writing communities, for example – or as a particular pedagogical approach – the use of conversational writing to develop more extended composition. However, in our observations and interviews with teachers, we discovered that many different theoretical orientations were at work and many different approaches used. There were almost as many different network activities as classes, and different student–teacher groupings to carry out those activities, including whole-class interactions both with and without the teacher, small-group interactions, and paired interactions.

There were also marked differences among the student populations at the consortium sites, ranging from precollege deaf students at Gallaudet to sophisticated juniors and seniors at CMU, with hearing students of basic and average writing ability in between at Minnesota, NYIT, NVCC, and Texas.

The institutions and individual classes differed also in terms of their learning goals, which included developing basic English proficiency, improving critical reading, and honing argumentative writing. Often these goals were defined by institutional gateposts, such as departmental exit tests, which also varied greatly. Finally, the institutional resources available to consortium members varied from site to site. Some institutions had considerable financial resources available to set up or improve their computer labs and trained technical staff to help the teachers. At some, teachers were given release time to develop their practice and had the support of key people in their departments. Other institutions worked with far fewer resources. (See Chapter 4 for a summary of the ways these constraints shaped ENFI at the different sites.)

When we compared elements of the original ENFI vision, what we might call the *idealized ENFI,* with what teachers actually did with the network in their classes, we encountered major discrepancies. Under a narrow conception of ENFI there were no real ENFI users. On the other hand, a conception of ENFI broad enough to include the various network uses in the consortium would no longer be descriptive; it would include a vast array of computer networking activities and projects that had nothing to do with ENFI and people who had never heard of ENFI (for example, all those who use electronic mail or bulletin boards in writing classes).

It began to appear hopeless to cope with the diversity within the ENFI Consortium. How could we evaluate ENFI's effectiveness if we couldn't even say what ENFI was? It seemed we needed either to force an arbitrary and unsatisfactory definition of ENFI or to abandon the study of an intriguing and potentially significant class of educational experimentation. We did neither, for we realized two important facts.

First, despite the diversity, the participants in the consortium believed they were in some sense doing the same thing, which they called ENFI. We were obliged to probe deeper to see what commonalities lay beneath the surface diversity. Although the term *ENFI* did not have a sharp technical definition, it served important social functions. Users of ENFI had shared goals and significant shared approaches to teaching and the use of technology. They collaborated with each other in formulating ideas and in studying their own teaching, just as they intended for students to do when they used ENFI.

Second, the ENFI situation exemplifies what happens when any innovation leaves the hands of the primary developers and moves into diverse settings, as described in Chapter 1. Individual users themselves act as agents of change and transform the innovation, often moving it far beyond what was originally envisioned. The fact that there were many ENFI's, and not just one, complicated our task considerably, but by no means made it unique.

Our solution was to cease trying to find or create a definition of ENFI and to begin to look at what happens when teachers at various institutions and in various classes set out to use written interaction on a computer network. To this end, as a first step toward a situated evaluation, we began to document and attempt to understand the various implementations of network use at the institutions involved in the ENFI consortium.

Research questions

In 1988 and 1989 we visited each consortium site at least once and if possible, twice. On each visit we observed ENFI classes and interviewed site directors, ENFI teachers, and ENFI students. Our primary goal was not to say whether ENFI was good or bad, nor was it to verify the extent and correctness of ENFI implementation. Instead, we wanted to be able to say what it was that people were doing when they claimed to be "doing ENFI."

We worked with a large set of research questions, starting with fairly simple ones about room layout and time spent on the network and moving toward more interpretive ones. Some of these are discussed at various points in this book, and others are addressed in articles about ENFI by participants in the ENFI Consortium (a bibliography is included at the end of this book).

First, we focused on the basic network configuration:

- How is the network room arranged?
- What computer software and hardware are used?
- How often and for how long is the network used?
- What activities is the network used for?
- What is the configuration of use: pairs, small groups, whole class?
- What is the teacher's role in the network interaction?

We also had questions about the nature of the online discourse when the network was used:

- What are the participation patterns on the network? Who "talks"? How much? What do they say?
- What is the content and quality of network discussions?
- Who has control of the interactions?
- Who is included in the interactions and who is excluded?
- How are these patterns similar to or different from those in more traditional classrooms, conducted orally or in sign language?

Because the original goal of ENFI was to enhance overall writing development, we also examined network writing in relation to other reading and writing activities in ENFI classes:

- How does network interaction relate to other classroom writing and activities?
- What kinds of literacy skills are practiced on the network?
- What kinds of literacy skills are not practiced?

Finally, we assessed as well as we could students' and teachers' interpretations of ENFI:

- How do different students and teachers interpret what ENFI is?
- How do the students and teachers react to the use of the network for teaching and learning writing?

Data sources

We had access to a rich, intertextual corpus of written materials for assessing realizations. These included survey data, writings by teachers about their classrooms, electronic mail discussing the implementations, student writing, and transcripts of interviews with students and teachers. Thus we relied to a large extent on what was already written about ENFI, which is typical when doing a situated evaluation and in most ethnography today (Clifford, 1986). But even with large amounts of text available, observations are essential to doing a situated evaluation. We made use of several kinds of data to approach these questions, none of which would have been sufficient alone.

Classroom observations

We observed, and in some cases participated in, selected classrooms using the network at each of the five consortium sites. In most cases we were able to visit at least two classes. Our site visits were planned according to the convenience of the site directors and teachers involved, but we did make sure ahead of time that we were visiting classes in which ENFI was well-established. We did not use a classroom observation guide, primarily because we did not yet know what we would find and did not want to limit what we saw with preconceived ideas of classroom processes. We wanted to be completely open to observe novel phenomena in this inherently new mode of discourse. We decided that our visits would be very open-ended, and we took open-ended field notes.

Interviews

We conducted formal interviews with site directors, teachers, and students. We interviewed almost all of the teachers involved in the project using both one-on-one and group interviews. Among the students, we tried to interview at least two who had claimed to their professor to like ENFI and two who had claimed not to like it. There were standard questions we asked at each site and common areas we wanted to explore, but we did not have a set interview protocol. Instead, we remained open to whatever people said, probed in the areas that were the most salient to the participants, and then documented carefully what we heard. Most of the interviews were tape-recorded and transcribed. Some took place informally during class time and were not tape-recorded; for those we relied on our notes.

Network transcripts

We also collected transcripts of network interactions for all the classes we observed. At some of the sites, we were told of other ENFI approaches that we were not able to observe, and were given illustrative transcripts. We are confident, therefore, that we had a comprehensive and nearly complete sample of ENFI implementations at the time of the study.

Survey data

To get a broader view of network use and the reactions of students and teachers in all of the classes at the consortium sites, we collected questionnaire data each semester on room layouts, course descriptions and goals, student characteristics, network activities, and teacher reports of strengths and limitations of ENFI. We made extensive use of these data, particularly teachers' written responses to open-ended questions about ENFI.[1]

Electronic mail communications

An electronic mail conference was set up for ENFI teachers and site directors in the consortium and used regularly to discuss activities, successes, problems, and solutions associated with ENFI use. As participants in this conference, we had access to all of the messages, which provide a rich corpus of information about ENFI implementation.

Reports by consortium members

We made use of reports and articles written by teachers and researchers at each site, and checked our perceptions against participant accounts in these documents.

[1] The results of the investigation are described in a series of project reports to Annenberg/CPB (Horowitz & Peyton, 1988a, 1988b; Peyton, Michaelson, & Batson, 1988; Solis & Peyton, 1989).

Participant feedback

Finally, we presented reports at consortium meetings, circulated drafts of our papers, and received feedback on the accuracy of our categories and descriptions. By soliciting the concerns, issues, and critiques of participants in the study, our evaluation was to some extent "responsive" in the sense defined by Stake (1990).

With these data collected and compiled, we were able to identify and categorize the various realizations of what the participants themselves called ENFI, a major first step of our situated evaluation. A brief description of these realizations constitutes the rest of this chapter; more detailed discussions from the consortium members themselves are in Chapter 6–12.

Realizations of ENFI

As discussed in Chapter 1, the disparity between well-established values and practices and those embodied in an innovation may present a challenge for those who decide to adopt the innovation. ENFI teachers embraced the innovation because they believed in the values and practices that it claimed to promote (discussed in the Introduction and in Chapter 5), but they needed to accommodate these within a framework of existing values and practices. As with any innovation, implementing ENFI at a given site involved resolving conflicts between old and new values.

For example, at CMU, ENFI entered an already computer-rich environment, with many excellent technological resources for teachers and students to use. A campuswide network of powerful personal computers was already in place. Nearly all dormitory rooms, offices, and classrooms had computers, which were connected to the network. Classrooms already had one computer terminal per student, so original class sizes and classroom layouts were retained. ENFI was simply inserted as an additional computer-based writing tool. The students at CMU are in general academically successful and fluent in writing. They do not need to work on basics such as how to write a sentence or paragraph, nor do most of them need to overcome initial reluctance to write or to use computers. Instead, they need to work on argumentation: how to step into an already rich and complex body of written discourse on a topic, organize and understand the major threads, make a unique contribution, and reflect with others on what they have done.

Concern for addressing needs such as these has been a hallmark of the writing research and pedagogy at CMU (Kaufer, Geisler, & Neuwirth, 1989). Given this setting, it is not surprising that ENFI use at CMU has emphasized critical, reflective response to published and student texts. Students typically work in pairs or groups of three, critiquing each others' work. The teacher is not present on the network at all, but in the room and available for oral consultation if needed. (See Chapter 10 for discussion.)

In contrast, few of the English classes in the General College at Minnesota had computers. A new lab was equipped specifically for ENFI classes, which were half the size of other classes in the college. Separate carrels were set up to inhibit oral communication, and the original software used at Gallaudet was installed (a CB Utility from 10-Net). The students involved were developmental writers who had demonstrated the need for additional writing instruction and practice before they could enter regular university English classes. Accustomed to receiving remedial instruction, they were surprised and delighted with the "special" treatment they received by being placed in a state-of-the art computer lab. Many of them were working on overcoming writing anxieties and blocks and developing basic writing fluency. ENFI in this setting tended toward more significant teacher involvement, with the whole class, including the teacher, working together on the network as a writing community. The purpose of the network interactions, which focused on published texts the students had read or on student compositions in progress, was to give them opportunities to express themselves informally in writing, to realize that written ideas originate with and are directed toward real people. (See Chapter 8.)

These two settings have led to realizations of ENFI that differ in terms of classroom layout, class size, hardware, software, educational goals and activities, number of participants in a discussion, teacher involvement, and relation of ENFI work to other classroom activities. The other sites discussed in this book, with their various ENFI realizations, differ in similar ways.

Across the sites and classes we visited, we identified 15 substantially different realizations of ENFI, which we grouped into 7 "families" – groupings of similar realizations. Here we present a brief description of each. Most of these realizations have been described in detail elsewhere, in most cases by the teachers themselves, either in chapters in this book or in other publications. Beil (1989), for example, contains papers about many different ENFI realizations, with extensive transcript samples. Sources for other descriptions are given with the specific realization descriptions here.

A. Discussion

This family includes the realizations that we observed in which students engaged in written conversations, often with their teachers. Students appeared as themselves on the network or used a pseudonym, but they did not adopt a persona as in a play. Although the purpose of the discussion may have been to support other extended writing in some way, the discussions were not necessarily tied to other texts. Instead, the discussion, which might revolve around open topics, controversial issues, data, or reading texts, was considered valuable in its own right for the ideas and manners of expression it provoked. These discussions took place among the whole class or small groups on separate channels and in the case of A-2, in pairs.

A-1. Open discussion. Open discussions had no prepared topic and little teacher direction. Students conversed on the network about personal issues, such as plans for the weekend, interacted with visitors to the classroom, or discussed current events, as those topics arose, and the teacher generally followed the students' lead.

A-2. Cross-age tutoring. The topics here were usually the same as those in A-1, open to student choice, but the participants were of two different ages (college and elementary school) or English proficiency levels, such that one participant provided a writing model for the other. Students typically worked in pairs on separate channels (described in detail in Peyton, 1989b).

A-3. Confrontation of issues. This realization is similar to A-1 except that one topic, some controversial issue, was identified and focused on. The teacher played a more dominant role than in open-ended discussions, introducing an issue and leading students to confront the questions it posed. The teacher also pushed students to articulate reasons or external sources for ideas that they might have stated first in personal or emotion-laden terms.

A-4. Analysis of data. Here students engaged in a discussion and analysis of data, such as a table of employment figures displayed by gender and ethnicity. They were grouped on separate channels (three to five students per group) to allow for focused discussion designed to reach reasoned interpretations of the data.

A-5. Discussion of texts. This was a common realization that, like A-1, typically involved the entire class. Unlike A-1, there was a specific topic, namely to critique or otherwise respond to a text all the students had read. Students typically had the printed text at their desks and consulted it for exact quotes and page references.

A-6. Therapeutic discourse. We chose this name for this realization because the discussions, which focused on literature texts the students had read, were akin to those that might occur in a group therapy session. Students were assigned to channels on the basis of personality types (introvert/extrovert, thinking/judging), using assessments such as the Myers-Briggs personality inventory. The teacher guided the discussion toward feeling statements ("This story makes me feel . . . ") and away from intellectualizing ("I think that . . . " or even "I feel that . . . ").

A-7. Brainstorming and prewriting. Topics in this realization could be open-ended or focused on a topic, reading, or issue, but the specific purpose was to generate ideas or preliminary text for subsequent student writing. This definition of purpose shaped the discussion (emphasis on expressing ideas, not on critical analysis) and the teacher's role (minimal, usually to keep ideas coming or to make relations among ideas).

B. Role playing

A second family of realizations is strikingly different from the discussion family. Participants on the network did not represent themselves, but rather the roles they had adopted, either by choice or by teacher assignment. These roles might come from published plays or novels the class was reading or from scenarios that the teacher constructed and gave the students ahead of time.

B-1. Dramatic production. Students, with or without the teacher, attempted to reproduce or create a dramatic piece on the network, adopting and maintaining specific network roles. The purpose of these productions was for students to reach a deeper understanding of a published play or novel by reenacting it, to learn about the art of dramatic production by producing their own creation, and to use language more creatively as they attempted to represent different cultures, periods, or personalities. (Described in Miller, this volume, and Peyton & Miller, 1989).

B-2. Role-playing scenarios. This realization is similar to dramatic production, except that instead of adopting roles from literature and focusing on the structure of the production itself, students took on roles for discussing business or policy questions or controversial issues that they would later write about more extensively. For example, one scenario that we observed involved a discussion of the destruction of the Amazon rain forest, with the students assuming roles such as "environmentalist," "land baron," or "government agent." (Scenarios such as this are described in Chapter 6.) In another scenario, for a full semester students in a business writing course assumed the roles of executive officers in a business and solved problems as they arose. The purpose of these scenarios was for students to understand the positions of various parties and to formulate, support, and criticize arguments. Because most scenarios involved three or four characters, students worked in small groups on separate channels.

C. Response to student writing

Although the realizations in families A and B may support other student writing in some way, they were not necessarily tied to any piece of student writing. In this responsive family of realizations, however, network discussions were clearly tied to more extended written text, centering on interactive written responses to compositions the students were working on.

C-1. Socratic tutoring. In this realization (named by Marshall Kremers), the whole class was on the network together, but the teacher engaged in one-on-one dialogues with each student, shifting from one to the next as a chess master would in playing multiple simultaneous chess games in an exhibition. In these dialogues, the teacher asked questions and challenged ideas to push students to rethink their arguments and support assertions they had made in essays they were writing. The dialogues were thus highly teacher directed (described in Kremers, 1990).

C-2. Peer response groups. This realization was typically carried out in pairs or groups of three to five. In one version, one student presented a printed version of a composition in progress for criticism and help from others. The teacher was often absent from the discussion, or switched from group to group (described in Sirc & Reynolds, 1990.) A more structured variation of peer response to compositions was Devil's Advocate, named by consortium staff at CMU, in which students typically worked in pairs or at most groups of three. One student presented a text he or she was working on and the other adopted the role of "devil," taking a consistently critical stance toward the first student's text and pushing and probing on weak points in arguments to ensure that the writer had considered all the possible objections to the text and addressed them accordingly (described in Chapter 10).

D. Language games

Network-mediated language games must be considered a separate category of realizations, even though we saw only one realization of them at the college level, because they clearly differ from all of the other realizations (language games are much more prevalent in elementary-level ENFI classes). We observed the language game Twenty Questions, in which all of the network discussion was in the form of yes/no questions ("Is it a man?" "Is he alive?") and one-word replies ("yes" or "no"), and the goal was to guess who or what the lead person had in mind.

E. Collaborative text production

As described in Chapter 5, one of the key features of ENFI for the developers was that it promoted collaboration, and all of the realizations discussed here involve collaboration in some way. In this family of realizations, however, the actual act of writing was collaborative. Students (with or without the teacher) produced together a text – a story, a play, an essay – by going around the room and writing one line, paragraph, or section each, building on previous contributions. A variation on this, used in a business writing course, was round-robin memo writing, in which one student wrote a memo and sent it to another, who sent that memo and a response memo to another, and so on, each memo influencing subsequent ones.

F. Distributed text

In this realization, developed and named by Diane Thompson at NVCC, students composed brief texts (10 lines or less in her class, which is what her network software allows) and broadcast them on the network to the rest of the class for oral discussion (described in Chapter 11). When students worked in groups to compose their texts, the writing that appeared on the network was much different than that in the other realizations. It was less spontaneous, because the group negotiated and planned what they would write before a group member typed it in.

G. Distance networking

Distance networking is as much a different technology as a different family of realizations, but it was implemented at one of the consortium sites using the same software used in the local-area networks. It was considered to be ENFI by the site director and the rest of the consortium. The activities over long distance can include any of the realizations described and were used for open discussion, brainstorming, and peer response groups. We consider it a separate family of realizations because it arose and has continued to be used as a distinct type of activity in a particular institutional setting, one in which the teacher was skeptical of the value of real-time written communication among people in the same classroom and was looking for a context in which such communication could be justified. Distance conversations provided the opportunity for students at one school (with a stable, working-class, southern, rural population) to interact and share experiences and ideas for writing with those at another school (with mostly military dependents in a transient, diverse community), who had very different values and life experiences (described in Chapter 11).

This typology covers all of the realizations of ENFI that we saw or heard about at the college level, but we are sure that it does not include all the potential realizations, or even all those currently in use. The process of implementation is constantly generative. As new people continue to use networks with new students, goals, and institutional constraints, new realizations will continue to proliferate.

Summary

The many realizations of an innovation reflect properties of the innovation-in-use, properties that emerge only in practice. These properties may seem ephemeral, based as they are on particularities of settings, but they are the only ones that matter for evaluation, for redesign of the innovation, for selecting appropriate settings of use, or for predicting future results of use. The examples in the chapters to follow show the power of the social context to affect the ultimate uses of a new technology. How the features of the technology interact with human needs, expectations, beliefs, prior practices, and alternative tools far outweighs the properties of the technology itself. Thus when we analyze the effects of an innovation, we must consider much more than an aggregate result such as the "average impact of the typical implementation."

We see situated evaluation as a new framework for understanding innovation and change. This framework has several key ingredients: It emphasizes contrastive analysis and seeks to explore differences in use rather than controlling difference and searching for commonalities. It assumes that the object of study is neither the innovation alone nor its effects, but rather the realization of the innovation the innovation in use. Finally, it produces hypotheses for further study supported by detailed analyses of actual practices. These hypotheses make possible informed plans for use and change of innovations.[2]

[2] See both Chapter 4 and site-based Chapters 6–12.

4   Pulling together the threads: Themes and issues in the network-based classroom

Joy Kreeft Peyton and Bertram C. Bruce

ENFI was developed in 1985 at one institution, Gallaudet University, and first used in two classrooms (a college preparatory English class and a sophomore composition class), by two teachers (Trent Batson and Steve Lombardo) who were later joined by a researcher (Joy Peyton). Its original qualities were shaped by that particular situation and by the personal and educational backgrounds, needs, and theoretical orientations of those particular participants (as described in Chapter 5). From there ENFI moved to other classes, professors, and students at Gallaudet, and then to other schools with different situations, professors, and students, who had different personal and educational needs and theoretical orientations. Most of this book consists of the stories of these participants in these situations. These stories tell of ENFI's evolution, in conception and implementation, from its origins at Gallaudet through its many iterations at the consortium sites. They provide an in-depth look at individuals and individual situations as their understanding and implementation of ENFI evolved over time.

In their individuality, the stories of ENFI suggest variation without limit – isolated phenomena from which no general observations can be drawn. Indeed, the contrasts among the implementations were what first captured our attention. Yet as we look across the various sites and the changes within those sites over time, some general themes emerge. These themes are not so much generalities about ENFI, but more about the process of creating diverse innovations, each labeled "ENFI" by the creators. What we see are similar ways in which existing practices, values, social relationships, technologies, resources, and institutional constraints transact with new pedagogical approaches. Whereas each transaction, and therefore each ENFI implementation, is unique, the mutual shaping processes have much in common, and may have much in common as well with the processes of adoption of other innovations. In this chapter we focus on some of the constraints that the ENFI Consortium members worked within as they implemented ENFI and examine the ways that ENFI evolved within those constraints – sometimes conforming to them and sometimes changing them. We draw from the descriptions given in this volume by educators implementing ENFI, from the other writings of

65

these authors and their ENFI colleagues in other project reports and published articles, and from our interviews with them and our observations of their classrooms (see Chapter 3 for a more detailed description of our data sources). Our goal is to identify the issues that situational constraints might raise for anyone attempting to understand and implement ENFI or, more generally, any nascent technology.

As discussed earlier, the ENFI vision was not applied to a blank slate or inserted into a vacuum. Instead, it grew out of a complex and already functioning educational system and entered others. At the same time that those systems were incorporating ENFI, they were also responding to well-established events and processes and absorbing other new visions and practices.

The vision for ENFI was for a transformed classroom – a classroom in which all communication occurs in writing, on a computer; a classroom in which writing has the power of conversation, done for real purposes and for real audiences; a classroom in which the teacher is not the center of attention, but a member of a learning and writing community, a facilitator; a classroom in which students have equal access to the ongoing discussion and participate equally (Batson, 1988a and this volume; Peyton & Batson, 1986). This vision took one shape at first, as described in Chapter 5. But many variables affected that shape as the vision moved into new contexts at Gallaudet and the other consortium schools. Here, we discuss five:

- The goals, practices, and gateposts of the institutions involved
- The theories, personalities, and practices of the teachers
- The characteristics and expectations of the students
- Features of the technology – hardware, software, room location and layout
- The resources available for setting up and maintaining the technology

We discuss each constraint separately, although the overlap among them is apparent throughout the discussion.

Institutional goals, practices, and gateposts

At Gallaudet and all of the other consortium sites, ENFI was used primarily for courses in the English department. The goal of the courses was to teach students to write extended prose – in some, personal narratives; in others, expository essays. In most cases, years had been spent planning curricula, choosing materials, and developing exit tests to assess students' abilities to perform these tasks. As is clear from the discussions and examples of network-based writing in this book, however, network writing is very different from the "essayist prose" (Scollon & Scollon, 1981) traditionally expected in these college English courses. In fact, it is less like solitarily produced, extended text and more like conversation, or "talk story" (Boggs, 1985). The differences between ENFI discourse and essayist prose contribute to both the excitement about ENFI and the conflicts in its implementation.

Instead of one author, there are many authors, each expressing ideas and building on or completely ignoring the ideas of others. Langston and Batson (1990) argue that network writing abolishes the notion of the original thinker, the solitary author producing a text, and gives rise instead to the image of "a precipitating solid in a supersaturated solution . . . the speck of dust around which crystals form" (p. 153). The individual in this new image is suspended in ideas and concepts that crystallize in a community. Sirc and Reynolds (this volume) describe network interaction as bricolage, a construction of meaning built from "a blend of one's own ideas, others' ideas, and material one has read or heard in discussion."

The writing does not result in a product in the traditional sense – a story, an essay, a term paper, or a dissertation. As one consortium member (DiMatteo, 1990) has pointed out:

The product of such writing is a text that reaches no conclusion. . . . Not only does no one have the final say, but even the notion of a final say is brought into doubt. The text, traditionally understood as a stable place of organized and fixed language, disappears. (p. 76)

The quality of students' network discussions often does not approximate what is normally considered literate discourse. In fact, students' network discourse has disappointed and shocked many teachers. As the authors in this book have described and illustrated with transcripts, the interactions are sometimes confused and off-topic, focusing on everything but the topic at hand. Rather than writing complex thoughts or extended, logical, thoughtful prose, students trying to keep up with the constant flow of language scrolling up their screens, and suddenly in linguistic competition with their classmates, may fire off humorous zingers and "graffiti-like messages" (Kremers, 1990, p. 40) or "cheap shots" and "easy insults" (Miller, this volume). Those who take the time to think and compose may be laughed at, criticized, or ignored and left behind.

Real-time written interaction seems to create an urge to engage in language play, to show off one's wit, to display one's verbal audacity. This dynamic can be valuable with students who are generally reticent to express themselves in writing, and in the early days of ENFI at Gallaudet this energy was unexpected but welcomed. At the same time, the result can be emotional and even confrontational and insulting dialogues, a phenomenon experienced in classes throughout the ENFI Consortium. A professor at NYIT, for example, found that students using the network for the first time began "to curse obsessively" in "a tidal wave of obscenity and puerility" (DiMatteo, 1990b, pp. 79, 80). Another described her students' initial network behavior as a "combination of unbridled bigotry and heady power" that produces exchanges "less interactive than interinsultive" (George, 1990, p. 49).

These qualities of network interaction have raised among consortium members serious questions about its role in the writing classroom and its viability as a way to help students do the kinds of writing that are expected of them.

The bottom line, after all, is that this is a writing class, and no matter what anyone says about the theoretically collaborative, social side of writing, ultimately it becomes a solitary act. (Sirc, University of Minnesota)*

The goal of writing as communication is not an expressed institutional one, while writing essays is, and ENFI does not have any very obvious impact on the writing of essays. (Thompson, NVCC)

[Network writing] is so revolutionary that it isn't at all clear whether or not there is any way to link [it] with success on an exit exam. (Kremers, NYIT)

One professor even mentioned the possibility that network writing might have an adverse effect on students' school-based writing, especially those students whose writing abilities are already weak:

Unfortunately, my ENFI class may be in a weaker position than my non-ENFI class when it comes time to take the departmental final, which involves writing an essay. My ENFI class tries to incorporate conflicting perspectives on an issue in their essays, because these perspectives arise in the network prewriting sessions. My non-ENFI students concentrate on their own perspectives. Their singleminded approach makes more traditional sense than the multiple-perspective approach, because it leads to a clear thesis and topic sentence. The skills the network promotes are difficult to assess through the traditional essay format. (Kremers, NYIT)

These qualities of network writing also raise questions about evaluation of students' writing in this new medium. How is this writing to be evaluated if there is no single author and measures of writing competence are based on individual performance? If network writing itself does not yield a text that can be evaluated, do the skills acquired in network interaction transport in any effective way to the essay and research writing that students must be able to do and that they are evaluated for?

The responses to these questions and the resulting ENFI practices that have been developed are very different. At CMU a strong theory-based writing curriculum was already in place for freshman students, and the goal of the teachers was to promote critical thinking, critical response to texts, and collaborative work. Thus the CMU staff working on the ENFI project asked bluntly, How will the practice of writing concurrently on a computer network facilitate the goals we already have in place? It was clear from the beginning of the ENFI experimentation at CMU that if ENFI activities didn't facilitate

---

* The quotations in this chapter not attributed to a publication come from interviews with and questionnaires completed by ENFI Consortium members.

those goals, ENFI would have no place in the program. The result of the work at CMU was a highly structured ENFI practice, with paired interactions and carefully delineated tasks (described in detail in teacher and student guidebooks; Neuwirth, Gillespie, & Palmquist, 1988; Neuwirth, Palmquist, & Gillespie, 1988). At this institution ENFI was adapted to fit the writing theory and curriculum that were already in place.

At Gallaudet the primary goal of all the English classes using ENFI is that students become proficient with written English, as demonstrated by performance on out-of-class essays and a departmental exit exam at the end of the semester. Doug Miller, one of the first teachers to implement ENFI, had spent years developing curricula, materials, and activities to accomplish this goal in his freshman and sophomore English courses. His first use of ENFI was an attempt to transfer those activities, primarily structured writing exercises and drills, to the network. When he found that those activities did not seem to facilitate his goals but rather to hamper them, he stopped using the network entirely for a time. When he returned to ENFI, it was in a completely different form, for dramatic productions ("script writing") in a more loosely structured summer course that had no preestablished curriculum and no exit exam. In the conclusion to Chapter 7 in this volume, Miller suggests that he wants to go even further and design a course specifically to exploit ENFI's potential. Thus, in Miller's case ENFI was eventually transported to a course that would exploit its qualities rather than being forced to fit an already existing course (see also Peyton, 1990, for a description of the evolution of ENFI in Miller's classes).

Like the ENFI team at CMU, the dean and two professors at the University of Minnesota set up an ENFI lab to accomplish the curriculum that was already in place in their department. This curriculum revolved around writing relatively brief texts about personal experiences. Through ENFI conversations among students about their compositions, Geoff Sirc and Tom Reynolds hoped to make visible the continual drafting and revising of text necessary to good writing and to encourage students to take greater ownership of their own and others' writing. In short, they hoped to create a community of authors. However, as they worked with the students on the network and began to study the network transcripts, flaws in the curriculum became visible. Their "time-worn" and "mode-driven" curriculum was no longer appropriate for their students, so they completely revamped it. In this case ENFI brought to light problems with the established curriculum and turned out to be an ideal medium for accomplishing the goals of the new curriculum.

Although at these three institutions ENFI came to have different relationships to the curriculum, in each case its basic nature remained the same – it consisted of real-time written interaction within the classroom. At NVCC even these basic features were altered. Diane Thompson believed that the institutional goal for her students, who were basic writers from working-class communities, was to teach them to "do school" – to function effectively within an academic environment and pass the school's required exit tests. As she describes in her chapter, she began her ENFI work by replicating as closely as possible what she had seen of ENFI at Gallaudet. But the apparently similar real-time interaction on the network assumed a new meaning in her new context. Writing to each other within the classroom seemed both cumbersome and unnecessary when the students and teacher could speak and hear. Thus, the faithful replication of ENFI was literally impossible.

Extending the interaction to include a class at a distant NVCC campus made more sense intuitively, but it was even more difficult to orchestrate, and both teachers questioned its value for accomplishing institutional and their own objectives. In the end, Thompson stopped conducting real-time network conversations altogether, both within the class and across a distance, and developed practices involving the non-real-time sharing of extended texts: orally negotiated paragraphs sent from group to group within the class, a common text file that students could contribute to when writing a research report, and an asynchronous public journal in a distance learning course. In Thompson's case the basic features of ENFI were changed, and "ENFI" came to mean something very general – "computer communications that encourage writing for one another" (Thompson, this volume).

The professors in each of these four settings started with the same body of information about ENFI conveyed at conferences, in papers, and in conversations with ENFI's developers at Gallaudet. But ENFI took four very different paths when it was merged with the constraints of their four institutions.

Theories, personalities, and established practices

Teachers are never passive recipients of new ideas, approaches, or technologies, but rather active agents in determining the shape those new technologies take. The way a teacher makes sense of and shapes a new idea, technology, or approach is a complex process influenced by that teacher's theories of teaching and learning, the teacher's individual personality and preferences, and the pedagogical practices the teacher already has in place (Bussis, Chittenden, & Amarel, 1976; Cohen, 1988; Cuban, 1986; Elbaz, 1981; Fullon, 1982; Hord, Rutherford, Huling-Austin, & Hall, 1987).

Counter to the all-too-common belief that teachers are atheoretical and make pedagogical decisions based on circumstances alone, in fact all teachers work within a theory or a set of theories about teaching and learning (Harste & Burke, 1977; Richardson, Anders, Tidwell, & Lloyd, 1991). The shape that ENFI took at the consortium sites was clearly influenced by the theories of those implementing it. For example, the original model of ENFI at Gallaudet grew out of language acquisition theory and the understanding that language – oral, signed, or written – is acquired through purposeful interaction with peers and more proficient language users (see Peyton & Batson, 1986; Peyton & Mackinson, 1989). This orientation shaped the initial goals for ENFI, understandings of what the teachers at Gallaudet were doing with ENFI, and, ultimately, the kinds of teachers who chose to work with ENFI. Those who shared this theoretical orientation became enthusiastic ENFI users. Others who followed more structural approaches to language acquisition (involving drill and practice, the desire for perfect performance and the need for constant correction, or the desire to deliver lectures) quickly became frustrated with ENFI and stopped using the network. This theoretical orientation also shaped understandings of what ENFI interactions were: They were considered conversations, and ENFI's "success" was determined on the basis of whether or not a successful conversation had taken place.

When the ENFI project expanded to include institutions with hearing students, new theoretical perspectives were introduced. For example, project staff at CMU implemented ENFI and asked their questions about its effectiveness from the perspective of writing process theory (e.g., Flower & Hayes, 1981). They hoped that ENFI would promote the production of "reader-based" prose (Flower, 1979) and facilitate the use of peer response groups (Freedman, 1987; Slavin, 1980). In short, the goal of network activities at CMU was to help individual writers produce better compositions.

For Fred Kemp and his colleagues at the University of Texas, ENFI made sense within the collaborative theories of writing development espoused by Bruffee (1984) and others. Therefore, ENFI practices at Texas focused on the power of collaboration and group work in the development of students' writing and on the ability of the network to promote "text sharing."

At the same time that teachers' implementations of new technologies are influenced by their theories, they are also influenced by teachers' personalities and the educational practices they have worked years to develop. Doug Miller at Gallaudet, for example, had always assumed the role of a showman, an actor, in his composition classes. He was used to standing at the front of the room, signing dynamically, walking around, using his body, and working with the blackboard and overhead projector in a kind of choreographed dance (Peyton, 1990). Over the years, he had developed a set of overhead slides, handouts, and exercises that he liked to use. When he started using ENFI, he felt deprived of the ability to orchestrate the class with his physical presence. He was stuck behind a computer, where he had to capture and maintain students' attention through print. He also found that his carefully prepared materials had become useless (Peyton, 1990):

What I've been doing is taking the materials for my regular freshman composition class and running to my ENFI class in the afternoon. I get them there and I think, "What am I going to do with these things?" I realize I can't even pass them out, because then the students will have to look at something else other than the computer screen. (p. 18)

The version of ENFI that Miller eventually developed revolved around his desire for showmanship, but now he shared the stage with his students, as a fellow actor in or director of their network "scripts." He and his students together strutted on the stage, and he once again had the power to lead and influence the direction of the interactions.

When Diane Thompson (Chapter 11, this volume) tried to replicate Trent Batson's teaching style in her classes at NVCC, she discovered that her own preferred style was very different:

Whereas Trent was able to focus on the topic of the discussion, I was constantly trying to make sure that each and every student felt included and responded to. My personality and teaching style made it harder for me to facilitate ENFI discussions.

After several frustrating attempts to conduct written discussions, both within her class and between classes at two different campuses, Thompson discontinued written discussion entirely and began having students send composed text to each other on the network, which they then discussed orally.

When Marshall Kremers first used ENFI at NYIT, he had to struggle seriously with issues of teacher authority and student power. His traditional, authoritative classroom style was challenged when his students took control of the network discussions and pushed him to the sidelines (Kremers, 1988). He was forced to either stop using the network entirely, in order to maintain his authority, or radically alter his teaching style to accommodate the new power the network interaction gave his students. He chose to do the latter, and has developed a series of ENFI activities in which students adopt roles and discuss current events, working in groups without teacher intervention. The version of ENFI that Kremers developed involved completely relinquishing the authority he had been so comfortable with for years and sharing it with his students (see Kremers, this volume).

Student characteristics and expectations

Just as their teachers did, students interpreted and shaped ENFI to accord with their own understandings of what teaching and learning involve. At every consortium institution, student reactions to ENFI were mixed. On the one hand, students were excited about the new technology and the new ways they could express themselves. In many classes students started coming early and staying late, and in some cases had to be asked to leave so the next class could begin (as Trent Batson, Fred Kemp, and Marshall Kremers report in their chapters). At the same time, ENFI activities did not fit many students' understandings of what schooling involves, and they felt they weren't really learning. At Gallaudet, for example, where the opportunity for deaf students to interact in English seemed to ENFI's developers like an obvious benefit, it seemed to the precollege students like playing around, a waste of time, a useless diversion from the "real work" of writing paragraphs, doing grammar drills, and practicing for the writing test they had to pass to enter freshman English. They expressed their frustrations frequently in network sessions (Peyton, 1990):

Will we do something different beside using the computer all the time??? I mean I would like to practicing our writing and to improve our vocabulary like some other classes do in Eng. 50.

We talk to each other through computer which doesn't have helped us alot. This class seemed like one of class being offered as Group discussion where we share our ideas not talking about our weakness in english grammar structure.

How can the computer helps me with use proper english which i want to pass writing test. I wanna to pass it so badly.

I want to write a paragraph often to improve my writing.

could you give us to write more not in computer. i feel i learned nothing in this computer. if i write more i would learn more because it helps me to remember etc. in english.

At the other consortium sites, the students were hearing and so were immersed in English all the time. Why did they need to communicate on a computer network? Kremers points out that professors at NYIT embraced ENFI because they welcomed the opportunity to explore new writing approaches, to engage students in collaborative writing communities, and to promote among students a more active role in their own learning. After three years of working out his ENFI practice, Kremers were satisfied that he had developed "a long overdue opportunity for real student growth." But even though his students "came to life in the ENFI classroom" and sat listlessly in the regular class, they still initially reacted to ENFI with "fear, confusion, anger, and distrust" (Kremers, this volume).

Some of the students at CMU did not see a connection between the informal ENFI interactions and the high-level academic papers they needed to write (Neuwirth et al., this volume):

I just print out a copy [of the transcript] and give it to the teacher. So, unless there's a memory benefit and seeing it on the screen – over hearing it – I don't know if there's really much of an advantage.

I don't see why you have to use the program – why you can't just say it. . . . I have a harder time typing – that's why . . . I'm not a good typist.

In interviews and written reports, teachers at all the consortium sites have reported that at least some of their students felt they were not doing real work:

Some students said they didn't think they were learning anything from using the network. They wanted more lecture. . . . It's a battle to get them to see that writing on the network is learning English and that it will help them pass the test. (Markowicz, Gallaudet)

The students' previous education in writing was so thoroughly grounded in drill that they . . . were initially disorient[ed] in the immersive, heuristic, free-writing environment of the ENFI course. (Collins, Minnesota)

At first, some [students] take to it immediately, thinking it's fun. Some of those fun folk also see the writing-related value beyond the amusement. For the rest, the fun pales and they wonder why they're doing this, why they're taking time away from "real" writing. (Sirc, Minnesota)

[For many students] ENFI was not an exciting innovation, but a new and empty space into which we threw them without explaining why. Already upset at being placed in a remedial course, they were less than eager to participate in an experiment that had no apparent link to the exit exam. (Kremers, NYIT)

In each case professors and students had to work together to find a significant role for ENFI interactions, an adjustment that often took a considerable amount of time, energy, and creative thought, as the stories in this book illustrate.

Features of the technology

As ENFI use expanded to new institutions and as it changed over time, it became associated with diverse hardware and software configurations (as described in Chapter 3). Technological capabilities, which in themselves reflected institutional resources and priorities, in turn shaped the forms of ENFI.

The different software interfaces have implications for optimal group size and the quality of class discussions. At the sites with a private composing window and group scrolling text, whole classes can communicate on the network. It was found early on at Gallaudet, however, that some teachers had problems managing more than eight or ten students, so early ENFI classes at Minnesota and NVCC were limited to no more than ten students. At NYIT, where class sizes were larger, students were grouped on separate channels.

At most of the sites, participants are limited to ten lines of text and must enter their contributions into a continually scrolling text stream to which many participants are contributing. Messages tend to be short so they do not exceed the space limit and so the writer does not lose the thread of the discussion. At CMU, where unlimited writing space is available and students can see each others' messages as they are being composed, only two or three students communicate at a time. They tend to take turns, waiting until their partner is finished before they begin to write. Thus they tend to write longer messages.

In some settings the Interchange software from the Daedalus Group in Texas tends to function more like non-real-time writing. It encourages writers to leave the continually building stream of discourse, to write within an unlimited composing space, and to publish the text (enter it in the electronic discourse stream) before returning to the public screen. This was especially so for an early version of the software in which text did not automatically scroll up the screen, and participants examined the file at their own pace. This setup created the impression that there was more time for reflection, and messages tended to be longer.

The manner of network interaction changes with different software, so it is not surprising to see different evaluations from network users as to its effectiveness as a learning tool. For example, although Diane Thompson stopped using synchronous written discussion at all within the classroom, Fred Kemp describes it as "the most notable classroom action in network theory" (Chapter 9, this volume). These contrasting evaluations are tempered by all of the factors discussed here, of course, but the software used certainly plays a role.

The layout of the lab also influenced what ENFI became. When the ENFI lab was set up at Minnesota, great care was taken to create an environment in which it made sense to write rather than talk to each other. The ten student stations were placed in carrels separated by walls. In contrast, at NVCC students were crammed into a room that initially did not even have enough computers for each student. Thus students were grouped at the computers, sometimes (if a relationship made it appropriate) even sitting on each others' laps. In that situation, it didn't make a lot of sense to communicate in writing.

The layout of ENFI labs has influenced the extent to which the original vision for ENFI, that the role of the teacher as authority figure be diminished (Batson, 1988a and this volume), has been realized. At Texas the computers face the front of the room and the teacher sits at the back of the room. At Gallaudet, NVCC, and Minnesota, the teacher sits at a computer station that looks no different from the students' stations and in most cases is not set apart in any way. At NYIT, however, the teacher sits on a raised platform at the front of the room. It is not surprising, therefore, that the most serious issues surrounding teacher authority have been raised at NYIT (e.g., see Kremers, 1988 and this volume; and George, 1990).

Room layout may even affect the success of ENFI in terms of student perceptions and performance. Terry Collins, the initiator of ENFI in the General College at Minnesota, is convinced that much of ENFI's success there is attributable to the fact that the students, basic writers who had experienced failure throughout their high school and college careers and who were used to getting second-rate treatment at school, were placed in a beautiful room (well lit, with one wall consisting mostly of windows overlooking a tree-filled park) full of state-of-the art computer technology. They felt they were being taken seriously, and they reacted accordingly.

Available resources

Implementing a computer technology like ENFI may require resources that were not necessary before: a separate room for the computer lab, additional computers, time for teachers to develop new curricula, and technical staff to support teachers and maintain the lab. Educational institutions may embrace a new technology because of purported pedagogical benefits and the desire to prepare students for a technological society, but not be ready to provide the complex network of resources necessary to assure that the technology succeeds. Even though there is a clearly perceived need at the institution for a computer lab and for the kinds of writing activities that computers support, that perception can be accompanied by considerable challenges.

In the ENFI Consortium, the resources available for implementing and maintaining ENFI had a considerable impact on what ENFI became at each institution as well as on perceptions of its success. When ENFI was introduced at CMU, a campuswide network and sophisticated, fully equipped computer labs were already in place. ENFI software was simply added to the existing network links and other writing software that were already available. The activities that took place on the network and in the lab were a crucial and respected part of the work of the writing program at CMU, and ENFI easily became part of the package.

In contrast, at the University of Texas the 50 computers available to the English department were relegated to two small, windowless rooms in the basement of the undergraduate library and ignored by most of the department faculty. ENFI was discovered and shaped by a group of graduate students who were far-sighted enough to see its importance and technically sophisticated enough to carve a place for it in the curriculum, but this work was initially ignored and unsupported. Therefore, whereas at CMU teachers and researchers carefully thought through the place of ENFI in the curriculum and wrote supporting manuals, the ENFI project staff at Texas finally left the university to form their own company and develop their ENFI software and practice from the outside.

Adequate and appropriate space and computers to support ENFI work was another crucial, but often challenging, factor in the shape and success of ENFI. ENFI instructors at Minnesota were blessed with a supportive dean who developed a sheltered environment for ENFI (a carefully designed lab and classes that were half the customary size in the department), but instructors at other sites had to piece together a lab as best they could. Cathy Simpson at NVCC began with four computers in the corner of a library, and Diane Thompson, also at NVCC, began her ENFI practice with seven networked computers for a class of 18 students. She had to divide the class into two separate sections, thus doubling her teaching load, and still the students had to work two to a computer.

A factor often not taken into consideration is the technical support necessary to maintain computer labs once they are set up. When ENFI was implemented at CMU, the computer lab already had highly trained technical staff who printed and distributed transcripts of class discussions, maintained the computers, and helped the teachers when they had problems. When NVCC decided to set up ENFI networks at three of their five campuses, they did not realize the challenge they were undertaking and the demand for technical support they had created: "We had not known that networks were complex, skittish, existing in a universe far beyond our technical capabilities" (Thompson, this volume). It quickly became evident that the one computer person on the entire NVCC staff, who was responsible for supporting all of the computer work on all five campuses, could not possibly provide the kind of technical support that was needed. The two teachers collaborating to develop ENFI practices were continually frustrated by the lack of technical expertise to implement their plans. Likewise, the decision to install eight computer classrooms at NYIT, without careful coordination and without consideration of the tremendous technical support needed to maintain the complex technology on that scale, "led to a host of problems" (Spitzer, this volume), and resulted in NYIT's inability to conduct ENFI classes or research for one year of the consortium's existence. In the end, NYIT's original plans for implementing ENFI were cut back significantly.

Finally, teachers need time to create new curricula appropriate for the technology. At some institutions time and financial support was built in for teachers to work closely with project administrators and researchers. The result (e.g., at CMU) was a carefully developed and well-understood practice, with supporting materials. At others, teachers had to find developmental time over and above their regular teaching load, and the result (at NVCC, e.g., in the development of distance networking between two campuses) was frustration and, eventually, a decision to discontinue the practice.

Conclusion

The processes of implementing ENFI have involved continual creation and recreation of the innovation. People started with what they understood about ENFI and what they believed to be its strengths for their students. They then incorporated it into the program they had in place, often making minor changes, such as reducing the class size at Minnesota and NVCC. In most cases, their first version was not satisfactory: The existing curriculum did not promote the kinds of interactions they wanted (Sirc & Reynolds); they could not make the connection between ENFI and institutional gateposts or their own teaching styles (Miller); or one of the basic features of ENFI – real-time written interaction within a classroom – did not seem reasonable for the student population or the teacher's goals (Thompson). This led to further changes. The result was a different "ENFI" in each case. This diversity, which is not particular to ENFI but accompanies any innovation, has major implications for all aspects of the implementation process – from deciding what the innovation is to designing an evaluation of it.

Just as an innovation does not take the same shape in all contexts, neither does it retain the same characteristics over time. Under the conventional view of implementation, there is a before state and an after state. The innovation is applied to the before (blank, unenlightened, undeveloped, primitive) state to improve, develop, or correct it. If the innovation "takes," the after state is better – richer, more enlightened, developed, more sophisticated. But in reality the before state is never blank, but a complex, functioning system that is continually changing. What actually occurs is continual change – many different after states. As Chapter 1 shows, there are many paths of change.

The diversity intrinsic to innovations presents challenges to our traditional understandings of evaluation. In these, methodological concerns related to defining pre- and postmeasures, selecting appropriate comparison groups, and identifying "objective" outsiders to conduct the evaluation are paramount. But these concerns are predicated on a well-defined conception of what the innovation is. More often than not, a close study reveals how ill-defined our conceptions usually are. Before assessing the effects of the innovation, we need to understand how the innovation is realized in different contexts of use. An effective evaluation of an innovation must include an understanding and critical analysis of its re-creations as well as of the outcomes of its use.

Following a situated evaluation, one may address the traditional goals of judging the innovation's effectiveness (summative evaluation) or improving its design (formative evaluation). These analyses can then be done with a deeper understanding of the innovation as it exists in use. Situated evaluation can also be useful after the summative evaluation. If overall differences are detected, researchers can study the origins of those differences. If differences are not found, as in Fowles' study (Chapter 14), they can examine why not.

Good evaluations must also include the perspectives of the users (see Stake, 1990). With the wide variety of ENFIs represented in this book, it is highly misleading to write an evaluation outlining across-the-board ENFI's strengths and weaknesses. Instead, the ENFI users themselves must help us understand the practices they developed, as they have done in their chapters.

Diversity also presents challenges for some models of teacher education in which teachers are "trained" in the use of specific methods or approaches. These models fail to account for the process in which teachers re-create an innovation based on an analysis of its potential, the institutional context, student needs, and pedagogical goals. For better or worse, the teacher is always an innovator, not a recipient of completed pedagogies. Innovation is a process that is initiated at times from the outside, but always completed by teachers and students in the classroom.

Because the innovation is constructed through its realization in an actual classroom, the role of the curriculum developer needs to be reconceived as well. Rather than attempting to articulate every step of the instructional process or establishing constraints that limit teachers' options, a more useful role may follow from conceiving a curriculum as a set of tools for the re-creation process. The technology of the curriculum then becomes a set of possibilities, including perhaps models and suggestions, but respecting fully the complexities of the classroom in which these possibilities are to be realized.

Innovations that call for significant changes are often abandoned or significantly transformed to accommodate classroom realities. We cannot avoid this process, but we can seek to understand it better and to support it in ways consistent with our pedagogical goals. In Part II we will read about teachers and students who accepted this challenge.

Part II

Creating the network-based classroom

In Part II we follow the ENFI idea from the original instantiation at Gallaudet University to its various realizations on other campuses. ENFI, at the beginning of the ENFI Consortium work, was thought of as the way that Trent Batson and a couple of other teachers at Gallaudet University used the network with the predecessor to Realtime Writer software, which allowed for full-group written interaction, the central feature of original ENFI practice. Although teachers at the other consortium sites began with this feature foremost in their conception of ENFI, they each found their own variations and preferences for their own ENFI work, and then proceeded to expand on those, allowing the ENFI idea to take different shapes at different university settings, like a plant adapting to different climates.

Part of the reason for the free adaptation of the ENFI idea may have been that it was being moved out of deaf education into the average college composition setting. Only Chapters 5 and 7 describe work with deaf students; at all the other sites mentioned in the other chapters, participants were hearing students.

It may be fairly obvious why a composition teacher would want to use a computer network to work with deaf students. The alternative, sign language, is not related to English, so class discussion would be quite removed from the target skill. But it is apparent from our interaction with uninitiated people in our field over the years that the reason to use ENFI with hearing students is not so obvious. Why shift to discussion in writing rather than in speech? What they forget is that spoken English is also quite removed from the target skill – writing. If one were starting from scratch to design a college composition setting and there was no history at all of teaching writing, most sensible people would look for a means of sharing text easily, just as sharing work with peers and teacher is a natural in an art class. The easiest way today to share text easily is on a computer network, so it would make sense for our hypothetical from-scratch designers to opt for a computer lab as the ideal place to teach writing. The bias toward *talking about writing* rather than *working with shared text* is probably based on our custom of doing that because we had no other choice before now. The *continued* bias toward talking is based on other factors, such as the typical teacher delusion that whatever he or she says is understood, mentally integrated, and then converted into practice by all students. This delusion is demonstrably just that, which is confirmed by nearly every student paper handed in, but as long as there was no reasonable alternative to mostly talking about writing (since text is so difficult to share with paper technology), the only solution seemed to be to talk more slowly, more dramatically, or more repetitively. Teachers also ask a lot of questions.

However, because the desire among some teachers to work more fully and ambitiously with student text is strong, the ENFI idea has spread despite the difficulties of working with a relatively new technology. In Chapters 6–12 the real struggle to adapt the ENFI idea, to understand it theoretically, and to support it technologically is described.

Many of the difficulties described here would have occurred even if the same people had simply moved from their regular classroom to a computer network lab, rather than trying ENFI (shifting not only to more student writing during class but from talking to writing to each other for all communication in class). In other words, ENFI was only one element in the switch, but the chapters talk only about ENFI. For those already working in a computer lab or already comfortable with collaborative learning, adoption of ENFI might not be so revolutionary, as Geoff Sirc and Thomas Reynolds confirm (Chapter 8).

A few of the teachers who have written chapters here tried ENFI, then gave it up, but came back after a semester or two to try another approach. It could seem that the encouragement to try a second time arose from participation in a funded project, as Diane Thompson mentions, but Doug Miller was not a participant in the consortium and he still came back.

Others explored a strictly limited version of ENFI. The group at CMU, for example, used small groups of students – usually two, but occasionally three or four – and never included the teacher in the on-line work. CMU was unique within the consortium in both using small groups and not including the teacher.

Flaming

Judging from the stories in this section, it seems that the power of ENFI for altering patterns of interaction may be greater than anyone expected. Unleashing students from their normal roles in the classroom seems to result in an explosion of energy, and that explosion can scare away even the most energetic and committed teacher.

The explosion is generally called *flaming,* a term widely recognized by people who use computer networks to communicate either within a classroom or over a distance. It occurs with both students and colleagues. Everyone who has dipped into network communication has experienced flaming.

In the chapters that follow, flaming from students emerges as a varying phenomenon, identified by the teachers here as when students write messages that are sexually oriented, insulting, or rude. However, in national network discussions among faculty, flaming is considered instead to be when someone delivers a harangue or uses an angry tone. In both cases, apparently the diminished social dimensions, immediacy, and ease of writing all encourage communication that is out of normal bounds.* Although flaming is the most sensational aspect of network communication, it is probably not as prevalent as one might believe based on the amount of attention that it gets. Only two of the participants in the consortium reported serious problems with flaming.

Is ENFI too slow?

Another pattern mentioned consistently in the following chapters is the speed or slowness of ENFI interaction. Some say it is too slow, but others say that it is too fast. To understand this paradox, it is helpful to compare ENFI to face-to-face spoken group interaction. As we all know, spoken communication requires turn taking; utterances may overlap, but in general people have to speak sequentially. Although turn taking creates a sense of order-through-time, it also means that most participants in a group discussion have to wait to speak, or be considered very rude. As they wait, sometimes they forget what they want to say, sometimes are lost in their own thoughts, and sometimes, therefore, may never say anything at all.

In contrast, the various forms of ENFI software allow everyone to "speak" at the same time, while the software creates a sequence after the fact; the transcript makes it look as though people have "spoken" one after the other, when in fact they may have been writing concurrently. In face-to-face spoken communication thoughts are concurrent among the members of the group, but expression has to be sequential; in ENFI thoughts are still concurrent, but expression doesn't have to be sequential. The ENFI network, then, gives us an interesting alternate view of the group mental map at any time. We are aware that not everyone is focused on the same idea at the same time in a group discussion – especially those who are quiet. Indeed, it may be a rare moment when there is unanimity of focus. As we look at the ENFI screen, however, we can actually get a sense of the multiple consciousness always present in a group, but normally hidden from us. But only a *sense,* for by the act of writing, participants may be more uniformly focused than if they were just "listening" (I use quotes because, as we all know, listening is often a euphemism for daydreaming).

Despite the appearance of chaos on the network, then, students may ac-

---

* The most often cited work regarding the effect of diminished social dimensions on the nature of written interaction is that by Kiesler, Siegel, & McGuire (1984).

tually be more focused on one general topic than when they are listening to a teacher's lecture. The traditional class may appear coherent, but really be a chaos of stray thoughts, whereas the ENFI class may appear to be chaos, but really be relatively coherent.

Thus the paradox about the speed or slowness of ENFI. If teachers try to achieve coherence in the ENFI lab the same way they did in the traditional classroom by controlling the written discussion, then ENFI is slow. People simply can't type as fast as they can talk, including the teacher. So a lecture or a teacher-led discussion on the network doesn't work too well. But if teachers instead allow for coherence of production – where everyone types what he or she is thinking – then ENFI is very fast. Thirty hands typing at once are in fact faster than one person talking. Therefore, ENFI is slow in creating the traditional coherence of control but fast in creating the coherence of individual thought and expression: slow for control, fast for idea production.

The ENFI environment has applications other than just for discussion, of course. ENFI can be used to create a simulation (a kind of improvisational drama to get students to work through an issue dramatically), to brainstorm ideas, to work in pairs doing peer response, and so on.

The evolution of ENFI

As you read the various chapters, it should be clear that people at the different consortium sites had great latitude to adapt a teaching idea to their own situation. We laid down no rules. The term *ENFI* itself is used in a wide variety of ways in this book. It becomes a *noun* ("the original ENFI"), an *adjective* ("an ENFI lab"), and a *verb* ("ENFI-ize" – a usage that unfortunately or not was deleted in one of our manuscript editing sessions). These usages echo the variety of ways that the idea behind ENFI was adapted. However, just to be clear, despite these usages ENFI is not software or hardware, or even a system, but simply an idea.

Two of us, Peyton and Batson, had invested hope in ENFI, so it was hard during our consortium work to see the original idea altered and, especially, to hear of failures or problems. At the beginning of the consortium work, no one else in the country was doing ENFI, so it seemed important to us to have it succeed, at least in some way. Yet when there were failures, they were spectacular, as described by Kremers, Thompson, Miller, and Spitzer. It is one thing to teach a traditional class and have it fizzle. One is aware of failure mainly because of silence or vacant stares. Once the hour is over, however, one can forget the class and look forward to better classes later in the day. In the ENFI lab, however, failure is not signified by silence or vacant stares, but by flying hands typing obscenities or insults, more like a skirmish than a wake. The sin is of commission, not omission. And then there's the printout, a lasting reminder of the failure. One can be quiet and hope to forget a failed class in a traditional setting, but the failure on ENFI is too glaring, too concrete.

It should not have been surprising that some of the sites experienced problems adjusting to ENFI. The traditional classroom and the ENFI classroom are both working environments, each with their opportunities and limitations. Some people work well in one setting, some in the other, a few in both. Because we teachers have years of experience in the traditional classroom, both as students and teachers, and because our entire conception of teaching writing (and other subjects) is steeped in the culture of the traditional classroom, we know how to prepare to teach there, how to avoid catastrophe, how to anticipate and correct most problems, and how to control the class. The students know what they are supposed to do as well. The ENFI classroom, on the other hand, is only a few years old. It introduces many new variables and eliminates many features of the familiar landscape of the traditional classroom. However, it is apparent that the teachers writing in this section of the book about their efforts to adapt to the ENFI environment have succeeded. Diane Thompson is the only one who eventually backed away from the ENFI environment altogether. We include her story because this book is not meant to sell an idea, but to describe how a technology-based teaching idea was re-created at various sites and how the re-creations can be evaluated through a situated evaluation approach.

None of us understood the magnitude of the undertaking when we started the ENFI Consortium work. The early work at Gallaudet had succeeded because of a lucky convergence of a teacher eager for the kind of activity ENFI encourages and a student body already accustomed to written interaction (via teletype devices for the deaf – TDDs). For this reason, and because of special needs at Gallaudet, the success there may have been foreordained. Nothing at the Gallaudet site could have prepared us for the complexity of moving the idea from Gallaudet to other campuses.

In the end, was the effort a success? Each chapter tells its own story, which must be weighed in the balance. It would seem that of the six sites (Gallaudet, Carnegie Mellon, New York Institute of Technology, Northern Virginia Community College, the University of Minnesota, the University of Texas), four had relatively good, if not trouble-free, experiences with ENFI, one had a good enough experience to want to continue ENFI work, and only one – NVCC (Thompson) – forsook ENFI altogether. Even after the consortium has ceased to work together formally, we know that many other colleges and universities around the country have adopted ENFI as well. So at least in terms of just moving the idea out of deaf education into the general mainstream of postsecondary education, we did succeed. Beyond the question of success or failure, however, the following chapters are rich stories of attempting to implement an idea within a complex array of local considerations. Each of these stories lets us see what is behind the grand, hopeful attempt to aid young students in learning to write and think.

5   The origins of ENFI

Trent Batson

Steve Lombardo and I were the first writing teachers at Gallaudet and, as far as I know, the first *anywhere* to teach a whole semester of composition by communicating entirely in writing through a computer network in our classroom. We were the originators of ENFI. We did what seemed slightly crazy to most people in 1985, which was to stop standing in front of our writing class and communicating in sign language (Gallaudet students are all deaf). Instead, we sat down at a terminal on a local-area network and had a group discussion or engaged in group exercises with the class by typing on the keyboard. Our classes met in a room just like traditional writing classes, but we didn't look at each other; we looked at the computer screens instead as we communicated.

What would lead us to do something as drastic as this? For me there were two reasons: dissatisfaction with teaching writing as I had been teaching it for 20 years and desire that my deaf students experience English in a natural – written – form instead of in its unnatural signed form. First, the dissatisfaction.

The role of the writing teacher

When I was in graduate school I was hired to teach writing in a department that handled the freshman writing requirement at Michigan State University. Very soon after I started, however, I found I didn't particularly like teaching because I didn't like being the center of attention. I just couldn't believe my students were learning much as I stood there and talked. I felt that I was on stage and the students were judging me; then they took their turn when they wrote a paper that I judged. We took turns performing for and judging each other (Faigley, 1989; Moffett, 1968).

On the other hand, I did enjoy the learning, both mine and my students'. I loved good discussions, one-on-one conferences, dialogue journals (Batson, 1990; Staton, Shuy, Peyton, & Reed, 1988), in-class work, and seeing students make progress. I loved anything that seemed like genuine interaction, or genuine engagement, and not a game. Unfortunately, there was too little interaction, and too much standing and talking. Teaching writing then, and for years after, seemed so constrained by the odd roles teachers and students were stuck in, that communication seemed strained and self-conscious – hardly the atmosphere to encourage good written communication.

A few years later, after a stint teaching at another university, I took a job with the U.S. Army and found myself faced with similar problems, but with new twists. In the Army the idea of a teacher performing was not just a tradition, it was a mandate.

My job was teaching soldiers how to teach. Now you might wonder why soldiers need to teach. The reason is simple: Turnover is a nightmare. How is it possible to train the steady flow of new volunteers to perform the complex skills to run the modern Army? As with any task, the Army has a system to deal with this problem: It trains individuals who know how to do something to teach those skills to the new recruits. I was one of those training the knowledgeable to teach the recruits.

We teachers were given sets of prepared overhead slides that consisted of the points we were to make during the class. A class was like a drill: It was preset. The people who carried out this drill were interchangeable. We had to rehearse again and again in order to give the lessons correctly. We trained ourselves to develop "enthusiasm" while delivering these set lessons. We had voice lessons, lessons in how to deliver a "motivational" joke at the beginning of a lecture, to write legibly on the chalkboard, to handle overhead projectors, and to follow correct military protocol at the beginning and end of each lesson (and training in every other aspect of class management as well). If we followed all that we had been taught, so the line went, we would be effective teachers and therefore good role models for those we were training.

This regimented approach seemed even more artificial than what I'd had to do on the two college campuses where I'd worked. Now I was not just following an implicit script but an explicit one. I began to think that teaching was not the easy personal interaction I had thought it to be when I was a student. As a teacher I found myself more and more constrained by the role I felt forced to follow.

I spent only a year working for the military, but before I left I learned something very valuable, not about overcoming role constraint but about directing or managing learning. Consider the problem our unit faced: We had only 2 weeks to teach someone to teach. On the surface this is an absurd notion. But, absurd or not, this 2-week workshop had been conducted for years and seemed to work. I think the reason was that it was designed to affect the *beliefs* of the students who took the course, and those beliefs would later affect how the students would behave as teachers.

Here's how it worked: Each student during the 2-week course would give a 5-, 10-, and 20-minute talk. The 5-minute talk came very soon after the class first met, say on the second day of the first week. Naturally, most men (they *were* all men then) did very poorly on that first talk. They didn't know the group, had almost no time for preparation, and had very little self-confidence. The 10-minute talk a few days later was only a little bit better. Five or 10 minutes is hardly enough time to feel comfortable with a group. The 20-minute presentation came at the end of the second week when everyone knew each other. They had many days to get ready for this talk, and 20 minutes allowed them enough time to feel comfortable in front of the group.

There is no question three practice sessions are insufficient to make a teacher, but the sessions did accomplish something very important. The 20-minute presentation was so much better in all cases than the shorter talks that the men left the program *believing they had made great progress.* Sham or not, the program succeeded in creating the one thing that was critical for these men – the belief that they had attained the ability to teach. I could see that what the teacher said was not so important as creating a belief, through this experience, that the students had made good progress. This was the first notion I had that the sequence of experiences a teacher sets up can be much more powerful than talk. I'd already begun to wonder about the effectiveness of talk anyway, and this experience in the military made me wonder even more.

By the time I was back in academia at Gallaudet University in the fall of 1968, I had some new ideas about teaching. The only question was how to put them into practice in the college classroom.

The first problem I faced was that the college classroom felt lifeless compared to the classes in the military. I'd forgotten how students in required writing courses in college seem to work hardest to remain as passive as possible. The students seemed to be saying, Make us laugh, tell us stories. Make the world simple. Most of all, don't make us change in any way. We're only here because we're required to be. I was teaching deaf students, of course, which made the gap between us more exaggerated, but still they were in many ways like the students I'd had at Michigan State and George Washington University.

To overcome the students' resistance to engagement, I again tried dialogue journals, introduced "relevant" topics for discussion (these were the sixties, after all), and had the students sit on the floor and face the wall so they could say how that made them feel. I tried techniques used in group cohesiveness training (one student who'd trained to be a priest led the class in some exercises) and went on weekend hikes with my students – anything that would get some mental activity going.

One semester I tried something radical to break the mental bondage of THE CLASSROOM and its associated behaviors: We became nomadic. We'd meet outside, in a lounge, in the campus cafeteria, or anywhere that seemed workable. At the end of each class we'd decide where the next class would be. (Students grew afraid they'd *lose* the class, so for the only time in my teaching career I had perfect attendance all semester.) One time, to teach perspective I led my class up a nearby hill from which we could look back and see the whole campus. Once on the hill, I asked them if the campus looked different to them.

But none of these methods was successful. I felt I had to work strenuously to make even the slightest impression on my students. So, predictably, after a few years I was burned out. I didn't know how to create an authentic learning situation, and I was stumped about how to create a sequence of experiences that would result in better writing or even in more engagement in writing. By the middle 1970s I had stopped teaching writing, turning instead to upper-level courses, like many another burned-out composition teacher.

Enter the microcomputer

In 1983 I took a sabbatical and had my first experience using a microcomputer. The experience was revolutionary: My interest in my own writing was rekindled. I could see myself finding more energy to write in ways I never had before. I revised more than I ever had before. Generating text seemed simple. I felt I had a new writing partner. In a few months my enthusiasm for writing on the computer was nearly unbounded. I came to believe that the computer could be my ally in the writing classroom. I didn't know how yet, but I could sense the potential. I thought maybe now I had a tool or device that would help me overcome student apathy in required composition courses.

Could the computer help with these problems? In those early days of my conversion, the "smart machine" seemed capable of anything. It was magical to me.

Microcomputer applications in 1983

Writing teachers on other campuses had begun to use computers in their writing classes even before 1983. I was intrigued by the things I read about their experiments. I saw the connections between the emphasis on the writing process (Emig, 1971; Flowers & Hayes, 1981) and word processing. Text could reasonably be considered "in process" when it was generated on the computer; on paper, it seemed more final, less in process. I was also intrigued by heuristic programs (see, e.g., Burns, 1979; Rodrigues & Rodrigues, 1984; and Rohman, 1965) that led students through the prewriting stages of thinking about their paper, grammar checkers that promised to relieve some teacher drudgery, tutorial programs that would give students individual attention, and even by drill-and-practice programs.

I attended conferences and heard about Wandah, later HBJ Writer, at UCLA, which was supposed to guide students to write better papers. I also heard about Carnegie Mellon University – "Computer U," as some of us called it then. I visited CMU in June of 1984[1] and met Andrew, the campus computing environment. I also spent part of the day with a prototype of Wandah and could see its limitations. The concept of Andrew's computing environment, however, intrigued me.

I began to see the options we had in our exploration of the new writing environment provided by the computer. My university was about to invest heavily in an expansion of computing facilities. I knew we wanted a lab, but I also felt that a simple "scriptorium," as Diane Balestri (1988) has described the computer writing lab, would not by itself make students better writers. The lab is only a place, after all, not a program. An additional difficulty at this point in planning for computing at Gallaudet was the fact that our students are deaf.

The inspiration for ENFI within deaf education

The idea for ENFI, as I said at the beginning of this chapter, might have seemed radical in 1985 to the average writing teacher, but within deaf education there were many antecedents to ENFI, so it was not so radical at Gallaudet. Not being able to hear the language of one's culture creates serious barriers to full participation in society, and these barriers have led to a number of inventive solutions over the years. If it seems that deaf people today face unusual barriers to full participation in society, one needs only read about what it was like for deaf people in earlier centuries to appreciate how far they've actually come.

A couple of hundred years ago, when the effects of deafness were not understood and the means to diagnose it unavailable, deaf people were in most cases outcasts, lumped together with the insane or mentally retarded. But even as the ability to distinguish deafness from these other conditions grew, deaf people still had barriers beyond misunderstanding and misdiagnosis to overcome. To really participate in a human society one has to be skilled in the language of that society. For deaf people, most of whom cannot hear even a glimmering of speech or produce it themselves (except with laborious and usually fruitless speech training), mastery of a language other than sign language meant, and means, mastering the written form.

For most adults with normal hearing, English written on a page seems like the same language we speak. We forget the steps we went through to make it seem so. When we first encountered print as little children, it did not seem in any way connected to speech. At first, print was merely marks on a page that had no meaning. However, even then, we who could hear already had

---

[1] Chris Neuwirth graciously hosted my day-long visit. She later joined our ENFI Consortium.

within our heads the potential for those symbols to come to life. We had internalized rhythms, patterns, and life associations with the words represented on the page.[2] We could infuse "dead" print with the life in our mind. For us, with our 5 or 6 years of total immersion in spoken English, the shift to print was hard enough, but not impossible.

A deaf person grows up with a very different linguistic experience. For her, there is often very little internal English. Her experience of English is not so word oriented as that of a hearing child. She receives English as a combination of lip movements, gestures, and nongrammatical signs (*home signs*) produced by hearing people as they speak (almost all deaf children have hearing parents who are ill prepared to deal with a deaf child). She has to rely heavily on context to make any sense out of this hodgepodge of communication signals. Because the communication is so laborious for both the parent and the child, they both may find ways to avoid it. By the end of her preschool years, this idiosyncratic experience with language leaves her, like most deaf children, poorly prepared to move easily into mainstream English *or* American Sign Language (ASL). Few hearing parents learn ASL, so a deaf child in most cases doesn't get practice even with what we might think is her native language.

Therefore, when the typical deaf child encounters print, the child most often doesn't have the same potential for linking his previous communication experience with the symbol patterns on the page. He's seeing *written* words, but he doesn't have *spoken* words in his head to connect the print to. The English he experienced was of course not sound based, as the symbols on the page are, but visual, either on the lips only or signed in one way or another. For the deaf child, therefore, the word sequences may have almost no mental analogue. A hearing child does have those spoken words in his head, of course, so he can make the phonetic connections. But miraculously, many deaf children still achieve a functional literacy.

Only in the past 175 years in the United States have we believed it possible to educate a deaf child in any way. A couple in 18th century America who had a deaf child would have only understood that the child was not normal. In the minds and emotions of her parents, she would be written off. The couple would have other children to compensate. The deaf child would be trained, if the child were at all viable, to use the pitchfork and the shovel. She would be a beast of labor. There would have been no other deaf children within miles, so her parents would have no other example to consider, no

---

[2] I especially remember the word *scarlet*. When I was seven, a movie serial played in our neighborhood theater called *The Scarlet Rider*. I admired the abilities and the deeds of the Scarlet Rider. I wanted to *be* the Scarlet Rider. Then, in school one day we were going through lists of words with our teacher in a small reading group. I happened to notice that one of the words was *scarlet*. Oh, I wanted to be the one who read the word and said what it meant! To me it had come to mean so much! I guess I was learning how words can take on new colorings, so to speak.

other approach. In a time when diseases took high tolls of human life, it was unlikely they or anyone else would take special pains with this one child. There was too much disaster already to focus on one new instance.

Only in the rare cases when a deaf child was born to wealthy parents would there be some attempt to understand and work with the child, and then perhaps only if the parents had few or no other children. In a real sense, the rescue of deaf children from this bleak fate began with an 18th century law in Spain that declared a child must be able to read and write in order to inherit property. Accordingly, the deaf children of wealthy parents in Spain, probably the first such lucky deaf children, were trained to read and write.

At that time no one outside of those undertaking the task of teaching the children in Spain believed such a feat was possible. But those teachers, taking a model from monks living under an oath of silence and therefore communicating with gestures, were able to teach deaf children using gestures borrowed from those monks. Some deaf children were actually taught to read and write sufficiently well to pass the legal test.

Because of the subsequent spread to Europe and America of the idea that deaf children could be educated, the situation for deaf children in 19th century America began to brighten, at least after 1817. At that time the first school for deaf children in America was founded in Hartford, Connecticut. The benefit of such a school for the children was not only lessons in the classroom, but the simple fact that they now were in contact with *other deaf children who used signs to communicate*. The deaf schools that began to pop up created a deaf community by serving as magnets to draw deaf people together (Lou, 1988).

Why was it important for deaf people to be together? Imagine growing up as most deaf children do, alone in a world of hearing people. They look around as everyone uses their lips to communicate, but they can't understand those lips. The children go for weeks understanding only the grossest communication signals, such as when people move to the table and the children smell food, or when people put on their coats to leave the house. Finer communication signals, such as why someone is missing from the table who is normally there, may be lost to them. The lips move and move but these children have no idea what those lip movements mean. It's hard to imagine the anguish of such deprivation.

Then imagine that one day, wonderfully, oh so wonderfully, one of these children is placed among other children who use their hands and bodies and faces to communicate. These children, all peers, make their ideas and feelings *visible*. They can now *connect* so much more easily to the reality of other people's experience! They are finally in a world not closed off to them.

I need to make it clear that parents of deaf children are not cruel or uncaring in making it so hard for their children to understand them. Most often they just don't know how to cope with a deaf child. What a child needs is constant exposure to an accessible linguistic system. Most of us would agree that such access is the birthright of all babies. No matter how impoverished, or poorly educated the parents are, most babies at least hear them talk, and thus they grow up in a world full of communication. Their minds, emotions, and knowledge of the world are formed by human interaction through language. It is this total immersion in the language of the culture that deaf children are deprived of.

I remember hearing an American Indian myth about bear cubs. The cubs in the myth are born as formless balls. The mother bear licks these balls and, after many days of licking, the cubs begin to form. Less and less ball-like and more and more cublike they grow as the mother licks them into shape. We use our tongues, too, through language, to shape our babies into recognizable human children. The problem for deaf children is that though the tongue of the mother may be able to lick, the baby cannot respond. This baby does not need the tongue – spoken language – but the hand, which can make language visible.[3]

Deaf children also need a community that uses a language accessible to them, a community that builds knowledge and history through that language. The value of bilingualism can be argued in many cases of spoken languages, but the value of bilingualism (ASL and English) for deaf children is much more obvious. Ideally, they will use their strong language base in ASL to bridge to English. Since ASL is much more accessible for deaf people, it is the logical language for deaf children to begin with. As they mature in their ASL-based concepts, they are then more readily able to broaden their language base into English or other spoken languages (Johnson, Liddell, & Erting, 1989).

The situation today

Many contemporary parents know that deafness is not necessarily a serious handicap. The handicap is to some extent created by the world's or the parents' unreadiness to deal with deafness. It is created by the ignorance and, until recently, the prejudice with which deafness is confronted. Because of the legacy of poor understanding of deafness, most deaf children are still deprived of transferable or usable linguistic input – either they experience the com-

---

[3] The baby can respond to the expression in the faces of his caregivers, of course, and to other body-language elements. In fact, because some degree of communication with a deaf baby is possible, parents are deceived and may not discover their baby's deafness until many months have passed. What they can't know is that the English sounds that they are caressing the baby with are literally falling on deaf ears. When they do discover that their baby is deaf (the deafness gene is recessive so may go generations undetected), their baby has lost precious months, even perhaps a year or more, of time when he should have been receiving finer linguistic input, building toward the time when he can begin to produce language himself.

munication hodgepodge I described or they get only the spoken English part. A lucky few grow up with caregivers who are skilled communicators, but these are rare. If a young person is denied access to language (signed or spoken), this truly is an affliction. Even a child with normal hearing would be handicapped who learned a linguistic system only she and her parents could understand.

Like the deaf children who spent their adult life shoveling manure in 18th century America, many deaf children even today do not develop as fully as they could because of their imperfect access to a signed or spoken language system. At the other end of the spectrum are the deaf children who grow up in deaf families where ASL is used. Most often, they move to English quite easily and are generally the most capable and successful deaf students.

Gaining access to English

English is, first and last, spoken. The written form was devised as a code for those who already know how to speak the language – who have already internalized the sound-triggered syntax of the language. Those who grow up hearing English every waking hour of every day develop an internal linguistic computer that is programmed for the sound patterns of English, allowing them to integrate, over time, the derived symbol system that is writing. They also bring to the written form the social content of the language built into the implied intonation patterns. They hear the music of spoken English in their heads as they read a text. Understanding the need to connect deaf people in some way with this music, with the living spoken form, and not just the dead written form (it most often *is* dead to those who do not have the living form already in their heads), educators of the deaf for 150 years have sought some means, from hearing aids to cochlear implants to cued speech, to make English more accessible.

It should be apparent, then, that for deaf people to live better lives – lives not so burdened by literacy handicaps – they need earlier and fuller exposure to standard linguistic systems. Even most deaf students who make it to college have not fully overcome their early language deprivation. English (and often ASL) is still unfamiliar and difficult terrain.

The deaf person in college

For most deaf college students, their linguistic acquisition started slowly (unless they had deaf parents), was characterized by an imperfect exposure to the patterns of any one language, but was then given a boost when they met their first deaf peers who signed to them. Their language development at an early age was then strongly bifurcated into a school language (English) that they repeatedly were told was important, and a social language (ASL) that was officially disregarded as insignificant. Imagine the assault on one's self-esteem and sense about life at this point! The language that you can understand and use for important communication among friends – making plans, sharing stories, becoming yourself – is "no good," but the language that you can almost never hope to use for any of those purposes is touted as the only "good" language.

English for these young deaf children is an experience largely limited to the classroom and lacking in real-life connections. This bifurcation in the language development process continues on through the elementary and middle grades and into high school, as most deaf students learn thoroughly and without question that ASL is their world, their identity (but it's no good), and English, the good language, is "out there," the language of that other world. Given the two avenues of linguistic development to follow in school – either ASL,[4] which is a language accessible and alive, or printed English, a language with few personal, internal antecedents – what avenue would a 6-year-old child prefer?

A hearing child also has to learn discourse patterns appropriate to both her social and classroom realms, but for a deaf child, the two discourses are so alien and separate that there is almost no mutual reinforcement, as there is for a hearing child. Also, the deaf child will probably put much more energy and enthusiasm into the ASL discourse than into the print, since his ASL discourse is interactive whereas his English discourse is largely one-way. His language task is much more complex, but at the same time he has less motivation for a large part of it than does a hearing child.

By the time a young deaf person arrives in college, then, English has most often been given short shrift, not out of contrariness, but simply because the living form of English, the social interactive part (the spoken form), is in-

---

[4] *Sign Language*, the popular term for the communicative and expressive hand movements deaf people use, is actually a catchall for several forms: first, American Sign Language (ASL), the actual *language* that deaf people use among themselves, which originated from the fusion of native American sign varieties and French Sign Language (Deaf people, interestingly, trace their linguistic heritage to France, not England, because only French deaf educators were willing to help Americans start their own deaf schools.); second, Contact Signing (until recently called Pidgin Sign English), which is what deaf people switch to when they communicate with most hearing people (except those hearing people who had deaf parents themselves or those who are highly conversant in ASL); and, last, various forms of signed English, which are almost exclusively limited to the classroom or other formal interactions between hearing and deaf people.

Naturally, there are many dialects in ASL throughout the United States and Canada, perhaps even more pronounced than those in English because ASL is not tied to a written form. ASL, however, does have its textbooks, encyclopedias, and linguistic studies (see, e.g., Klima & Bellugi, 1979).

In contrast with their rich linguistic experience with ASL, deaf people see English communicated in a sign form that is not natural to hearing people or to them, because signed English is not used in any personal spheres of life. Thus, for them, the actual living form of English (except for that which is written) is represented in sign as an orphaned, unnatural, and awkward form. No wonder that many deaf students think English is dull.

accessible to him. English remains an only partially known land and deaf college students (and most deaf people in general) are not residents but tourists in that land.

Technological efforts to meet language needs

Many attempts had been made to bring deaf people into the flow of living English, its spoken form, for at least a century before ENFI. When deaf education began in the United States in 1817, deaf educators believed that the royal road to English mastery was ASL itself (a belief resurfacing now). Later in the 19th century after the Civil War, educators did an about-face and came to believe that *denying* deaf people access to ASL would force them to learn English. The few deaf people with enough residual hearing to benefit from this "oral" approach misled educators for decades into believing that the oral approach was the best way. During most of the 20th century, too, the oral approach has dominated, with deleterious results: The English proficiency levels of most deaf people remain painfully low (Allen, 1986; Charrow, 1974).

In the context of the oral approach, inventors worked on hearing aids, and are still doing so, of course, hoping to bring sound into the lives of deaf people. Hearing aid technology has moved from ear horns to cochlear implants, a recently developed surgical intervention for deaf adults who still have the proper nerve endings to which the implant can connect.[5] Another approach appears in some classrooms and auditoriums: the *audio loop,* a device to amplify ambient sound for deaf people wearing special hearing aids.

Still another way to offer access to "living English" was to create sign systems that would represent English. Various forms have been used, even, in one case, moving all the way to complete finger spelling of English (imagine hearing a lecture in which every word was spelled aloud!). This is indicative of the lengths deaf educators have gone to in order to address the problem of English access.

One offshoot of the attempt to represent spoken English visually is *Cued Speech,* a system using cues or gestures on the face to show what kind of sound is being made. This system is designed to aid in speech reading (often called "lip reading").

Another method was based on a ring of overhead projectors in a classroom. Each student and the teacher had his or her own projector on which to write. The projected writing, encircling the room like a ring of wisdom, would be real-time communication in English.

Another similar proto-ENFI approach was based on teletype machines donated by the Associated Press in the 1960s. Again, the ring of wisdom, but

---

[5] Cochlear implants are being used for deaf children now, but for a number of reasons this seems premature and perhaps unwise, which is why I say "for adults." The implant is proven to work only with adults who were once hearing.

with this method there was no general access as with the overhead projectors. All communication was funnelled through the teacher. This attempt, too, died an early death.

None of these oral-enhancement techniques have had much demonstrated impact on English acquisition for the hundreds of thousands of young deaf people in America. Nor have most of these techniques lasted more than a few years.

The current generation of teletype devices for the deaf (TDDs) and closed captions on television have provided glimpses of the "natural form" of English referred to in ENFI (ENFI originally meant *English Natural Form Instruction*) – English used conversationally, interactively, for real communicative purposes in daily life. But neither of these technologies – TDDs or captioned television – is easily transferred to the classroom. (Real-time captioning on closed-circuit TV has been used for many years at The National Technical Institute for the Deaf in Rochester, New York, because deaf students there are often mainstreamed with hearing students. They must watch a TV monitor with captions to follow the spoken classroom interaction. Because this method relies on the services of a court stenographer, however, the cost is prohibitive for most schools.)

The discovery of ENFI

It should be clear that I had more than the usual motivation for change that the average composition teacher had in 1983 when microcomputers became common and affordable enough to be available to the typically financially strapped college English department. I had the history of deaf education and the many attempts to make English accessible to deaf students to draw upon. Also, since my year immersed in the pragmatism of the Army, I'd been quite willing to try almost any technique.

This *virtual environment* (still a new concept to me then) made possible by microcomputers seemed to me more like the kind of classroom I'd been desperately looking for when I led my class on its nomadic wanderings through the campus. With the virtual environment, we could stay in one room while we imaginatively moved to another place.

Many different elements came together for me in 1983 and 1984 that led me toward the use of computers for teaching composition. In a way, I was lucky to be working with deaf students because, ironically, I was freer to try something radical. Radical problems require radical solutions.

The value of ENFI

My English department colleagues and I were primed to see different kinds of opportunities with microcomputers than were writing teachers at other colleges. To us the computer network was simply a more capable set of teletype devices. We saw that this network might be able to make English into a living thing for deaf students. People *typing* to each other over the wires in a room full of computers could simulate a spoken conversation and thus, for the first time ever, allow deaf people to directly experience and participate in a live *group* discussion in English. Because this electronic conversation would be visible and therefore accessible to deaf people, and because this accessible flow of English would be using the natural written form of English – not the stilted signed English deaf people generally experience – we called this grand new experiment English Natural Form Instruction (ENFI).[6]

We set up our first microcomputer local-area network in the fall of 1984 at Gallaudet. After a couple of months of practice using the system, we awaited our first ENFI classes in January 1985.

As I sat at my teacher station in the lab a few minutes before the first students were to arrive, I of course had no idea how this wild notion would fly. How would it seem, sitting in a room together, but not talking or signing to each other? Wouldn't that in itself seem terribly artificial, the very barrier to student engagement I was hoping to eliminate?

The students arrived, I explained our procedure (which seemed odd to them, of course), and we started typing. To my delight, once they saw their messages on the screen, and those of others, the students reacted with glee, one of them writing, "Wow, look at this ping-pong English!"

It seems slightly ironic to me [I wrote 11 months later] that the computer, which for 25 years has been perceived as anti-human, a tool of control and suppression of human instinct and intuition, has really humanized my job. For the first time in a long time, I have real hope that we might make some progress. After so many years of dealing with my own sense of failure, that small hope I now have is extremely invigorating and allows me to start the new year [1986] with a greater measure of professional hope and pride than ever. (*EnfiLOG* 13, 12/13/85)

Broader Implications

ENFI worked! In fact, it worked even better than we had hoped.

Very quickly it became apparent that the move to the network was not a simple shift from signed to written English; it led to a social shift as well. My role as teacher became very different once I was but one line on a screen and not the dominating presence at the front of the room. I also could see new

---

[6] When our project grew far beyond deaf education and it was clear we had to change the name, which was appropriate only within deaf education, we struggled to find new words that fit the acronym ENFI. If Electronic Networks For Interaction is not as memorable as English Natural Form Instruction, it is probably because of the history of its development.

energies emerging in our classroom interaction that had never occurred in my classes before.

I began to suspect that I had something pretty big here – front-page news. I also began to think that what I had discovered, as exciting within deaf education as it was (and is), was more universally applicable. ENFI might be the way that all students – deaf *and* hearing – should be taught writing. As I continued working on the computer network in the first weeks of that semester, I had a growing sense that I'd found the answer to my two decades of dissatisfaction.

I now know there are a number of conceptions of ENFI, but then I only knew that, on the network, my students were writing to communicate with me and with each other (not to perform) and seemed unusually interested in their writing. I also found that in these ENFI sessions I no longer feared running out of things to say. I was no longer in the spotlight. I actually had time to think during the class, because I was no longer frantically trying to get a "fire" going. Also, I no longer had to be reminded, class after class, that I am not a very entertaining performer. Perhaps if I had been a good performer, I might not have been so eager to change my approach to teaching writing. And, of course, if I had been a good performer, it may be that lots of learning would have been going on. But of course I don't really believe that. What I do believe is that most teachers delude themselves into believing that a good teaching performance leads to a change in student writing.

Horizontality in the writing classroom

What I discovered in the ENFI classroom was *horizontality*. The traditional class is vertical, or, to use the more common term, hierarchical. The teacher is *above* the students, both literally and figuratively. Communication moves up and down; the teacher filters and processes all communication. It is as if the learning process is occurring mostly in the teacher's head, and the students are supposed to follow along.

My problem in writing classes seemed to be that during class we worked vertically but the students were expected to write horizontally; or pretend to write horizontally. In other words, Don't address me, the teacher, directly, taking into account what I know and don't know, and that I am going to grade you and all that, but pretend to be writing to some vague audience out there who doesn't know about the story we've just read. Oh, this audience knows *something*. Maybe you can assume they *do* know the story, but are just waiting for someone to tell them what they should *think* about the story, which is what you think the teacher wants you to think. The class works in a jungle gym of surmisals, a let's pretend authenticity. It's a highly convoluted communication structure, yet we expect students to take it in stride and work within it.

Some teachers, sensing the vertical-horizontal discrepancy in the traditional classroom, sit in a circle with their students, hoping their physical position on a level with the students will make the class's communication more democratic. They may also use collaborative writing and peer critiquing for the same purposes. These measures may help, and are more in keeping than the lecture with current views about how learning takes place. Collaborative work involves an interactional process between the teacher and students, with the stress on the "action" part of "interactional." Collaborative work also is in keeping with our current view of writing as communication and as occurring in a social context (Bruffee, 1985; Elbow, 1973, 1981).

In my experience, however, these decentralization efforts in a traditional classroom had failed to make me, at least, a less dominant presence in the classroom. There is something about the basic communication dynamic of the traditional face-to-face classroom – the heavy presence of the teacher – that supports, perhaps demands, verticality. The teacher is the expert and is far more experienced than the students. It is therefore inevitable that a sense of verticality or hierarchy will prevail in a traditional classroom.

In many other subject areas (e.g., history, sociology) verticality might not be a problem. It might be better for the student if the expert – the teacher – is in control. In a writing classroom, however, where sense of audience is critical to good writing, verticality is indeed a problem. And the efforts to impose horizontality (teacher's physical position, collaborative work, peer critiquing) in an essentially vertical social situation may simply add to the sense of inauthenticity of the writing classroom. Imposing democracy in an essentially hierarchical social situation may only add another level of let's pretend.

Finally, in January 1985, I discovered one kind of horizontal classroom, the classroom where horizontal is the default and vertical hard to achieve. There in LE60 of the Learning Center at Gallaudet, we seemed to move out of the social and psychological constraints imposed by the traditional classroom. I could stay *in* the classroom physically, but be *out* of it psychically. No more nomadic wandering, hoping to escape the inescapable.

Virtual reality as a social equalizer

We did sit in a circle, each of us behind our display screens (occasionally peeking around to get a glimpse of our partners in crime), but in a sense we were not actually there. The physical setting in the room, oddly enough, had little effect on how we related. We had moved into a kind of virtual reality. The surrounding room slipped out of our consciousness. We were drawn into the screen, where we found ourselves talking as if we were whispering in a dark room. Our physical reality had diminished to such an extent it was as if our minds were talking directly among themselves. Social trappings, the hierarchy that defines and confines us, had diminished and quieted. I talked to my students as never before. We had found "neutral" social space.

In this space I could work in wholly new ways. I could think "out loud," writing ideas to my students that were tentative and exploratory, not definitive and authoritative. We negotiated our way through class. I could play, tease, shift roles and personas. I had become the artful dodger. Freed of having to be the cardboard figure at the front of the classroom, I became a person again, with foibles, feelings, and fantasies. We were more democratic and open with each other than in any other writing class I'd had. And, most amazing of all, our entire social interaction was occurring in writing.

I liked that I could be just Trent with the class. I became a collaborator in their learning, not the authority, the one who could do no wrong, the great evaluator, the director of all learning, the knowledge giver, the protector of the purity of the language, and all the other absurdly contorted roles we are thrust into as teachers in the traditional writing classroom.

Recently, Maxine Hairston of the University of Texas told me that the only time in her long professional life that a student had ever called her Maxine to her face was in an ENFI class. John Slatin, Hairston's colleague, says that in his traditional classes he is Dr. Slatin, but in his ENFI classes John (Batson, 1990). This is an attribute of the horizontal class, one that I think indicates how much less contorted the communication structure is in an ENFI class.

Listen to William Condon of the University of Michigan commenting on ENFI after receiving unusually good student evaluations in the spring semester of 1991:

Now, I think I'm a good teacher, and my evaluations are usually gratifying, but I've never experienced such universal approval in my life. I think the technology had a lot to do with that. . . . First, the technology [an ENFI network] put me in closer touch than had ever before been possible with my students, and at more of a "talking across" level. They e-mailed me outside class, we talked in Confer [a campus conferencing system] and really got to know a lot about how we all think, etc. Even though our course includes a half-hour conference for each student each week, I felt the difference: I was in closer contact with my students. (MBU-L@TTUVM1.BITNET 25June91 from USERLCBK@UMICHUM.BITNET)

Why do teachers and students feel closer in this environment? A few conjectures:

- The teacher no longer filters all communication (at least not so obviously); instead, the network does, so the teacher is released from being trapped as constant arbiter.
- The normal face-to-face social controls are diminished by communicating in writing – a rebuttal or criticism in writing for most people doesn't have the same primal emotive force as it does when spoken, so more risky communication is possible.

- Communication is with the screen in front of you, which is in your private social space, not with a person many feet distant, out in public space.
- The disparity between student expectations of the classroom setting, expectations of traditional teacher authority, and the actuality of the network communication, a seemingly more democratic arena, causes a release of student energy (as if a dreaded meeting were being postponed).
- The teacher is not able to control the floor.
- Student-to-student communication is permitted.
- Pauses in the interaction are more sustainable. Instead of the whole class sticking to the "beat" of the normal flow of class time (studies show a teacher can't, or typically doesn't, wait more than 3 seconds for a response to a question), each participant is freer to follow his or her own beat. Interestingly, because pauses are more permissible on the network, participants may enjoy more leisure during which to think about the discussion and present thoughtful ideas.
- The class is like a studio or lab yet a conversation is going on.
- All participants can "talk" at once.
- Perhaps most importantly, because no one can control the conversation, no one can lead it, making it clear that *all* participants have responsibility for keeping it going.

These are all aspects of ENFI I've noticed, but I think there are others. It is clear that the move into virtual space, which doesn't occur with a stand-alone computer and seems to be most powerful with real-time written group discussion when the participants are in the same room, radically changes the way that people experience each other. I had no idea the network would affect the group psychologically, but once I saw it happening, I knew that we writing teachers had a new source of energy to work with. We had a new ally.

Building a writing community

The writing I saw on the network gave me more insight into my students as writers than a couple of semesters of essay writing would have (essays in the traditional manner of composing, that is). I could see in writing how my students thought, how they handled ideas, how they picked up cues from me or others. I saw their true intelligence at play; the curtain between us was raised.

Working in this new, wonderful space we had discovered, I finally felt that we were communicating more as people, not as students and teacher. I had tried so desperately to escape the writing-class game for 20 years and had only occasionally seen glimpses of what it would be like to truly break free, but those glimpses, unfortunately, were almost always during an *oral* discussion. (It's hard to trace the connections, if any, between group oral discussion and individual composing.)

In those pre-ENFI years, I treasured those occasional moments, those moments when my class and I communicated with each other in common pursuit of an idea. Finally, in January 1985, on the computer network, I experienced hundreds of such moments; I was showered in gold.

My students and I found ourselves saying things we'd never said in writing classes before. We felt skittish as we experimented to find the limits, the contours of this seemingly neutral social space. We tried improvisational drama, role playing, changing our names and becoming new people. We found ourselves able to expand the range of our social personalities. Some of the students contributed more in the first week of class than they had in the previous several years. For all of us, English class became fun. My students showed up early and stayed late. We felt we shared a secret. One of my female students challenged me to a wrestling contest (and my persona on the network took her up on it, though my off-network persona did not). To this day, when I see one of these students who has come back to campus to visit, we smile at each other, remembering the great time we had that first semester of ENFI.

I was very gratified to find that the students I had that semester did remarkably well on a standard writing test given at Gallaudet. But I was not surprised. (All students improved in a pre- and posttest, but some improved more than any students in years in such a short time.)

If ever learning had been painless, it was that semester. We didn't simply play on the network, however. The students wrote essays and I graded them, we read books, and we worked on exercises such as sentence combining on the network, writing opening paragraphs of an essay (again, on the network), working on variations of expressing the same idea, on the concept of persona, cohesion, and so on. The difference was that all this work was infused with the lightness of play and all done through some activity, not through lecture. Even off-topic, we were on-topic in the sense that we were writing to each other and still working, unknown to the students, on persona, cohesion, diction, tone, irony, and other attributes of writing that I could model as we seemingly wandered off topic.

Conversation vs. discussion

I came to sense the power of human conversation (Bruffee, 1984) while using ENFI. In school we call conversations discussions, but *discussion* is not a fun word. It connotes a serious intention. Conversation seems focused on the pleasure of interaction, whereas discussion seems goal-bound. Conversation also suggests following social rules; with discussion, the implication is that the rules of logic, not social rules, are primary. If I say about my class that we had a conversation, I appear to be saying we just chatted, and didn't focus on our work. The contrary is true if we had a discussion.

The problem with "class discussion" is that it now implies a teacher-led interaction, which may mean that the teacher does 85% of the talking. A conversation is more democratic. A discussion in class is vertical, but a conversation is horizontal. What occurred in my ENFI class, then, was not discussion, but conversation.

An archetypal form of communication

I realized I had found a way to have a conversation in writing class that was productive. I had resurrected the oldest forms of teaching, conversation and modeling, through thoroughly modern means. The computer-created virtual space was bringing to the forefront something essentially human. I came to see that students are really very eager to talk to us teachers but are prevented from doing so by social forms, by hierarchy, by the physical presence of each other. In Catholic churches, this problem of hierarchical barriers to communication has been addressed by using a confessional: The priest is a disembodied voice who invites the disembodied or true voice of the penitent to speak. Our network seemed to be our confessional: It also removed the troubling physical presence of a teacher. Our once so obvious social roles and social differences became much less obvious on the network.

I had no doubt that we had found a new archetypal form. ENFI has primal energy. It is privileged talk, much like that between doctor and patient, lawyer and client, or priest and parishioner. The video-display screen before you is a wandering eye, which you can direct to any one member of the class or to all. It is also your Charlie McCarthy, your dummy who speaks for you. It is your inebriated self (the alcohol made me say it – *in vino veritas*). It is an altered state. It is powerful enough that even now teachers talk about ENFI as if it is a minefield where sudden flaming occurs.

Some people have noticed similar effects in computer conferencing at a distance and even in e-mail exchanges. ENFI is more pronounced and more useful instructionally because the interactions occur nearly in real time, and ENFI is an alternative classroom, an actual space within which to work in real time.

Discovering the power of ENFI as I did, without any inclination or knowledge beforehand of what was waiting for me, was like stumbling upon King Tut's tomb, or cresting that last mountain ridge and catching sight of the Pacific Ocean, as did Balboa. One thing was very clear to me: My 20-year quest for a sense of human authenticity in my classroom had brought me far more than I had bargained for. I now had authenticity and a whole lot more. I had found a way to tap into latent human energies that had implications far beyond just teaching writing.

Spreading the word

Within a few months I started a newsletter about ENFI, which I called *EnfiLOG*. In *EnfiLOG*, and in other things I wrote, my main effort was simply to explain what I was doing. Few people in 1985 could grasp ENFI, even after painfully laborious explanation, and even those who did understand would ask me, But why do that?

Nothing is more frustrating than finding THE TRUE WAY only to find that no one recognizes your discovery. Soon, though, enough people understood that ENFI was a different kind of computer application that I was accepted to speak at conferences. At those conferences I generally had 20 minutes to present ENFI. This is a very short time in the best of circumstances, but with a radical new idea, the 20-minute limit was excruciating. I had to spend 15 minutes just to make it clear what I was talking about. Inevitably, then, all that came across was having a conversation in writing. I had no choice but to focus on the most obvious feature of ENFI in order to get the idea out in the marketplace of ideas.

I also knew that until someone experienced ENFI, he or she would have no idea of the power behind it. If one has never gone to a confessional in church, one might have a problem explaining the psychological dynamic at work; the same is true of ENFI. Consequently, as I talked and wrote about ENFI, I felt the frustration of not being able to convey, no matter how dramatic my language, the reality of the ENFI phenomenon.

I knew then, which has partially come true, that ENFI would become a standard option as an environment for teaching writing. Thus I felt highly disturbed when again and again people would ask, But why do it? I always wanted to ask back, On the contrary, why do it as you do now? Why would anyone teach writing by *talking* about it? To me, the strange approach was teaching writing in the "traditional" manner.

Speaking and writing

Those of us who teach writing are working in the secondary form of our language. The first is speech. For a number of reasons, we approach the secondary form differently than we do the primary. Almost everyone learns to speak and to use speech productively throughout life, but the same is not true of writing. We think of speaking as natural (though it is not), but of writing as learned (which, unfortunately, it often is not).

In the writing classes I had in high school and college, we used speech most of the time. We had discussions. In the evenings, with my portable typewriter, I had to face the chore of writing. When I started *teaching* writing, I followed the same pattern. During class discussion I found myself striving to create a process of thinking that would carry over to writing. I had no idea how the transfer was made from class discussion to individual composing. I thought that if the discussion was hot enough a few embers might remain when the students were writing. They could use the embers to rekindle the fire of our discussion.

But that belief was pretty unspecific. How did the transfer occur, if it did? The great frustration of teaching writing, it seems to me, is that it all occurs in the head, so it's invisible. And we who teach it don't even know how we ourselves go about writing, at least not very well. Therefore, because it's invisible and not well understood, we can't easily *demonstrate* to the students the thinking/writing process.

In addition, we've recently become more aware of how important the context for writing is. We see that writing is communication, just like speaking, so it's important to know one's audience and purpose (see, e.g., Lunsford, Lunsford, & Lunsford, 1984). In other words, it may be that for writing to be good the whole writing situation has to be worked with.

But the writing classroom, and class, is inherently artificial. Students are expected to write to the teacher about something that in most cases the teacher already knows. They are also expected to write as if they are communicating when in fact they know they are writing to be evaluated. It's nearly impossible in the traditional classroom to overcome these and other factors that create a sense of artificiality in the writing class.

At times, however, during a really good discussion, students seem to forget the artificiality of the situation and get *engaged*. Something about social interaction, having a real audience, using language to communicate, and not being evaluated (or corrected!), tends to draw in the whole being.

It's this magic suspension of disbelief, this moment of engagement in discussion, that writing teachers hope will carry over to composing. But, alas, the magic usually slips away. With a blank piece of paper in front of you, especially if you haven't internalized a sense of audience, it's hard to re-create the enthusiasm you had in the oral discussion. (Besides, as my students said to me once, Why say it over again? We already said it in class.)

Thus the central irony of the writing class: The occasion when the class seems most engaged (during a good discussion) is precisely when the work is most distant from the goals of the course. After all, the purpose of freshman composition is not to teach the discourse of oral discussion but of autonomous text. How can we reduce the distance between the two? How can class discussion and individual composing be brought closer together? It was this that I thought I had done with ENFI.

Because social interaction and composition had always remained problematically separate, but could now be linked much more directly, I stressed in my conference presentations about ENFI that it is a group written conversation (sometimes using *discussion* to make it clear we had a serious, not frivolous, purpose). I didn't describe it as peer critiquing or as collaborative writing or as modeling because it seemed to me beyond a mere technique. I knew about ENFI's special magic, and knowing about it kept me flying around the country like a peripatetic preacher, ready to set up my soapbox wherever I found an audience.

Beyond speaking and composing

To sum up, what I found appealing in the ENFI environment is the way it decenters the classroom, moves me away from the knowledge transfer model of learning, and allows me to use collaborative learning. ENFI constructs a more understandable audience for the students, seems to increase the fluency of novice writers by giving them more practice, and shifts the teacher's role from great evaluator to coach/participant. It has allowed me the pure pleasure of *working in the medium I'm teaching*.

I was happy that ENFI seemed to have the blessing of the college composition research community, which was publishing articles on these issues and a whole new area of concern, the social construction of knowledge. This new movement seemed especially appropriate in an ENFI environment where the voices of the students had so much more leeway and power (Gergen, 1985; LeFevre, 1987; Rafoth, 1988).

Joy Peyton's influence on ENFI

When Dr. Joy Kreeft Peyton joined me in mid-1985, a few months after my electrifying experiences as I began ENFI, she brought with her a background in linguistics, second language learning, and her research with dialogue journals. She saw in ENFI, as I did, a way to put into practice her ideas about language learning. We reinforced each other's enthusiasm for this new arena for teachers who worked with language in any way, and Joy provided an important "scaffold" – to use one of her favorite terms – to help me build a conceptual structure for ENFI.

I had been seeking a sense of authenticity during the years I taught writing. I'd also learned that the environment I created and the sequence of experiences for the students were as important as what I actually said. But my credo, my set of beliefs about teaching writing, was idiosyncratic. I was also less a researcher in 1985 than an innovator. In order to convey my front-page news, I had to find a way to describe this new thing – ENFI – in terms understandable to other composition instructors on both my own campus and other campuses.

Joy worked with me to build a theoretical framework for the hybrid discourse form we had discovered (and she works with us still). We found very early in our work together that we had compatible theoretical orientations about language and writing (although mine was based on personal beliefs developed in the trenches over 20 years of teaching and hers was based on formal research). At that time she had worked for several years with dialogue journals and so was immersed in the theory supporting *interactive language use* as a successful approach to building increased fluency. She also was aware of the research supporting the writer's need to have *real purposes* for his or her writing, including writing to a *concrete and immediate audience*. She gave me the terminology for my beliefs, telling me how to identify the elements of what I had always called "authenticity."

As we talked in the first months of our collaboration, I saw that Joy's conception of learning to write was like mine in stressing learning through doing, through action. We also agreed on the need to pay attention to the thinking going into the writing and to allow formal elements to develop along with maturing thinking. I learned from Joy that most students will write better when they write interactively rather than in solitary production, which coincided with my own beliefs. Mostly, we agreed that the artificiality of the classroom was especially inappropriate for improving language use, because language is so personal, so much a part of one's identity.

I was of course delighted that the credo arising from my experience and reading over many years seemed to have a basis in research and theory. But what I found especially appealing was finding a research community that provided value and guidance to our work with the computer network. We could begin to map out a research strategy; we might even be able to understand some of the dynamics of the network classroom and so help others who wanted to try ENFI.

The early conception of ENFI

After two years of working together, Joy and I had developed our own concept of ENFI as we started our work with the ENFI Consortium in 1987. During the first two years of ENFI, I had pretty much set the ENFI teaching pattern because Joy and I were the only people talking about ENFI. (She was a researcher with the ENFI Project, not a teacher, so she followed my lead about what constituted ENFI.) We described it as the class shifting entirely to written interaction. We also had in mind one particular software implementation. Results had been good, and a number of other teachers at Gallaudet had adopted "the Batson Method." Also, a few people around the country – Terry Collins at the University of Minnesota, Diane Thompson at Northern Virginia Community College, Fred Kemp at the University of Texas, and Mike Burton at Floyd College in Rome, Georgia – were in the process of "going ENFI," so we had little reason to suspect at that time ENFI could mean anything other than what we knew it to be.

Because of the importance to me of what I was calling authenticity in communication, and how deadly I had seen its lack to be, and because I saw that the traditional role of the teacher in the writing classroom was one of the sources of inauthenticity in the writing classroom, I believed strongly that the network, with its special magic, should remain central in writing classes. In addition, because I worked with deaf students and I was aware of the language confusion between English and ASL in traditional face-to-face classes at Gallaudet, I had a second powerful reason for meeting 100% of the time on the network where we could use only written English.

Thus our vision of ENFI was that it was in itself a new space within which to work, where human communication took on special new aspects that were helpful across the full range of language-related learning, from basic literacy to advanced composition, with both hearing and deaf students. This is still my own vision today, but during the 3 years of our ENFI Consortium work, many other people found their own ways to work with the network software tools. Despite the apparent loss of the purity of my vision of ENFI, I did come to realize that each of the variations of ENFI potentially pointed to new uses of the environment: Each brought into play new combinations of teaching style and environment. I had to hold my vision (and my tongue) in check while I allowed others to explore the environment for themselves, without prescription or proscription.

Fortunately for me, my vision of ENFI was not unique. Others, some within the consortium and some without, perhaps with similar years of dissatisfaction behind them, took up the ENFI banner while I shifted from proselytizer to project director, necessarily speaking less as the advocate and more as the evaluator. The Daedalus Group of Austin, Texas, developed new ENFI software (Interchange) that operated differently than Realtime Writer (developed by Realtime Learning Systems of Washington, DC), the software we had used for years at Gallaudet. Interchange became common on college campuses and many of the new users of Daedalus's Interchange now sound oddly like the Trent Batson of 1985–86. Thus I am reassured that the vision of ENFI from those years will not fade, even if I don't resume my role as flag bearer.

The original vision of ENFI has not remained static, however. When I first began working with ENFI, I used this environment as a launching pad for traditional individual composing, much as class oral discussion is used. We conversed and carried on exercises on the network, but my students composed alone at home as they had always done. Now, however, I see that actual group composing is possible and helpful for students (it both spurs them on to better writing and is realistic preparation for the collaborative writing done in the workplace). Consequently, much of the composing work in my current classes is done in class and we have our electronic conversation on the campus network outside of class time; we've basically reversed the old pattern of discussion during class and composing out of class. In other words, though my original conception of ENFI as a new archetypal form of human communication remains, how I use ENFI to pursue our learning goals has evolved. I still believe that the class should meet almost all of the time on the network, but instead of so much free conversation with exercises and modeling woven in, I now set up a sequence of prewriting activities for the whole class to follow. We even use separate, integrated software programs so that the sequence is palpable and managed appropriately for that stage in the group composing process. I have been as active in altering the original Batson vision as anyone.

The vision now

At Gallaudet about half of the 50-plus members of the English department, and a number of faculty members from other departments as well, have taught in one of the ENFI labs. Even though ENFI has been here for many years now, it continues to provide significant challenges to whoever ventures in. Many other colleges and universities also have computer labs and many are networked. ENFI, and its cousins, will continue to be experimented with and used.

The chief challenge, I think, and the one I'd like to see addressed, is in our basic conceptions about how to create coherence through group interaction. We all know how coherence has always been created in the oral- or paper-based sphere, but new technologies have a way of confusing us with new realities. Many of us, for example, have had the slightly awkward experience of a conference call involving a number of people: Who's in charge? How do you take turns? What register do you use? How do you say goodbye? Conference calls are new enough that many of us aren't familiar with the contour they should take.

ENFI is even more disorienting, especially to our conceptions of coherence. We are accustomed to having a person in charge in a group situation, be it a composition class or a business meeting. That person is responsible for creating coherence, the coherence of the dominant voice. Even in the most egalitarian gatherings, one person is almost always dominant, whether by authority, habit, or default. Yet in the ENFI environment, it is very difficult for anyone to control the interaction. Without control, how can coherence be created?

But should we even link control and coherence? Should we be limited by traditional notions of group coherence? Perhaps by imposing the traditional notion of coherence on ENFI we are missing its essential value. The price we pay for traditional coherence is often the loss of contributions by the group: Each group member in a traditional meeting experiences some disjunction between his or her own thoughts and what's being said at the moment. Each has to wait for a turn to speak; many participants say nothing; peer pressure forces out some threads of discussion; and some who might "discover" what they really think by speaking out loud never do, so their thinking is lost to the discussion.

In other words, though the traditional meeting may appear to be coherent, each individual member may be experiencing internal incoherence. In a classroom, where the teacher is so much more articulate and knowledgeable than the students and more experienced in speaking, the discrepancy between the leader's (teacher's) experiences and the group's (students') is even more pronounced. Traditional means of creating group coherence privilege the leader's conceptualizing at the expense of each member's. In contrast, ENFI privileges individual coherence building.

In practice, in an ENFI session there may be clusters of two or three conversational partners who build temporary collaborative coherence, and these clusters may last for only a few minutes before other clusters form (these patterns are currently being studied). Within an ENFI environment it is much more difficult to build coherence the traditional way, and we are not yet sure how new kinds of coherence are built.

It is the necessity to create alternative coherence that is most challenging for a teacher coming from a traditional classroom into an ENFI lab. As more and more people experience multivocality and new kinds of group coherence building, ENFI will cease to be quite so challenging. In the meantime, the development of this new environment continues to be exciting. I expect that its various social and psychological effects will continue to baffle and engage us for many years to come.

6   Student authority and teacher freedom: ENFI at New York Institute of Technology

Marshall Kremers

I discovered the true power of ENFI in 1988, the first time I tried to lead a class discussion in real time on one of our new local-area computer networks (LANs). Expecting that my students would follow me in discussion, I found instead that they much preferred to converse with each other, forcing me to the sidelines. I could not imagine that happening in my conventional classroom. No student had ever tried to take over the discussion in all my 20 years of teaching, even during my progressive period, when I arranged the desks in a circle. I had always set the direction, and the students had always done more or less what I wanted. But interaction in real time on the LAN was totally different because it seemed to give all the power to the students, who outnumbered me 20 to 1 (Kremers, 1988).

Reform and radical change

At first glance, adapting to ENFI seemed fairly easy. A new classroom structure would be accompanied by an innovative pedagogy based upon current theory about the social construction of knowledge. It would provide a natural writing community in which students would learn to work together, sharing in a conversation that would eventually lead to greater individual reflection and discovery. After writing together, students would become more literate and thus would know better how to prepare an essay. The LAN would model the networked arrangement of desktop computers and terminals in offices where these students would soon find themselves at work. It even seemed that the term *computer lab* would disappear, since with just a bit more equipment and available space, we could meet all our writing courses on the LAN all of the time, making the traditional classroom obsolete.

At New York Institute of Technology (NYIT), we welcomed the formation of collaborative writing communities. Students would work with each other more and more – and teachers would dominate the learning less and less. Such an arrangement would free writing teachers to create and plan a context for writing in which students would teach themselves. All of this would be easy to accomplish because the network would automatically create a writing community. Writing in real time meant constructing a shared conversation, and so we expected that no one would refuse to write or read, that no one would hang back for long.

This was a paradigm shift away from the traditional classroom on which the entire curriculum of our college is based. We were proposing to create an environment in which the teacher no longer dispenses all knowledge and arbitrates all disputes, but one in which the students become active learners. We expected to draw traditionally marginal students into the center. Even the weakest students would have space in which to take chances, to experiment with language, to work past writer's block. In ENFI, Tony DiMatteo (1990) saw opportunities for a deconstructionist reassessment of our composition pedagogy, a reformed classroom where knowledge is "pluralistic and conflict-ridden," where the sense of community is "based on dissent, and where turbulence transforms, rather than represents, knowledge."

Change does not come quickly to educational institutions, however, and theory alone does not lead automatically to reform. To revise a pedagogy one must take into account, and sometimes challenge, long-standing departmental goals. ENFI did not sweep through our department, and for a variety of reasons, many writing teachers at NYIT chose not to use the LAN in their courses at all, leaving those of us who were ENFI researchers to design our own projects and see what we could do to test the theoretical waters.

Practical realities

During my first two ENFI years, I developed an approach based on a single principle: sharing control of the LAN with my students. After my students' first attempt to take control of the LAN, I decided that it might be useful to direct their energy in positive directions, rather than attempt to stifle it (Kremers, 1990). However, the remedial composition course I taught with ENFI was set up as a 3/2 split (3 hours in lecture, 2 in the lab), so I had to decide how to use two very different, often contradictory, environments. On the one hand, I was using the LAN to give my students plenty of free rein, while on the other, when meeting in the conventional classroom, I was controlling the discussion. As if to compensate for my dominance in the lecture, I was coming more and more to see my own presence in the ENFI class as a kind of intrusion.

It was a very confusing time for all us. Though I tried not to get in the way of the written dialogues, I often had no choice but to intervene because the conversations were so degenerate. That is, in the ENFI class my students seemed to have little sense of how to be civilized.

Wondering how to exert control while still encouraging freedom of expression, I decided to create role-playing scenarios for each ENFI class based upon daily newspaper stories. Usually about well-known people, these stories provided the characters for the scenarios. Students worked on these scenarios in small groups on different channels. As much as possible, I wanted the role playing to become a way for my students to explore underlying public issues.

My rationale for using role playing was based on three assumptions: that I could bring out creative impulses that self-consciousness about composing so often defeats; that group prewriting activities could help students to become more open to discovery and more willing to play with words; and that group writing would stimulate centers of creativity that are lost in solo composing. Although the students had fun, I saw little evidence that they understood the issues, or that creating a persona for, say, Michael Milken or George Bush stimulated anyone to write more thoughtfully about business ethics or presidential politics. Sometimes the conversations became ugly. Once, for example, I unwittingly created a scenario about San Francisco that led immediately to an attack on homosexuals; it was so vile that I threw out the whole transcript for that session. On such occasions the discussion spiraled inexorably downward, and no one was able to pull the group out of it. There were no leaders, no one to rescue the discussion and turn it toward a productive end. When I got a scenario right, when it seemed to strike a chord, it wasn't unusual for my students to work synchronously on the LAN for a full hour. They clearly enjoyed ENFI work. But for all of the successes there were twice as many failures, sessions that died as soon as they got started. It was difficult to find the formula, to figure out in advance what would work, since each group responded to a scenario differently. Although I tried my best to strike a balance between control and freedom, that ideal proved elusive.

To look more closely at these conflicting forces, I began my third year with ENFI by asking Sylvia Broffman, Associate Professor of Speech at NYIT, for help. Sylvia had interviewed selected ENFI students on audiotape since the beginning of the project at NYIT. She suggested making a videotape of typical student behaviors in both my classrooms, oral lecture/discussion and ENFI, in addition to conducting more interviews. My role in the non-ENFI classroom would be familiar: to lead a discussion in which I would do almost all of the talking by lecturing, asking questions, and jotting ideas on the chalkboard. For the ENFI classroom I would continue to create scenarios for small-group role playing. In both settings my instructional goal was group prewriting prior to the individual planning and drafting of a short essay.

The videotapes are instructive. In the conventional class my students sit passively and respond only when I press them on a point; a few take notes while I list items on the chalkboard. They look like uncomfortable captives, grudging and reticent. At one point during the semester, I asked the class how they would feel if the New York Yankees were sold to a Japanese corporation such as Mitsubishi (Mitsubishi had just purchased a 51% interest in Rockefeller Center). I asked them to discuss their feelings and write an essay about them. (Earlier, Sylvia had suggested that this group in particular, some of whom were members of the NYIT baseball team, might do better in oral discussion with a subject they care about and understand.) But what the tape shows is behavior that is no different from all of the other non-ENFI sessions: While I talk, the students yawn, scratch, fidget, and stare off into space. They seem to be trying, but their hearts clearly aren't in it.

In direct contrast, these same students come to life in the ENFI classroom. Our computer labs are equipped with monitors that rest below desk level in cabinets with plexiglas tops, so it's easy for students to talk to each other. While I hand out copies of the scenario I have prepared for the day, they chat quietly. Because I am not standing at the front of the room with a piece of chalk in my hand, I am not in a good position to talk. I say very little. They read my instructions, stop talking, and start typing. The room becomes quiet as everyone gets to work. Some students are fast typists who can fire off messages in half the time of the others, so while they wait for responses they go back to chatting, often about things that have nothing to do with the assigned writing task. From time to time they glance down at their screens, and if a new message has been sent, they write a response. They don't stare off into space, and they don't sneak glances at their watches.

Meanwhile, I go to my workstation, where I have a range of options: (1) intervene by joining one of the small groups; (2) sit at my monitor and observe what is happening on the different channels without participating (that is, I lurk); (3) act as discussion leader in any one of the dialogues; (4) join in a dialogue as a "masked" participant (under a pseudonym); and (5) invite selected students to join me in one-to-one dialogues. Or, of course, I can do nothing. The conversants have a task and a powerful means of communicating at their fingertips, so I can, if I choose, leave the room.

During all three ENFI years, I experimented with each of these roles, always trying to find the right formula for a particular group. Sometimes the work went so well that I had to ask my students to quit, to make way for the next class scheduled for the LAN. On task or not, the ENFI class was always a community, a student-centered environment, a place full of small talk and laughter. ENFI seemed to provide a long overdue opportunity for real student growth.

Emotional barriers

Yet when we looked a bit closer at Sylvia's interviews, we discovered a deep vein of ambivalence in these students. Whereas they welcomed ENFI because it was always fun, they did not necessarily like the freedom that went with it. They expressed feelings of fear, confusion, anger, and distrust – feelings they had hidden from me.

For many of these students, ENFI was not an exciting innovation, but rather a new and empty space into which we threw them without explaining why. Already upset at being placed in a remedial course, they were less than eager to participate in an experiment that had no apparent link to the exit exam. For one thing the ENFI class was disorienting in contrast to the conventional classroom. Why didn't the teacher lecture or lead a discussion? Were the rules for measuring performance the same in both classrooms or were they different for ENFI? If so, what were they? ENFI work seemed not to be graded, but non-ENFI work was. Did that make ENFI "play" and the other serious work? For these students the teacher in the new environment was not a meddling controller but rather a much-needed and reassuring presence, the adult in the group who understands why and how ENFI relates to the goals of the course. If ENFI should lead to chaos, the teacher must be ready to call a halt and figure out ways to resume an orderly progression of activities. So it is not surprising that these students reacted to ENFI with mixed feelings.

Sylvia and I also discovered that many negative behaviors – flaming, ignoring the teacher, profanity – were sometimes expressions of a generalized anger rooted in feelings of abandonment. In the case of one remedial group in particular, I decided to leave the classroom often during the semester because I sensed that they were far too dependent on me for direction. They said nothing to me, but later Sylvia discovered that my absence upset them a great deal; they thought that I didn't care about them, that I was too busy. Other students felt isolated within the class when they were left on their own because the teacher had always been for them the agent of group cohesion, the arbiter of disputes.

Freedom, authority, and empowerment

These feelings should prompt us to reflect on how students understand us when we say that we want to liberate them. There was much evidence in the interviews to suggest that my students did not wish to be liberated, certainly not in the sense of taking full responsibility for their actions in the relative chaos of real-time interaction. Their acting out seemed prompted by quite reasonable questions: Where is so much freedom of expression granted to us elsewhere in the college? Why don't we do ENFI work in non-English courses? What are the rules of network civility? If we are as free as you seem to be saying, don't we get to make our own rules? Laurie George (1990), also at NYIT, has written that in her ENFI class the dialogues contained *verbal wilding,* a term she took from the rape and beating of a female jogger in Central Park by a group of youths who said they often went out "wilding" – that is, attacking people in the park at night. She also coined the term "interinsultive" to describe her students' tendency toward personal aggression on the LAN. However, as negative as such behaviors were, Sylvia and I came to believe that our students' emotional outbursts were not directed at others so much as at a situation in which the old rules did not seem to apply. We saw their behavior as rebellion against a system in which the guardians of authority, the faculty, had apparently abdicated their traditional responsibility for classroom decorum.

The problem of giving authority to students who are not used to it is real, but the potential of ENFI is impressive nonetheless. ENFI helps students to become authors by granting them freedom of expression, while it frees their teachers to create a more stimulating climate for learning. ENFI students are self-motivated and able to work without dependence on the teacher. An ENFI classroom is student centered. What's more, by suggesting greater *empowerment,* a reformist political notion, ENFI draws attention to the gap between progressive change and what the system will allow. At the very least, ENFI invites everyone – students, teachers, administrators – to look at the implications of granting greater powers of expression, greater empowerment, to students in writing classes.

According to William Safire (1990), empowerment means "giving people the opportunity to gain greater control over their own destiny through access to assets of private property, jobs and education." That is hardly a radical notion in itself, but ENFI empowerment is revolutionary, because it puts more weight on learning to cooperate with others than on individual destiny. ENFI work is radical because it is shared and communal, thus presenting an implicit challenge to a long-standing pedagogy based on individual achievement and reward. As I discovered when my students took control of the network, ENFI can alarm the most enlightened of us. If a college administration allows the English department to use a LAN in a substantive way in its writing courses, then that means it fully understands and welcomes radical change. And when a college grants such empowerment to its students, then clearly it must trust in their ability to act responsibly.

Yet, as Gail Hawisher and Cindy Selfe (1990) have pointed out, where they threaten the established order, networks "may actually be used to dampen creativity, writing, intellectual exchanges, rather than to encourage them. Computer-using teachers seldom talk . . . about the instructors who are using networks to deliver drill-and-practice software exercises to students" (p. 8). Thus, by challenging the status quo, ENFI draws attention to a contemporary paradox. How, in a system that rewards individuals, should faculty evaluate work done by groups? How can they give grades to "group text"? Where does the individual end and the group begin? What is plagiarism if everyone is borrowing ideas and facts freely from each other? These questions remain to be addressed by ENFI users.

Implementing ENFI

There are several strategies that can be used to implement ENFI effectively, at least within an educational context like ours at NYIT. First, it doesn't make sense to split time between two kinds of classrooms, where the teacher dispenses knowledge one day and appears to withhold it the next. How does one adequately explain what amounts to a contradiction? ENFI renders terms such as computer lab obsolete, because the computer classroom can now become the primary educational environment. The goal of ENFI is to hold all class meetings on the network. Recently I heard someone complain at a conference on computers and writing that he would be happy to use a computer lab to teach technical writing, but he just did not have time because there was too much course material to cover. He meant that the real work is done in the conventional classroom, and that computer labs are nice if you have the luxury of time. That is not the idea of ENFI, which involves everyone learning from each other in a collaborative environment.

Second, it will help if we can get past the notion that "serious" writing must be done in isolation. After their ENFI sessions, which were always fun no matter how purposeful, my students returned to the conventional classroom more at ease, better prepared to work in groups, and more confident about writing in general. They were less worried about failure and less afraid of each other, of saying something stupid, of being pressured to break their silence and speak. The reason was obvious: ENFI involves group work in which everyone sees that their writing is connected to a common goal. Because the writing is spontaneous, taking each writer in directions that are impossible to predict, ENFI is ideally suited to prewriting. ENFI writing is a group heuristic. The old grading rules don't apply to ENFI, because the voices blending together express ideas that come from every side. There is no plagiarism because everyone is openly taking from each other.

Third, ENFI opens new pathways for creative interaction, for breaking out of the passivity that so often grips students in the teacher-dominated classroom. Role playing, for instance, allows students to generate an organic conversation that closely parallels dramatic discourse. Miller (this volume) describes how he uses the LAN to create play scripts with deaf students at Gallaudet (see also Peyton, 1990). I also discovered the power of on-line dramatization when, during my first year of ENFI, I had my students expand on a discussion they were having about the Brazilian rain forest. I divided them into groups of four and assigned them parts that represented the major sides in the dispute over who is responsible for stopping the fires there. To my surprise, what started out as a sort of roundtable turned into a narrative to which everyone in the class contributed, a lurid tale of greed, deceit, and eventually murder. ENFI provided a means of unlocking creative impulses that would have remained hidden in a conventional setting.

And fourth, ENFI role playing allows students to test their attitudes toward controversial issues in ways that oral discussions cannot accommodate. That is, network roles provide a mask behind which one can become invisible, an anonymity that many students need when they are afraid to say what they really believe. For instance, to demonstrate ENFI recently for a group of teachers attending NYIT's annual conference on computers and writing, I prepared this scenario:

The scene is the Oval Office, 1600 Pennsylvania Avenue, where the president, the vice-president, and the chief of staff are preparing for a news conference to be held later in the day. They expect questions about what the United States might do to stop the burning of Amazonia; all agree that it is in our interest to stop this destruction. However, there is a problem. The president wants to err on the side of caution by calling for more research on the relation between the fires and atmospheric damage. The vice-president, who is 25 years younger than the president and wants to make a run for the White House before the end of the decade, wants an outright condemnation of the Brazilian government. The chief of staff, as usual, wants to look at the polls before going forward.

Instructions: Develop a discussion in which you try to get your two colleagues to agree that your strategy for the news briefing is correct.

I had chosen a political theme to show the participants, mostly high school English teachers, the potential of ENFI to stimulate cross-disciplinary discussions. As usual, the room grew quiet as everyone started to write, people typing away furiously as soon as I handed out the instructions. However, one group – Bill, Sam, and Linda – caught my attention because the sparks started flying between them even before they got started on the network. By coincidence, Bill and Sam were friends who taught at the same school, but Linda did not know them. When they were discussing who should play which role, one of the men made a chauvinist remark, Linda became furious, and then insisted on being the president. Here is an excerpt from their network dialogue:*

LINDA: What the American government will do is send a fact finding mission down to the Amazon jungle to investigate what we want to know. What we want to know is that there is no problem down there. There are some Brazilian construction difficulties, but there will be no problems that we will have to get involved with. Got it???

SAM: I say we fold 'em. Call in their loans. Tell 'em the pigs in the poke, the gig is up, I – mean you – are calling their hands. I say we call in their debts and TAKE those forests as COLLATERAL. That'll show 'em. They ain't gonna fool with me; I'm the Vice-President.

LINDA: Listen moron, if we call in their loans, my retirement and the others in the cabinet will fold, because our government will fold. Do you get it????

SAM: Mr. President, to err on the side of caution is erring on the side of caution. Let's not err on the side of caution. And besides, say we nuke 'em, wouldn't you want to go down as the man who didn't err

---

* All dialogues are reproduced as originally typed, without benefit of proofreading and editing.

on the side of caution? As the man who pushed it for trees, and for the American way of life?

BILL: Jill, let's go to channel 1. Press Alt-C and respond to the prompt.

LINDA: Listen pin head . . . The American way of life is green, green money. Money is being made in the Amazon. Your future depends on agreeing with me and agreeing with me is agreeing with the American people. Just say yes.

SAM: Yes.

Clearly, this was no empty, make-work exercise, but the interplay of basic human emotions. Linda took control of a power game, both as "president" and as a woman who had just been insulted by two men. By developing such a strong persona, she successfully maneuvered Sam into a position of submissiveness and rendered Bill nearly mute. I wonder if she would have felt so free to do that in oral conversation.

My final suggestion is that it helps to be flexible in designing activities because every ENFI group is different. Some groups can go right to real-time writing, but for others I prefer to show them more gradually how the network assists group work. For instance, I will ask them to run a word processing program (we use Microsoft Word and WordPerfect on the LAN) and then to write something for discussion. I will ask for a volunteer and use the video-switcher to display that student's text on all the other screens. Or I will ask one student at a time to let me look at what he or she is writing by displaying the text on my screen at the main workstation. At other times, I will write something on my screen for everyone to see and then show how I tend to make revisions. It is important to plan time so that students can work alone, in small groups, and in larger groups.

Conclusion

Gary Tate (1990) has called those of us who teach in computer-assisted classrooms the new Romantics, the purveyors of "HyperKeats." I have always thought that by using networks we are simply recognizing reality and adjusting our pedagogy to match it, that ENFI helps students to cope in the world they will enter when they go to work. But Tate is correct. We are indeed breaking out of oppressive patterns we have fashioned in the writing classroom through our dominance of the conversation. Under such a system it has been impossible to empower or liberate anyone. When Trent Batson (1990) says that ENFI teachers are "using the energy of chaos to build coherence out of diversity," we understand better the potential of ENFI to promote change. I sum up this chapter, then, by reviewing how ENFI transforms traditional pedagogy.

ENFI allows students to work as hard during class meetings as their teachers. After viewing the videotapes of my conventional classroom, I was surprised by how much of the work I did; I would have guessed that the ratio of my talking to the students' talking was 60:40 but it was at least 90:10. I was also surprised by the blank looks on their faces, the stubborn refusal to participate even when the discussion turned to baseball. At one point in the tape, Tony, sitting in the front row where Sylvia asked him to move in order to get everyone into the picture, answered my question and then turned to look at Brian, the class leader, as if to apologize for being a good student, the teacher's pet. After the taping, Tony went back to his accustomed place in the back row. ENFI classes have no back rows, and students don't have to apologize for playing along with the teacher, because they are busy doing their own work. In the conventional class my students get up and leave after 10 minutes or so if I am late, but my ENFI students start right in whether I am on time or not.

ENFI teachers can enter into substantive, extended conversations with their students. One day I worked in the ENFI class only with Ralph, a bright student who had arrived late. While the others worked, I asked Ralph to join with me in a role-playing dialogue in which I would be a party official in Prague and he would be Ivan Lendl in Greenwich, Connecticut. A brief excerpt:

KREMERS: Good morning, comrade Lendl. We miss you here in Prague. You could have done a lot for the cause of reform. Why did you leave?

RALPH: I left because I felt my talent was not being appreciated there. And I knew if I came to America I would not only be able to show thousands of people my talent but also make a good home for my family.

KREMERS: You did it for yourself, Ivan. You are selfish. You only care about getting richer and richer. Here in this country everyone is the same – equal. I hear you have a big wall around your estate in Greenwich. What are you afraid of?

RALPH: It's not that that's all I think about I love what I do, playing tennis is not just a career it's something I love doing. So I don't see why you think I'm selfish that's probably one of the reasons I left because you probably would have kept me from playing tennis. And the reason I have big walls around my estate is not because I'm afraid for my life it's just that I like my privacy.

KREMERS: In this country, we have no walls around our estates – no one lives on an estate. We don't have to worry about privacy either because we have nothing to hide.

RALPH: but the reason I live in an estate is because I'm a public figure and if you are a public figure you find it hard to go out a lot without people coming up to you for autographs or just to talk to you or for a picture so I have my estate so that i can stay home but still go for walks and be able to go outdoors. And that's why I worry about my privacy because I don't get too much of it.

This dialogue continued for at least 30 minutes, neither of us knowing beforehand where the conversation would take us. What impresses me about Ralph's prose is its fluency, his use of polysyndeton (the repetition of conjunctions) to move his thoughts along. He is exploring a complex subject, the confrontation of capitalism and socialism, the rationale for acquiring personal wealth, the conflict between nationalism and internationalism. I am engaged with him in a new and different way, because I have no notes to work from, no lecture outline to follow. I am Ralph's correspondent, his interlocutor, as interested as he is in what he will write next.

Finally, ENFI makes teachers better able to listen to what their students are saying. I have found it useful to join in a group dialogue as a masked participant, an arrangement that simply calls for having everyone log on under a pseudonym. The masked approach is liberating because it allows teachers freedom to experiment, to create personas, and to join students in discussion as an equal. I have come to think of it as "jumping in," in the sense of joining a game of jump rope.

Trent Batson (1990) makes the point that ENFI allows time for reflection, for both collaboration and individual space, for writing and thinking about how one's message fits into the ongoing conversation. As teachers, we need to sit and engage in that kind of reflection with our students on occasion. In my teacher-dominated classroom I had thought that by leading a discussion, by using the Socratic method, by polishing my notes, I was having a conversation. In my ENFI classroom I started out thinking that lots of verbal interaction would lead directly to greater fluency, more mature ideas, and, eventually, better essays. What I did not fully understand is that radical change needs time. But it wasn't difficult to recognize the potential of a good idea. Before ENFI I did not understand what it means when the teacher is standing while everyone else is sitting down. Now I understand what it means to trade the traditional posture of power and influence – standing, talking, interrogating – for the humbler role of fellow scribe, member of the group, writer in the writing community.

J. Douglas Miller

This chapter grows out of 4 years of using the local-area computer network at Gallaudet University as a medium of instruction for deaf students. The most significant part of my experience involved the process of re-creating ENFI – that is, the process by which I abandoned the originally intended version of ENFI in favor of what seemed to me a more logical, more natural, and more dynamic use of the network. My experience in using the network and in re-creating ENFI as an instructional approach has led me to various conclusions about what I now consider to be one of the most appropriate ways a computer network can be used as a medium for classroom teaching.

The discussion here falls into two general periods: early experiences, in which I attempted to incorporate ENFI into a conventional curriculum, and later experiences, in which I found ways for the curriculum to grow out of the powerful capabilities available in the network.

Fitting ENFI into an established English curriculum

My initial goal for ENFI was to help facilitate the curriculum goal of the standard course in freshman composition offered by my English department. I had two classrooms available in which to meet my classes: a conventional classroom complete with blackboard, desks, and overhead projector, and the ENFI microlab complete with 13 IBM PC computer terminals networked together for use with the software package Realtime Writer. I met in the conventional classroom during 50-minute class times on Mondays and Wednesdays and normally reserved the Friday session to meet with students on the network in the microlab.

During the ENFI sessions I attempted to use the network in three primary ways: as a medium for giving students drill-and-practice exercises in vocabulary building, sentence structure, and paragraph coherence; as a device for conducting discussions on various writing topics in preparation for composing essays on those same topics; and as a tool for a number of role-playing activities, again involving topics that students would then use for their compositions. Each of these various kinds of practice had the aim of helping

124

students become generally more proficient with written English and of helping them discover and develop ideas for their out-of-class essays.

In addition, the activities conducted both on the network and in the regular classroom were intended to help students pass the final exit essay exam at the end of the semester, an exam given under strict supervision. This essay exam required students to write two compositions – a comparison-contrast essay and an argumentative, or opinion, essay. All students enrolled in the course had to receive a passing grade on one of the two compositions in order to proceed to the next course in the sequence of required English courses.

The network software used at Gallaudet has a private composing window at the bottom of the computer screen and a public area in which all typed messages are displayed as they are sent from each computer connected to the network. Messages are queued in the order in which they are sent, so there is generally some delay between a given message and any response to that message.

Anyone who has worked with a network of this kind knows that meaningful interaction demands careful attention to what appears on the computer screen and a quick and appropriate response to a given message. Generally speaking, the number of messages sent on the network grows in proportion to the number of users interacting on the system. The greater the number of active participants, the more complex becomes the text that is generated in the public area of the computer screen, and the greater become the demands placed on the attention and concentration of those using the network.

My initial experiences with ENFI were well intentioned, but generally ineffective and frustrating. I attempted to use the network in a way that perhaps most instructors hope to use any new technology – as a means to help achieve the goals of the "standard" curriculum already established in my particular academic department. I attempted to use the system as a tool for helping students become more proficient writers of English composition.

I believed I could use many of the drill-and-practice exercises in paragraph development and sentence structure that I had previously used with my students in the conventional classroom setting. Such exercises are commonly found in freshman grammar-rhetoric textbooks, and I intended to use them as collective class activities on the network. In the conventional classroom I had used either the blackboard or overhead transparencies as the public arenas in which I could discuss possible answers to specific items in these exercises, make corrections of student work, and offer suggestions for improvement. I planned simply to transfer these activities to the network.

I almost immediately encountered unmanageable problems that were not present in the conventional classroom. For one thing, if students on the network responded to my messages or questions at will – that is, without taking turns – their responses would appear so quickly on the computer screen that I could not field all of them. As student responses came hot and heavy, it was too easy to lose track of what had been said and of which student response I had singled out for comment. On the other hand, if students responded in turn, the entire process was too slow; while one student attempted a correct response, the other students passively waited for their turn.

Using the network to discuss printed material proved equally disastrous, for students had to look in their textbooks or read from distributed papers, thus losing eye contact with the computer screen. Because my students were deaf, I could not simultaneously talk to them while they were reading, so when a student offered a comment on the computer, I could not get the other students focused back on the computer screen quickly enough to read the comment before it scrolled off. At times the students' responses were so slow and the whole process so cumbersome that I found myself in the ridiculous predicament of asking and then impatiently answering my own questions. I longed to return to the blackboard, overhead transparency, and sign communication.

In addition to these problems, an even more serious and perhaps more interesting problem arose – that of the great temptation for students to engage in *flaming*, electronic discourse characterized by inappropriate or excessive emotionalism, bluntness, or hostility (Sproull & Kiesler, 1991). As one ENFI instructor has stated, "A flamer is a network user who has not developed a socially acceptable network persona, who intrudes commentary which would usually be kept to oneself" (Collins, 1989, p. 55). I consider flaming to include any kind of clearly inappropriate communication on the network, ranging from idle gossip to more direct sabotage of an established communication context by using vulgarities or wisecracks. Whether it is used intentionally or not, flaming has the effect of undermining the stated or, more commonly, the unstated rules of conduct within a given communication context. Flaming typically interferes with the logical flow of ideas by drawing unwarranted attention to trivial and often vulgar irrelevancies, which many students are only too keen to pursue (see also Kremers, this volume).

My own experience and that of others who have used a computer network for instruction is that the tendency to engage in flaming on the system is a persistent and powerful force. Research suggests that disinhibition occurs more readily on electronic networks than in face-to-face communication (Kiesler, Siegel, & McGuire, 1984; Siegel, Dubrovsky, Kiesler, & McGuire, 1986), and that the tendency to flame results from "the lack of nonverbal cues about physical appearance, authority, status, and turn taking" (Rice & Love, 1987, p. 50). The important point is that students in ENFI classes consistently experience the powerful urge to flame, and the instructor is left to devise ways to control or to channel this urge.

As the semester progressed, I became especially nervous because I felt that the instructional activities we were attempting on the computer network were doing little to help prepare students for D day, the day on which they would be required to demonstrate their competency in English composition by writing their final essay examination. I began to sweat.

I realized that my prepared writing exercises were not working, and I could not find a suitable alternative. My primary problem was finding an effective way to focus, organize, and control class discussion. While I tried to conduct orderly discussions of my prepared lessons, students would begin talking to each other about dates, campus events, trips to the zoo. When I did manage to get their attention fixed on a particular exercise, they would sometimes sprinkle their responses with light-hearted obscenities. If I became incensed at their insolence and threatened them with failure, they stiffened momentarily, but soon relaxed into their customary chitchat.

In trying to impose control on my ENFI classes, I sometimes felt like the cartoon character who frantically runs about a burning forest stomping out flames with his boots. Every time he successfully extinguishes one fire, others start in the underbrush. Soon the entire forest is a storm of flames and the ineffective but well-meaning fire fighter must plunge into a lake to save his hide. Unfortunately, in my case no such lake was immediately available. I simply had to wait until the long semester slowly burned itself out.

After these early frustrating and largely unsuccessful experiences with ENFI, I abandoned the network altogether for about 1 year and returned to the conventional classroom where I used my more familiar tools of blackboard, overhead projector, and sign communication to teach students the fundamentals of expository writing. At the same time, though, I had a feeling that the temptation to engage in flaming could become a powerful, creative resource, *if* properly controlled and channelled. I felt that the urge to display one's verbal audacity, which is at the root of flaming behavior, might have great potential for overcoming many of the inhibitions to writing that students often experience in formal classroom settings.

Adapting the curriculum to fit the technology

After a year of suspending my use of the network, I had the opportunity to use it in a course very different from the one in which I had initially used it. This new opportunity involved teaching creative writing to a group of advanced deaf high school students in a summer program offered at Gallaudet. Of course the goals of this course were very different from the goals of the freshman composition course in which I had first used the network. For one thing, there was no established curriculum in the summer course – no final writing examination, no established syllabus. Together with my students, I was more free to innovate, to experiment, and to explore various ways to use language as a means of tapping the latent imagination. The results of using the network with this class seemed the precise reverse of my previous experience. Here I encountered surprising success, where before I had found consistent failure.

It was almost by accident that I hit upon what I now believe to be an application of ENFI more suited to the capabilities of the network technology. This new approach, which I still use, was to give students a scenario – a dramatic situation, a setting and characters – and ask them to flesh out the script on the network.

The final goal of this script writing is collectively to generate a dramatic production on the network. This activity places great demands on students' abilities to read attentively and to respond quickly by using comments that drive forward the story line. Students have multiple options for participation. They may give themselves stage directions. They may "speak" to the stage directions given by other characters in the production. They may initiate and create dialogues with one or more other characters. In selecting among these options, students learn to play various challenging, creative roles. They are collaborative authors of the scripts they produce. They are one or more characters in the scripts that are being generated. They are their own audience. They are their own directors, aside from minimal spontaneous coaching provided by the instructor. Successful participation in the script means that students must skim the many comments that rapidly appear on the screen and then quickly make decisions about what comments to respond to. They must pick up cues from other participants. If the action sags, they must find appropriate and effective ways to revitalize it.

An ENFI script – the result of an on-line dramatic production – looks something like a conventional dramatic text, but it also has significant differences. Unlike a published dramatic work, an ENFI script is strewn with all sorts of mistakes produced in the thick of spontaneous, imaginative interaction. These mistakes involve typographical errors of all sorts, miscues, misunderstandings, misspellings, malapropisms – the same kinds of mistakes in written English that might occur in the creative heat of a first draft for an actual dramatic script. However, beneath these mistakes, or lying among them, I have consistently found gems of verbal interplay, prodigious feats of imaginative wit, layers of figurative meaning that rarely appear in more commonly used creative writing exercises.

A transcript of any given ENFI production can be printed out and copied for later class distribution. The copied transcript can then be studied, discussed, and edited. Various exercises in which students must rework and edit their own text appearing in the original ENFI transcripts can be useful writing assignments and help instill in students a sense of responsibility for what they compose on the network.

Despite the great success of the script writing approach, I encountered one serious obstacle, an obstacle that I had previously faced in my initial experiences using the network – the strong temptation for students to engage in flaming when communicating on the system. In fact, the sense of creative freedom that the script writing approach engendered led to even more spectacular examples of flaming than I had hitherto experienced and, if left unchecked, could clearly interfere with the success of a script.

In addition to flaming, I found that other influences can contribute to the quality of an ENFI script. For example, the nature of the scenario I give to students and the relative complexity of the story line seems to have some bearing on whether or not an ENFI production is successful. I have found that some scripts fail when I have fed too much information into a scenario. Consequently, students seem overwhelmed with too many choices at the outset. They do not get on with the major events. They become bogged down in details or relatively unimportant concerns, the result being that the action sags and the momentum is lost or never begun.

Another important influence that seems to affect the quality of an ENFI production is the amount of classroom preparation given to discussing the scenario and possibilities for character roles, stage directions, and story line. Some amount of prior classroom discussion of these issues is beneficial in helping students to focus their thoughts before going to the computer terminal and creating the ENFI script.

I provide here one example of a script I consider to be unsuccessful and then an example of what I see as a successful script. These two examples were among many produced in the creative writing course during the summer of 1990, and I offer them in the same sequence in which they were produced. In the first example (the unsuccessful script), flaming clearly got out of control. In the second example (the more successful one), there is no evidence of flaming. It may be that classroom discussion concerning the drawbacks of the first script, combined with careful classroom preparation for the subsequent script, helped make it a more satisfying performance than it might have been otherwise.

The scenario I gave to my students was as follows:

Situation: A nice, respectable, middle-class community on earth is being invaded by mutant aliens. These aliens are the offspring of humans, who long ago were transported to the planet Roto because they had been contaminated on Earth by nuclear radiation.

On planet Roto, the nuclear radiation promoted longevity instead of death because of certain atmospheric conditions existing on Roto. The offspring of the radioactive humans were born with extraordinary physical and mental abilities. Some of these mutant, alien children have returned to Earth, but to what purpose? Do they want to save the human world? Do they want to destroy it? Have they come merely to experience fast food and video arcades?

Characters:

Nuclear physicist	Army General
Little girl (human)	Big alien (Roto Major)

Girl's mommy   Small alien (Roto Minor)
Girl's daddy

The ENFI production of this alien invasion script was conducted on two separate network channels; in other words, the class was divided into two groups, one on each channel, and two separate scripts were created simultaneously. I changed channels to enter and exit each of the scripts as I desired. I played a more active character role on one of the channels than on the other. It was on the channel from which I was most frequently absent that the flaming became the most intense. I quote from the script about midway into the action. The student playing the role of General initiated the flaming in answer to the question in the scenario, "Some of these mutant, alien children have returned to Earth, but to what purpose?" (I am playing the role of Daddy.)

GENERAL: They came here to get laid, satisfy them if you want to get rid of them.

I immediately attempt to deflect the flaming from the General:

DADDY: (To his daughter) I think they are just hungry, darling – why don't you make some nice tuna fish and catsup sandwiches for them – the kind you like.

ROTOMINR: yeah

ROTOMAJ: SHUT UP

MOMMY: HEY WHY DID YOU BLOW UP MY HOUSE???? (shouts at general)

NUKEPHYS: (boiling angry) no nuclear weapon war here, what hell do you think you are doing? (to mommy)

After several lines of general indirection, Mommy finally picks up the General's cue with the following:

MOMMY: I WILL HAVE TO GET RID OF YOU BY STRIPPING MY CLOTHES AND DANCING IN FRONT OF YOU AND MAKE YOU SO HARD.

ROTOMINR: yeah!

ROTOMAJ: "YEAHH"

ROTOMINR: you take (the girl) I take her

GIRL: nooooo!

ROTOMINR: OK

MOMMY: WE SHOULD TRY TO USE OR LOVE POWER.

ROTOMINR: (as I move towards mommie i jumped into the couch)

GIRL: You can't catch me! I am a fast runner!!!!! And yes use our love power!!!

MOMMY: NO NOT WITH YOU, I WANT TO DO IT WITH THE GENERAL!!!!!!!!!!!!!!

Mommy:	OK DO IT
Rotominr:	too late bitch
Mommy:	FUCK!!!
General:	(general grabs video camera to video tape a possible porno movie that he can make millions from)

The flaming became even more heated before the class period mercifully ended.

Following this largely disastrous ENFI production, I felt the pressing need to discuss with students the meaning of pornography, which I loosely defined as works of art using profanities or vulgarities without redeeming literary merit. We discussed how the presence of sex and violence in this particular script might have been used in more imaginative, more intellectually complex ways. I cautioned students to control the urge "to have sex on the computer" – especially when it is mindless sex. I pointed to examples in the transcript of prurient comments and explained how the effect of such comments undermined the quality of the script being generated.

From the unsuccessful alien invasion script, we proceeded to an ENFI production of *Little Red Riding Hood*. I chose that particular story in large part because I felt the need for control and structure after the chaotic results of the prior production. Yet I had some reservations about using *Little Red Riding Hood* as the basis for script writing because it seemed too simple. I was fearful that students would become bored quickly and begin deriding their character roles or sabotaging the action. Therefore, I was especially careful to discuss the story first in the classroom. We diagrammed the important parts of the story on the blackboard and drew a map of Red Riding Hood's journey from Mommy's house, through the forest, and finally to Granny's home. This preparation feeds the imagination of students but does not overwhelm them with too many details; it leaves options open so that students can use their own originality in fleshing out characters and in shaping the action.

In our classroom discussion I made sure that everyone had knowledge of the basic story line, and we discussed some possible variations of the basic plot. We discussed the characters, pointing out that all of the characters could become sympathetic ones. The wolf, for example, was not necessarily totally evil; after all, he was behaving according to his nature. We agreed that we might even commend him for his cleverness. We discussed possible meanings of the story – especially the symbolic possibilities such as loss of innocence, the search for independence, the problem of deception versus honesty, and so forth. I purposely avoided discussing possible sexual overtones that could be found or inserted in the story because I saw these possibilities as a tempting source of flaming.

After our classroom discussion of the story, I passed out the following handout as a guide and reminder of what I expected from students in their handling of this particular script:

ENFI PRODUCTION OF LITTLE RR HOOD

You will recreate the story of "Little Red Riding Hood" on ENFI. I WANT YOU TO GIVE YOURSELVES PLENTY OF STAGE DIRECTIONS AT THE BEGINNING. YOU CAN ADD MORE STAGE DIRECTIONS AS THE STORY DEVELOPS. DESCRIBE YOUR APPEARANCE, YOUR ACTIONS, YOUR SURROUNDINGS, AND SO FORTH.

Remember that you are free to make imaginative, clever changes to the original story.

Especially try to give your character originality. Here are some of the kinds of questions you might consider:

Wolf – What is he wearing? What is his goal in life? What kind of home does he have? Does he have a wife and hungry children to feed? Does he have friends or is he a "lone wolf"?

Red Riding Hood – What does Red look like? How does she feel about always wearing her red cape and red hood? Does she have friends at school? Does she always obey her mother?

Granny – What does Granny's home look like? Neat as a pin? Smelling of ginger and rum? How does she feel about being a senior citizen? Is she a sweet old lady or is she moody and grumpy?

Woodcutter – Is he a stereotypical lumberjack, a macho kind of guy? Is he the silent, sensitive type? Does he smell of bark and wood chips? Does he have a happy home life? Is he a conservationist at heart or is he a callous destroyer of forests?

For the production of this script, we used three separate channels so that we had three Red Riding Hood stories going on simultaneously. I jumped from one to the other to follow bits of the action in each and to participate in the role of Author. I have selected an excerpt from one channel as an example of a script that has many fine creative moments and that kept the story line moving in a constructive and imaginative fashion. I have deleted parts of the original script in the interest of space:*

RRHOOD: (RED RIDING HOOD IS A SMALL, SKINNY GIRL WHO IS BRIGHT, CHEERFUL AND IS POPULAR WITH THE CHILDREN IN THE VILLAGE. SHE IS PREPARING TO GO TO SEE HER GRANDMA IN HER RED CAPE THAT HER MOTHER HAD MADE HER.) Mummy, do you have any flowers? I am sure Grandma would like some.

AUTHOR: (Author appears in the audience – wearing typical author's clothing – tweed coat with elbow patches, horned-rimmed glasses, mop of hair falling to the side.) Good RRHood (feels excited about seeing his characters come to life.)

---

* To demonstrate the coherence of the story, I have omitted some of the text within the script. Ellipses are inserted where omissions occur. Otherwise the excerpt is represented here as it was produced on the network.

WOLF: (WOLF WAS VERY HUMOROUS, GOERGOUS, COOL, AND KIND. HE ALWAYS WEARS ANY T SHIRTS WITH LEVI JEANS AND NIKE SHOES. HE IS SO BRIGHT AND INTELLIGENT IN SCHOOL. HE CAN BE HELPFUL SOMETIMES. HE MIGHT MAKE DESPERATE PEOPLE TO THINK HAPPY AND POSITIVE. HIS BEST FRIEND WAS RR HOOD. THEY HAD DONE ALOT OF GOOD TIMES TOGETHER.) . . .

WOODCT: The woodcutter is a very unpleasant man. He is covered with grease and dirt. He smells like the inside of one of those porta-toilets. He has not shaven or taken a shower for months. He is isolated from civilization and is psychotic. No one knows what could happen should he meet anyone in the woods. At the moment he is busy chopping wood in the middle of the forest.

AUTHOR: Very good, Woodcutter!!!! (Sits on the edge of his seat, eyes bulging with intense interest.)

RRHOOD: Goodbye mummy, i will give Grandma you love. BYE!

WOLF: (Wolf meets rr hood and they decided to go to the store and buy some candy together then go to rr hood s granny house) . . .

GRANNY: Granny is a hip granny. She rides on a motorbike and wears a leather jacket. Yet, she is a very sweet, old, petite lady with short, grayed hair. She is a very energetic old lady for a 80 year old woma. She lives in a cottage in the middle of the woods.

RRHOOD: (Meanwhile RRHood is walking along the path that will lead her to Granny's house when she meets the wolf) Good day, Wolf. How are you? Do you not agree that this is a lovely day today?

WOLF: yeah gday and sure this is a lovely day today and weather was perfect!!!

WOODCT: (Hears voices in the distance, stops chopping for a minute, then continues to chop) . . .

RRHOOD: (To Wolf) i cannot stay long, Granny is expecting me. So long!

WOODCT: (rrhood and wolf walk into view of woodcutter. He stops chopping and stares intently at them as they come closer)

WOLF: (OK GBYE SEE U LATER AND HOPE THAT YOU HAD A NICE VISIT TO SEE YOUR GRANY BYE!!!!)

GRANNY: (In meanwhile, at her home, Granny mutters to herself.) Wher is that darling little Red Riding Hood? I'm home sick in bed. I should not have gone out on my motorbike on a chilly day.

WOODCT: (woodcutter sees the wolf and licks his lips and slowly lifts his axe.)

RRHOOD: (Thinks to herself) there is that horrible woodcutter, mummy told me not to talk to him.

WOODCT: (woodcutter heads toward wolf, picking up speed.)

WOLF: (wolf heard some noises behind and looked around and saw the horrible woodcutter and ran so fast.

WOODCT: (woodcutter breaks into a run, axe high over his head)

WOLF: (WOLF YELLED, HELP!!!)

WOODCT: (gives off a horrible, crazy scream) yaaah!

AUTHOR: (Becomes increasingly excited – absorbed in the action – forgets himself for a moment.) Ohhhh – THAT AX – THAT HORRIBLE AX!!

WOLF: (aaaaaaaaahhhhhhhhhhhh)!!!

WOODCT: (woodcutter is only 3 feet away from the running wolf)

AUTHOR: (Settles back in his chair exhausted from his sudden outburst) Oh, good Wolf!! "aaaaaaaaahhhhhhhhhhhh" is a good choice of words. . . .

GRANNY: (Granny still muttering to herself – "Where's that darling girl, it has been a hour and I'm starting to get real concerned. If only I hadn't been that sick, it would never have happened. Come on, little darling, please be all right."

AUTHOR: (Worries about the wolf – forgets what he had written in the script) Lemesee now – does the wolf die or does he eat the Woodcutter – I forget!

RRHOOD: RRHood continues walking in the direction of Granny's house when she turns to see the wolf being chased by the woodcutter. RRHood then hears this big crying of HELP! She turns and rus after woodcutter shouting: LEAVING HIM ALONE, STOP CHASING HIM, HE'S DONE NOTHING WRONG.

WOODCT: (woodcutter swings, just missing by a hair) . . .

WOLF: nooooooooo stops and said look there a pretty girl is walking toward you look!!! . . .

WOODCT: (the woodcutter is now chasing RRHood and the wolf to granny's)

AUTHOR: (Continues biting his nails – eyes bug out in excitement – breathes spastically, sweat breaks out on his forehead) I can't stand the suspense!!

RRHOOD: RRHood cathes up with the woodcutter and grabs him by his hair, as he tries to throw her off, she screams a high piercing scream in the woodman's ear. (GRANNY HEARS THE SCREAM)

The suspense continues to build until the woodcutter, in an apparent attempt to free himself from Red Riding Hood's grasp, brings his axe down on her. The wolf manages to flee to Granny's house to alert her of the mad woodcutter. Granny exits her house with a machine gun aimed at the woodcutter. The script ends with Granny slaying the woodcutter and the wolf weeping over the frail body of his dear friend, Red Riding Hood.

Despite some problems in usage and idioms, this script shows much creativity and coherence. I was especially pleased with the care students took in giving themselves stage directions and in picking up cues from each other. The demise of Red Riding Hood could have been handled more subtly, but I felt that the appearance of the woodcutter's axe and the ensuing chase gave an element of suspense that involved some complex decisions. We wonder who will be the woodcutter's victim, and, ironically, the woodcutter decides to let his axe fall on Red Riding Hood rather than the wolf. The woodcutter, of course, comes across as something of a homicidal maniac, but this character depiction was established in the student's initial stage directions for him: "He is isolated from civilization and is psychotic. No one knows what could happen should he meet anyone in the woods." I see much of the wolf's subsequent behavior as a rather clever extension of his initial character portrayal as well.

I chose these two examples of ENFI scripts because they occurred in convenient chronological sequence and serve to show a clear contrast between a largely unsuccessful example of script writing and a more successful one. Using this approach in other subsequent English classes, I have participated in several more successful ENFI scripts, as well as additional unsuccessful efforts.

Although every script writing performance on the network does not produce dramatically satisfying results, this approach does offer clearly demonstrated value as a tool for enabling students to experience the power of written English in a collective creative activity. The fundamental and primary value in the script writing approach is that it taps the magic, the enchantment inherent in computer-mediated communication. It draws upon and encourages ways that humans seem naturally driven to communicate on the system. It allows for and stimulates a fascination in playing with words to express feelings and emotions. It allows students to experiment with guises, with personas, and to explore parts of themselves that they may not normally reveal in everyday face-to-face discourse. It allows for students to become other characters in an elaborate and spontaneous act of imagination.

As is clear from the ENFI scripts produced by my students, much of the exciting and dazzling displays of language and wit that occur spring from natural tendencies to engage in showmanship with language. However, I believe that the more satisfying results over the long term will occur when students are given proper guidelines and some intelligent classroom coaching in using this approach. The spontaneous and random urge to engage in flaming can be a powerful creative force, but some preliminary planning is advised in order to help control and direct the creative sparks.

I have recently begun distributing to students the following guidelines for script writing on the network. Each guideline requires clarification and discussion in the classroom:

1. One of your primary goals is to establish a presence, a creative personality, a "speaking voice" in the script. This dramatic presence will probably be somewhat different from the "actual," everyday person you normally are. You will need to find a presence that comfortably matches your concept of your character role.

2. Try to imagine that everything you communicate is happening on a dramatic stage or in a fictional world. You cannot "speak" to other characters as you would offstage or outside this fictional world. Your every utterance becomes part of our script.

3. You are not allowed to kill yourself in order to avoid participating in the script. If you die by your own hand or by the hand of another, you must continue your participation anyway – perhaps as a spirit or as some other dimension of your former self.

4. You share in the responsibility to keep the script going – to create believable and interesting conflicts, to generate a story line, to present and to follow up cues as the script is being created.

5. Options you have: You can give yourself stage directions that describe your appearance, your gestures, your movements, your thoughts, your feelings. You can speak to other characters by commenting on their actions, their appearance, what you assume to be their intentions, and so forth. You should normally respond to characters who speak to you. You can comment on other characters not immediately present in the script.

6. Use vulgarity only if it helps the script. Do not be obscene or profane as an end in itself.

These guidelines are directed at a fairly sophisticated student population, and most of my successful experiences have been with bright and literate students. Students who have more fully developed schemata about the world, about the nature of fiction, and about dramatic conventions seem to adapt more readily to the script writing approach. However, because this approach draws heavily on students' raw and latent imaginations, students whose schemata may be lacking in formal areas of knowledge may still find success with this approach.

The individual and combined personalities of students using the system is certainly an important consideration. Students who have greater confidence in themselves and are more socially adept seem to participate more frequently and more intensely in the dramatic interplay that the script writing activity requires. This confidence factor covers a variety of skills from typing proficiency to English language fluency. Students who are generally more reserved seem to participate less actively.

Contrary to these reasonable assumptions, I have found that the degree of natural shyness a student exhibits in everyday discourse does not necessarily carry over to the script writing activities on the network. Students who seem passive and lethargic in conventional classroom settings may virtually come alive in the ENFI script writing activities.

Conclusions

Looking back at my adventures, frustrations, and elations with ENFI over the past 4 years, I am left with the following important conclusions. First, I found it necessary to discover what I consider to be the natural, latent power in the network technology and then to find a course compatible with the technology. I found ENFI to be exasperating, cumbersome, and unproductive when I tried to force my use of the network into a curriculum that was unsuited to its nature and potentialities. Second, and equally important, I needed to find effective ways to help students understand and channel the powerful urge to engage in flaming when using the system. In those instances in which network use is matched with an appropriate curriculum and in which the temptation to flame is nurtured artfully and intelligently, remarkably rich and exciting interplays with language can result.

I believe that the script writing approach offers a logical and natural application of ENFI as a pedagogical tool. However, we need to journey still deeper into the intriguing possibilities for helping students give expression and life to their latent imaginative resources by means of this powerful technology.

8   Seeing students as writers

Geoffrey Sirc and Thomas Reynolds

In our culture we have generally agreed-upon notions about reading. Oh, So-and-so, we say, she's a real reader. We associate reading with pleasure. It is desirable to read to one's children. On vacation we bring along something to read. Over lunch at work we discuss our recent reading experience. Magazines run summer reading issues. However, we have no corresponding positive thoughts about writing. We think, instead, I can't write. We don't know enough about the cultural values and practices that surround writing. Such knowledge, though, seems important for those of us in the business of designing and implementing effective instruction in writing.

For the past few years we've used ENFI at the University of Minnesota. This work has helped us understand better how writing functions culturally. The young people we taught in our ENFI classroom had many opportunities to discuss writing over the network – they talked about writing in general, about the subject matter for papers about to be written, and about what they thought of each other's papers. The records of those discussions, verbatim printouts at the end of each session, proved highly significant to us. They served as a record of what the person in the classroom (the academic counterpart to the man in the street) feels about writing in general and how specific parts of a writing curriculum are worked through in practice.

The significance of those records was in the antidote they provided to our theoretical notions about writing and its instruction. Too often, before our ENFI work, we found ourselves swept away by some new theoretical conceptualization of what writing is or what students are or what they need, but had no way to tap into students' needs and processes to get feedback on our theory. Our classroom use of ENFI enabled our students to communicate articulately with each other in writing and about writing, providing an archival record of that communication. Watching the finely grained picture of student self-disclosure and interaction that emerged over the ENFI network allowed us as educators to see more of how our students functioned as writers. It allowed us to see what students meant when they spoke of writing, revealing points of strength and of confusion in their conceptualizations. Moreover, seeing the pressure points in graphic close-up was evidence that our writing

138

curriculum needed redesign away from vague perceptions of students to a better mesh with actualities. ENFI became the impetus to implement improved instruction in writing, based on actual rather than perceived needs.

Our goals

The students who use the ENFI classroom in University of Minnesota's General College are from the lower half of their high school classes. Their writing histories have not been successful by traditional measures, and they scored low on the verbal sections of their college boards. General College's mission for its students is to prepare them for successful transfer to other degree-granting units within the university, to turn out students capable of succeeding in their postsecondary education. To fulfill the first-year writing requirement in our college, students must take a two-quarter course sequence, whereas a single writing course satisfies the requirement in other units. We believe that our students, as basic writers, are better served by a more intensive first-year writing experience.

The original goal of our writing curriculum in the college, when the ENFI network was first used, was to offer students experience in writing in several common modes – descriptive, narrative, expository – drawing on their personal experience. The assignments were fairly brief – long paragraphs of description and one-page character sketches. We assumed that such assignments would give students a chance to encounter focused writing tasks in which they could learn about formal concerns and strategies without being overwhelmed by other rhetorical demands. The challenge for our students was to use the familiar, and the personal, while learning the conventions of university writing. We also believed that many of the skills they would learn in these assignments were transferable to more academic writing. Developing detailed content for a descriptive paper, for example, seemed to us important for many kinds of writing; the organizational problems to be solved in narration would give students practice in learning matters of textual arrangement. Because the topics were personal, we thought students could concentrate on writing without having to be burdened with the evaluation of outside information. Our experience with ENFI, however, led us to think differently about this curriculum and about our incoming basic writers' needs.

When we first implemented our networked writing technology, we had the luxury of being able to run sections of 10 students. In terms of our teaching styles, we are both casual and personable with our students, trying to provide a student-centered classroom, so the chaos that some have pointed to as a result of interactive network dialogue in a writing class (e.g., Kremers, 1988, and this volume) was not a major concern.

We were fascinated to see systematically, through the transcripts of networked discussions, how students interacted, how they spoke about writing and its concerns, how they engaged in discussions about individuals' texts or subject areas, and what language they used. At the outset we determined we would offer three kinds of opportunities for ENFI-talk in the course:

- An initial conversation (or two) about writing and writing classes in general (what students thought about writing, what made it hard or easy, what students thought about writing classes, what made them hard or easy)
- Brainstorming sessions for various assignments
- Peer-response sessions on drafts

The first two opportunities we planned as conversations for the class as a whole, whereas the peer-response work would be done in smaller groups.

Initially we were drawn to the use of ENFI transcripts in the classroom because we felt they would allow students a concrete way of thinking of the composing process – from early discussion and brainstorming, through initial drafts, to feedback on those drafts, up to the final paper. We felt the system had the possibility, through the trace of discussions of topics and drafts, to clearly reveal the various parts of the process. This would make the process clear for the students, who we hoped would then be able to conceptualize the process as a whole – a particular problem for our students, who often stumble on a particular step in the process and lose their way. We hoped that over the network students would offer each other pointed suggestions on early drafts, and then the printout of their conversations would act as a heuristic (prompt) for later revisions. We thought that through ENFI's process of peer response, documented in hard copy, students would learn revision. We expected network "talk" like the following, in which Jim offers Jerald a suggestion on how he might provide a more vivid picture for his readers in the memoir he wrote about the summer he helped his uncle as a sharecropper:

JIM: Jerald, maybe a few more details about the ride out to the field, such as:
The warm sun and the sound of the highway combined to lull me into a nap.

Besides serving as a medium to help each other draft papers, the transcripts of talk over the network acted as a key component in a larger pedagogical heuristic, one that leads students to a richer and stronger view of writing. This ideal kind of student collaboration (peer response) seemed more likely on the network. Our vision was of ENFI as a system that would save students' early, exploratory discussions of a topic; let them use that record in initial drafting; then save a record of peer-response commentary on those drafts, which they could use, along with teacher commentary, to finalize their papers. We both view writing as bricolage, as construction of meaning from what is at hand: We were struck by the way ENFI might allow students to see how writing is really a blend of one's own ideas, others' ideas, and material one has read or heard in discussion, with elements of emotion, controlling images, and revision directed by an outside source or editor. The system, we felt, could become a living drama of the way in which writers draw on various cultural sites (sources) to produce a text. By having a variety of discourses lead up to the final "discourse" (namely, the ultimate speech act that is the finished paper), students would see how writing involves basic elements used in a variety of combinations and situations to generate new meanings. Also, we hoped such an embodied metaphor might lead students to a formal, academic conception of writing. Barthes (1985) captures this notion in his own reflections on the phenomenon of transcribed speech:

What transcription permits and exploits is a thing repugnant to spoken language and classified by grammar as *subordination:* the sentence becomes hierarchical; in it is developed, as in the staging of a classic drama, the difference of roles and stage positions; in becoming social (since it passes to a larger and less familiar public), the message recovers a structure of order; "ideas," entities so difficult to delineate through interlocution, where they are constantly overwhelmed by the body, are put here in the foreground, there in image-repertoire appears, that of "thought." Whenever there is a concurrence of spoken and written words, to write means in a certain manner: I think better, more firmly; I think less for you, I think more for the "truth." (pp. 5–6)

It was this change in conception to a focus on thought and content, along with a concern for the formal arrangement of discourse, that occurs in writing in conversational transcripts. We planned to use those transcripts as key course materials that could trace formal concerns – how ideas emerge, how they are received, how they are refined analytically – in the immediate context of the students' own work, rather than through models of expert writing.

We desired also to demystify the writing process for our students and to show them how writing operates collaboratively. We started out with what we thought were the best collaborative learning methods. Following such thinkers as Wiener (1986), we thought our students would learn best in smaller writing groups of four or five. Through an active learning process facilitated by the network system, we envisioned a steady movement toward better versions of individual pieces of writing. ENFI offered the opportunity for students to see other students carry out their writing process, giving them real models of *writing* in its dynamic form rather than in its finished form as we've done unsuccessfully in the past (Horatian forms as writing teacher – the hope that, somehow, when students saw good writing, they'd be able to imitate it). The importance of what actually happens in the classroom would be heightened, we felt, when valued as a lesson in how writers solve problems. And because we were working with students who were basic writers, we imagined the task to include more than a simple here's-how-we-do-it approach. We hoped that student interaction in the writing process would increase our students' confidence.

What actually happened

Upon analyzing the transcripts and seeing how our students discussed writing, we became convinced that the task we were setting was wrong. Their first conversation, in which they spoke their mind about writing and writing classes, was permeated with frustration and confusion. "I usually go crazy when I write," said Kevin. "I try to avoid writing," said Jim. Jerald offered that "writing is sometimes fun if you have a good topic." And Jennifer confessed that "my ideas are there but they are not clear." "There is no real standard form," she goes on to say, expressing a desire for a template that would make things clear and simple. Their first peer-response drafting conferences showed that they were not just talking a bad game; their attempts both to write and then to talk about writing consistently misfired. For her first descriptive paper, Jennifer chose (maybe trying to keep her subject simple) to describe eating her favorite flavor ice cream. In her group's discussion of her draft, Dean starts by focusing on a misspelled word in her paper, and things devolve from there to Jennifer's even further bafflement:*

DEAN:	whats blubbery Cheesecake
JENNIFER:	cheese cake with blue barries
DEAN:	oh
JENNIFER:	it's great you never heard of it where do you live? on the farm [?]
DEAN:	yes
JENNIFER:	nothing wrong with farms
DEAN:	we don't call it blubbery just regular cheesecake
JENNIFER:	this is regular but with topping
JOHN:	I liked it but think you could have described the taste of the ice cream a bit
JENNIFER:	how do you describe it? john
DEAN:	I agree with John
JOHN:	I've never eaten it
JENNIFER:	how describe vanilla ice cream or any it is not easy you are here to help each other
DEAN:	I don't understand when you say your fingers have to experience the ice cream and not just your mouth.
JENNIFER:	the cold and sticky haven't you dripped before all over your self

* Network discussions are reproduced here as the class produced them, unedited for spelling, punctuation, or structure. Occasionally students made comments on other topics, which were interwoven with the topic at hand. These comments have been omitted, to represent a single topic thread.

DEAN: no
JOHN: its extremely rich and creamy and sweet
JENNIFER: sorry i'm a mess[y] eater
DEAN: just kidding
JENNIFER: john knows what's up thanks
DEAN: Its kind of confusing the way you say it
JENNIFER: so I should elaborate it more and explain on the eating or on the
            mess or on both or on none
JOHN: not a heck of alot more
DEAN: just make it less confusing

Jennifer, who has already gone on record in an earlier class discussion as a person for whom writing is difficult, needs to have the tangles in her writing straightened out. She has chosen a topic that is personally meaningful to her, and now watches as it misfires right from the start for her two readers. She can't even get across the name of the object she's describing. When John suggests she describe the taste a bit, Jennifer asks how. John confesses he's never eaten it. Poor Jennifer, she has to get feedback on her descriptive paper from a person who has never experienced the referent. "It is not easy," she says to the group, to herself, to the teacher, to the world. Then she reminds her group they are "here to help each other" (meaning, in this case, her). What she receives from her group is a litany of negativity and absence: "you could have . . . never . . . I don't understand . . . no . . . it's kind of confusing . . . just make it less confusing." Her head spinning from confusion (witness the multiple conjunctions in her last comment), she is told simply not to be confusing. The rhetorical level of the commentary she receives is that of the old vaudeville joke: Doctor it hurts when I do this. Well, don't do that.

Even worse was when the confusion boiled over into confrontation. When Nick, for example, by far the weakest writer in the class, has his paper, "The Long Road to Class," critiqued by his group, they offer him a combination of pointed and arbitrary commentary that Nick takes defensively. The commentary's focus soon leaves strictly rhetorical matters and becomes an emotional struggle over classroom "face":

JIM: Nick, your first sentence about your obligation to attend class doesn't
         really fit with the rest of the paper where all you talk about is the
         cold.
NICK: I put for my title, a Long Road To Class? I just talk about my
         jou[r]ney to class.
KEVIN: Nick you should have started your first sentence off different.
JERALD: Nick that long Road Too Class is not a very good title you are talking
         about getting out of bed [about] you having an obligation. By walking
         to class how did you re[a]lize how important it was to walk to class
         every day.

NICK: Chris are you up now? It's about time. The title of my story does
          not have to fit your liking jerald

JERALD: Nick you had alot of spelling mistakes and grammar mistakes. I [think
          the] title should fit the writing correct

JIM: Nick's title was OK but the sentence about the obligation to attend
          class didn't fit.

NICK: I feel that MY title was a little weak, Title of storys doesn't alway
          have to fit. I also feel that you should get your eyes fixed becuse
          your too one sided. jerald

JERALD: There is only one side to your paper Nick the bad side. But to be
          positive you need a little word on sentence forming and grammar

NICK: NOthing good to say, well maybe your [ ] is too big? [The euphe-
          mistic brackets in this turn were typed by Nick.]

After other papers are discussed, Nick, still smarting, ends the conference
with a parting shot at Jerald, his fellow football teammate: "I thought I had
a friend jerald, just goes to show you that your really a fat nasty." Nick's
paper is dismantled in broad strokes, according to the lore his readers remember about topic sentences, suitable titles, and surface errors; but to Nick
this just seems like malicious judgment based on personal preference ("does
not have to fit your liking"). Backed into a corner, he admits he's a weak
writer, then lashes back at personalities, the only outlet he has. Jerald, seeing
his authority has triumphed, can't resist a quick kick when his opponent is
down.

Nick comes to the next peer-response session prepared, not with a paper
he put extra effort into, but with a hook on which to hang his attacks on
Jerald. He and Jerald had come into class that day arguing about taste in
shoes, and as soon as Nick gets an opening, he continues that argument in
the drafting commentary. They're deciding how Kevin can better describe
the sound of a slamming door in his paper. "Man," Kevin remembers, "you
should have heard that door. It sound[ed] like a big can crusher." Nick, first-
year football player on the university team, has found his opening: "Like
jerald's shoes [can crusher]," he offers. That thread is carried through the
rest of the session: "jerald what about your shoes," Nick insists, a few lines
later. "Avia," Kevin smirks, adding, "get rid of them didn't you say you had
them ever since jr high." The remark on how long Jerald has owned them
prompts Nick to comment, "Jerald you do smell like you want to be alone,
and so does your shoes . . . those shoes smell so bad that they don't even want
you." The conference ends with sexual boasting about who was dancing with
the prettiest young woman at the campus bar the other night. Such critique-
turned-clash was surprisingly common throughout our first year of conversations in the ENFI classroom.

A snippet of dialogue from Chris's group's discussion of his paper shows another important finding resulting from what we initially thought was the students' confusion about how to respond to writing. This finding concerns the propensity of peer groups to shift the discussion away from a given paper to overarching cultural concerns stimulated by the paper's topic. How do student writers learn to use collaboration when the discussion seems at best tangentially related to helping them get the paper done?

Chris was a first-year writer who came to Minnesota from Ohio as a recruit for our school's football team. He wrote a fairly successful paper that described the pain he felt when running his practice drills. His group, though, gave Chris commentary that did not reinforce the success of his paper or show him how to build on it, but rather simply suggested other things he could have also described (cf. John's suggestion to Jennifer about how she "could have described the taste of the ice cream a bit" in an earlier network dialogue; such an open-ended gesture toward random possibility became a standard tactic in these conversations). Chris, however, didn't buy such vague possibilities because he knew they didn't fit with the focus of his paper:

DEAN: Describe the good results of running maybe

CHRIS: What do I need to use them for.

JENNIFER: when you finish you should say sorta the pain has left and a fantastic sensation of nothing hurts any more or something of that sort of utopic feeling

CHRIS: My title is The Pain of running.

Chris's readers then use his topic to go off-task and discuss running in contemporary culture:

JENNIFER: running is a yuppy sport a fad around the states these days

DEAN: I run and I am not a yuppy

JOHN: are you planning to be

JENNIFER: you run because you like the fashionable clothes your mother told me

DEAN: Of course I love those tight pants, chicks dig em

JENNIFER: I knew it

JOHN: I thought all college kids were upward mobile

DEAN: Is that like the gas station

It wasn't just in difficult moments that students preferred to talk more about the world than their papers. Often the mere topic of the paper held sway over draft-specific commentary. For example, after his group nitpicked Drew's paper in which he described the 1950 Chevy truck he restored, he and his group got to their real agenda, talking about trucks:

JERALD: Drew I would like to see your truck someday

KEVIN: DREW what color was the upolstery in the truck.

DREW: chocolate brown leather
        the outside will be sunset red
KEVIN: Is that metallic paint the one with the little crystals in it
DREW: no, polyurothane
        i did a 68 camaro with metallic paint and was disappointed
KEVIN: Sounds pretty mean, what kind of mags are you going [to] put on it
        craigar centerlines [?] are you going to give it a low profile.
DREW: yes Kevin
KEVIN: kick ass!!!!!!!!!!!!!!!!!!!!
        that's going to be mean as hell.
DREW: except for the engine
KEVIN: are you going to run nitro drew
DREW: it has a 99 horse power slant six

One response to this interaction might be to work with Drew to show him how to draw on that off-task discussion, using it to revise his paper. But, admitting that we want to teach our student writers how everyday events as well as traditional elite culture are appropriate as topics for college writing, how do we actually help them decide which of those events are appropriate at the moment? Given the propensity they showed for abandoning the agenda we set, it is clear that they don't feel connected to the writing assignment. Strategies are needed that allow the vitality of their popular culture discussion but tie it into a writing assignment.

After our initial surprise at the level of confusion, confrontation, and off-task commentary we saw in the transcripts, we began to compare these rough draft commentary sessions with the final papers the students submitted. We were further puzzled to see that even though a fair number of good suggestions were offered to writers by their peers (and later available in print to review), almost none was used to guide further drafting. Derek, for example, makes this needed structural comment to De regarding the brevity of the paragraphs in his draft:

DEREK: De man, not every sentence has to be a paragraph. Go into specifics
         more and add some examples.

Not only does De, unsurprisingly, take this suggestion as a personal insult, responding in kind:

DE: DERECK!! I don't know how to tell u this . . . but here it is your
         paper died, kicked the bucket blew its last wistle,

but his resultant final draft shows no improvement regarding paragraph development. Such resistance to feedback, a refusal to consider the advice given in their subsequent text production, was endemic among our first-year writers. Rather than learning to draw on students' comments in composing, they manifested a stubborn tenacity to complete their papers from their own individual perspective. Their social mesh is explicit in many areas, as witnessed in the examples, but it remains latent in their formal written prose. De, then, is not prepared to draw on Derek as a source or colleague who can aid in text production, although the two young men would probably blend beautifully in their analysis of, say, a Vikings game.

One reason for the students' unwillingness to take seriously the suggestions of others might have been that the students still saw themselves writing for the teacher. Their greater freedom to write what they wanted, when they wanted, didn't automatically get them engaged in the writing assignment. De might wonder, Why should I listen to Derek's suggestion? He's not the one who's going to grade this. Our students were not opened up by ENFI to a conception of writing as speculative or discursive; they remained locked into a conception of school writing as a course that had to be run in a certain way, one they wanted to spend as little effort as possible completing. Because we were the ones judging their performance, they would jump the extra hurdle of peer response we put on the course, but they wouldn't follow the new route suggested by one of their fellow runners – they would stay on the track they perceived to be the one we laid out. Students were acutely aware of our presence on the network, even when we weren't participating directly in the conversations. One student went so far as to warn her fellow members, "hey you guys this is amy our conversation is also on toms computer sooo beware."

When we did participate in network discussions, attempting to model language and rhetorical strategies for students, our comments sometimes seemed to head off more genuine discussion in favor of our own concerns as readers and teachers who "know better." So when one of us asked Sara if her paper argued for two contradictory points, she replied, "Okay, maybe I should reread my paper over. Is this writing today going to affect the grade I'll receive?" Then, immediately following, she asked, "Can't we talk about Julie's paper now?" Sensitive to the fact that her writing was being "shown up" by the teacher in front of the others in the group, however tactfully done in actuality, she reacted first by trying to determine just how important this exercise was to what she was interested in (a high mark for the paper) and then by shying away from further discussion of her paper. It's not that she didn't appreciate the implied suggestion for revision – she talked to the teacher privately on this point afterward – but rather that she felt uncomfortable with what she seemed to perceive as the teacher wielding his heavy-handed red pencil over her rough draft in the public "margin" of the network computer screen. This situation was exacerbated by the unquestionable power of this ultimate reader who can determine the grade she'll receive. What's the point of further discussing this paper with the rest of the group, she may well think, if the one I'm mostly writing this paper for is available in a private conference?

Because we wanted our students to view their writing as produced for an audience that was wider than ourselves, we increasingly chose to coach them outside the discussion groups. Gradually we learned that their discussions could work better without us being on-line; for example, in one such discussion when Julie suggested to Betty that points cut from an earlier draft of Betty's paper might be better left in, Betty answered, "Yes, Julie, the points about MLK will be a part of my final draft." Direct, helpful suggestions for revision, we were reminded, do not always need a teacher's prompting.

How we responded

Instead of completing successfully the task we had set for them – offering helpful feedback to each other on their drafts and then using that feedback to produce successful papers – students overwhelmingly preferred to focus on the topics of those papers or the people who wrote them. They chose the communicative (personal interaction) over the metacommunicative (critiquing the paper), despite our expectation to the contrary. A paper about Y gave them license to talk about Y, not the paper, or to clash with the writer of the paper. We've discussed this phenomenon at length elsewhere (Sirc & Reynolds, 1990), but here it's important to note that such a response did not cause us to rethink our students' abilities (we had never assumed basic writers could enter a first-year classroom spouting dialogue out of *The Paris Review*); rather we began to locate their rhetorical confusion and preference for off-task socialization in our assignments. Was it a good thing to have them doing what we had them doing, we wondered? We had been reading the work of Mike Rose (1983), who suggests that "the writing topics assigned in [remedial] courses – while meant to be personally relevant and motivating and, in their simplicity, to assist in the removal of error – in fact might not motivate and might not contribute to the production of correct academic prose" (p. 109). Rose notes that the simple assignments that we give basic writers, such as describe your favorite place, are perceived as juvenile by students and, hence, fail to motivate them. They realize that such a topic is not the complex, challenging task they expected of a college writing course, and they turn off – to talk about Camaros or each other's clothes. We would add to Rose's critique another possibility, that topics thought to be simple are not simple at all. We have often watched in sadness how the open-ended, expressive nature of our curriculum has further muddled our students' writing. Describe your favorite place may be as difficult for some students as describing running, restored Chevy trucks, or one's favorite ice cream was for our students.

The odd misfirings in our students' classroom conversations became proof of our need to rethink the entire expressivist tenor of our developmental curriculum at Minnesota. Kevin, in the initial What do you think about writing? discussion we had, offered an off-hand comment that ultimately loomed large in our thinking. "Being that I'm not a good writer," he said, "I try so hard to express myself that I just go crazy." Why should our students have to dredge up authentic, creative examples of self-expression when, at our university, that is precisely what they will never have to do? The other units on our campus have very set notions of what academic prose is. It concerns writing to various forms, using certain scholarly methods of argument and development. What we offered as assignments to teach writing were exercises in creativity, with no formal strategies or rules to learn. Descriptive writing, for example, is almost a whimsical thing for which to delineate expectations or requirements (e.g., "Describe vividly, so that the reader can picture in his or her mind . . . " Such direction only further mystifies writing for our already mystified students, turning it into a creative, generative endeavor beyond them). "It is harder for me to describe an object then a scene," Drew admitted as the paper on his truck was initially carped about (with the group complaining he forgot to tell the year of the truck and the original owner). The parameters by which to judge such prose weren't there as a group notion. Caprice, confusion, and confrontation ruled the discussion. Our students' interactions on the network became more important than we had hoped. In their redefinition of both the task and the activity, they showed us the need to redefine them for ourselves.

If our focus going into our ENFI classroom was on peer response and poststructuralist notions of text, coming away from the first year's work we were more aware of the limits of our curriculum. What we thought would help students feel comfortable with any writing demand seemed to be making them even more uncomfortable or unmotivated. We decided, therefore, given the way our writing tasks were being thoroughly rejected, that we had to substitute writing that honestly reflected the academy's demands. Using our transcripts as evidence, we discussed the problem in meetings with our department's writing committee. We noticed something that other teachers were noticing; namely, our curriculum was not challenging our students to write and think on a level that would approximate academic discourse. In addition, there was a growing dissatisfaction with the ability of our incoming student placement exam to successfully place students into either the first-year course or further remedial courses. A sweeping reform, eliminating the placement test and making the first-year course required for all incoming students (with performance in that course acting as a placement mechanism), was initiated.

Our research office surveyed the other academic units to see what sorts of writing assignments students would be expected to do throughout the rest of their university career. The survey showed that they would be expected to read and evaluate complex material critically, and use such material in their own analytical writing. So, with the help of our staff, we redesigned our first-year writing course, substituting more expository writing based on reading and discussion. Our ENFI transcripts, highlighting as they did the undeniable reality of the students' lives outside of school – their interests, their passions – helped us realize that we had to balance preparing them for their college career with awareness of their background. Our current curriculum, as a result, mixes the scholarly with the contemporary. For example, a student might read passages from Louis Althuser or Dick Hebdige or Michel Foucault to learn about a concept such as ideology, and also study the lyrics of popular rap groups – those played on the radio and those excluded from radio airplay – to see how ideology actually plays itself out in our national discourse.

The ENFI transcripts also showed us the truth of the work of scholars such as David Bartholomae (1985), who realize that much of writing is simply accommodation or acculturation to the academic institution and its textual demands. We could see from their network commentary that our students were not yet willing, or able, to internalize the goals of the institution. Our students' personal world is far more there for Nick than the academic world is. In their on-task talk over the network, students often seemed to be characters in a drama not written by them.

We did not want simply to wipe out the students' own social realities and substitute in their place our "empowering" notions of academia. We didn't want to substitute more complex academic assignments for the ones we now thought were simple; that might just be substituting Bridge for Crazy 8's. It would do no good if students still thought of our new curriculum as a game that had no connection to their lives. So our new curriculum aggressively attempts to deal with the perceived need of academic acculturation by preserving and drawing on students' own strongly formed social identities. We read Malcolm X's autobiography, for example, to see how one person went from a position outside of the dominant, intellectual culture to inside the culture, while managing to preserve his identity and difference. We even look at the writing of Allan Bloom and E. D. Hirsch, Jr., so students are better able to see and judge the way they are represented in the academic culture; such texts also give them examples of academic writing and allow them to take their own position toward it.

Current status of our networked classroom

After almost two years of our new writing program, we're happy with the results we see in the transcripts. Students may not always enjoy the reading and writing assignments we give them, but they see the logic of them and, most importantly, they are always willing to discuss ideas and concepts. It's almost as if they were just waiting for the chance to play "serious student." ENFI has a value we never dreamed of before in our strictly expressivist curriculum; it turns out to be a marvelous medium for discussing reading. The transcripts now have the archival function we had always wanted. Students frequently keep the highlighted copies of their reading discussions next to them as they write papers based on the books and articles under consideration. It is this use of the ENFI printout that shows the truth of Barthes's observation on transcribed speech cited earlier: There is a dynamic revealed in the transcripts of conversations on the readings that is a record of a journey through cognition to meaning. No more are the conversations just records of personality clashes or confusion; as Barthes observed, the archival nature of the enterprise keeps the focus on "*think[ing] better* [italics added], more firmly . . . less for you . . . more for the 'truth.' " For example, the record of a discussion of *The Closing of the American Mind* is like watching a time-lapse film of human thought development:

GEOFF: Allan Bloom – thoughts?

THOMAS: What a joke

JEANA: Some of what he says is true in a lot of cases, but he makes to many generalizations

DOUG: I think he had a real bad attitude towards the way Americans gain their knowledge

DAMON: After reading it in class I was opened up more to how close-minded HE is

JEANA: I think he is too old fashioned

COURTNEY: His ideas on music were stupid, relating everything to sexual intercourse.

DAMON: He generalizes people and only has one view on a broad variety of personalities

JEANA: He tore Mick Jagger apart

THOMAS: I think he is way to much like my mother

GEOFF: Is that good or bad, Tom?

THOMAS: Bad
she is a nagger and a winer

COURTNEY: In fact hes got that same snobbish attitude he accuses others of having.

JACKIE: I think in some sense he is correct about saying that students don't read as much as they could but I don't like how he generalizes everyone together

GEOFF: Does anyone really think rock is "commercially prepackaged masturbational fantasy" (p. 75)? I mean, that's pretty crude.

ANDREW: He's simply generalizing America instead of researching each separate faction

DOUG: He totally disregards the fact that you can learn a great deal from parents friends and just experiences you have

GEOFF: Yes, Andrew, there is just a lot of unsupported generalizations in here – like that rock is worse than porn (p. 74) for example. Is music a drug you are addicted to?

THOMAS: no.

ANDREW: thats a generalized moral for a generalized topic

TERRECE: HE MUST BE VERY OLD FASHIONED AND THINK AMERICA'S YOUTH ARE FALLING APART

CHARLIE: Ma St ur bational – someone should tell him about Rock -n-ROLL – music can stimulate the imagination as well as decay it.

GEOFF: Yes, Terrece, old-fashioned is a good word – I think he is hear-kening back to a time when things were a lot simpler.

ANDREW: before there was a change

COURTNEY: he is just clinging on to his last desperate ideas

JEANA: almost everything Bloom says is negative toward change

GEOFF: "but as long as they have the Walkman on, they cannot hear what the great tradition has to say. And after its prolonged use, when they take it off, they find they are deaf." (p. 81) But what is Led Zeppelin is the "great tradition"? Who knows what the great tradition is? Did it stop or is it still going?

NATE: Geoff could you explain this list of books Bloom thought every-one should read.

GEOFF: Plato, Aristotle, the Bible, Shakespeare – basically it's the so-called classics, Nate.

JEANA: Bloom thinks he has the right to classify what the proper tradition is

CHARLIE: What if Blume was just unforgivably JEALOUS of Mick Jagger

"Allan Bloom, what a joke" is precisely the kind of unreflected, nonacademic thesis our students are tempted to make coming into our class. But being able to discuss and refine why they think he's a joke, to cite the pages in the text that justify their thinking, allows them the reflection they need to turn their initial response into a considered one: snobbish attitude, generalizing America instead of researching each separate faction, clinging on to his last desperate ideas. These are notions that fit in an analysis of Allan Bloom, and are written in a style worthy of formal prose. Responding in a written medium also gives students a record of what others bring to the reading from their own personal worlds into the common group – the image of Tom's whining mother, for example, or an Allan Bloom jealous of Mick Jagger, might be just the sort of once-private, now-shared image that will be a catalyst for another writer. We frequently hear responses to this effect: "Remember in that one conversation when Jessie said such-and-such? Well that gave me the idea to write about . . ."

ENFI, then, exists as a splendid environment for class discussions on specific readings or general topics. It is a vehicle that affords systematic, recorded immersion into the text. Nascent ideas that might prove evanescent in an oral dialogue become more articulated, more formed, more on that hierarchical level Barthes spoke of, when students realize they are working in an archival medium, one that allows for verbal articulation and storage. It's almost as if students, in discussing readings concerning significant issues in our larger culture, can see – both while they engage in the discussion and later when they read over the transcript – that such issues really are worth discussing.

Then their writing assignments reflect this logic – they act as the students' long, formal turn in the ongoing cultural dialogue around that topic.

Our peer-response sessions work a little better now, given that students have a different curricular agenda. Rose (1983) felt remedial students would be better served by teachers who were "presenting [them] with intellectually worthwhile problems, assisting them as they work through them, offering them strategies with which to explore them, showing them how to represent and, when necessary, reduce them" (p. 118). That not only seems intellectually justifiable to us, but the discussions our students are now having on papers, discussions in which they are trying to solve those problems and learn those strategies, seem like a better expenditure of class time.

Becoming literate in a new area is, of course, a gradual process, and students do not automatically become folk-theorists of writing just because they are given more complex things to read and write about. Lori asks Jen, "What is going to be the point of your paper?"

JEN: My point or elijia muhammads point and malcolm xs point at the same time was black was superior and evil white man was created of evil and knew no other. my question was is this justified[?] is there enough evidence[?] and i am looking from references in the book the auto-biography, and from the bible and from elija muhammads writings from the library as it coincides from the book.

Jen's answer shows uncertainty is still present, but it's an uncertainty that has some conception of the text to be written – the state of cognitive dissonance that comes with learning a new idea – unlike the confusion present in our earlier Jennifer, who had no notion of what a description of ice cream should look like. There is confusion that allows for possible solutions, that has entryways back into the text, and there is confusion in which things look hopeless. Jen is learning both the degree of difficulty involved in academic writing and a little of how to solve it.

The significance of a discussion carried out on ENFI is that it keeps the personal as part of the student's writing process. Associating objectivity with the specialized literacy in academic culture, a literacy that they as basic writers hold only in part, this group visualizes their response task as an unfortunately frustrating activity surrounding the concept of writing. Further, entering into the language of the objective implies for them a restraint on what they consider they do have, their subjective voice (in the sense of Can I put my opinion in? as we hear many of them say).

Such results remind us again that offering up their papers to a group of peers does not necessarily provide students the supportive initiation into the university's language of the objective (no matter what the medium, ENFI or otherwise) that we might have hoped. To some degree the activity remains under suspicion: Not only does it not automatically lead to awareness of academic discourse, but it makes them wary of holding any opinion at all. If for us peer response amounts to a sound pedagogical tool, for our students it often represents little more than a bewildering disenfranchisement, another way to not know how to write. Understandably, they react as we often do when we don't understand the rules of a game – they make up their own. We see, for example, that Jason succeeds in his reformulation of a task when the consensus that ends a peer-response conversation is that they all "pretty much agree with each others papers." In fact, they've talked very little about the papers; what seems to be agreed upon is that they would rather talk about the difficulties of writing than about the writing itself.

When we compare this situation with earlier off-task tendencies, we feel more confident in our use of the ENFI technology. Our original goal was incomprehensible to our early students, and so it often wasn't even addressed. The network succeeds, however, in at least creating this forum for communication of the personal side to writing. For our writers this is significant, because they have often failed in writing earlier.

We do not wish to present a picture that all is rosy now in our new ENFI-supported curriculum. Our students still have a difficult time integrating the ideas of others into their final papers. But we now see this as a larger problem concerning their inability to synthesize seemingly discrete, disparate sources or sites of information into their text, their inability to conceive of a text as a coherent whole formed from layers of variously determined meaning. When we discuss issues in Malcolm X's autobiography with our students relative to who controls the agenda for our national dialogue, they are halting and more silent than chatty. When we discuss the censorship of 2 Live Crew, they are nonstop in their enthusiasm for the discussion. Yet when they write about the issue in their ideological analysis, they forget to use elements of the ENFI discussion.

ENFI as sampling

ENFI, then, is not a magic pill that will bring students to a poststructural conception of writing. Frankly, we're surprised, because our students are very savvy about another method of composing popular today in contemporary music, the technique of sampling. As music critic Kyle Gann (1990) defines it,

Sampling – digitally recording performed or prerecorded sound for potential manipulation – has hit the music world like a sonic boom and opened up thousands of unforeseen possibilities. Linehook your sampler to a CD player and the world of recorded music is your oyster: Coltrane's horn, Phil Collins's drumming, Fischer-Dieskau's voice all at your disposal. (p. 102)

Our students, very big fans of contemporary music (as Allan Bloom bemoans), are well aware of this omnipresent recording technique; in fact, we overhear discussions before and after class where they try to identify which previously recorded material was sampled in which current hit.

This sampling technique is precisely the manner in which academic texts are constructed:

A major skill in academic writing is the complex ability to write from other texts – to summarize, disambiguate key notions and useful facts and incorporate them in one's own writing, to react critically to prose. Few academic assignments (outside of composition) require a student to produce material ex nihilo; she is almost always writing about, from, or through others' materials. (Rose, 1983, p. 118)

Our task, then, is in part to help teach students writing-as-sampling. They currently live it in the culture of the musical remix, but they can't as yet theorize it. Here, too, we think the ENFI transcripts will be a great help, as we show students how to mix in prewritten text from the transcripts, the reading, and the culture at large to form their texts. ENFI gives us valuable, class-specific prerecorded material, material made of the students' own discourse.

What Baudrillard (1983) says about the masses (and the "imaginary representation" we have of them) may be true for our students as well:

According to their imaginary representation, the masses drift somewhere between passivity and wild spontaneity, but always as a potential energy, a reservoir of the social and of social energy; today a mute referent, tomorrow, when they speak up and cease to be the "silent majority," a protagonist of history – now, in fact, the masses have no history to write, neither past nor future, they have no virtual energies to release, nor any desire to fulfill: their strength is actual, in the present, and sufficient unto itself. It consists in their silence, in their capacity to absorb and neutralise, already superior to any power acting upon them. It is a specific inertial strength, whose effectivity differs from that of all those schemas of production, radiation and expansion according to which our imaginary functions. (pp. 2–3)

Students as we conceive of them in the classroom are always "to be": They are potentialized not actualized, on their way to becoming experienced. "You have the choice of thinking like a student or like a writer," Donald Stewart (1986, p. 17) tells the student users of his writing textbook, neatly revealing how mutually exclusive our discipline finds those two terms.

ENFI exists for us, then, mostly as a counterpoint to the traditional student "imaginary," the standard representation of the student writer. Standard measures of writing quality and traditional measures of metalinguistic ability are increasingly unsatisfying to us because we know they don't fully capture our students' strengths (or weaknesses). Transcripts from an ENFI class become an important classroom text that illustrates how students create meaning, interact, pose questions, offer answers, respond to each other's work as well as their own, and become interested and bored by the classroom enterprise. It is active, living literacy.

At first we were convinced that ENFI went only so far – nice adjunct, we thought, but it ultimately doesn't make good on the promises it seems to hold. We were tempted to find support in an incident that occurred during the end of one of our two-quarter ENFI course sequences during the students' last peer-response session. The instructor gave them the option to either discuss their papers on the network for the last time or break up into small groups and discuss their papers orally. All students in the class chose *not* to use the network, but rather to talk orally among themselves.

The instructor figured this showed the ultimate limitations of ENFI until he started eavesdropping on the group closest to him. It was animated, lively, the students having amazingly rich things to say about each other's papers. People who had previously demonstrated no visibly powerful network face turned out to be fascinating composition theorists. Was it that ENFI had them reined in too long? that the network was an artificial medium for them on which they could only cut loose and get no serious work done? that oral, face-to-face conferencing is more natural, more productive? Ultimately, the instructor of that course thought no. He was convinced (because he had never, in 15 years of teaching, experienced such a productive oral conversation) that the rich interchange came about *as a result of* the 15-plus weeks on the network, that the students had, through much off- and on-task network interchange, built up a history of interaction. Bonds were formed electronically and students were as anxious to talk to each other in person about their writing as pen pals who are giddy at the prospect of meeting face-to-face for the first time.

You can found a course on network interaction, we feel, but you must let it all ride on the interchange, lift off the lid and see for yourself, and let students see for themselves, what sort of exotic things are under there. We have to look at ENFI as a writing technology in the strictest sense, as a multivocal, multicultural word processor, producing texts of a kind of "environmental writing." It belongs to the same family of technology as e-mail, amateur press alliances, CB radio, party lines, 900 numbers – the technology of polyphony, of heterotopia.

Conclusion

We began this paper with a discussion of reading and writing in our culture, and we close by thinking about painting. The network transcripts (polylogs), as vox pop, as de facto forms that bubble up from a nontraditional formal source, have something in them of the initial promise of pop art, about which Huyssen (1989) said,

From the very beginning, Pop proclaimed that it would eliminate the historical separation between the aesthetic and the nonaesthetic, thereby joining and reconciling art and reality. The secularization of art seemed to have reached a new stage at which the work of art rid itself of the remnants of its origins in magic and rite. In bourgeois ideology, the work of art – in spite of its almost complete detachment from ritual – still functioned as a kind of substitute religion; with Pop, however, art became profane, concrete and suitable for mass reception. (pp. 48–49)

Such texts, unmediated by the filter of a specific writing assignment and informed by the everyday materiality of students' lives, are key for the writing teacher in the way they represent records of student behavior around the notion of writing. Like postmodernism's reclaiming of pop art, we too stress a kind of reverence for these previously degraded forms. The ENFI conference fractures the conception of the traditional writing class, making events in the classroom seem more like everyday life, where students talk and work and play and sleep and help and hurt.

Destroying one agenda reveals a new one: In their sheer rejection of the agenda presented to them, the students who worked in our ENFI classroom told us something about the writing curriculum we thought was a good one – that it, in the words Marcus (1989) uses to describe the British punks' rejection of hegemony, "comprised a fraud so complete and venal that it demanded to be destroyed beyond the powers of memory to recall its existence" (p. 18). The ability to say fuck you uncategorically to a teacher's writing task is what we saw our students discovering over the network; they appropriated the technology for their own ends. It's a power more useful, we suggest, than most of the writing assignments we urge on them, in the hopes of some vague empowerment, can bring about. But it's a scary power for us because, as happened in our writing program, it puts under question our entire enterprise.

To continue our analogy with pop art, we began to see our students in the same light as a Robert C. Scull. Scull, a cabdriver turned executive and pop art collector, invested early in pop artists, and his nouveau riche, arriviste vulgarity thoroughly rankled the traditional fine arts crowd. He is the kind of man art critic Sidney Tillim spoke of (in Hebdige, 1988) when he profiled the pop audience as

involved with art in a way that I think no American art public has been involved before. It is concerned less with art, with quality than with the release of a spirit that has been repressed by its subservience to an idea of culture essentially foreign to its audience. The pop audience is tired of being educated, tired of merely *good* art. (p. 119)

Our first wave of ENFI students showed us how tired they were of merely *good* writing and of being educated in the institutions that taught it. Stewart (1986), again, opens his textbook with a telling example that replaces the blue-collar cabdriver image with beer drinker:

Harold, the son of rancher Spangler Tukle in Robert Day's *The Last Cattle Drive,* has this observation on living the full life: "You only go around once.

... Give it all you got. Take your very best shot." Punning on the name of
an instructor, Buddy Jenkins, he comes up with this "original" observation:
"When you've said Bud, you've said a lot." Aside from the fact that the
young man is the obvious jerk his creator intended him to be, what specifically
are his difficulties? He thinks and speaks in the language of TV beer commercials. As a speaker (and, we may assume, a writer), he has two serious
deficiencies: he lacks versatility and authenticity.

I seriously doubt that there are many Harolds among today's college students, but I know from experience that there are many who have Harold's
language problems. They have not been taught how to respond to a wide
variety of composing occasions, and their written work lacks an authentic
voice. (p. vii)

Our students are those beer-commercial-speaking ruffians who have been
set loose in the halls of the liqueur-sipping mandarins. They're cabdrivers
who dare speak art in their own bastardized lexicon. Our goal becomes to
lead them away from speech and writing that are media determined, to a
prose style worthy of E. B. White – a prose style that, even though so much
of the curriculum is based on prose models and teaching to forms, we can
still call "authentic." But has not authenticity become a questionable value?
Will not Stewart have problems with the clichéd nature of every observation
in a postmodern world?

Indeed the very criterion for determining authenticity is how well it reminds
us of something we like, how well it approximates language mediated by other
sources, more prestigious academic sources rather than beer commercials.
It's a question of style, not authenticity – style, which, as Bartholomae (1985)
reminds us,

is the evidence of mediation and, at times, of a writer's consciousness of that
mediation. It is language that mediates, that stands before the writer and
determines what he will say. When a student, for example, is asked to write
an essay about "How I Learned a Lesson," that essay, in a sense, is already
there in the institution, with its understanding of what a lesson is or what
learning is, with its available introductions, transitions, and conclusions, with
its language appropriate for such a narrative. (p. 72)

We don't really want the authentic, we want the familiar, the always already
available. And when students are unmediated or mediated in a way that seems
foreign (and threatening) to us – as do beer commercials, for example – then
we say they are still students and not writers, because we don't recognize the
mediation.

Our task as writing teachers, we now feel, entails finding the right balance
between the academic and the contemporary, between the social and the
scholarly, between beer commercials and Allan Bloom, because, frankly, as
happy as we are that our students' ENFI conversations now seem more academic, we miss the furious spirit of those earlier discussions. We want stu-

dents to be able to discuss each other's expository essays with the same vital passion with which they critique each other's wardrobes. Of course Allan Bloom reminds you of your mother; that's the whole point. ("Maybe you're just like my mother, she's never satisfied. . . . ")

We imagine most writing instructors have the same attitude toward the "goof-off" off-task transcripts we now remember so fondly (and prize so highly) as that of an audience member in a conference presentation one of us gave (Sirc, 1990), who characterized the interchange of Nick and Jerald and their conference group (discussing Jerald's shoes) as "five guys whacking off." Again, we are reminded of the historical reception of pop art. For most art critics, as Hebdige (1988) has noted, pop was

a temporary aberration from the proper concerns of responsible artists, a silly, wrong-headed or empty-headed, essentially callow or immoral digression from the serious business of making serious statements – the business which these critics imply should preoccupy committed artists of whatever persuasion – academics, formalists, propagandists and populists alike . . . [T]hat dismissive critical response merely reproduces unaltered the ideological distinction between, on the one hand, the "serious," the "artistic," the "political" and, on the other, the "ephemeral," the "commercial," the "pleasurable" – a set of distinctions which pop art itself exposed as being, at the very least, open to question, distinctions which pop practice set out to erode . . . [P]op's significance resides in the ways in which it demonstrated, illuminated, lit up in neon, the loaded arbitrariness of those parallel distinctions, lit up in neon the hidden economy which serves to valorise certain objects, certain forms of expression, certain voices to the exclusion of other objects, other forms, other voices, by bestowing upon them the mantle of Art. (p. 126)

Those distinctions are too much with us in writing theory – academic versus nonacademic writing, the university versus nonuniversity, experienced writer versus inexperienced writer, obvious jerk versus authentic writer, serious writing student versus five guys whacking off. We are still shoring up that bankrupt intellectual "hidden economy." Baudrillard (1990) speaks of the dangers inherent in such autonomization; we enforce various arbitrary categories onto settings that are otherwise undifferentiated by those categories. So we can speak of things like collaboration or invention or text production or whatever in a writing classroom where before there was nothing, or in Baudrillard's words, "uncontrolled, unstable, insensate, or else highly ritualized forms" (p. 40). We read a situation, in this case a writing classroom, according to these new truth criteria, which promise to reveal what was previously hidden in the situation. It is "the incredible racism of the truth, the evangelical racism of the Word and its accession" (p. 40).

We began to look at our earlier students' off-task network commentary, in which they took a break from the serious work of straining for textual commentary and meaning, in the same light as Degas's pastels of ballet dancers – adjusting costumes, idly waiting, preparing for otherwise determined moments – scenes in which the real action is off-stage. Our students, in the lovely pastel sketches of them in their off-stage moments that ENFI was able to capture, showed us something important about what they wanted to do in their grand, dramatic, center-stage solos in our classrooms. It turned out they knew more about the dramaturgy of a writing classroom than we had ever suspected.

9 The origins of ENFI, network theory, and computer-based collaborative writing instruction at the University of Texas

Fred Kemp

In 1982 Maxine Hairston, professor of rhetoric and composition at the University of Texas at Austin, in a famous if not notorious article declared that a paradigm shift in the teaching of writing had occurred. Hairston argued that a "static and unexamined approach to teaching writing" (p. 76) had given way to a new model, one that emphasized process over product, writing behaviors over prescriptive rules. Recently I included this essay in a graduate course I was teaching at Texas Technical University called Computers and Writing.

My graduate students exchanged position papers every class period through electronic mail. These are messages responding to the reading or to previous electronic and face-to-face discussions. One of the students, after reading the Hairston article, startled me a little by writing derisively, "some paradigm shift." Another pointed out with equal disdain Hairston's 1982 dismissal of computer-assisted instruction as, in Hairston's words, having "faded from the scene" because it was "too limited and impersonal."

I tried to defend Professor Hairston on both points. First, the shift from handbook rhetoric to process-based rhetoric was a major conceptual move that is even now far from accepted everywhere, no matter how enlightened some graduate students may feel. Then, too, anyone who has heard Professor Hairston's presentations at the Conference on College Composition and Communication (CCCC) in Chicago and at the Sixth Computers and Writing Conference in Austin can have no doubt that she enthusiastically embraces the concept of computer-based writing instruction and teaches regularly in the networked classroom at the University of Texas.

But my graduate students may be steeped in a completely different paradigm from even the presumably radical one Hairston outlined in 1982. This new paradigm has been gained from a familiarity with and immersion in computer capabilities totally foreign even to the pedagogical adventurers of the early 1980s. Among these capabilities I would put at the top of the list computer-mediated communication, or what is more commonly called computer telecommunications or area networking. When the team I worked with at the University of Texas at Austin thought of computer-assisted writing instruction in the mid-1980s, we did not include networking in the picture, and many still don't. But the inclusion of networking changes greatly how computers can be used in writing instruction and encourages the formulation of a new rhetoric, a network-based rhetoric, which is as radical a departure from the process model as the process model was from the static, rule-based model of formalist or current-traditional rhetorics.

Seymour Papert (1980), in his book *Mindstorms,* calls computers "naturally heuristic." One of the things he means by this is that it is impossible to put a process, any process, onto a computer without exploring and thoroughly understanding that process. So when we put drill and practice on a computer, we are forced to understand drill and practice in a way and with a psychological intimacy not experienced previously. Even those who, like me, had always and somewhat blindly accepted the efficacy of drill and practice in whatever form, can be quite shocked at what we see when we start writing the computer code, mapping the screens, inserting the decision points, and actually seeing at close hand the terrible, mechanical reductiveness of running people through a drill-and-practice process. The same kind of consciousness raising occurs when one tries to put any instructional method on the computer. The old methods are made strange, and we see them in different lights. We more clearly recognize their failings.

Early computer use at the University of Texas

The English department at the University of Texas (UT) at Austin received, in the fall of 1985 and throughout 1986, some fifty IBM microcomputers as a part of an IBM grant program called Project Quest. The principal stipulation that governed the grant was that the department use the computers for the development of innovative instructional practices, not merely as writing devices. Accordingly, responsibility for handling the computers was given to English Professor Jerry·Bump, and he assigned me as a graduate research assistant to supervise specifically how the machines were to be used. I was in my second semester as a doctoral student and got the job simply because I showed up at a general meeting and perhaps overstated my familiarity with computers. I had done a very small amount of programming in BASIC during the summer I was preparing to enter the Ph.D. program. The prejudice against computers was so great in the department that I was assigned to babysit the new computers mostly by default, and it was one of the most fortunate things that has ever happened to me.

The first group of microcomputers we received were housed in the department's writing lab, but space limitations (and general dislike of the computers) required that we move elsewhere. Professor Bump acquired space in the basement of the university's Flawn Academic Center, which housed the undergraduate library, and we moved into two rooms that had once been the offices of English department lecturers and graduate students. The two rooms were located across a hall from each other. The room on the north side of the hallway we designated our laboratory, and the room on the south side of the hallway we called our computer-based classroom. We consciously avoided the term *computer-assisted,* because we wanted to avoid the implication our facility was intended simply to support traditional classroom activities.

Although I found out later that no one realistically expected me or whatever staff I could put together to satisfy the conditions of the Quest grant, I intended from the start to discover new and powerful ways to use the computers as classroom devices, not merely as new forms of audio-visual or tutoring aids. But as I wrote program after program in BASIC designed to operate as a diagnostic or tutoring program, I realized the inherent deficiencies of computers in managing natural language.

The new technology could not be pasted onto the old methods. This was made clearer to me when Paul Taylor and Locke Carter joined the project later in the year, and we began our investigations in earnest. Since drill and practice in grammar was a predominate (if repeatedly denounced) method of teaching writing, computers were immediately put to use as drill-and-practice machines, and that is what we did with them. Because essay grading was presumably at the heart of a writing instructor's efforts, we longed for a *Writer's Workbench* that would truly grade essays. A step up toward more legitimate instructional practices occurred when we developed invention heuristic software based upon the model of Hugh Burns's *Topoi,* the original version of which had languished on the university's mainframe since Burns's 1979 dissertation, *Stimulating Rhetorical Invention through Computer-Assisted Instruction.* But there was still a sense that we were simply trying to force computers into standard precomputer classroom lessons. Instead of "turn to page 47 and do numbers 1 through 20," we were saying "let's go to the computer now and do module 14," or "let's go to the computer and run the question prompt series, 'Starting the Policy Essay.' " When in January of 1987 the Computer Research Lab hooked up a local-area network, it became even more obvious that we were forcing the round peg of networked computers into the square hole of traditional writing instruction.

It wasn't until Taylor and I observed a presentation by UT graduate students Valerie Balester, Wayne Butler, and Kay Halasek at the College Conference of Teachers of English (CCTE) at Corpus Christi in March of 1987 that our fundamental mistake became clear. Balester, Butler, and Halasek had worked in graduate student offices not 40 feet from the doors of the Computer Research Lab for over a year, but it wasn't until all of us went to Corpus Christi that we shared our ideas. Their group presented a session on collaborative instruction and the pedagogy of Kenneth Bruffee (Bruffee, 1985). Although Butler remembers being worried by all the nudging and whispering Paul and I were doing in the audience, we were actually responding to what was being said with a great deal of excitement. Here was the classroom theory to fit the network, and it represented, to us at least, a considerable shift from what we had always thought of as the proper way to teach writing. When later that month at the CCCC in Atlanta I saw Trent Batson describe synchronous electronic discourse, the principal mechanism of his ENFI project syllabus, I felt sure that an integrated package of networked computer features could be assembled that powerfully supported a collaborative pedagogy.

Since all of us at the Computer Research Lab (Taylor, Butler, Carter, Balester, Halasek, and Nancy Peterson) were graduate students in rhetoric and composition studying under such notables as Jim Kinneavy, Maxine Hairston, James Berlin, Lester Faigley, and John Ruszkiewicz, we felt an insistent demand to develop practices consistent with the best rhetorical theory. I have on occasion been chided for my emphasis on the theory behind what happens in the networked computer-based classroom, but I believe that without a theory that maintains a continuity with mainstream research in rhetoric and composition, the practices that result are in danger of being thrown willy-nilly at the student, justified only as the products of a glamorous technology. Although Batson's ideas, tossed upon a screen from an overhead projector in a meeting room, seemed terrific, I quickly realized that my scholarly community would look for more theoretical support and firmer ties to the research of the rhetoric and composition community.

The move to theory-based network instruction

On the evening of Batson's presentation of ENFI methods at CCCC, I attended a demonstration of real-time discussion hardware and software given by a vendor high above Atlanta in a hotel suite. Working with me on the linked IBM computers, by chance, was someone I had met only once before but who was to become a colleague of mine at Texas Tech, Professor Thomas Barker. He and I sent synchronous messages back and forth between the networked computers and grew more and more excited by the instructional possibilities. Here, I felt sure, was the best means to employ networking and the Bruffee curriculum I had seen earlier that month.

Upon returning to Austin, I called a war council with Paul, Locke, and lab director Jerry Bump. I described what I had seen in Atlanta and suggested that although we could not afford the equipment and software the principal commercial supplier of Batson's ENFI Project was offering, we could write our own software to run on the Token Ring network of the Computer Research Lab (CRL). Paul, our most capable DOS programmer, was quite dubious. It seemed like a tricky technical requirement, to have a room full of computers all contributing comments to a shared text stream.

I left the group for about 20 minutes to demonstrate our computer classroom to a group of visiting junior college instructors. When I returned Paul and

Locke were already drawing flowcharts of computer code, their previous reservations forgotten. Two days later Paul showed up at the lab with a prototype program that provided a crude but workable ENFI classroom.

Two weeks later Valerie Balester, a graduate student in rhetoric and composition and one of the proponents of a Bruffee collaborative pedagogy, walked into the CRL, sat down at a table next to me, and said she and two other graduate students, Kay Halasek and Nancy Peterson, wanted to team teach three freshman English courses the first summer term in the networked computer-based classroom. It is hard now, looking back, to see that offer as an act of courage, but it was. None of the instructors had been associated with the CRL before, and before the CCTE meeting had never seen a connection between their pedagogical interests and ours. Although all three were computer users, none had used local-area networking, the software the CRL was writing, or computers as instructional support.

That move would be akin, I think, to having a teacher successful in the traditional classroom consider teaching on a sand-filled playground replete with jungle gyms, swings, teeter-totters, and tether-ball poles. How, this teacher might ask, are these things going to support writing instruction? Balester, Halasek, and Peterson might well have asked the same of e-mail, heuristic prompting software, and synchronous electronic discussion. No one, as far as we knew, had ever implemented a pedagogy consistent with current rhetorical theory in a networked environment.

That summer session was a mangle of software crashes, net crashes, ruined diskettes, and teacher and student confusion. The commercial word processing software we were using, billed as specifically intended for college writing, was much too difficult for students. I have learned that any command gap in any software acts as an irresistible attractor for students. They'll find it, get lost in the software, and sit there helplessly waiting for the instructor to come and pull them out. Documentation, good or bad, is very rarely any help at all. Then, too, the Bruffee (1985) assignments, in which students focus primarily on what each other has to say in response to tasks set by the teacher and examine the ways they and other students make judgments and arrive at decisions, underwent a considerable warping when forced into the networked computer environment. Student opinion alternated between being in love with and hating the computers. We made wholesale shifts in the syllabus as the courses proceeded. This all occurred in a 6-week summer term.

It was the most active intellectual period of my 20-year teaching experience. If we weren't crying, we were dancing around doing high-fives. When the classroom worked, it bristled with activity and student energy. When it didn't, the room died and the instructors felt helpless. Those of us who weren't teaching hugged the doorway to the classroom, intent on how our software, our machines, were helping or hurting what the instructors were doing. We had arguments, some quite serious, between the instructors and the CRL staff, and the staff had arguments among themselves and so did the instructors. The questioning and challenging was vibrant; the solutions weren't obvious.

What was obvious, clearly obvious, was that none of us would ever teach writing the way we had before. With computers or without computers, we had seen something happen among a group of people that had made the effective teaching of writing the same as climbing a difficult peak. It could be done, and it didn't take super humans, but it did take teamwork and a sense of mission.

The physical layout of the computer-based classroom

The size of the room we were using as a classroom required a very squeezed arrangement of equipment. We had 25 IBM PCs, each with an old-fashioned expansion unit, an EGA color monitor, and an Epson dot matrix printer. The expansion units were simply PC boxes with a 10 megabyte hard disk and a cooling fan. So by doubling the computer box and its electrical demand, we added 10 megabytes of storage. We considered ourselves lucky at the time. A workstation was composed of a CPU and an expansion unit side-by-side, with the monitor on the CPU and the printer on the expansion unit. We fitted two of these clumsy workstations on a utility table, and fitted 13 of these tables into the room, all lined up facing the wall opposite the door in a traditional classroom format. The aisle that ran down the middle of the room between the rows of tables was barely wide enough for us more sedentary researchers to navigate unembarrassed.

Because each workstation required four separate electrical wires and plugs, the wiring, even before the network was installed, was nightmarish. The electrical drag was so great that the classroom blew breakers a number of times in the 6 months before Bump could get the room rewired, and because the location of the breaker boxes was a secret jealously guarded by the university maintenance crew, any outage effectively brought the room down for an hour or more. We placed the rows of students facing the back wall so that anyone entering the door would not see the viper's den of cables at the back of the computers but rather the brilliant color of the EGA monitors, and for promotional purposes we programmed the most colorful title screens we could.

The forward row of computers was pushed right up against the wall, so that an instructor who wished to address the class had to stand in the aisle, practically locked into position. In order to satisfy the ever-present demand for a blackboard, I filched a portable blackboard from the English department, but had to remove the wheels and wheel brackets in order to fit it between the front row of computers and the wall. Somehow, at the front of all that powerful computing equipment, our amputated portable blackboard managed nevertheless to define the facility unmistakably as a classroom.

At the rear of the room stood another utility table upon which we placed a PC dedicated as a telephone bulletin board. This computer, once we had installed our Token Ring network, allowed students to call in and enter our local-area network and perform some of the classroom functions from a distance.

There was no instructor's console, or indeed, no computer designated as an instructor's machine. Usually the instructor would begin a particular classroom computer activity and then sit down at any available machine in order to participate. In the software we were developing and in the later Daedalus Instructional System software, developed quite independently of the CRL, it was an important point of theory that the instructor not have any technical advantage over students in terms of an ability to manipulate a student's access to the text stream or an ability to direct specific instructions to a particular student. The reason this is important is that collaborative theory presumes that it is the classroom reader, not necessarily the instructor, who prompts and guides revision. The instructor who retains all the obvious trappings of classroom authority, who emphasizes that peer authority is simply a fiction and that the one reader – indeed the one *person* – who counts in the classroom continues to be the instructor, undermines the character of peer response. Consequently, the network collaborative classroom resists placing teachers at special computer stations with special technical authority.

Many of those who first consider the concept of networked instruction consciously or unconsciously picture the networked classroom as a clone of the foreign language lab, in which an instructor works a console and a bank of switches that allows him or her to control what individual students hear, to monitor the students' responses (usually modeling pronunciation), and to tutor individual students at will through the audio network. Students do not know, at any given time, whether they are being monitored or their individual efforts are being recorded. It is not until the teacher's voice suddenly comes through the earphones that the student realizes that the teacher has been monitoring his or her particular station.

It was our intent at the CRL, and continues to be the principal emphasis of those working with the Daedalus Instructional System, that computer networks should encourage responsibility in students and a greater sense of participation and engagement, and to do that students need to be given a stronger awareness of their own power to intervene and comment during classroom action. Having an instructor at a console capable of disconnecting individual computers from the net or, worse yet, able to insert the instructor's text into the document the student is composing, seems antithetical to our particular instructional emphasis.

During synchronous electronic conversation with the software Taylor, Carter, and I developed, an instructor's comments come across with the same physical capabilities and appearance as any student's comment. Obviously, students are realists and know who gives the final grades, but the networked computer-based classroom pulls the instructor down from the podium into the group of students, seated at a random monitor, facing the same direction as them all, and entering comments into the same scratchpad with the same technical abilities and limitations as any student.

As the instructors were conducting class either in their cramped space at the blackboard or on a computer communicating synchronously or asynchronously with students or groups of students, one or more of the research assistants assigned to the CRL would cross the hallway and stand in the doorway observing the class. Because the students' backs were to the door, the researchers/programmers could observe the computer screens without themselves being noticed, though the students were always aware of how easily the programs could be altered and actively participated in the refinement. Many times students or instructors would encounter problems with a particular function or feature, exhibit the frustration that would bring an anxious programmer to their side (usually an expletive of some fashion), and ask for a different prompt, another color on a particular menu bar, a different kind of screen shift, or just that a tiny (but always aggravating) glitch be corrected. The programmer, in many many cases, could retire to the lab across the hallway, fix the lines of code, and have the new version on the file server in a few minutes. He then would return to the complaining student or instructor with instructions to reload the program, and then bask in the general amazement that computers could be "fixed" so easily and quickly.

For years the staff of the CRL advocated that graduate students who studied computer-based instruction develop programming ability. By doing so, we left ourselves open to much criticism that English majors didn't, by the nature of things, involve themselves in such reductive behaviors as computer programming or managing equipment. Often (although this problem is growing less) people in English studies exhibited a technophobic elitism that prompted them to denigrate the computers themselves and certainly the technical capabilities of those who spent significant amounts of time programming and managing them. It was and remains our contention that an effective blend of classroom, theory, and computers cannot be realized without classroom skills, knowledge of rhetorical theory, and intimate knowledge of the computer and software all being combined in the same team working very closely together, and ideally combined in the principal members of that team.

How network theory differs from other rhetorical theories

When my colleagues and I first decided to try using networks in writing instruction, we settled on adopting a collaborative pedagogy drawn from the work of Kenneth Bruffee (1984), Peter Elbow (Elbow & Benaloff, 1989), Anne Ruggles-Gere (1987), and Patricia Bizzell (1982). Essentially, these writers focused on collaborative pedagogy that values group work and the commitment and engagement the writer discovers when writing to peers rather than writing to instructors. It seemed reasonable to us that a pedagogy that privileged the computer capability of moving files between computers should support group work and peer critiquing.

I was, frankly, not enthusiastic about peer work. I had for a number of years in the precomputer classroom tried to make peer editing successful but had never been able to apply the theories, no matter how convincing, without massive complications the theorists never seem to emphasize strongly enough. Simply distributing student text required vast amounts of photocopying, or reading aloud (an unsatisfactory means of encouraging peer editing), or complex schemes for collating student critiques. But the network presented the opportunity of managing student interaction in entirely new ways, and so my colleagues and I made the effort and I'm very glad we did. The resulting scheme of instruction I call *network theory,* and although it shares many instructional assumptions with the collaborative theory generally propounded by Bruffee and others, technology allows network theory distinct and powerful advantages.

In what follows I briefly describe the theoretical antecedents to network theory: formalist theory, process theory, and collaborative theory. Formalist theory, or what Dick Fulkerson (1979) has called "formalist instruction" and Jim Berlin (1982) has called "current-traditional rhetoric," privileges error elimination and manuscript organization. The principal instructional process is "prescribe and test." Rules are prescribed in textbooks and handbooks and are strengthened in the student's mind through drill and practice. The student's mastery of the rules is then tested in the writing of academic essays. The teacher grades these academic essays as performance; that is, he or she looks to see if the essay demonstrates an appropriate application of the rules. If errors remain, especially errors the teacher feels have been adequately identified and drilled upon, then the essay grade suffers.

Proponents of process theory, those who follow the problem-solving strategies and process flowcharts of Linda Flower (1985), quite correctly deride formalist theory as missing the point. Writing is simply not rule driven. Therefore, process theory rejects attempts to duplicate good writing by applying rules of grammar and coherence, and instead concentrates on the expert behaviors that have produced such good writing. It doesn't matter so much what the essay seems to be as what the writer seems to have done to produce it. Rather than trying to duplicate good writing, students should be trying to duplicate the actions of good writers. Hence process theory privileges things like invention, revision, and multiple drafting, the expert behaviors supposedly derived from protocol analysis.

Collaborative theory says process theory is fine as far as it goes, but it still misses the point, though not nearly so badly as the despised formalist theory.

What is important is not so much what writers actually do, but what they are trying to do, and central to what they are trying to do is influence an audience. Writing behaviors are not nearly as important as writing intentions, and writing intentions are strongly dependent upon the writer's notions of his or her audience, purpose, and the general presentational situation. Both formalist theory and process theory generally hold up the same audience, an audience of one: the instructor. Students may be told to imagine different kinds of audience, and in some fashion include an awareness of such audiences into their writing decisions, but they nevertheless still write their essays to the instructor. Collaborative theory says, and I believe quite correctly, that until a type of instruction can provide something more closely approximating real-world readers than English teachers, all instruction will devolve into the teaching of writing as performance rather than the teaching of writing as proficient and effective communication.

So what's wrong with teaching writing as performance? Writing that is presented to the instructor as a performance is constructed and judged on the basis of performance markers. In the case of formalist theory, those performance markers are correct pronoun-antecedent agreement, proper modifier placement, and so forth. In the case of process theory, the performance markers are less visible and more individual to each instructor, but reflect the emphases the instructor has declared (or implied) as the proper result of the writing process. In either case, as James Britton (Britton, Burgess, Martin, McLeod, & Rosen, 1975) and many others have described, the writing has not been written to be read, but written to be judged. This teacher, as Britton et al. (1975) have emphasized, is not a reader but an examiner. Whatever performance markers the instructor has asked for will be included by successful students, and the resulting academic essays will succeed in the usual way, but the actual writing would fail in any environment but the classroom. It will probably be, as Ken Macrorie (1970) calls it, a kind of "engfish."

The sine qua non of collaborative theory, on the other hand, is the real-world reader, or its closest approximation in the classroom. How nice it would be if our students' essays could be published in the community in a local newspaper or magazine. Very few teachers should fail to see the power that would be infused into what was previously academic writing, and the resulting and certainly startling change in the intentions of our student writers. But the institutional demands of large-scale education make community publishing in any major way impossible.

If the class is to provide a real-world reader, then the reader must be in the class itself. Students must publish for each other. This, then, is the principal tenet of collaborative theory: Students must write to each other in order to encourage the intentionality that is a necessary part of real-world writing. But those who have attempted peer work in the traditional classroom have come to realize that managing the classroom publication, actually directing the heavy traffic of drafts and feedback from writers to readers and back to writers in a continuing process, is a draining if not debilitating procedure.

What I first conceived as the major step forward of network theory over collaborative theory was simply in the management of written text. Networked computers could move large amounts of student text in complex but controlled patterns between student writers and readers with very little effort on the part of the instructor. Menuing shells could be incorporated into the text-sharing software that would allow all kinds of student text – essays, critiques, brainstorming, position papers – to be moved instantaneously between individuals, among enumerated groups, in any conceivable combination of students within or across class boundaries or even between campuses. But I soon found that network theory, or the application of collaborative theory to networked computers, actually stimulated a significant improvement in not just the operating procedures of collaborative instruction but also in the instructional paradigm itself.

The difficulty with collaborative instruction, as we quickly realize, is that if the writer's intentionality is to be honestly influenced, the student or peer reader must actually be reading and commenting on the written text in some effective manner. Writing to a zombie is no real improvement over writing to a teacher. So if collaborative instruction is to work, either in the traditional classroom or in the computer-networked classroom, we must ensure that students can read critically. We must further ensure that such critical reading can be articulated effectively in peer responses. Peer responders must not only know how to find good and bad things in a text, they must be able to express those good and bad things back to the writer in a rhetorically effective manner.

When I talk about this need for critical reading, I am often confronted by the statement, "Oh my lord. Can't we just teach them to write? Do we have to teach them to read too?" But it doesn't take too much pondering to realize that good writing is a direct function of good reading, especially if we buy into process theory. How in the world is a writer going to revise a text effectively if he or she can't read that text critically?

Collaborative instruction in traditional classrooms requires that students read their papers aloud, then discuss them face-to-face, orally negotiating the markers of effective and ineffective writing. Herein lie many of the management problems of collaborative instruction in the traditional classroom. But in the computer-based networked classroom, almost all of the interaction among students takes place on-screen and in written text. Essays are sent to students or groups of students on-screen and in text. Critiques are written using split-screens and mailed electronically to the writer, in text. Negotiations concerning the markers of effective and ineffective writing are written and distributed to a student or a group of students on-screen and in text. And all of this text is saved and retrievable by any student practically at any time to read and review and reread.

I have called all this reliance on text in the writing classroom a "textualizing" of the instruction. Herein lies the most visible difference between collaborative theory itself and network theory. Collaborative theory privileges negotiating both textually and orally, but network theory privileges negotiating almost exclusively in written text. If our principal mission is to develop critical readers, then the emphasis on text in the networked classroom is of vital importance. I don't believe you can teach students to write or read by telling them how to do it. Nor can you teach students how to write or read by showing them how to do it. Both of these methods Papert called "teaching by advice," or top-down instruction, and for many reasons this kind of instruction simply doesn't work with present-day students, who tend to be much less receptive to prescriptive methods than the student populations of years previous. You can, however, teach students how to write or read by making them do it, lots of it, and then requiring them to react to it in successively more sophisticated ways.

What networked computers allow us to do in the writing classroom is emphasize reactions in text to text. These reactions, of course, are based on critical reading. The student is immersed in text, from the detailed daily class instructions that arrive on-screen, through the progress reports delivered from the instructor in e-mail, through electronic discussion, to the freewriting, essay drafts, essays, and critiques themselves. Class and homework time are almost completely taken up in reading student text and writing student text and writing about student text.

There is, therefore, in the networked classroom a vast amount of writing being directed by the software from student to student in whatever interactive combinations the instructor wishes. A student can write to a student, a group, or the entire class, and conversely, a student, group, or entire class can respond to a student's text. Students can work in pairs or groups for weeks at a time, or change readers with every draft. Students can freewrite critiques, or critique drafts according to heuristic prompts. The critiquing prompts exist as text files called up by the software, and can remain the same for a semester, strongly emphasizing a particular set of criteria for critical reading, or the prompts can be adjusted for each critiquing session, allowing the instructor to alter the criteria as the course progresses.

Collaborative theory has been both praised and criticized for reducing the role of the instructor in the classroom, but whereas the instructor may indeed lecture less using group work in the traditional classroom, the chances are he or she must still be a powerful presence in the classroom to provide the bottom line in terms of student motivation. This motivating "presence" in network theory is assumed by the software and the manner in which class assignments configure the features of the software. Whatever the student does in response to the day's assignment and in terms of manipulating the collaborative features of the software, he or she is always aware that every character or line of published text can easily be reviewed by an instructor either presently or in the future. This means that every distributed draft, critique, message, or comment has, in the student's mind, the possibility of being read by the teacher and collated into an evaluation of the student's effort. In reality, of course, very little of this material is reviewed by the instructor, although the instructor always has the option of intensely scrutinizing the work of individuals, and the complete text of any semester's class is always available for more scholarly discourse analysis at a later time.

What happens in the computer-based networked classroom

The classroom that has evolved from my early experiences with ENFI has no boundaries in the sense that the teacher is restricted to one activity or another. But an example of an instructional process illustrates the possibilities.

The instructor decides upon an issue to write about, say, the dress code in public schools. She initiates a synchronous discussion in class concerning dress codes, perhaps with a provocative statement such as "dress codes promote the kind of behavior that helps students learn in school." Very quickly (with this topic especially) the screens are alive with comments about individuality, basic rights, and so forth. A student decides to make a comment and brings up an electronic scratchpad on the screen and enters his remark. The editor used is a full-screen editor with the standard capabilities of most word processors and no practical limit to the length of the student's entry. When the comment is ready to be "published" to the class, the student hits the command key and the comment is displayed in the "text stream" on every computer in the room. Soon after, another student's comment is tacked onto this text stream immediately following the first comment, both entirely visible to the whole room. Other comments follow, attached to the text stream as the students issue the publish command. Students who are viewing the text stream may scroll back to previous comments, cut and paste particularly relevant comments to a save file, and even make up and enter conferences separate from the main conference, so that several students may, if they wish, create an electronic discussion involving only themselves. All conferences are open to anyone, however, and students soon learn not to try to escape the requirements the instructor has outlined by hiding in created conferences. After about 20 minutes of comments added to the text stream, the instructor declares an end to the discussion, and tells each student to download the discussion to his or her diskette for further perusal.

The entire class discussion is downloaded as a single text file to each student's diskette. The student brings up the discussion, cuts and pastes as necessary, and develops a thesis based upon the comments of the class as a whole. This thesis is pursued and supported by citing remarks (direct quotations, of course) by classmates as experts. The resulting draft is uploaded to the class database, and a message is sent to the peer critiquer that the writer would like feedback. The peer critiquer comments, either in free form or using a critiquing heuristic feature of the software, and e-mails the response back to the writer. A writer can have one, two, or five peer critiquers, depending upon the predilections of the instructor and the time constraints of each assignment.

A new draft can either be resubmitted for further peer critiquing or submitted to the teacher for grade evaluation. These submissions, of course, are simply a matter of uploading text from the student's diskette to the class database. The student can use e-mail as a query device, and the teacher can critique the student's work at any time. The specific path of how a student submits a draft and receives comment, and so forth, is flexible and entirely up to the instructor. The flexibility, of course, is the major strength of the pedagogy. Communication among students and instructors, within classes, across classes, or across campuses, is much much easier using network links. Writers and readers are joined in much more useful ways than before.

As I write this description I am aware of how restrictive it is, of how many times I have seen instructors do quite different things with the network and the synchronous and asynchronous messaging features. The network and the appropriate software (I use the Daedalus Instructional System) provide not so much a variety of lesson plans as a capability of interaction in text that would have been inconceivable before computers. Over the 5 years I have used network theory as a pedagogical base and observed others bend the equipment to their own emphases, I have seen text sharing employed in a startling variety of ways. For example, one type of interaction included in network theory is the synchronous classroom discussion. The classes I have had most experience with have used the Daedalus feature called Interchange and DOS computers networked with Novell, though at Texas Tech we are currently also using a new version of the Daedalus Instructional System developed for Macintoshes and Appleshare. The synchronous classroom discussion is the most notable classroom action in network theory and is what is usually thought of when the term *ENFI* is mentioned.

As described, synchronous messaging allows everyone in the room on computers to share the same text stream. That in itself is quite significant, for the following reasons:

1. The classroom discussion has been textualized. That is, whatever dynamic that traditionally supports the free exchange of ideas in a classroom is now filtered through writing. The students feel the need to express themselves to the issue of the moment, but must do so in writing. In writing classes, this seems advantageous.

2. The discursive action is parallel, not sequential. In oral discussions, one person speaks at a time, the others listen. No matter how excited a student becomes, he must wait for his turn or vie with others for attention. Many students simply succumb to passivity. In the ENFI discussion a student may enter a comment at any time without any fear of being cut off in mid-thought.

3. The comments are edited and published only when the student is ready to do so. Especially thoughtful students don't have to spend agonizing minutes preparing their words, gearing up their courage, and hoping against hope that their ideas come out the right way. In an ENFI discussion the student enters the comment, changes and edits it in whatever fashion she deems comfortable, and then either sends the message or cancels it. I have found that the ability to cancel a message (although very few messages actually get cancelled) is a great psychological aid to some students.

4. Also of great comfort is the fact that the students are facing a video screen reading words, not exposing themselves to the social complications of face-to-face utterance or the sometimes frightening prospect of speaking extemporaneously before the class. Some critics of ENFI have complained that this dehumanizes the discourse, but I find the filtering process of networking ideas a very humane process indeed, especially for less socially dominating students. It is the general belief among those who have experience with ENFI discussions that participation is more evenly spread among the students than in oral classroom discussions (Batson, 1988b).

5. The comments that enter the text stream can be studied and referred to repeatedly. Unlike oral remarks, the remarks made in an ENFI discussion can be read and reread. A remark can be and often is referenced by succeeding remarks, and no one need depend on the vicissitudes of short-term memory. This "archival" capability has several good features. For one thing, participants need not get engaged in arguments about what was actually "said." It's there for all to read. For another, what is said and understood becomes a function of writing and reading, and the critical abilities that play such an important part in good writing are given full practice here. The sense of audience so necessary to good writing looms quite important in this form of writing, and the lesson is driven home again and again.

6. As a continuation of point 5, the discussion produces a transcript, a stored text file that may be used in a variety of ways. In a prescriptive sense, the simple knowledge that one's participation in a discussion can be easily demonstrated tends to encourage students to participate. The file itself, as described earlier, can be provided to the students to be used as an invention device or a means of directly citing classmates (also encouraging thoughtful comments in the ENFI session).

I have noticed other happy things that go on during Interchange sessions, such as students jumping up to share a monitor and a particularly funny or stimulating comment, or students unwilling to leave the program even when the instructor tells them to, but the list of numbered points describes the most pedagogically useful effects of synchronous messaging.

The criticisms of synchronous electronic discussion probably should be mentioned here also. Some say the whole process, a room full of students clacking away at keyboards, seems cold. That coldness, however, is a perception of the person who remains outside the discourse, who is standing at the back of the room away from a monitor. Once that person enters the discussion, he or she quickly sees why students almost always respond more excitedly to this classroom activity than any other.

Another criticism is that electronic discussion privileges those students who type faster, and it is therefore unfair. This criticism is valid, but I would point out that traditional classroom discussions in traditional environments also privilege certain students, those more articulate or who have certain social characteristics, and that the lack of typing skills can be more readily overcome than shyness or underconfidence. In any case, the characteristic of synchronous messaging that I have described as parallel versus sequential expression allows such an increase in participation that any perceived exclusion because of typing ability can be discounted.

The expanded ability to examine writing behaviors

A major tenet of research in writing instruction is that a greater knowledge of what influences student writing will result in better teaching methods. The networked computer-based classroom provides a greatly expanded research capability over the traditional classroom because of two factors: (1) Almost all classroom interaction and certainly all writing is in text and saved in a single electronic format, and (2) almost all classroom interaction is through the computer, which affects student behavior and attitudes in instructionally interesting ways.

To expand on the first point, a semester's class in freshman writing can generate up to 3 megabytes of text, or about six times my 250-page dissertation. A portion of that text will be the students' classroom essays, of course, but other portions include drafts of those essays, free-form and prompted peer critiques of student essays, freewriting and prompted invention drafts, individual asynchronous e-mail messages about essays or grades or topics or anything, and transcripts of synchronous electronic classroom discussions (ENFI). The conventionality of the writing extends from the formal essay to the quick conversational response on Interchange. The ability of the researcher to investigate this text and the interrelationship among the various stages of writing and brainstorming and the effects of collaborative influences should be obvious. Further, analysis mechanisms can be programmed to process this comprehensive classroom text to reveal statistical patterns of development that can complement (but never replace) traditional human discourse analysis.

For instance, although I have never had the time to fully explore the analytic aspect of the networked computer-based classroom, I have written software that counts word length, sentence length, paragraph length, punctuation ratios, ratios of transition words, and a number of other aspects of text that are relatively easy to count. The data that results from such processing of the huge amount of writing done over a semester's time should, in the hands of researchers fully aware of the limits of computer analysis, provide insight into how network theory performs. Unfortunately, comparable material cannot be retrieved and analyzed from traditional classrooms so easily.

The second point, that most classroom interaction is directed through a computer, allows interesting research into the nature of student and instructor attitudes. Because students are not communicating face-to-face, many of the dynamics of such interaction are muted and other aspects of behavior revealed. Pseudonyms can provide students facilitating, if hazardous – they may abuse their invisibility by engaging in flaming – courage in the expression of their ideas and allow a huge variety of role playing and gender shifting, the limits to which exist only in the researcher's imagination.

Jerome Bump, first director of the CRL, performed a series of experiments using ENFI in literature classes during the fall of 1987 and the spring and summer of 1988 (Bump, 1990). He employed pseudonyms using parts of social security numbers and organized discussion conferences by sex. Using the Myers-Briggs scale and a dependence measure developed by the University of Texas counseling center, Bump was able to conclude that interaction in the three courses produced "a truly egalitarian, student-centered interchange which supported relatively democratic discussion by all concerned of the goals and methods as well as the subject of the course" (p. 54). Bump further reported that "when conferences were organized by sex some people were liberated but the stereotypes became quite clear. With all the men in their own conferences, some women in the freshman class felt more able to be heard" (p. 58). Students reported that the male and female conferences showed consistently different emphases and remarkably different readings of the same literary text and characters.

Bump also experimented with focused on-screen reading of poems, in which specific lines of poetry were presented for student reaction in instructor-controlled fashion. Some students were frustrated by their lack of ability to read the entire poem at will, but "this format slowed students' reading so much, making them ponder the significance of each individual word, that it soon became apparent that few would even finish reading a 60-line poem in 75 minutes of class time!" (p. 59). Nevertheless, when asked, 12 of 17 students voted to do more focused reading of the poems. Bump performed his "most radical experiment" in 1987–88 – the collaborative exam. As he reported, all of his freshmen and 8 of 11 graduate students asked that all exams be given on Interchange.

Lester Faigley, a well-known researcher in rhetoric and composition, investigated student behaviors using pseudonyms on Interchange in 1988 (Faigley, 1990). Among Faigley's findings in an intense reading of a single Interchange session was what he termed "changes in the network of power" (p. 306). Regarding his own role in the discussion (calling himself by his first name), Faigley comments:

Lester has hardly been a force in the discussion since message 1, in part because of his continual direct references to the text which the others do only indirectly. By the end of this section we see a reversal of roles with the teacher replying and students making evaluative comments. . . . The paradox, of course, is that the class discussion has gone much farther and much faster than it ever could have with Lester standing at the front. (p. 306)

Faigley agrees with many of Bump's observations, that "not only is the discourse structure radically different than what goes on in a typical classroom, but so too is the level of participation" (p. 307). In a particularly revealing passage, Faigley notes:

In each of the four college classes I have taught using a computer network, one student has objected early in the semester to using Interchange. In an Interchange session they have asked: "Why can't we just meet in a regular room and talk?" Each time they have found no support from the other members of the class. And each time the complaining student has been a man. (p. 307)

From this Faigley concludes that men prefer oral discussions and the attendant ability to exercise traditional authority, and my experience tends to make me agree. In his remarks concluding his study, Faigley makes a most powerful observation regarding network theory:

Too often we know little about the potential of students as researchers because we have been deaf to the possibilities of student dialogue. . . . The play of language in Interchange subverts authoritarian discourse by showing human discourse is composed of many voices. A student in another Interchange said it better: "When I first came to this class, it seemed abnormal to participate all the time. Now it seems abnormal to sit still and listen to a lecture for an hour and a half. (p. 310)

It is not my intention to summarize the results of Bump's and Faigley's studies, or to review the equally stimulating conclusions presented by Wayne Butler (1991), Valerie Balester and Kay Halasek (1989), Locke Carter (1989), Paul Taylor (1989), and others who have in presentations and articles described the electronic classroom discourse at UT. I hope, however, that these brief descriptions emphasize my point that the ENFI classroom presents a wide range of research opportunities for rhetoric and composition.

Problems with ENFI at the University of Texas

Most of my descriptions so far have been fairly rosy, but in fact much of what I and my colleagues were able to accomplish in 1987–88 regarding networked writing instruction came with great difficulty. Chief among all problems was the one of anticomputer bias among both faculty and graduate students in the English department. There was (and to a lesser degree still is) a sense among traditional English scholars that technology itself is spiritually reductive. This thinking, to my mind, is a clear reflection of romantic prejudices against science harkening back to the very early 19th century and the struggles among science, theology, and aestheticism. It is dangerous, because carried to the extreme it will eventually place English studies outside the basic concerns of modern society.

The forms of such a bias are many, from a writing center director who feels that computer cables are "nasty," to graduate students who despise typing in their names on a computer screen because of Orwellian fears that somehow it will be used against them, to faculty who dislike departmental e-mail because feedback as to whether departmental mail had been read or not would deprive them of "plausible deniability" in disregarding memoranda. Once, visiting western Tennessee in order to assist a small teaching college set up a computer-based writing classroom, I had an English professor, a person I had met one minute earlier, pointedly turn and walk away when it was announced I was there to help with the computers.

Accordingly, recruiting research assistants to help Jerome Bump and me fulfill Project Quest requirements was tough. The English department was willing to assign such graduate assistants, but for the students themselves, working with computers was assumed to be a professional dead end. Paul Taylor, a person of extraordinary personal strength and, like me, an older-than-usual graduate student, found my oft-repeated demonstrations to the graduate students interesting, and moved to the CRL at first chance. I had to convince Locke Carter, younger than us all and the only person attached to the CRL in those early days who actually had programming training, in Jim Berlin's kitchen one night during a party for James Kinneavy. I ended up that night simply handing him a key to the lab and telling him that he could come use the computers, or steal them, or do whatever he wanted, because I was desperate for graduate students to know we existed there beneath the undergraduate library and that we had a marvelous amount of powerful technology just waiting for someone to take advantage of.

In late 1987 it became evident to the ten of us actively involved in the CRL that neither the English department nor the university could understand, much less actively support, the type of instruction we were creating. We therefore formed a company in February of 1988, the Daedalus Group, Inc., in order to maintain our close personal and professional association past graduation and to create commercially viable software. Our mothers and fathers and friends bought stock in our little S-Corporation, and with that money we bought computers and began programming an entirely new piece of software that became, eventually, the Daedalus Instructional System, an Educom/ NCRIPTAL award-winner for the best writing software of 1990.

Other academic disciplines have been allowed, even encouraged, to work with the society at large, with its technological emphases and its commercial advantages. One could hardly imagine university departments of business or engineering or natural science not having contacts with real-world companies in terms of hiring expectations, grants, or knowledge acquisition. But English studies, because, I think, of the biases I mentioned, sometimes seems to consider itself above the practical world. For this reason, I felt the need to reach outside academic English departments in order to do what I felt most personally and professionally advantageous.

Conclusion

Before I entered the Ph.D. program in rhetoric and composition at the University of Texas at Austin, I had taught English and other subjects some 9 years. I had been called, and thought of myself as, a successful teacher. But I was highly dissatisfied by my own feelings that I was reaching only very few of my students, that my "success" was based upon the expressed feelings of my most successful and articulate students. I had the definite feeling that I was teaching to 20 students, but the only 5 who ever said anything said I was a great teacher, and those 5 were going on to good colleges, and the other 15 were accepting the judgment of those 5 because they themselves had no real entry into the learning process or the evaluative process and had no confidence in their own judgment. Their discourse, as Faigley suggests, had been discounted so thoroughly by the system that they themselves discounted it.

The use of networked computers and the ENFI process that I learned from Trent Batson changed my feelings of discouragement to new excitement about an instructor's ability to influence learning. A whole new instructional environment clicked into place. There is no "solution" to education, just as there is none to raising children or discovering happiness. Expectations and processes and requirements are constantly shifting in accordance with the shifting nature of society itself. But a system of instruction that shifts with those expectations, processes, and requirements has a good chance of working across all spectrums. Letting students define their own working environments through computer-mediated communications seems a good beginning.

10   Why write – together – concurrently on a computer network?

Christine M. Neuwirth, Michael Palmquist, Cynthia Cochran,
Terilyn Gillespie, Karen Hartman, and Thomas Hajduk

Why write – together – concurrently on a computer network? This question was central when, in 1987, Carnegie Mellon (CMU) was approached to participate in the Electronic Networks for Interaction (ENFI) Consortium. Several characteristics of the CMU setting made it impossible to give the same answer to this question as other consortium members. For example, our student population was different: Gallaudet University, the site of the original ENFI innovation, had pioneered using concurrent network communication to create opportunities for deaf students to interact in English and to model competent English in the context of genuine communication (Peyton & Batson, 1986). Clearly, their answer to Why write – together – concurrently on a computer network? could not be our answer, because the majority of our students have different needs than Gallaudet's.

On the other hand, there was a body of theory and research that allowed us to construct some plausible "stories" about ways in which concurrent network communications *might* be useful for CMU students. For example, one story we told ourselves was that writing together, concurrently on a computer network might help our students see the need – more vividly than they did with traditional methods of instruction – for some of the forms and structures of written communication that help manage the absence of nonverbal cues. Research indicated that nonverbal cues are important in coordinating and comprehending messages efficiently (Kraut & Lewis, 1984; Kraut, Lewis, & Swezey, 1982). People have great difficulty conversing when they cannot make eye contact, nod the head, murmur "uh huh," and so forth. Indeed, the absence of these nonverbal cues is one probable cause for anecdotes concerning the difficulties of computer conferencing. However, it is precisely this skill – the skill of communicating effectively in the absence of nonverbal cues – that is one of the goals of much instruction in writing, for example, instruction that aims to help students produce "reader-based" prose (Flower, 1979). We speculated that if students interacted with other students on the computer network and experienced communication difficulties due to the absence of nonverbal cues, they might get a better sense of the comprehension problems their readers experience when nonverbal cues are absent and, as a result, be more aware of the need to supply written structures in order to compensate.

A second story we told ourselves was that the written transcript of the network interaction might help teachers monitor peer groups more effectively. Instructors are divided as to the efficacy of peer response groups (Freedman, 1987, p. 91) and report that students in such groups experience numerous difficulties, including the following (cf. Bishop, 1988):

- Uncertainty about the purpose of the group
- Uncertainty about the nature of roles within the group
- Failure to provide each other with adequate response
- Failure to remain on task
- Failure to use the peer response effectively in revisions

A written record of the peer group interaction would allow the instructor and students to study the complete text of the interaction and develop a response to the interaction based on concrete incidents and examples. Such response might also improve the effectiveness of the peer session, because research suggests that it is important to structure cooperative learning activities so that each individual's performance is evaluated (Slavin, 1980). Likewise, the instructor could ask students to hand in an analysis of the session transcript with their revisions. The analysis could detail students' reasons for accepting or rejecting each of their peers' suggestions for revisions. Such analyses might help the instructor and students understand how students are thinking about the session when revising their papers.

On the other hand, there was a negative story to be told as well. The little empirical work already done on interactive computer-mediated communication suggested that there might be serious negative effects of writing together concurrently on a network. In particular, in an important experiment on the effects of concurrent computer-mediated communication, Kiesler, Zubrow, Moses, and Geller (1985) found that people who communicated concurrently by computer evaluated each other less favorably than people who communicated face-to-face; they felt and acted as though the setting was more impersonal, and their behavior was more uninhibited (more impolite statements, swearing, flirting, expressions of personal feelings, etc.). Kiesler et al. (1985) began their study with the observation that computer-mediated communication relies on text alone, thereby reducing to a minimum nonverbal feedback and information about the social context of the message. Based on this starting point, they theorized that participants in computer-mediated communication would focus greater attention on the message and on manipulating the message, and less on the people with whom they were communicating. They reasoned that in an *interpersonal communication* task (getting to know the other person), the reduction of nonverbal feedback and information about social context would negatively affect performance – and indeed, their findings concerning less favorable interpersonal evaluation, more impersonal feelings and actions, and more uninhibited behavior indicate that it did. But would a similar result obtain when the task was a *writing* task? We did not know. Although there would surely be *some* focus on the other person in a writing task, presumably the focus in a writing task would be more on the message and less on the person than in an interpersonal communication task, so the negative effects Kiesler et al. found for an interpersonal communication task might or might not be found for a writing task.

With initial stories that established a prima facie case *for* ENFI and some doubts about the case *against* it, we thought it would be worthwhile to ask teachers and students at CMU to work with us in putting to the test our speculations concerning the potential of concurrent network communications in learning to write, and so we agreed to join the consortium. In this chapter we present some results of that exploration, describing teachers' and students' answers – as well as our own – to the question, Why write – together – concurrently on a computer network?

The technological context

A series of earlier technological and related pedagogical developments in educational computing influenced the ENFI project at Carnegie Mellon. At the start of the ENFI project, CMU was in the midst of a transition from central time-shared computers to a campuswide network of powerful personal computers, called the the Andrew system (Morris et al., 1986). The existence of the campuswide network influenced the ENFI project team's decision to design and implement Andrew-based software to support concurrent network interaction.[1] Although CMU had a cluster of IBM PCs on a local-area network (LAN) that would, in principle, run the system that other sites planned to use to implement ENFI, the IBM PCs would not fit well with existing educational computing practice in the English department, a practice that employed the Andrew system heavily. Teachers in computer-based sections of writing were already using the Andrew electronic mail and bulletin boards[2] in their classes. In addition, these teachers were using several Andrew-based writing tools developed by the Center for Educational Computing in English (CECE). Among the tools was Comments, a program that supports *non*concurrent communication about writing (Neuwirth, Kaufer, Keim, & Gillespie, 1988). Although there were interfaces from the IBM PC to the campuswide mail and bulletin boards, there was not one to the Comments program, and building one would be very time-consuming. If CMU were not to build An-

---

[1] The project team consisted of the ENFI site director, research assistants, and programming staff, all of whom were members of CMU's Center for Educational Computing in English.

[2] There are presently over 2,250 bulletin boards, both internal and external, on campus.

drew-based software but use IBM PC–based ENFI software, students would either need to use two systems (Andrew and IBM PCs), or the other practices would have to be curtailed. Given that one of the goals of the computer-based writing sections was to minimize the time spent teaching students about computers and dealing with computer problems, the first alternative was not attractive. Given that teachers and students were enthusiastic about other network tools, especially Comments, neither was the second.

Thus, our primary reason for designing and building Andrew-based ENFI software was one of compatibility with existing practices at CMU. A secondary reason was that Andrew-based software to support concurrent network interaction also represented an opportunity to explore concurrent communication that would be more broad-based: If there were ENFI software on Andrew, students could use it not only within a classroom, but from the public computing clusters or their dorm rooms[3] to interact with their teachers in their offices or with students elsewhere at any time.

Pressures of implementation time,[4] existence of a software toolkit on Andrew to support rapid implementation, and the prior existence of a concurrent "talk" program on campus significantly influenced the form the program took. The Andrew Toolkit provided the basic materials on which the rest of the software was built. This toolkit provided a user interface that looks much like that of the Apple Macintosh and other high-resolution, mouse-driven user interfaces. It gave the developers windows, menus, dialog boxes and all the text-editing tools. The developers drew upon the toolkit and the already existing talk program to rapidly create a similar program that kept a log of the interaction.

The Andrew-based program for concurrent network interaction, called CECE Talk, allows concurrent network communication among workstations connected to the Andrew network. Unlike ENFI software being used at other sites, CECE Talk does not have a private window in which participants first compose messages and then send the already composed messages to a public conversation window. Instead, each participant is assigned a window on all other participants' screens in which the participant types messages to the other participants in the conversation (see Figure 10–1). As the message is typed, the characters appear on the screens of all participants in the conversation. In addition, participants can respond to messages at any time; they

---

[3] There are currently about 500 network connections activated in dorm rooms. CMU has a total enrollment of approximately 4,300 undergraduate students.

[4] In the initial organization of the project, as discussed in the proposal to the Annenberg/ CPB Project, the development of ENFI software for CMU's campuswide network was to proceed *separately* from the activity of integrating ENFI activities into writing courses. However, we could not get the IBM-based ENFI software to run on the campus local-area Novell network. This led to the use of an Andrew-based prototype (CECE Talk) *in conjunction* with the first pilot course, so the group needed to get something running quickly.

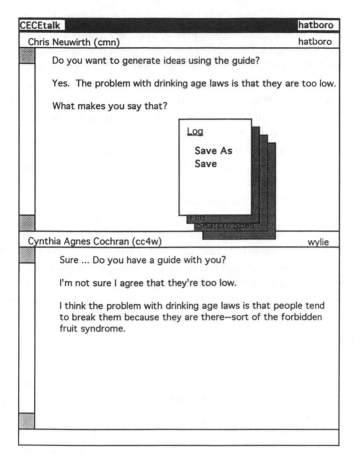

Figure 10-1. CECE Talk program screen with one participant in the upper panel and the second participant in the lower panel

need not wait until other participants have finished typing to compose their messages.[5] All participants have independent control of scrolling in all the windows displayed on their screens. Like other ENFI software, the "transcript" or "log" of the session is stored on disk and participants can print or edit it.

[5] Users of CECE Talk sometimes used these features of the system to engage in a sort of "cooperative overlap," in which participants would begin to compose responses to a message while the writer was still writing it, sometimes indicating that they knew where another participant's message was headed by responding to it before it was finished. This phenomenon is in contrast to face-to-face interaction, in which overlap is relatively rare, because speakers must interrupt each other to talk simultaneously. There is a related phenomenon, however, also called cooperative overlap, in which listeners show encouragement or understanding by issuing "uh huhs" and other "re-

Unlike other ENFI sites, the CMU site evolved during the initial semester to the use of very small groups for most activities, usually pairs[6] or at most a group of three or four. One reason for this difference in sites may be due to the different ENFI technology in use at CMU, which employed separate windows for each participant rather than one private compose window and one global conversation window.[7] It may be more difficult to understand an interaction when a large number of messages appear in many separate windows, rather than appearing in a single window.

Technical differences are not the only reason for differences in group size between the sites, however. During the pilot semester, the project team explored alternatives such as the size of group for collaborative interaction, both with the instructor and with students. The project team felt that a large number of students on the network rather than a small number had the disadvantage of being confusing and failed to identify a corresponding advantage. (Other sites, of course, had identified advantages to offset the disadvantage. For example, at Gallaudet, larger groups, in particular, whole-class discussion, allowed teachers to model competent English for students in the context of a real communication.) The team failed to find any research that examined the effects of various group sizes in writing groups.[8]

The classroom context

The ENFI project team began integrating concurrent network interaction activities into writing courses at CMU with a single pilot section of Strategies for Writing, the writing course required of all incoming freshmen in the university except those students who exempt based on high SAT and AP scores.[9] Enrollment in Strategies is set at 24 students per section maximum,[10] with approximately 15 sections offered in the fall, 10 in the spring.

The Strategies course has two goals. The first is to introduce students to processes of composing. The course asks student writers to examine their thinking and composing processes in order to gain more control of the strategies they use for both learning and writing. Students look at the processes that underlie effective writing to help them develop more powerful strategies for planning, drafting, and revising. The second goal of the course is to

---

sponse cries" (Goffman, 1981) or indicate that they know where the speaker's sentence is headed by finishing it (Tannen, 1985). The cognitive and social consequences of such cooperative overlap are not well understood.

[6] Sometimes students worked in series, first with one partner, then a second.

[7] The workstations that participants used had large (approximately 19 × 19 inches), bit-mapped displays that could hold up to 20 windows.

[8] The team did find research on the effects of size in brainstorming groups (cf. Stein, 1974).

[9] In the academic year 1987–88, approximately 12% of the freshmen were exempted.

[10] Sections that meet in computer labs are typically limited to 20 because of the number of seats available in the lab.

introduce students to three major kinds of writing they will do in college and in their professional lives: writing an analysis of a problem, writing a paper that defines and supports a thesis, and writing a proposal (which includes an oral presentation). To increase the transfer of the skills taught in this course, students also examine how each of these three kinds of writing functions in its academic, public, and professional contexts. The course is set up so that there are three major graded writing assignments – with multiple drafts and between-draft response (cf. Beach, 1979) – that reflect the three kinds of writing. The text for the course is Flower's (1981) *Problem-solving strategies for writing*.

Given the need to coordinate a university-wide course with multiple sections, the course director expects instructors to follow the course goals and assignments,[11] but they have a great deal of latitude concerning strategies and tactics. For example, many instructors rely heavily on small-group response to writing; others rely more on whole-class response. Instructors teaching the course for the first time attend a two-semester teaching practicum that meets weekly to discuss, among other things, course goals and suggestions of ways to implement them, but the teaching suggestions – though usually supported by theory and evidence from research – have the force of suggestions, not commands.

With the exception of one or two sections taught occasionally by faculty or adjunct faculty, all sections of Strategies are taught by graduate Ph.D. students. The instructor who taught the pilot ENFI section, a beginning Ph.D. student in rhetoric, was recruited from the pool of Strategies teachers on the basis of prior experience in teaching computer-based writing courses at another institution and her interest in teaching a computer-based section of the Strategies course. Although she had some prior teaching experience, it was her first time teaching Strategies. Similarly, other ENFI instructors in subsequent semesters volunteered to teach computer-based sections; they had varying degrees of experience in teaching writing and in the particular courses they were teaching.

There were 15 students in the pilot section at the beginning of the semester, 4 females and 11 males ranging from 17 to 19 years of age. Students reported the following high school grades in their most recent writing or writing-related class: 3 A's, 9 B's, and 3 C's. Five students reported planning to major in engineering, with the rest reporting majors in business, psychology, prelaw, and writing. During the course of the semester, one student dropped the class.

We asked the pilot instructor to participate in three activities: (1) the development of activities for concurrent network interaction; (2) definition and review of software requirements and designs; and (3) interviews about

---

[11] This is not to say that instructors cannot influence course goals and assignments – they have had substantial influence – but because of the multisection nature of the course, that influence is generally felt in a subsequent semester.

her course. In addition to the normal teaching stipend, the instructor received additional support to compensate for the extra time these activities required. With one exception, other ENFI instructors in subsequent semesters typically had less intense interaction with the project team and received no additional compensation. The development of concurrent network writing activities at CMU can be divided into four phases: (1) exploration of designs, (2) formative assessment of the experience, (3) codification of the experience, and (4) summative assessment. These phases, however, like subprocesses in the composing process, were actually highly interactive and recursive during the course of the 3-year project.

Exploration of designs

During the pilot semester, several members of the project team met weekly with the instructor to discuss her goals for the upcoming weeks and possible concurrent network activities. Given the institutional context of the Strategies course, the group decided to try to follow, as much as possible, the standard curriculum and course goals, attempting to use ENFI to enhance existing goals rather than introduce new ones. As the instructor observed in a post-semester interview:

One of my major goals . . . was to blend the two themes [process of composing and kinds of writing]. . . . Secondary to that . . . was . . . to find activities that would complement what I was trying to help them [the students] to do.

The meetings were spent thinking of ways concurrent network activities might be useful in helping students, then asking the following critical questions:

- How does the activity meet the goals for the course? Specific instructional goals?
- What theory and research support the activity?
- What are the advantages and disadvantages of doing this activity collaboratively compared to alternatives (e.g., lecture or demonstration by the teacher, whole-class discussion)?
- What are the advantages and disadvantages of doing this concurrently on a computer network compared to alternatives (e.g., face-to-face, nonconcurrently)?
- What other instruction and support is needed to make this activity most effective?
- In what ways can the activity be improved?
- What other teaching goals can/cannot be met using this activity?

Drawing upon a cognitive process model of composing (Flower & Hayes, 1981; Hayes & Flower, 1980), the group explored, over the course of the semester, the following collaborative activities that students might engage in concurrently over a network:

- Representing the writing task
- Representing the task environment (e.g., purpose, audience)
- Acquiring knowledge
- Generating ideas (e.g., brainstorming, peer questioning, role playing)
- Setting goals
- Planning
- Organizing
- Drafting
- Evaluating
- Revising

Some of these (e.g., collaborative drafting) seemed a long reach, given a course structure in which students were assigned grades for papers individually. Others (e.g., collaborative knowledge acquisition) seemed less appropriate for concurrent network interaction. The decision to use any particular activity was, of course, the instructor's.

As was often the case, the instructor's goals shaped the group's discussion. For example, one of the instructor's goals was to help students consider others' perspectives in their papers:

I want them to be better critics, to really be able to understand when you look at somebody else's piece of writing that . . . the kinds of response that you would give someone else could be incorporated.

Previously, the instructor had relied more on teacher-led, whole-class response, but was trying to incorporate collaboration as a means to increase the immediacy with which students could obtain audience response:

The collaboration I saw as providing audience, kind of set up a response type system where they immediately got feedback or . . . got some response to whatever they generated, and for the most part tried to make . . . it attached to an assignment.

But the instructor reported difficulty with getting students to engage in appropriate dialogic writing:

What may make a lot of sense to me – and certainly this came out – it would make sense to me to ask the question "What does this word mean to you?" But that question in itself . . . has a lot more meaning to me than . . . to the students, so if, for example, one of the students asked the other "What does this mean to you?" they may just . . . say something back – a non sequitur or some off-the-wall comment like, "Well, it doesn't mean anything to me" and "What time are you going to lunch?"

Research suggested two things about this dynamic. First, the instructor's goal to develop students' sensitivity to various perspectives was an important one: Students' ability to consider others' perspectives contributes significantly to the quality of expository writing and, to an even greater extent, persuasive writing (Rubin & Rafoth, 1986). Second, her students' problems were not unique: Inexperienced college writers and basic writers engage in far less thinking about their readers' thoughts, beliefs, and knowledge than expert writers (Flower, 1979; Lunsford, 1979).

To focus student response on others' perspectives, the project group developed the idea of a role-playing activity in which students would play devil's advocate to each other – an activity in which a partner would take the opposite point of view to a writer's points. We hoped this activity would make students more aware of the divergent points of view of their readers.[12] Using conversational partners to help students see other perspectives and to elaborate their own positions is a widespread technique in teaching writing (see Rubin & Dodd, 1987, for a review). Although research that specifically addresses the effectiveness of the technique for writing and for different sorts of students is scant, the research that has been conducted is encouraging (Chandler, 1973; Wagner, 1987).

Once the group decided to try an activity, they explicitly discussed whether or not it was appropriate to do it concurrently over the network, analyzing the design trade-offs among various alternatives such as doing the activity face-to-face or nonconcurrently. Although the goal of the project team was to integrate concurrent network activities into writing courses at CMU, the project team wanted to avoid seeing ENFI as a "technological imperative," that is, restricting the design choices and design criteria to concurrent network activity alone, so that classroom activities would be subordinated to the technology (cf. Cummings, 1981).

The group discussed the following costs of using a computer to do any assignment rather than working face-to-face: It is much slower to communicate in writing than face-to-face,[13] it is more difficult to be responsive to another person's ideas (Kiesler et al., 1985), and there is the likelihood of technical problems. The group also discussed the finding that people communicating by computer generate more conflicts than those communicating face-to-face (Kiesler, Siegel, & McGuire, 1984). They were unable to agree, however, on whether the finding would apply to the proposed devil's advocate activity and, if it did, whether the result would be negative (students would flame) or positive (students would be more willing to generate opposition).

Next the group discussed whether this activity should be done concurrently, rather than using a nonconcurrent network tool such as the Comments program. Although the pressures of concurrent interaction would give the participants less time to think about their responses than they might noncon-

---

[12] The devil's advocate activity was one of many that the group explored during the pilot semester. In the following, we use it to illustrate the development of ENFI at CMU.

[13] Kiesler et al. (1985) report "the face-to-face pairs said 9 times as many words as did the computer-conversing pairs, . . . they made 6 times the number of remarks, . . . but answered just twice as many questions directed by the guide." On the other hand, Fondacaro and Higgins (1985) report studies indicating that written messages are more efficient, concise, and nonredundant than oral ones.

currently, the group identified two reasons for doing the devil's advocate activity concurrently. First, the give-and-take of a concurrent interaction, in which the writer responds *immediately* to the devil, seemed as though it would make it easier for the devils to modify their opposition, in order to take the writers' counterstatements into account (e.g., concede a point), with the result that writers would be more likely to feel that the devils were opposing their *actual* positions. Second, the nonconcurrent interaction requires the students to write their lines of argument down *before* interacting, whereas the concurrent requires only that they be able to sketch a line of argument *during* interaction. Because of the effort involved in producing a written draft for a line of argument before interaction, some of the writers might be quite committed to their drafts and thus less likely to change them in order to respond to the devils' perspectives. Although not concerned with commitment generated through the effort involved in writing, a study by Kiesler (1971) indicates that people who advocate their own opinion on an issue are more resistant to subsequent counterattacks on their position if the circumstances surrounding the production of their messages increased their commitment to them.

For the devil's advocate activity, the instructor decided to use the network rather than face-to-face communication so that she could more easily monitor students' interactions to see whether the activity was "working" for them. She decided to use the concurrent network tool rather than the nonconcurrent tool because she wanted students to work with sketches for lines of argument developed during interaction.

Formative assessment of the experience

In addition to discussing course goals and ways to meet them, the project group meetings involved evaluating the success of ENFI activities that the instructor had tried in previous weeks. The group attempted to come to a mutual agreement on the usefulness of the activity generally in light of the instructor's pedagogical goals, the instructor's strengths and weaknesses as a teacher, and other classroom constraints such as problems with the technology and so forth.

The basic strategy for gathering material for assessment was a combination of field and laboratory research methods. In the pilot semester, members of the project team tracked a small number of students and their teacher with open-ended interviews (Dexter, 1970) and observed the ENFI classroom (Goetz & LeCompte, 1984; Lofland, 1984).

The interviews were open-ended to allow for unanticipated response, but included questions about perceived problems writing with the computer network and questions about students' perceptions of the effective, social, and cognitive consequences of using a computer network. The interviews, which were tape-recorded and transcribed for analysis, focused on four students, the maximum number that the project team felt they could follow effectively. These focus students were selected on the basis of their performance on a diagnostic essay given in the initial week of class. The project team chose two higher achieving and two lower achieving students who also differed in gender. The interviews formed the basis for creating a closed-form questionnaire that was administered to the remaining 10 class members at the end of the semester.

Classroom observers attempted to be minimally obtrusive and nonreactive. One of the members of the project team attended classes, recording impressions of the verbal and nonverbal interaction between the teacher and students. The team also collected ENFI transcripts and student drafts.

The following sections present the results of our interviews and observations for the devil's advocate activity. The discussion is divided into two major sections: (1) results of writing together – responses to the devil's advocate activity itself, which can influence responses to doing the activity on a network; and (2) results of writing together concurrently on a computer network – responses to doing the devil's advocate activity with concurrent network communication.

Results of writing together

The responses of the students and the instructor to the devil's advocate activity itself were, on the whole, positive. The following excerpt from a concurrent network transcript illustrates an interaction in which the project group felt students had moved beyond mere rote performance for the teacher to one in which they had been empowered to learn from one another's perspectives:[14]

STUDENT 1: I plan to do my proposal on the problem of tuition. CMU plans to raise tuition next year and I don't think it is necessary. . . .

STUDENT 2: What are you going to do when they say they are raising it because of rising costs that they have to meet or inflation?

STUDENT 1: I am not sure but, I think that tuition is too high already. I might propose that they spend the money more wisely. They might be using the money for one thing when they should be using it for another.

STUDENT 2: I agree, one thing you might say is the money that was spent laying the new track down last year. It was not even used by the track team once. It now going to be ripped up, I am sure that investment cost near 100,000 dollars, this is an example of spending money nonwisely.

Not all students were successful, however, with some expressing uncertainty in the interviews about what they ought to have been doing:

---

[14] Excerpts from students' writing on the network are reproduced as written, with typos, mispellings, and so forth.

We had to wait until . . . [the instructor] came around and like we had to ask her exactly what she was looking for. So that was more a problem with the assignment than really with the computers. But then again, too, by the time we got started we didn't have that much time to work on it. [S12]

The transcripts suggested that even the most successful pairs were not always engaged in the devil's advocate task, although what they were doing was generally on the task of formulating a proposal and perhaps helpful:[15]

STUDENT 2: My proposal is the possibility of getting a computerized bulletin board so as to get rid of the messy bulletin boards and litter on campus.

STUDENT 1: This sounds like a good plan, it would be a good idea to cut down on the litter from the bulletin boards we have now. You also might want to talk about the problem of bulletin boards we have now. There is a lot of competition among the frats to get party signs up. Rival frats tear each others signs down.

Despite these difficulties, the instructor thought that the devil's advocate role-playing activity facilitated social processes of learning that she had not been able to fully realize before using collaborative activities in which students were free to give any response rather than play a role:

I asked them, "Okay. Well challenge so-and-so's idea. Give them the other side of it." When they did that, they had to become involved. In a sense, they had to look at what the other person said and, in some way, frame a question that was going to take on someone's view. And it caused them to engage with the text for a little while at least. And I felt that got them more involved in what they did.

Focus students also saw role playing as more useful than free collaboration because it motivated them to elaborate and justify their opinions. They saw it as helping them to locate specific points in their texts where they needed to make substantial changes, or even places where they needed to reassess the validity of their own points of view:

I think that was a good activity because a lot of times, if someone is going to be taking something that you do, they don't tend to put in things like that – like playing devil's advocate. They tend more just to tell you, "Well, this sounds a little wordy, this sounds a little confusing, get a stronger idea, get this, get that." But with something like that – where you're playing devil's advocate – I think it helps to really make you see that you have to make your point stronger or that you have to change certain things or you really have to explore something deeper. . . . So I think that's a help. [S12]

The activity seemed also to increase their awareness of views other than their own, as expressed by another student:

[15] The value of this kind of substantive facilitation in learning to write is unknown (cf. Scardamalia & Bereiter, 1985).

Well it seems like it's a good idea because I get a sense of what other people might be thinking about my paper and what specific questions I'll need to address. . . . We had to take into account what our audience – what knowledge and attitudes they're going to have – and . . . – I'm just guessing really – by playing devil's advocate my partner was able to give me more information and a clearer idea of what people – what types of questions and what types of knowledge and attitudes that other people will have. So I'm able to get – I'll know more of what I need to address. [S1]

For another student, the activity seemed to have helped him see, perhaps for the first time, a crucial rhetorical premise – his interpretations do not necessarily match his reader's – a premise that is most likely necessary for the development of audience-centered communication:

I saw how what I think isn't always right. What I understand about other ideas and what everyone else sees isn't always – how when I run into something, I'll interpret it and I know exactly what I'm trying to say, but when someone else reads it, they might not get the same message from it that I'm thinking. [S9]

Results of writing together concurrently on a network

Besides seeing the devil's advocate activity itself as valuable, the instructor felt that doing the activity on a network was extremely useful because the transcripts substantially increased the ease with which she could obtain information about the activity's success:

I had to see the transcripts because there's no way I could judge other than the sense when you're walking around the room of whether or not . . . they are on-task. Once I could see the transcripts, then I could make some evaluation as to whether it really was a successful activity. How well did they participate and what did they get out of it and how well could that carry over into future writing assignments?

The instructor saw the concurrent network activity, in particular the resulting transcripts, as a way to clarify and refine students' collaborative skill – one of the central skills of the course. Although the instructor valued the transcripts as a means for her to monitor and facilitate students' acquisition of this skill, none of the focus students shared her perceptions. Many were clearly uncertain about the utility of working concurrently on a network, seeing only limited value or no reason at all why it was useful to do the activity on a network rather than face-to-face:

Well, . . . I just printed out a copy and gave it to the teacher. So, unless there's a memory benefit and seeing it on the screen – over hearing it – I don't know if there's really much of an advantage. [S1]
I don't see why you have to use the program – why you can't just say it. . . . I have a harder time typing – that's why. . . . I'm not a good typists. [S9]

The following sections explore students' perceptions of the negative and positive aspects of writing together concurrently on a network in more detail.

Negative aspects of concurrent network interaction

Negative aspects of concurrent network interaction include problems with the technology and problems with discourse production on the network.

Increased problems with technology. Kling (1980) observes, "Computing technology is often portrayed as a 'problem solver,' but in routine use it is as much a 'problem generator.' " Because instructors at CMU have complete discretion over their use of computing in classrooms, problems with technology can play a significant role in the spread of any computing innovation. The project team identified three problematic aspects of the computing systems design that influenced the patterns of concurrent network interaction and the quality of classroom life: the complexity of the network technology, the instructor's and students' computer literacy, and classroom computing access.

Complexity of network technology. Relying on a personal computer network can introduce more computer problems to the classroom than relying on stand-alone personal computers. A network crash disrupts a computer-based classroom to a degree that a single computer crash does not. In trying to use concurrent network interaction, students and the instructor confronted the frustrations of network failure. As one student reported:

Well, first of all, ours was a disaster because that day most of the computers weren't working [the Andrew network was down] so we were just supposed to work on it, you know, just speaking as a group [face-to-face]. [S9]

Computer literacy. Carnegie Mellon's educational computing environment is diverse and complex (with vendor-specific LANs as well as a campuswide network, IBM PCs, Macintoshes and advanced function workstations, DOS and Unix operating systems, etc.)[16] Not surprisingly, some training to help members of the campus community negotiate and manage such a diverse and changing environment is critical. The nature of this training – both for students and their teachers – affected ENFI at CMU.

All freshmen who do not exempt are required to take Computing Skills Workshop (CSW) in their first semester. The one-credit course introduces them to IBM PCs, Macintoshes, and Andrew mail and bulletin boards. Partly as a result of this training, almost every CMU student uses computing in

---

[16] The research and administrative computing environments add further diversity and complexity.

some way. For example, most students in the Humanities and Social Science College use computing for word processing and many use it for statistical analysis and for communicating via electronic mail and bulletin boards. For students taking writing in the first semester,[17] however, the training co-occurs with their use of writing tools in the computer-based sections. Moreover, students learn the various systems at different times: Some learn Andrew first, others the Macintosh first.[18] In addition, the instructor, although experienced with computer-based classroom teaching, found learning the diverse and complex CMU system problematic. This state of affairs led to minor but disturbing turmoil in the classroom as students and teachers struggled with the basics:

Well it seemed that for, for the first few sessions people weren't clear on how to get on [the Andrew system]. I mean a few people had done it in CSW and had learned how to do it, so there wasn't *much* problem, but . . . [S1]

Because training in computing systems is concurrent with writing classes, there was some goal displacement: At the beginning of the semester, the instructor spent some class time teaching computing rather than writing.

Computer lab scheduling. Carnegie Mellon does not have dedicated computer classrooms. Instead, instructors can schedule classroom time in public clusters. The total number of reservations per cluster per semester, however, is limited and reservation requests are filled on a first-come, first-serve basis. Moreover, reservations must be made at least 2 weeks in advance, although it is sometimes possible to have exceptions made. In response to this policy, most instructors usually schedule their computer-based classes to meet twice a week in a traditional classroom and once a week in the computer "lab." This arrangement had some dysfunctional consequences in the pilot section: Sometimes the instructor did not do a concurrent network interaction activity because she was not scheduled for the lab on the day she would have wanted to do the activity; at other times she cancelled the lab meeting and held class in the traditional classroom because the activity she wanted to do was not suited to concurrent network interaction.

Decreased discourse production. Besides the negative aspects associated with computer network technology, the project team's interviews indicated that students were perceiving some negative cognitive effects. For example, some students, even self-reported good typists, mentioned a drop in the effective-

---

[17] In general, students *elect* to enroll in a computer-based writing section; they are not required to do so.
[18] Attempts in earlier semesters to schedule all students in the computer-based writing sections into a CSW section that taught Andrew first did not work due to conflicts with students' schedules.

ness of their discourse production, sometimes explicitly alluding to problems with memory:

STUDENT: It's just I can't express my train of thought as well, you know, typing it down because it's just too slow by the time you type it out and I can't explain it as well as I can verbally. So it's easier for me to like explain something to someone and let them take whatever little notes or whatever, you know, reminders that they need to re-mind them later on of what I said. [S12]

INTERVIEWER: Now is this because of typing or is it because of writing?

STUDENT: No it's just like, I mean, even though it's not a significant amount of time – it's just – it's not my typing skills because they're fine. It's just like the amount of time. I don't know. I just think I express myself verbally better than I can, you know, written. [S12]

Students' reports are consistent with empirical research. Forgetting what one was going to say may be a more significant factor in writing than in speaking because of short-term memory loss brought on by the slower rate of production (Bereiter & Scardamalia, 1987).

Positive aspects of concurrent network interaction

Although students reported numerous problems with concurrent network interaction, they reported some benefits as well: decreased communication anxiety and increased dialogue comprehension, both during and after the interaction.

Decreased communication anxiety. One student, who seemed to experience a significant amount of anxiety in face-to-face interaction, felt that computer-mediated communication was less threatening and helped him maintain his personal dignity:[19]

Sitting face-to-face is a little more threatening than being at the computer . . . um . . . your voice doesn't break up . . . your, you know, you don't – if you break out in a sweat the other person [mumbled] and you can be as calm and collected as you wanted to be. . . . [N3]

The reduced communication anxiety for this student may have helped him be more responsive to his devil's advocate partner:

The [computer-mediated interaction] was a little easier because I could take the ideas she was giving me and . . . um . . . kinda refute them. I didn't ask any questions in the [face-to-face] session . . . in the [concurrent network] one I asked her – for example – she said . . . that . . . that she could never possibly believe how hard it was to come to college . . . so then I asked, "Well, if you

---

[19] This student was a participant in a study of the devil's advocate activity, not a focal student in the pilot section.

had the chance would you come to it again . . . to Carnegie Mellon?" . . . to see – because she, you know, I . . . I found that like kind of contradictory . . . because she said that . . . she said that it's such a wonderful place . . . not really contradictory . . . I just wanted to see her explanation. . . . " [N3]

Kiesler et al. (1985), however, found no support for their hypothesis that subjects engaging in computer-mediated communication would feel less anxious and threatened than in face-to-face communication, perhaps because face-to-face communication produces very little anxiety in the first place for most people.

Increased dialogue comprehension during the interaction. Several students reported that having the dialogue available for review promoted their ability to comprehend it and reason about it during the interaction itself:

STUDENT: You can see what you've said and you can go back and look at your different comments or his comments and they're up there for as long as you need to look at them. So that's nice. [S9]
INTERVIEWER: Did that help you for this particular assignment?
STUDENT: Yeah, it did because he'd [my partner] make a new comment about a new idea and I'd say – I looked up at the computer and – "You said you would do this before. Now you're saying you agree to do this," and so it's useful to see the whole dialogue on the screen. . . . That's one of the advantages of a computer over conversing . . . once it's up there though you can look at it and break it down and ask questions about certain parts of it. [S9]

Students' reports are consistent with historical research. Historians of literacy have argued that because the permanence of writing permits review of what has been written and reflection upon it, it facilitates logical analysis and even changes the shape of discourse itself (Goody & Watt, 1963; Havelock, 1976).

Increased dialogue comprehension after the interaction. Research suggests that the labels communicators give to messages can result in later distortion of the actual content of the message, so that the recalled message is compatible with the message *label* rather than the original message (cf. Bartlett, 1932; Higgins, McCann, & Fondacaro, 1982). Consistent with this research, our exploratory observations suggested that students who talk face-to-face tend not to jot down remarks with which they disagree, and they tend not to address those points in revisions of their drafts. Because the interaction is verbal and ephemeral, it is difficult for participants to reflect on their own interpretations of the interaction, even when they try to take notes.

Thus we were very interested in seeing whether having a written record of collaborative interactions would benefit writers by enabling them to refer to remarks, reflect on them, and address them while writing. As in other problem-solving tasks, such a written record would act as an external representation that might significantly influence participants' success.[20] In the pilot semester, however, even students who reported revising their papers to reconcile other's perspectives did not report using the written transcript:

STUDENT: Well I changed what he didn't find clear to make it so anyone could actually understand it, or interpret it. [S9]

INTERVIEWER: Okay and... how exactly did you go about using the comments, did you...?

STUDENT: Well I just remembered, and... I just circled them [in the draft] ... – things that I would probably change. [S9]

Students' decisions to forego using the written record may have been due to problems with the software that surfaced in actual use. Although the technical problems under the project group's control were alleviated by the end of the semester, they seem to have contributed to students not using the logs, as evidenced by this student's comments:

I did it from memory. I haven't used any [logs], because a couple of my logs didn't even work and then a couple of times the computers were down and I think that once, too, something was wrong with the memory in her [my partner's] computer and it wouldn't print and she had logged into mine and so there always seemed to be some type of problem when I was using the printout. So either I'll just make a note to myself after class or, you know, I'll just remember it and when I'm, you know, working on the paper do it. [S12]

During the course of the semester, the instructor, who was concerned that the network activities were not intelligible to students, increased her efforts to make the transcripts meaningful by telling them about the uses she saw for them, for example, in revision:

One of the things I definitely learned was... I had to make them [the students] responsible for the transcripts – so the transcripts meant something to them, so this written record they were producing had some significance.

Although it was late in the semester, the team found some evidence that these efforts were having an effect on students' perceptions:

One thing that I consider useful is that... now I can go back and look at what his [my peer reviewer's] points were, whereas if he was just talking I doubt that I would have written down really what he had said. [S1]

Codification of the experience

An important period of work with ENFI activities occurred after they were being used with students. At this point, the project group began discussing

---

[20] See Neuwirth, Palmquist, and Hajduk (1990) for a study that examines this hypothesis systematically.

what needed to be changed so that students would find the activities more useful. This process of trying to understand how to make ENFI activities more useful led the instructor to reassess her pedagogy, especially her communication with students about what they were supposed to be doing and why they were doing network activities:

What I didn't anticipate is to set up an activity. . . . I had not . . . give[n] them [the students] the whole sense of theory as to why they were doing it. . . . And so, you know, what I see now is – if you say it in a whole context, give them an example, a reason, and say why you're doing it – model it before – then when they're performing the activity . . . then they've seen it demonstrated – they see the context for it . . . and it takes on a whole meaning.

Together with the project team, the instructor developed the following tactics for improving the usefulness of concurrent network activities, drawing upon techniques of "reciprocal teaching" (Palinscar & Brown, 1984), reflective processing (Scardamalia, Bereiter, & Steinbach, 1984), and "cognitive apprenticeship" (Brown, Collins, & Duguid, 1989):

- *Talk with students about the advantages and disadvantages of the activity on the network.* This talk usually took the form of whole-class discussion, both before and after any concurrent network activity.
- *Provide students with example interactions to study before they work on the network.* These took the form of annotated transcripts.
- *Model the process for students.* Sometimes the instructor modeled an activity with another student in front of the class; sometimes the instructor asked a group of students to model the activity while the instructor coached them.
- *Guide students' practice.* This usually took the form of the instructor actively using the transcripts to comment on students' performance – sometimes in small groups, sometimes in whole-class discussions.
- *Show students how to use the transcripts when writing drafts of their papers.* This tactic took the form of giving students example, annotated transcripts, having whole-class discussions, and working one-on-one with individual students.

These tactics were codified in a set of supporting materials for class use (see the appendix at the end of this chapter for an example of the devil's advocate material). One motivation for producing these materials was a long-term goal of maintaining concurrent network activities after the ENFI contract had ended. The practical significance of any technical innovation is dramatically improved if it can be implemented under conditions approaching those of a normal classroom, one in which members of the project team would not meet weekly with instructors, for instance. The institutional context also motivated the project team's development of these guides. The freshmen writing courses involved in the ENFI project are primarily taught by graduate students in the department's two doctoral programs: Literary and Cultural

Theory (LCT) and Rhetoric. Members of this group vary considerably in their experience as teachers, in their attitudes toward technology and experience with it, and, consequently, in their ability to reason about how to use it effectively. The existence of technical problems was also a motivation. If students could do the concurrent network activities on their own, outside of class, like they did word processing and nonconcurrent network activities, then instructors would not have to deal with disruptions of entire classes due to technical problems (e.g., slowness due to unfamiliarity with the system, network crashes) and might be more willing to ask students to try ENFI activities. Although students working alone would face similar problems, individual help for students working in the labs is available,[21] and there would not be additional problems arising from students not having enough time to complete the activity in class, for example, students who know the technology well having to wait for those who do not.

Finally, and perhaps most importantly, the research findings of Kiesler et al. (1985) concerning the negative affect of informal computer-mediated communication also motivated the project team. Experience at our site as well as at other ENFI sites suggested that uninhibited behavior (e.g., swearing) on the network indeed occurred in classrooms and was highly disturbing to some teachers and students (cf. Kremers, 1988). This phenomenon raises serious concerns for teachers and researchers interested in the potential of computer-mediated communication for teaching writing. Our own experience suggested, however, that such behavior significantly decreased for more structured writing tasks. In addition, the project team conducted a partial replication of the Kiesler et al. study, with a more structured writing task rather than an informal, interpersonal communication task and failed to find effects for negative affect and uninhibited behavior[22] (Neuwirth, Palmquist, & Cochran, 1989). Given the potential for negative impact of computer-mediated communication, members of the project team felt that it was important, especially for a population of inexperienced teachers, to provide strong models for effective uses of concurrent communication.

Members of the project team eventually produced a set of instructor and student guides for using concurrent network interaction (Neuwirth, Gillespie, & Palmquist, 1988; Neuwirth, Palmquist, & Gillespie, 1988). These materials were intended to give students reasons for both collaborating and collaborating on the network and to model collaborative activities so students' uncertainties about what they were supposed to do would be reduced.

The instructor's guides provided suggestions for working with concurrent

---

[21] CMU computing labs are staffed by consultants to help students deal with technical problems.

[22] A post hoc analysis indicated a high probability that the study had enough power to have seen a difference, had one been there.

network activities and implementing specific activities, emphasizing the following reasons for doing collaboration on the network:

- More effective monitoring of collaborative activities because of the written record
- More detailed response to the group's performance because of the availability of concrete incidents and examples
- More detailed response to individual's performance (Slavin, 1980, for example, underscores the need to structure collaborative learning so that individuals are accountable.)
- Better understanding of the response dialogues and better revisions because of the opportunity for reflection and review

The activities in the guides were those that the project team and students judged most useful:

- Brainstorming
- Role playing, including Devil's Advocate
- Questioning, summarizing, requesting clarifications, and predicting by a reader
- Discussing a draft of a paper with a partner

The student guides provided an introduction to the activities and their purposes, a discussion of the advantages and disadvantages of doing the activities on a network, annotated examples, and a discussion of how to use transcripts in writing papers.

The project team continued to incorporate changes in the materials during the following semester. This in itself is not surprising – incremental course revisions are not atypical in any teaching. But modifications and refinements, although part and parcel of teaching, may also reflect the project group's being able to see so easily – via the transcripts – what students were doing with the materials.

Summative assessment of the experience

During the pilot semester, the project team was continually trying out activities and developing instructional supports for them in response to numerous problems. The instructor's assessment, although positive, alluded to only some of the difficulties:

It was a good trial run. I ended up – a lot of it – it's difficult to separate how much of the problem came out of my not knowing how to deal with computers – how much came out of my not knowing how to deal exactly with collaboration, and how much came out of my not knowing how to teach that to a real class because – the units and everything. . . . I'd say it was problematic but it was problematic in a constructive way in that I learned a lot from it and I don't think the students, you know, were irreversibly harmed.

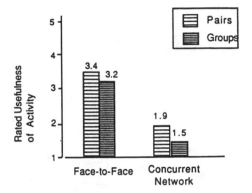

Figure 10-2. Students' ratings of usefulness of face-to-face versus concurrent network activities for pairs and small groups in the formative semester

Although students' evaluations of the course as a whole were positive, as were their evaluations of face-to-face collaborative activities, their evaluations of concurrent network activities were negative. The project team asked students to rate the usefulness of activities on a 6-point scale (0 = *not useful*, 5 = *very useful*). As Figure 10–2 depicts, students' mean ratings ($N = 10$)[23] of working together *face-to-face* were positive, both for pairs (3.4, *SD* = 0.8) and for small groups (3.2, *SD* = 1.0). However, their mean ratings of working together *computer-mediated* were negative, both for pairs (1.9, *SD* = 1.4) and small groups (1.5, *SD* = 1.3).

Although not encouraging, the project team felt that the numerous problems associated with learning how best to integrate concurrent network activities into the curriculum had influenced students' overall assessments of the usefulness of those activities. The project team knew that some problems, such as the nature of computer literacy training at CMU and the stability of the Andrew computer network, were outside their control and direct influence and would remain so. The project team thought that other problems, however, such as the students' uncertainty about what they ought to do and why they were doing it, had been significantly reduced over the course of the semester. The team decided to give ENFI another try in the spring semester. They believed that with the primary structure of ENFI activities developed and with the additional instructional supports in place, students might see some value to ENFI activities and, indeed, this turned out to be the case.

In the spring, members of the project team and the Department of Social

---

[23] We did not survey the four focal students because they have been interviewed. One student dropped.

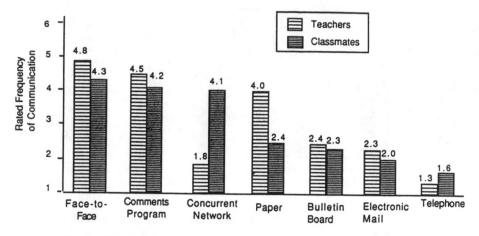

Figure 10-3. Students' ratings of frequency of communication with their teachers and classmates for various communication modes in the summative semester

and Decision Sciences pooled resources[24] to conduct a study of classrooms using network software, including ENFI (Hartman, Neuwirth, Kiesler, Sproull, Cochran, Palmquist, & Zubrow, 1991). The study examined the effects of using network technologies in learning to write on teacher–student and student–student interactions. Two sections of Strategies for Writing used traditional modes of communication (face-to-face, paper, phone); two other sections, in addition to using traditional modes, also used electronic modes, both concurrent (ENFI) and nonconcurrent (e-mail, bulletin boards, and Comments program). The research team measured patterns of social interaction at two times, 6 weeks into the semester and again at the end of the semester, by asking students to rate their frequency of communication with their teacher and with other students via the various modes on a 7-point scale (1 = *never*, 4 = *sometimes*, 7 = *very frequently*).

Results

Students' mean ratings of their use of the different communication modes at the end of the semester indicate that in the networked sections ($N = 36$), students interacted with their teachers via the concurrent network mode of communication only rarely (1.8, $SD = 1.3$). As depicted in Figure 10–3, student–teacher communication in the networked sections at the end of the semester was primarily face-to-face (4.8, $SD = 1.3$), paper (4.0, $SD = 4.0$),

[24] CMU's Committee on Social Science Research on Computing (CSSRC) provided additional funding to carry out this study.

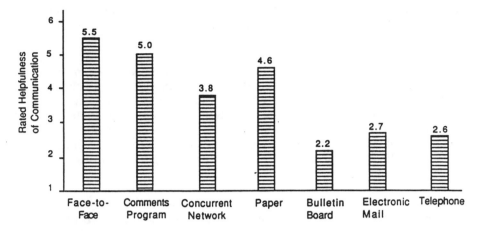

Figure 10-4. Students' ratings of helpfulness of communication for various communication modes in the summative semester

and nonconcurrent network communication via the Comments program (4.5, SD = 1.8).

On the other hand, students' mean ratings of their interactions with their classmates in the networked sections (N = 36) indicate that at the end of the semester they used face-to-face (4.3, SD = 1.5), Comments (4.2, SD = 1.6), and concurrent network (4.1, SD = 1.8) most frequently (see Figure 10–3).

Students were asked to rate the helpfulness of the various modes of inter-action (both with teachers and with classmates) on a 7-point scale (1 = *not at all helpful*, 4 = *somewhat helpful*, 7 = *very helpful*). As depicted in Figure 10–4, students in the networked sections rated the concurrent network as somewhat helpful (3.8, SD = 1.5, N = 33), but selected paired comparisons indicated that they rated it significantly lower (p < .05) than their ratings of face-to-face (5.8, SD = 1.4, N = 35), Comments program (5.0, SD = 1.5, N = 36), and paper (4.6, SD = 1.1, N = 34).

Discussion

The relatively low involvement of instructors on the network can be under-stood because their goal was that students would learn how to collaborate effectively – independently of the instructor. As one instructor reported telling students:

Try to look at this class not as just trying to get through here [the class], but [ask yourself] what kind of skills can you [the student] learn in here that would help you collaborate throughout the rest of your writing experience in any capacity.

The guides for using ENFI, which were in draft form, emphasized this conception of the teacher's role on the network as well, and interviews with instructors confirmed it:

And when you're wandering around the room trying to check groups, you miss so much of what's going on and the transcript gives me a chance to go back.... Sometimes when I see what they're doing, I'll say, "Hey. Take a look at your transcript. Something really great came up in there and you missed it." So, it gives me a handle on what's happening in the groups and I can see what they're doing and then that gives me a chance to kind of help work them back into ideas. And some of it's garbage, but most of the time they're on-task.

Students' perceptions of ENFI as only somewhat helpful compared to other modes (face-to-face, Comments, and paper) could be related to the low involvement of teachers in concurrent network interaction relative to their involvement in the other modes, given the tendency of the students to see their teacher's responses as most helpful (because teachers give the grade).

This study formally confirmed the pattern of interactions that we informally observed for teachers and students at CMU throughout the ENFI project.

Summary

Integrating concurrent network interaction into the writing courses at CMU involved four phases: exploration of designs, formative evaluation, codification of the experience, and summative evaluation. The addition of concurrent network interaction did not change the basic aims and structure of the courses in which it was implemented. Although it would have been possible to develop specific writing assignments with concurrent network interaction activities in mind, none were introduced. Rather, the development of the innovation at CMU strongly reflected the existing course goals and assignments, especially the goal of learning to collaborate effectively.

Students' perceptions of the value of concurrent network interaction varied, with some seeing no advantage over face-to-face interaction, and others seeing some use for increasing their comprehension of the unfolding dialogue and aiding their revisions. Students perceived disadvantages such as slowness, reduction in the effectiveness of their discourse production, and technical problems. Overall, students judged concurrent network interaction to be somewhat useful.

Instructors valued most highly the computer's ability to keep a record of the interaction, in particular, for its role in helping them to nurture an intellectual community through student-directed discussion of writing. Because of the disadvantages of concurrent network interaction and the existence of nonconcurrent alternatives, instructors tended to use the concurrent network for activities in which computer-mediated concurrency was *desirable,* not just possible.

The following are the hypothesized advantages and disadvantages for concurrent network interaction in educational settings similar to CMU:

Advantages	*Disadvantages*
More effective monitoring of collaborative activities because of the written record	Lower communication efficiency because of the written medium
More detailed response to group's performance because of availability of concrete incidents and examples	Less effective discourse production because of the written medium
More detailed response to individual's performance	Greater emotionality and more uninhibited remarks because of the written medium
Better understanding of response dialogues and better revisions because of the opportunity for reflection and review	Less reflective responses because of the pressures of interactive communication

Concurrent network interaction demonstrated a limited but positive value, but only when its disadvantages were counterbalanced with advantages and when instructors worked actively to supply needed instructional supports.

Appendix: Devil's advocate activity

The following is an excerpt from *A Student's Guide to Collaborative Writing with CECE Talk* (Neuwirth, Gillespie, & Palmquist, 1988):

A *devil's advocate* is a person who takes the opposite point of view for the sake of argument. As everyone knows, a person playing devil's advocate can quickly become a nuisance by constantly disagreeing with what you say. Although you wouldn't want to put up with this type of person for any extended period of time, responding to such an antagonist while discussing a paper you have written can often produce new and different insights for you. In addition to opening your eyes to new ideas and viewpoints, carrying on a discussion with a devil's advocate forces you to do your best at explaining and defending your position. In reviewing the log produced by the talk program after such a discussion, you may find that you have stated your position much better while discussing it than you had in what you had actually written.

Playing the role of devil's advocate can be a lot of fun, and is really quite easy. In general, you want to challenge the assertions made by the writer. The writer will then have to elaborate the point, by presenting arguments and evidence to support the stated view. When the writer begins to present solutions to the problem, you [should] propose alternate solutions (possibly far-fetched ones) so that the writer will have to argue why the proposed solution is better than the ones you offer. You may also propose a solution that the writer had not considered before, and [that] may be quite helpful to the goals of the paper. One important point to remember: When the writer has done a good job of stating a point, concede the argument and move on to another topic. Arguing a point to a stalemate will not be helpful to the writer. Below are some sample exchanges between a writer and a devil's advocate.

WRITER: In my paper, I say that the administration needs to do something about the quality of students' lives on campus.

DEVIL: I don't think it's the job of the administration to make improvements in the quality of life for the students on campus. What makes you think that the administration can do anything about it? (*State an opposing viewpoint: i.e., it's up to the students, not the administration.*)

WRITER: Well, I think that part of the reason the quality is so bad in the first place is because the administration places so much emphasis on academics, and not enough on the other aspects of a student's life. I think the administration can help balance these things out, by emphasizing the other aspects as well.

DEVIL: The students come here for academic training – that's what the school is here for. If they want to develop other interests, I would say it is up to the individual students to do this for themselves. (*Propose alternate solutions: i.e., The solution is not to have the administration de-emphasize its role, but instead, the students should take charge of their lives and develop other areas on their own.*)

WRITER: Well that might be true. But if the students are forced to spend so much time and energy on their studies, they don't have any spare time in which to pursue their other interests.

DEVIL: OK, I'll give you that small point! (*Concede to writer.*) Tell me what you think would improve the quality of life on campus. (*Move on.*)

WRITER: Well, first I say that one problem students have is lack of spare time. As a way of addressing this smaller problem, I suggest that the administration provide more activities on campus, so that it will be easy and quick for students to get to an event. This will also address a problem often cited by students – they can't "get" anywhere to do anything because they don't have transportation.

DEVIL: Oh, come on. I don't think that is a valid complaint for students to make. After all, there are buses or they could catch a ride with someone who does have a car. (*Challenge assertions.*)

WRITER: That may work for some of them, some of the time, but what about the others? I contend that if you consider the lack-of-time problem for some students along with the transportation problem for some students, you will see that the end product is still a problem. And this problem can be eased, if not solved, by the administration offering more events of interest to the students on campus.

DEVIL: OK, you win. I'll admit that more events on campus would contribute to an overall improvement in the quality of life on campus. *(Concede to writer.)* But that seems like a rather small effort on the part of the administration. What else do you propose they do? *(Move on.)*

Several points to remember

1. When the writer has done a good job of stating a point, concede the argument and move on to another topic. Arguing a point to a stalemate will not be helpful to the writer.

2. Even if you do agree with what the writer has stated, try to disagree by coming up with other ways of viewing the point, other possible solutions, etc.

3. When the writer is explaining his or her views, evidence, and solutions, ask for further information and clarifications as a way of helping the writer further elaborate the points of the paper.

11   One ENFI path: From Gallaudet to distance learning

Diane Thompson

After observing ENFI classes at Gallaudet University, I acquired an ENFI lab for my campus writing center at Northern Virginia Community College (NVCC). I ran my first ENFI classes closely imitating what I had seen at Gallaudet, but I was soon disappointed to find that ENFI did not work particularly well in my classroom. It was cumbersome, technically demanding, and not as obviously useful with hearing students as it had been with the deaf students at Gallaudet.

Consequently, I began to experiment with alternative ways of using the networked environment that supported ENFI. First I tried distance ENFI with groups, connecting my class to a similar class on another campus. This made sense in theory, because the distant students could only communicate in writing. However, the logistics of this two-class (and two-teacher) real-time connection were excessively complicated, and the actual connections were too difficult to coordinate.

My next attempt was to use the ability of the network to distribute text instantly from one student station to all student stations within the classroom. The students worked in small groups at a terminal, orally discussing and composing in writing a short text that was sent to the whole class for discussion. This was a modification of the original ENFI that worked well in my classroom.

Moving out of the classroom and beyond class time, I developed two further realizations of network communication that kept the spirit of ENFI (computer communications to encourage writing for one another), but were very different from the original ENFI pedagogy. One was the use of shared text files, so that groups could work on a single long file (such as a group research project), but each member could do at least some of the work at his or her convenience. This method used the ENFI network equipment, not in the class itself, but during open lab hours.

My final (so far) adaptation has left the ENFI lab entirely and uses the college mainframe, modems, and students' PCs to support a distant learning class that uses an asynchronous computer conference as a Public Journal. Students post assignments to this journal, read one another's assignments,

210

write comments to one another, and write back and forth to the teacher at any time they please.

These applications (and others to come, I am sure) have grown naturally out of the original ENFI inspiration – students could communicate with one another in writing – and the original ENFI environment – a networked computer writing lab. The common thread is computer-mediated written communication.

Discovering ENFI

I first heard of ENFI at the Conference on College Composition and Communication in 1985, following a session on collaborative classroom writing using word processors. Trent Batson introduced himself and told me about a computer network he was using for teaching English to deaf students by means of writing. He called it ENFI.

A few weeks later I visited Trent's ENFI classroom at Gallaudet University. Although in the midst of a poor section of Washington, DC, Gallaudet looks like a traditional college campus, lovely in the spring and wonderfully quiet. I was enchanted by the stillness, which was the silence of the deaf, not the silence of those with nothing to say.

The network was in a pleasant room. Five or six students, Trent among them, sat at computers arranged in an arc. Trent began writing, and students responded in writing. Their writing was direct, rough, even hostile at times; it seemed stronger and more free than the kind of writing generally found in a traditional English class. I was witnessing a miracle – deaf students actually conversing in English! I had a powerful desire to join in the network talk. My hands were yearning to write on the network, possess the network, teach on the network.

From that moment I was converted – a believer, blissfully unaware in my ignorance of either the realities of deaf communication or the complexities of computer communication. I was hooked.

I returned to my ordinary, unmagical, suburban community college campus absolutely determined to get a network like Trent's. For a few weeks I bothered everyone I knew at the college who had any power in such matters. I told them about the ENFI network, how it would revolutionize the teaching of English, how the college simply had to have networks. Then, out of the blue, the college set aside funds to establish new writing centers. My chairman asked for my equipment recommendation, and of course I said ENFI.

ENFI fit into the kind of teaching I was already doing: collaborative, computer-based, interactive, expressive. I felt certain that ENFI would help weak writers learn to generate written text; it seemed to be the perfect bridge between spoken and written language. I was experienced in teaching writing using stand-alone microcomputers, and it never occurred to me that networks were any different from bunches of computers strung together like beads on a wire.

Three of our five campuses bought ENFI-type networks for their writing centers. These were the first academic networks purchased by our college. We had not realized that this would be a problem, because we did not know that networks are complex, skittish, existing in a universe far beyond our technical capabilities. We had only one person on the entire college staff who was able to set up network directories, and he was responsible for the computers on all five campuses. There was no one on my campus who had ever managed or even used a network, no one to run to for quick advice, no one who could handle the complex directory of a network server. I have written at length elsewhere about the problems we had setting up and maintaining these networks (Thompson, 1990b), so I will focus here on my experience implementing ENFI as a teaching methodology.

Bringing ENFI to Northern Virginia Community College

I teach at the Woodbridge Campus of NVCC, an open admissions institution. The Woodbridge campus serves about 5,000 students in day and night classes, on and off campus, including two local military bases. Most of our day students are young, recently out of local high schools, and often plan to transfer to four-year degree programs at various Virginia colleges after a year or so at our campus. NVCC provides its faculty with a great deal of freedom to experiment because of the nature of the campuses and the general organization of the college, which is composed of five campuses, each with its own developmental English and/or English department. Although all five campuses cooperate on curriculum through collegewide discipline clusters and curriculum guidelines, each campus has a great deal of autonomy when it comes to setting the tone and form of particular courses.

Writing courses are taught either by full-time faculty or by lecturers. Because we have no graduate assistants, there is no group of junior instructors to be supervised. Furthermore, because we are a two-year school, the majority of our English courses are in writing, not literature, so there is no literature elite to dominate the writing program, as is often the case at senior colleges. Consequently, there is no person or group of persons to tell the rest of the composition teachers what to teach or how to teach it, and there is great scope for individual variation, experimentation, and creativity.

My campus is especially congenial to experimentation. My provost and my former and present division chairs have all supported computer applications in the humanities. My division is strongly egalitarian and supports individual faculty's rights to design and implement courses according to their best judgment. Consequently, faculty are able to use any textbooks they select, or no books at all, teach in a computer lab, send students to a computer lab, or use no computers at all, depending on their estimations of the course and student needs.

Replication of "classic" ENFI

Those students who do not pass our department's English Placement Test enroll in Developmental English. This is an intensive writing course that focuses on developing expressiveness and fluency in writing, not on grammar as such. It has a desired class size of 17. This course is smaller than our regular composition courses and more amenable to experimentation because the students do not have to be graded, nor do they have an exit exam to force the teaching of grammar rules. They only need to write sufficiently better by the end of the course to be able, in the teacher's judgment, to do the required work in Freshman Composition at the level of a "C" student. These developmental students are also more willing to collaborate than those in Freshman Composition, since they welcome the support of their peers and are not competing for grades.

Our new writing center had been able to afford a total of only seven networked computers to start the lab, so I divided one developmental class into two sub-sections, one of 6 students and one of 12, and met them at different times in order to teach ENFI as Trent did it at Gallaudet. The smaller class was able to have one student at each computer station; the larger class had two students at each station. Because these two sections were in fact only a single class, I still had to teach four additional classes to make up my five-class teaching load. Consequently, these tiny classes could only be an experiment, not a standard method of teaching.

My goal was to imitate Trent's ENFI pedagogy, where each student and the teacher sit at a terminal and converse with one another by writing messages in real time. The jointly produced text is read by all participants and stimulates further written discourse, providing a bridge between immediate interactive speech (or, in the case of deaf students, sign) communication and more formal writing.

My first two ENFI classes were as close to perfect imitations of Trent's (which I now think of as "classic" ENFI) as I could make them. I did not even speak on the first day. I sat at a computer and wrote a welcome to the students as they entered the classroom. I waved them to the computers and wrote to them to start writing. Our network conversation began as follows:[1]

DIANE: I am your teacher and this is english 001 you can read what I write
           and you can write to me to get a message sent, just press the key

---

[1] In this and following examples some lines are omitted for brevity's sake. Otherwise, responses appear exactly as they were typed.

labeled "F10" it is in the lower left hand side of your screen well, doesn't anyone have anything to write/say? Tell me your names and where you come from for a start

JOHN	JOHN
DIANE:	My name is Diane and I like to teach writing on computers because it is easier than by hand
ANDREA:	my name is andrea, I LIVE IN DALE City.
DIANE:	do any of you have a computer at home? hi andrea, I live in Reston
JOHN:	no
DIANE:	John, have you ever used a computer?
ANDREA:	YES, but I don't know how to use it.
JOHN:	no but i have typed before.

I went on to explain in writing what ENFI was and why it would help them to become better writers. We wrote to one another throughout that first period and much of the ensuing quarter.

This approach was exhausting for me, since I took on the burden of responding to each student's comments. I had quickly realized that if I did not respond to each student, his or her comments might disappear from the screen without anyone responding to them. This would make the students feel bad, and me worse. Consequently, I was continually carrying on six dialogues, one with each workstation, instead of a single-group discourse (Thompson, 1988b). By the end of a class session, I was weary from the concentration it took for me to keep track of and respond to multiple dialogues.

Most of the students seemed to enjoy the class, and they were certainly doing a lot of writing, both on and off the network. Part of their enthusiasm, as well as mine, was probably a response to my constant boosterism as I explained (in writing) over and over how much this sort of interactive writing would help them to become better writers.

The smaller class of six, which had only one student at each terminal, remained eerily silent, rather like the class I had observed at Gallaudet. The students stared quietly at the screen as we wrote. We wrote stories and brainstormed and generated beginnings for various papers. I was very satisfied with their work. This was ENFI as Trent did it; the students were indeed talking in writing, or so I thought at the time. Following is a typical example from the second ENFI session of the smaller class:

DIANE:	First, I wonder how many of you have jobs Could each of you write a sentence or two about what you do to earn money?
ANDREA:	I work at Pizza Hut, in Dale City. This is my way of earning money. Sometimes I will babysit to earn money.
DIANE:	How many hours a week do you work, Andrea?

ANDREA:	About 19 to 20 hours per week.
JOAN:	Inorder for me to earn money I learned to manage it. With the money that remains I can use as I see fit.
DIANE:	That's a lot of hours when you go to school. How many credits are you taking?
JOHN:	I am working at Ross store as a sales person.
DIANE:	But how do you earn it in the first place, Joan? John, how many hours do you work? What is Ross store? What do you sell there, John?
JOHN:	I put in about 27 to 30 a week.
MIKE:	Is that store at Potomac Mills Mall John?

Joan, an assertive older woman in the class, complained that the network talk was a waste of time, but the other five members of this class went along cheerfully and quickly learned to enter into the discourse, as Mike did when he asked John whether the store was at Potomac Mills Mall.

The larger class of 12 was more of a problem. The two students at each workstation inevitably talked to one another about what they were reading on the screen and conferred about what to write. This was not classic ENFI, but I felt I had no alternative, because the students had to talk in order to write together. Even these students, though, spent much of their time staring rather quietly at the screen and writing obliging responses to my many questions, as in this example from the eighth week of instruction:

TEACHER:	ok, hello everyone, sign on and tell us who you are
SUSAN:	Hey, I'm Susan and I'm fine.
PETE:	Hi I'm Pete Smith and that about it
LEE:	lee and Robert
JAMES:	I'm James Peterson
CARL:	Hi, my name is Carl Grimes
TEACHER:	Hi, Susan and Pete and Lee and Robert and James. Who else is there?
CHEE:	h
TEACHER:	Hi, Carl and chee ok, today I want you to think about something you have an opinion about How many of you like lieutenant Oliver North? Do you know who he is?
PETE:	no
JAMES:	no
CHEE:	No
LEE:	no
CARL:	I think he is just a skapp goat.
TEACHER:	Pete, have you heard about the arms we were selling to Iran?
PETE:	yes

SUSAN: I don't know about him enough to say
LEE: hes helping hostages

The students did what I asked of them – they wrote responses to my questions. But their oral conversations with their partners used up as much or more time and words than their written discourse with the class on the network.

Because they orally discussed each question I asked before responding to it in writing, the written discourse built slowly; this slowed down my ability to manage the discussion. For example, using the network instead of speech, it took me a while to realize that Irangate was not a useful topic because the students were generally unaware of the hottest political issue of the fall of 1986. If we had been talking, the sudden silence and blank faces would have quickly informed me that this topic was not going to get us anywhere, but on ENFI I kept the class on the topic for a while longer, until I was quite sure that we were getting nowhere, slowly.

Despite the unavoidable deviation from classic ENFI and the slowness of the process of writing instead of talking, I was satisfied with the progress of the larger class too. I was sure that the writing of both classes was improving, and it seemed to me that these ENFI students wrote more papers and did more revisions than the students in any previous developmental classes I had taught. I was pleased, yet weary from all the effort I was putting into the interactions.

I also had come to realize that a significant component of classic ENFI as Trent did it was Trent himself. He was a splendid group facilitator who took on various roles easily and happily, including Ogre. As Ogre, Trent was able to prod and stimulate students during network discourse. I began to realize that whereas Trent was able to focus on the topic of the discussion, I was constantly trying to make sure that each and every student felt included and responded to. My personality and teaching style made it harder for me to facilitate ENFI discussions.

Further, I found it awkward to express complex ideas on ENFI. It took too much time to write them out, and once they were sent, a few casual responses pushed the original message up off the screen, which made it difficult to keep a discussion focused on a previous statement. For example, when discussing revision, I started with a deliberately blowsy sentence to encourage students to revise it:

DIANE: Say I write a long clumsy sentence about wanting to talk about
            revising and then I ask you to revise my sentence. What would you
            do?
CONAN: simplify it.
DIANE: good, conan. How would you simplify it?
JOAN: rewrite it
DIANE: Yes, joan, but what do you do when you rewrite a sentence?
CONAN: take out works that don't really mean anything.

GUMBY: that right conan
DIANE: Yes, take out words that don't really mean anything. Good. What else?
What if, even if my sentence is long, it doesn't tell the reader enough to make sense to her?

At this point, the 14 lines available on the screen were used and the original long clumsy sentence was scrolled up off the top of the screen to make room as new messages appeared at the bottom. It was possible, using the scroll function, to retrieve the earlier sentence, but while that was going on, no new writing could be done. A paper copy of the sentence, handed around for discussion, would have been a more effective way to post it for revision. Consequently, I tended to develop narrative discussion topics for the ENFI classes, such as story generation, rather than analytic topics that required remembering what had been written earlier.

One day late in the quarter, feeling tired and frustrated, I simply turned my chair around and started TALKING to the class! We were surprised. I was elated. I had truly forgotten about talk. I could talk. My students could talk. There was no need to make communication more difficult by writing everything to each other when we could simply turn around and talk. What a relief. Once I started talking, my use of ENFI dropped off; there were so many things to talk about and so little time left before the end of the quarter.

During the Christmas break, I studied the transcripts of those two ENFI classes. I had been exposed to discourse theory and analysis at a National Endowment for the Humanities Institute on Linguistics in the Humanities, so I approached the transcripts assuming they would mirror conversation and exhibit the increasingly egalitarian writing community that was one of the theoretical hallmarks of ENFI (Batson, 1987). To my dismay, the transcripts did not mirror conversation; instead, they mirrored a typical teacher-led classroom discussion where "the teacher asks almost all of the questions" (Peyton, 1988, p. 163). The transcripts were dominated by one person – me. Whether there was one person per terminal or two, whether it was a jolly story writing activity or a serious topic analysis, I did most of the "talking." During the 10 weeks that I taught those first ENFI classes, I had 40% of the total turns and 60% of the total lines (Thompson, 1988b).

Frustration with ENFI and the return to word processing

I was seriously discouraged. Indeed, I did not teach on the network for the next two quarters, and no other teachers on my campus were interested in trying a complex new system that had already given me, the resident "techie," so much difficulty. But the machines did not go unused. We had designed the writing center to be both an open lab and the classroom for Developmental English. Classes were regularly scheduled in the room, there was an attendant to help with the computers, and teachers incorporated word processing into their developmental classes. Students learned to use a simplified word processor, spelling and style check programs, and even some grammar CAI. The lab was a success; ENFI seemed to be a flop.

Besides my frustration with the day-to-day difficulties of running an ENFI class, my decision to drop ENFI as I had envisioned it came down to dollars. I was not willing to teach six courses for the price of five again in order to follow the ENFI model, especially since that model had not worked very well in my classroom environment. Nor could I think off-hand of any way to use ENFI that did not require tiny classes, near total silence, and excessive teacher time and effort. ENFI would have probably remained unused for good at my campus had I not received outside funding for release time so that I could experiment to discover other appropriate ways of using networked computers in an English classroom. This outside funding also provided release time for a colleague at another NVCC campus who would work with me to develop network applications that made sense to us in our community college environment.

Distance ENFI and collaboration

Funding came from two sources: the college and the ENFI Consortium. The college provided a small grant so that Cathy Simpson, the director of the writing center at the Manassas Campus, and I could experiment with connecting our two networks for written conversation using modems and a phone line. This was during a period of temporarily declining enrollment at our college, and the idea of connecting small classes on two campuses, so that one teacher could eventually instruct both simultaneously, seemed attractive. This later proved to be both impractical (one teacher could not control two distant classes simultaneously) and unnecessary (enrollments shot back up again), but it stimulated us to collaborate on the use of our networks for distance interaction. The grants provided each of us with one course release time and money for the phone line connection. We spent the summer of 1987 planning how to coordinate two pairs of connected courses, one pair in Developmental English and the other pair in Freshman Composition, and struggling with the initially unreliable phone line connection.

At the same time, our participation in the ENFI Consortium encouraged us to take a second look at ENFI. I had great hopes for connecting classes at distant campuses for written discussion, because that seemed to provide a genuine context for writing as communication, not as an artificial substitute for speech. Conducting all of our communication in writing within a classroom, as I had tried to do, seemed finally odd when we could always speak. However, when two classes are at different sites, it makes good sense to exchange ideas in writing, and network writing is far more attractive than letter writing for connecting two distant classes, because the response time is so much faster.

Cathy had even fewer networked computers than I did. She started with four workstations, and the first year they were in the library, not in a classroom, so she never even tried to emulate Trent's ENFI methodology. From the start she had used the network for occasional group work and had developed certain activities that she liked, such as collaborative story generation and peer-editing activities.

Cathy and I had in common many years of experience with group work with students before we started with ENFI. I had been grouping students at computers to compose collaboratively, used teams to solve problems and/or generate arguments, had groups compose dialogues at a single computer, team taught with a counselor in the classroom to develop group career research projects, and used peer groups to read and respond to student papers. Cathy had been working in her developmental classroom for many years with a counselor who presented a series of values clarification exercises that led to group problem solving and then to individual composition.

Cathy and I also shared a common understanding of writing instruction as process based, social, and communicative. Our commitment to connect the two networks led us into intensive discussions of how to use the equipment, how to coordinate the classes, and how to extend the interactive writing on the network into collaborative composition.

By the end of that summer our plans for use of the network were pretty well hammered out. Students would do some interactive messaging within the classroom to brainstorm and discuss topics. When connected to the other campus, they would dialogue to get acquainted, have a few whole-class discussions with both teachers on line, and mostly break into small paired groups, one from each campus, connected by their own channels, to discuss papers, topics, research findings, and the like.

Because we had so few computers, students would have to work in small writing groups at each terminal, reading received messages, discussing them orally, and collaborating to send messages in response. This collaboration was an inevitable result of our few computers; however, we planned to encourage students to work together on their other writing as well. Each writing group would write a number of short texts collaboratively and produce at least one graded collaborative paper of more substance.

Problems

Unfortunately, real-time distance communication among groups is more attractive in theory than in practice. Not only did Cathy and I have plentiful problems with the actual connection, but an inordinate amount of connected time had to be spent letting students get acquainted, discussing what we were doing, trying to hold the students on-topic, and easing the inevitable hostilities that erupted between groups of distant students and even between the students in one class and the distant teacher of the other class.

If both classes were connected as one superclass including perhaps 40 students, the amount of writing generated was so great that the messages flew up the screen and away faster than most students could read them (this became a more serious problem as we acquired more workstations). Nonetheless, this whole-class discussion was needed to introduce the classes to one another, to create a sense of two classes communicating, and to help the teachers to coordinate the activities at the two sites.

The two activities we concentrated on when connecting the whole classes were getting acquainted and brainstorming, as in this example from a freshman composition class in the fall of 1988:[2]

GROUP1W: you are supposed to be identifying topics for your documented argument paper
GROUP9W: Gay rights
M1:   kkk
GROUP6W: ME TOO
GROUP8W: You tap keggs too
M9:   Remember that this is an argument paper and not a research report
GROUP7W: I'm glad DUFUS didn't win
M6:   what gay rights?
GROUP9W: your gay
GROUP5W: who is for kkk
GROUP6W: who's m9
GROUP2W: Kill the KKK
GROUP7W: Gays don't have rights
GROUP8W: Who's Gay
M2:   gays have none
M1:   white supremisists or transvestives
GROUP6W: so are you

Such discourse can stir up a number of ideas, but is too quick and superficial to develop any of them. As can be seen from this brief excerpt, the content can easily offend some students and degenerate into hostility, although this particular session did not do so.

Perhaps the best whole-class connection we had was when Cathy and I led a discussion on the nature of paragraphing and I took one point of view while she took the other. The students were encouraged by our dissent to express

---

[2] GROUP1W is the teacher at Woodbridge, M9 is the teacher at Manassas. Entries designated "GROUP" are at Woodbridge and those designated "M" are at Manassas.

their own ideas instead of handing back the teacher's, and this session turned into a surprisingly lively discourse considering the unexciting topic. Despite the success of this session, many of our whole-class connections were filled with idle chatter, attempts to make dates, and exchanges of vital statistics such as cars, hair and eye color, marital status, and phone numbers. Often Cathy and I were unable to hold the discourse on-topic, and occasionally we even cut off the connection in the middle of a session because it had become a waste of class time.

When we broke the students into smaller groups and connected pairs of groups on separate channels, it was even more difficult to keep the student discourse on-task. We teachers were not on the channels with the students, but on a separate channel of our own trying to coordinate the timing and activities in the two classrooms. Some groups worked fairly well together, brainstorming for topics, exchanging information about their research projects, and doing peer review of papers, as in this example from a freshman composition class in the fall of 1988 where the instructions were to "discuss your documented argument paper with members of your research group at both sites":

1M:	we found out that most people who work with under age drinkers think the drinking age should remain the same because teenagers are not mature enough to handle alcohol
CHANEL1W:	that's interesting. I know people that work with me who get alcohol for minors.
1M:	what responsibility does an 18 year old have go to war right to vote
CHANEL1W:	able to vote, able to be drafted, convicted as an adult, able to enter legal contracts
1M:	why not raise the ages of those instead of lowering the drinking age
CHANEL1W:	Because 18 year olds are informed enough to vote, able bodied to fight, some are on their own without parents and so should be able to sign contracts by themselves
1M:	people my age want to be treated like an adult. but do they act like adults. i don't think getting drunk and then driving is very mature of them
CHANEL1w:	also they are aware of what crime is and should know not to commit it So adults drink and drive. sometimes more often

These students worked effectively together in this exercise, addressing their ideas to a real, distant, interested audience.

However, other groups simply did not like one another or had difficulty communicating in writing. These groups easily became hostile, and not infrequently their communication degenerated into insults and outright anger, as in this example from a first small-group connection between two developmental classes in the fall of 1988 (*GROUP* designates Woodbridge students):

GROUP3:   Hello, my name is Charles and this is Karen
          HEY, WHAT'S UP! THIS TOMSON AND THIS IS SUSAN.
CHRIS: Hello our names are Alice, Helen, Bill, Ernie and Dora. Yes were
          the Fatboys! To bad you guys don't drink! . . .
CHRIS: Of course we drink beer and etc. . . .
GROUP3:   Are you guys single.
CHRIS: some of us are and some of aren't
GROUP3:   What is the etc.
CHRIS: Bill has been divorced 3 times and he's only 18.
          Etc. . . . is other types of alcohol!!
          Ernie does crack!!
          Dora does Dallas!!!
          Bill smokes candy!!
GROUP3:   Susan is married lives in the slums and she has 8 kids all from
          different and I am gay
          Helen shoots up!!
          Do you have aids!!!

Although this started as a friendly game of insults, it quickly degenerated into more hostile exchanges including this refusal to exchange phone numbers:

CHRIS: We don't know you well enough to call you!!
GROUP3:   I DIDNT WANT TO TALK TO YOU ANY WAY WITCH
CHRIS: Listen wench if we don't want to talk to you then we DON't want
          to talk to you!!!
GROUP3:   SORRY WE ARE OFFENSIVE. YOU ALL ARE NARKS
CHRIS: fuck you
GROUP3:   Hey our teacher here was right here reading everything that you
          guys have written!!

Despite GROUP3's warning, the teacher was definitely no longer in charge. She might walk around the room overlooking the group exchanges, she might even get angry and warn students to shape up, but she had very little input into the actual writing, and student group exchanges could quickly get off-topic and out of bounds.

Although distance ENFI had seemed to offer the ideal necessary situation for interactive real-time writing, it was finally no solution to the problems I had found with classic ENFI. It was clumsy, time-consuming, potentially hostile, and extremely difficult to organize and coordinate. In addition, collaboration became even more difficult. Collaborative work is demanding enough under ideal conditions within a single classroom. When two distant classes are involved, the chances become remote that all students will be ready with their share of the work at the agreed-on time. For example, if small groups were working together on a research project, three out of four members of a group at one site might be absent or unprepared on the day they were scheduled to connect with their opposite site group to narrow their topic and divide the research responsibilities. This would turn the scheduled connected session into a waste of time and irritate the more responsible students who were present and ready to work.

After using the network both locally and at a distance for over a year, I was still firmly committed to finding ways to encourage students to interact about texts, both orally and in writing, but I was equally committed to the need for a structured environment for doing so. I wanted students to share writing, to work as groups to read, talk about, and respond in writing to texts, and to research and write collaboratively. These activities required rapid distribution of writing, access to shared texts, and far more organization than I was used to providing in the classroom. The confusions and coordination issues of the distance connection had made me especially sensitive to the need for structure in the classroom. I began to look at the network itself for other tools that were already in place to help me facilitate and structure written interaction and student collaboration.

New versions of ENFI

The two network capabilities that I found most helpful for structuring interactive writing sessions within a class were the ability to distribute text and the ability to share text files. The network could distribute text by sending the contents of one screen to all the screens on the network. The network could be used to share texts by setting up word-processing text files that could be read and written to during open lab hours by a group of several students, each working according to his or her own schedule. For distance communication, I found asynchronous conferencing to be much more effective than synchronous.

Distributed text

By splitting the network screen in half, instead of into the small write and large read window that I had been using (see Chapter 3 for a description of the network screen), I was able to provide a place for student groups to compose limited texts, such as a summary of a story, a retelling of a poem, or a plan for a research paper, for distribution to other students' screens.

Each group would compose a brief text (a maximum of 10 lines, which is what the software allowed) in response to my instructions. They would talk freely within the group, write their text collaboratively, but wait to send it until all the groups were finished. Then the groups would send their texts,

> I am writing the story to show that the American dream is a joke. Willy is just an unfortunate character I used to explain this point of view by. No matter what your expectations are, we are never fully satisfied. Through Willy, I am showing the destructions of a family because of the unattainable goals forced upon them by their own conscience. By comparing ourselves to others we are unable to understand who we are and become instead the role we are portraying.

> I worked hard all my life to succeed and become the best. It seemed that the harder I worked, the harder it was to get ahead. I was tired of failing. I began to realize that I would never succeed and the only way I could provide for my family was to discontinue my life. It really seemed like the only way my family could get ahead. With the insurance money, Biff would finally have the chance he needed to get a start on his success.

Figure 11-1. Distributed text activity

one at a time, reading each text aloud and discussing it before going on to the next (Thompson, 1989a). This procedure provided the kind of structured balance I was seeking between teacher-led activities and discussion and student freedom to interact within a specified context.

Figure 11–1 is an example of such a distributed text activity. After reading *Death of a Salesman,* student groups were asked to take on the persona of one of the characters in the play or of the author, Arthur Miller, and write about the ending. Two of the student entries are shown. The upper one, from the viewpoint of the author, is currently visible to the entire class. The lower one, from the viewpoint of Willy, has not yet been sent, so only the author group can read it.

Another helpful aspect of ENFI for distributing text was the ability to send live text from the teacher's station to any or all of the student stations. (Using a video switch, the teacher can transmit one computer screen to the others in the class.) This was ideal for teaching revision, because I could broadcast a student's (or my own) text to the whole class and involve them in a discussion of what changes could be made, why and how to make them, and then show immediately the changed text. After a few such modelings and discussions of how to do revision, student groups could then work on revising their papers without further intervention (Thompson, 1989b).

Shared text files

Shared text was the other network capability that fulfilled my desire for balancing structure with interactivity. During the winter of 1988, students in my English 112 class (the second quarter of Freshman Composition) had complained bitterly about composing collaborative research papers; they had found my instructions inadequate, had trouble meeting with group members out of class, disliked sharing their grades, and resented those group members who did not participate fully. I knew their objections were largely valid, but I was not sure how to deal with them.

During the following summer, I heard Cynthia Selfe give a paper on students using a bulletin board to share written comments in an advanced grammar course (1988). This bulletin board concept seemed to be part of the answer to my needs. I went back to my network and set up shared text files so that students could enter their research whenever they were able, instead of having to always get together with the members of their groups.

In order to provide adequate structure, I adapted Ken MacCrorie's I-Search format (1980) into a We-Search project. The I-Search approach focuses on the process of identifying a topic and searching out information about it; students write about the search itself rather than focusing exclusively on findings. I had each student group identify a common topic and divide up the research activities. I wrote extensive, specific directions for this process. The idea was to have all members of a group write a series of entries, such as article reviews and interviews on their common research topic, in the shared file. The group would also write some entries collaboratively, such as a plan for future research, a statement of what they had known before beginning the project, and a summary of what they had discovered. The final research report could be written individually or collaboratively, depending on the wishes of the students involved (Thompson, 1990a).

Although the complaints about collaboration had come from English 112 classes, I first tried the shared text file project with a developmental writing class. It was surprisingly successful. The students liked the mixture of sociability and freedom to work at their own pace. I was impressed by the sheer amount of writing they did and by the support they gained from working in a collaborative group. I am currently adapting this method to college credit writing and literature classes.

Asynchronous conferencing

My negative experience with classic ENFI and the coordination confusions of real-time distance ENFI led me to search for a nonsynchronous computer conference for student written communication from distant sites. Steve Ehrmann, our ENFI project officer from the Annenberg/CPB Project, suggested that I might use dial-in conferencing as a way to do this. Dial-in was not available on the ENFI system in my writing center, so I went to our Extended Learning Institute (ELI) and asked if I could develop a distance course for them that used computer conferencing. They immediately agreed and I collaborated with an instructional technologist, Bob Loser (who did all of the programming and most of the conference design), to develop both the conference and the course – Technical Writing.

This course has been running continuously since the summer of 1989 and is a delight to teach. The students are able to communicate with one another and/or the teacher in writing, but there are no coordination or time issues to struggle with. The course is designed to use a computer conference called the Public Journal for communication. Students enter a series of specific assignments onto the conference, read entries on the same topics written by other students, and write responses to some of the other students' entries. I read all the entries and write comments as I see fit.

The students write whenever they please. I read the conference at my convenience. Because this use of writing to communicate is a best possible solution for distance learners, students do not waste their time irritating one another or playing dating games, as did the students in real-time distance communication situations.

Although asynchronous conferencing is not classic ENFI, it has been, for me, an outgrowth of my experience with ENFI and the ENFI philosophy. Both use computer communications to connect students and/or the teacher so that they write to and for one another. Both encourage the concept that writing *is* communication, that writing is *for* other people. Both constantly publish early stages of writing and provide a medium for rapid feedback from other students as well as from the teacher. The main difference is time. Classic ENFI works on real-time interaction. Writing must be done quickly, read quickly, responded to quickly. This encourages spontaneity and speechlike exchanges in writing. In contrast, asynchronous interactive writing allows students and the teacher to take their time, to read others' writing at their convenience, and to answer as the spirit moves them. It invites reflection as much as responsiveness. As such, it is further from speechlike writing than classic ENFI and closer to letter writing, with each letter posted to a whole group of interested readers, any of whom may respond. Classic ENFI messages are evanescent; a few more lines of writing and even the wittiest message is gone. Asynchronous messages, however, remain indefinitely available and can be reread at any time by anyone.

I suspect that the teacher's temperament might incline her or him to prefer either classic ENFI or asynchronous conferencing. I personally like time to think about what I am reading and write a response when I feel ready. Consequently, I prefer asynchronous conferencing. Another person might prefer to make a quick response, placing more value on spontaneity than on reflection, and hence prefer classic ENFI. Student needs might also be a factor in choosing one or the other. Developmental students seem to be especially happy using classic ENFI, and they seem to get a lot of much-needed writing experience from using it. The very immediacy of the experience supports their use of writing to communicate. However, more advanced students may prefer to think *before* writing, and may appreciate the opportunity to read the writing of other students over time. In this situation asynchronous conferencing might be the appropriate medium.

Finally, the class situation must be a factor in deciding which kind of interactive messaging to use. Class size, purpose, level, and type all need to be considered. Computer communications, like any technology, should be used when they offer a best possible solution to the needs of a particular class. Once computer communications are decided upon as the medium, the particular form of communication should be selected that best fits the teacher's purpose and the students' needs within the context of what is possible in the institutional environment.

Conclusions about ENFI at NVCC

ENFI did not take me where I thought I was going, but it has helped me to travel very far indeed along the pathway to computer-supported education for the teaching of writing. Once I was able to break free of my initial limiting mindset of imitating my understanding of classic ENFI, a model designed to teach English communication as a second language to deaf students, I began to look at the network as a toolbox, a set of capabilities that could help me to achieve my ENFI goal of encouraging and facilitating a wide variety of interactive written communication activities. Perhaps symbolic of the change in my understanding has been the change of the words that the acronym ENFI stands for. In the days when ENFI was used only with deaf students at Gallaudet, the letters meant English Natural Form Instruction. Now ENFI's letters stand for a broader and more general concept – Electronic Networks for Interaction. That change in words accurately reflects the multiplying realizations of ENFI that are spreading through English classrooms.

12 Institutionalizing ENFI: One school struggles to implement ENFI across the writing program

Michael Spitzer

New York Institute of Technology's (NYIT) use of ENFI began in the fall of 1987 in a computer classroom consisting of 12 networked and 8 stand-alone microcomputers. Managing the ENFI environment during that first year was relatively easy. Three faculty members used ENFI for a total of 4 hours per week as part of the Annenberg/CPB-funded ENFI Project, and two other teachers experimented with ENFI on their own because it appealed to them. A single student proctor (an undergraduate with computer expertise) was either present or on call during every ENFI class session that met in the lab. The proctor knew the machines and the networking software, managed the file server (an AT-compatible clone), prepared student diskettes, and assisted the instructor and any students who had difficulty in the lab.

Expanding computer use

With this modest ENFI activity in progress, other developments at the college had an impact on the extent of ENFI use. This included a recommendation by a collegewide task force in October 1987 to expand the use of computers into all core curriculum courses. The English department was already using computers in developmental and freshman composition and business and technical writing courses, so the major change for English faculty involved migrating from Apple IIe to MS-DOS computers, which were chosen because, as a career-oriented college, NYIT wanted its students to become familiar with the hardware and software they would use in their professional careers.

At the same time, the college was awarded a Title III grant to revise the core curriculum courses in accordance with the recommendations of the task force. In order to accommodate the increased use of computers on campus, the college was prepared to purchase approximately 200 machines and set up new computer classrooms. Already the leading users of computers on campus, the English faculty recommended that the new labs be networked and equipped with Realtime Writer (RTW) software. Our initial experience with the local-area network (LAN) had been positive, despite some problems, and

228

we felt that the time was right: The college was ready to purchase equipment and would probably be much more likely to buy everything now than to invest again in networks at a later date. The benefits of networking appealed to other departments, and they supported the recommendation. Because class-room space was scarce, the only way we could find the room to install the computer labs was by scheduling classes to meet in them for one class session each week – precisely what we wanted to do, although we would have pre-ferred moving more slowly.

A faculty committee recommended that local-area networks and RTW be installed in labs containing Zenith clones. We selected Microsoft Word, which at the time was vying with WordPerfect for the lead as the industry standard. We chose Word because we judged it to be the easier program to learn.

Institutional decision making often follows a serpentine political route, one that is hard to understand and even more difficult to explain. In the case of our institution, the decision to install eight computer classrooms (most with 23 student stations, some with more) was finally made in late July of 1988. Instead of purchasing Zenith clones, the college chose to buy IBM model 25s for the student stations and model 70s for the file servers. Some of the class-rooms, however, would use already-owned Zeniths and other clones, and one was to be equipped with more powerful 286 machines by Commodore.

This decision led to a host of problems. For example, all the new computers came with 3.5" disk drives, whereas our older machines and all the computers available to faculty used 5.25" disks. Faculty therefore had difficulty preparing materials on disk that they could bring into the lab for use in their classes. Also, the model 25 IBM computers required a different, more complex video cabling system than the one available from our network vendor, so installing the video switching component that allows instructors to view students' screens was delayed for months.

IBM was chosen to provide the computers in part because the company promised that it could deliver the machines in time to be installed during the first week of September. This would allow us to provide training to faculty just before the start of the fall semester (mid-September for us). Unfortu-nately, the computers did not arrive until early October, which meant that classes were disrupted so equipment could be installed and the networks could be set up. The training we provided to faculty had to be conducted on the Zenith machines already in place, rather than on the machines they would have in their classrooms.

We had no time to shake down the equipment, so, not surprisingly, we encountered several significant problems. Some of the IBM machines, in-cluding two of the file servers, simply did not work. We had difficulty getting Microsoft Word to function properly on the networks, either because we were using the model 25s, or because the software did not run well on this particular network. IBM's field representatives blamed the network or the utility providing electric power, and the network vendor blamed IBM or the word-processing program. In any event, the networks would crash with alarming frequency, for reasons we could neither diagnose nor prevent. We were unable to toggle back and forth between Word and RTW. We had had this problem during our first year, using the Zeniths, but had been assured by the vendor of RTW that it would be corrected in a later version of the software. It wasn't.

We discovered as well that to run eight labs on three campuses we needed a much more structured and complex support system and more than 100 trained student proctors. Because of our late start we were unable to train them sufficiently, so many of the proctors arrived at classes knowing less about the software than the faculty did. This problem diminished as the semester progressed, and we gradually developed a more effective administrative system for managing the computer classrooms. We now have a collegewide LAN manager, a LAN manager for each campus, assistant LAN managers, and proctors. Providing staff for the computer labs has remained one of the more challenging tasks we have faced, one that has proven to be more difficult and expensive than anyone at the college had anticipated.

Our faculty, whose expectations had been raised by promises of wonderful new labs with state-of-the-art equipment and dazzling software that could revolutionize their teaching, reacted to the various troubles in the computer classrooms about as well as one might expect. We quickly retreated from our goal of involving every faculty member in ENFI. The networks were not working properly, the support staff could not support the endeavor, and both faculty and students were frustrated by the numerous system failures. Although we continued to provide training to faculty in both Word and RTW, we asked all faculty except those whose classes were part of the ENFI Project to use the computers only for word processing. None of them complained. Our most knowledgeable and talented proctors were assigned to the few ENFI classes, but we still had trouble getting the network to function smoothly.

We continued to offer training sessions to faculty and the proctoring staff throughout the semester, and we hoped that during intersession we could eliminate all the remaining bugs in the computer classrooms. The spring semester started with the labs working more effectively, but after a few weeks a computer virus somehow infected one of the labs. It quickly spread from lab to lab and campus to campus. Regardless of how often we eradicated the virus, it returned. Our attempts to use the labs and RTW were seriously undermined.

During the summer of 1989 we implemented a new computer security system to combat viruses. We also concluded that some of our problems were caused by Word. Switching to WordPerfect 5.0 alleviated these problems. We still have problems with RTW, but they are minor compared to those we had in the past, and WordPerfect has been fine.

During the 1989–90 academic year, the labs began to function more or less as we had hoped when we installed them, although the LANs remained much slower than we'd have liked. Loading software from the file server can take several minutes when a whole class begins working at once, and at the end of class, when many students want to print at the same time, there is a bottleneck at the printer. However, faculty became confident enough to feel they could conduct classes effectively. They are not required to use RTW, but they know it is available to them, and those who feel comfortable using it have been doing so. At our Old Westbury campus, where four faculty members have been using RTW as part of the ENFI Project, about 10 other teachers have used it to a greater or lesser extent, and a few of these have embraced it enthusiastically. At the other campuses, where we do not have resident gurus, it has not yet spread. We expect, however, that as they see the benefits of ENFI, other faculty will begin to use it in the future. Given our earlier experience, we are quite willing to let them adopt it at their own pace.

Effects of ENFI at NYIT

Has our investment in networked computer classrooms been worthwhile? I believe so. ENFI has had positive effects on our faculty and our students. Has ENFI improved students' performance? Several specific responses are given to this question elsewhere in this book and in several studies conducted as part of the ENFI Consortium.* In this chapter, which focuses on effects on faculty, it is sufficient to say that student attendance improved in ENFI classes, that students' grades were higher in ENFI classes, and that students enjoyed using ENFI – although many of them did not think their participation in networked writing helped them. I believe they felt they were having too much fun to also be learning.

Apart from the value that we believe ENFI provides to students, we find that it has benefited faculty in two important respects. Faculty in our English department teach both composition and literature. For the most part, the research activity of these faculty had been in literature. Because ENFI provides such fertile ground for studying what happens in the composition classroom, more of our faculty are now engaged in research in composition, and several regularly give presentations and publish articles related to their work with ENFI or on computers and composition. Discussions about composition theory and pedagogy are more common and more informed than in the past.

Faculty who have used ENFI in more than a cursory way have had to learn

---

* See studies by Bartholomae (Chapter 13) and Fowles (Chapter 14) for reports on the effect of ENFI on student writing at several project sites. An NYIT-specific study, *Effects on ENFI Freshman Writers: A Research Report*, compares first drafts to revisions of ENFI students and students in a control group. The report is available from Gallaudet University.

how to make this new classroom environment work effectively. To teach comfortably in a networked classroom, the instructor must fumble and stumble first, constantly experimenting. Only this first-hand experience can correct preconceptions and enable the teacher to achieve a synergism among people, technology, and pedagogy. The experience is energizing. As revealed by the presentations and articles of several of our faculty (see, e.g., DiMatteo, 1990; George, 1990; Kremers, 1990), they have found that they have to rethink what they do in the classroom and why they do it. As they observe the effects of ENFI on themselves and on student behavior and performance, they think about the relationship between their practice and the theories that support their practice.

If used appropriately, ENFI can transfer power from the teacher to the class. Even when the teacher controls the network discussion – as some studies of turn taking on the network suggest can happen (e.g., Thompson, 1988b) – the teacher has less control of who responds to teacher questions. In an oral classroom discussion, the teacher can select the student who will answer. On the network any student who wants to respond can seize the shared screen. It is the teacher's job to recognize the possibilities inherent in ENFI and to make sure that students benefit from the transfer of authority.

To use ENFI as a tool that empowers students, faculty find they must change their classroom methods, as is described clearly throughout this book by ENFI teachers. If ENFI permits discussion in writing, then the structure of writing courses is affected. Some of our faculty report that ENFI-type behavior carries over into the regular (noncomputer) sessions of their courses (e.g., Kremers, this volume). The result of these changes is an invigorated, modified pedagogy that makes our writing classrooms more student centered. Faculty have devised new assignments and sequences of activities. The changes in their teaching methods accord with the latest theoretical work in composition studies on cognitive theory (Flower & Hayes, 1981) and social construction and collaboration (Bruffee, 1983, 1984; LeFevre, 1987), so that theory and practice can go hand in hand in our ENFI classes. Over the long term our writing program has been strengthened because of our participation in the ENFI Project, our involvement with ENFI, and the way ENFI promotes a symbiotic relationship between theory and practice.

NYIT is an institute of technology, so the fact that the English department is the largest and most visible user of academic computing, and has integrated that use more thoroughly into the curriculum than any other department, has had a positive effect. Primarily a service department, English has gained respect from colleagues and all levels of administration. Even in a tight budget year, resources are more available than they would otherwise have been. The college's writing program, despite its problems – and many problems remain – has been praised internally and by outside visitors and evaluators. Not only have we changed how we teach writing, but improving student writing has become an important institutional goal, with new efforts at writing in the disciplines and with faculty in English providing guidance to colleagues in other departments.

Some of these changes might have come about if we had not embraced computers in the writing program, or had not networked our classrooms, but they might not have. Certainly, we would not have accomplished as much without ENFI.

Part III

Assessing outcomes across realizations

Chapters 5–12 reveal a varied set of complex practices associated with ENFI use. They show, as no formal definition could, the living, evolving meaning of ENFI for a community of teachers and researchers. The stories reported by the participants in this community constitute the core of the situated evaluation of ENFI, for they show how the innovation came into being as social practices in each setting.

Our study of the ENFI community and other studies of this sort, cited in Chapters 1–4, suggest that the variety of ENFI practices indicates not weaknesses of implementation, but the essential process of integrating new ideas with ongoing institutional and social systems. Minimizing the variety or characterizing it in a unidimensional fashion would mislead those who might wish to use the ENFI ideas or learn from the ENFI experiences.

We hope it is clear by now that the obvious, practical question – Is ENFI a good way to teach writing? – cannot be addressed solely on the basis of one type of classroom experience, one approach, or one set of test scores applied across the board. Nevertheless, there is a legitimate need to ask what *can* be said about the ENFI experience as a whole. We made one effort along those lines in Chapter 3, in which we presented the taxonomy of ENFI practices, and another in Chapter 4, in which we pulled together some of the threads of the ENFI experiences.

In this section we approach this question again, here with a summative evaluation perspective. Bartholomae (Chapter 13) reports a qualitative analysis of the writing produced in three of the ENFI classrooms in this study, asking whether and how compositions written in ENFI classes differ from those written in non-ENFI classes. Bartholomae found, as we did in our situated evaluation, that the social and academic contexts varied greatly from class to class. This variety in contexts for writing had an influence on the compositions that students produced. Because network writing is simply another way of communicating, can be entirely open-ended, and is shaped by the factors we have discussed earlier in this book, many different types of on-network interaction and off-network composition evolve. Student writing can take one shape when the focus of a class is on social decorum and academic

235

correctness, which seemed to be the case at NVCC, and another when students are encouraged to break from convention and challenge other authorities and texts in their writing, as they were at Minnesota.

At the same time, Bartholomae was able to make some statements about "the ENFI experience as a whole." When the network writing was treated as *conversation* and students were allowed and encouraged to interact openly and aggressively with the teacher, each other, and the texts they read, their compositions tended to be more conversational, more informal, more un-predictable, more aware of their audiences, and more aware of themselves as part of an ongoing discourse. Students seemed to be more engaged in a negotiation between "the language of conversation . . . and the language of written academic discourse." Bartholomae hastens to point out that these features of writing in ENFI classes do not *necessarily* constitute better writing or smarter students. They are different from writing in non-ENFI classes, and it is up to the teachers and students involved to decide the value to place on those differences. He found many of these features to be very compelling, however, and not always possible with more traditional approaches to writing instruction.

Fowles (Chapter 14) reports a standard writing assessment, with before and after writing prompts used uniformly at five participating sites. Interest-ingly, she finds no significant differences in scores between ENFI and non-ENFI writers. Evident differences occur, instead, among the different sites. Does this result force us to conclude that ENFI doesn't work and is not worth the trouble and expense? Fowles believes that no such conclusion is warranted, and we agree. Instead, this result argues against trying to make a judgment about "ENFI as a whole" or any innovation across the board by treating it as *one thing* and applying one standard measure in all situations. We are brought back again to diverse contexts and the need to be sensitive to this diversity in any measure of success.

In searching for commonalities among ENFI practices, these chapters stand apart from, but also complement and complete, the situated evaluation. The analyses of off-network writing reported are essential to understanding net-work interaction within the broader context of a *writing* classroom and all of the goals and efforts that that entails. By looking across sites with the same lens, we are able to bring together otherwise isolated accounts of each site. The contrasts and similarities among sites found here highlight the distinctive features of the innovation created in each setting, but also give us a sense of a community of teachers, students, and researchers moving together in similar directions.

13 "I'm talking about Allen Bloom": Writing on the network

David Bartholomae

I was invited to join the ENFI Project as an evaluator. My job was to read around 3,000 pages of prose written by students from three sites in the ENFI project: the University of Minnesota, Northern Virginia Community College (NVCC), and the New York Institute of Technology (NYIT). (For a variety of reasons, we did not include Carnegie Mellon and Gallaudet in part of the evaluation.) About half of the 3,000 pages came from students in ENFI classes, the other half from students in similar non-ENFI classes (in some cases in matched classes) at each site.

My goal as an evaluator was to see if there were differences in the writing produced by students in ENFI and non-ENFI courses (differences in the prose produced in the later stages of the courses, differences in the ways writing developed over a semester or quarter) and to evaluate the ENFI students' writing in relationship to the general hopes and ambitions of consortium members and to the specific instructional goals at each site. If Chip Bruce was the outside observer (see Chapter 2), I was the outside reader, the person other than the instructors who would pay close attention to what the students actually wrote, who would use the students' essays to tell the story of what was happening in the courses, and, perhaps, what was happening as a product of using the networks.

Methods

I began with the assumption that the opening set of ENFI essays and the complete collection of non-ENFI texts would be *normal* – that is, that they would be similar to essays students would be writing in entry-level courses (courses with similar goals or approaches) across the country. I found this to be true. It is worth noting, however, that the students at the three sites I reviewed would generally be classified by the profession as *basic* writers – that is, they were not well-prepared or accomplished writers. They did not have the skills or the fluency assumed by most mainstream freshman writing courses. Most universities have two tracks in the writing curriculum for in-coming students: one for students who can produce the usual freshman theme

237

and one for students who can't. The sample I read was skewed in the sense that it predominately featured students who couldn't. I might have come to different conclusions than I do in this chapter if I had read the work of more accomplished writers using the networks. It may be that ENFI is particularly suited for basic writers – for students who write hesitantly, for example, or who feel they have nothing to say. My experience as a teacher and as a program evaluator tells me that this may very well be true. Because I didn't review essays from ENFI sites with more skillful writers, I am left without a specific point of comparison.

I began with the assumption, then, that the writing in the non-ENFI courses would look like writing I had seen before in similar courses, and this was in fact the case. The non-ENFI courses differed one from the other, but they were a representative sample of what you would see if you observed composition courses across the country. And I began with the assumption that the ENFI courses were different and that I might see different features in the prose after the opening set of essays. After I read through the full sample the first time, I prepared a tentative list of the key differences I had seen.

When I read through the second time, I did so slowly and skeptically. In a sense, I had learned how to read these essays in the first reading. I had learned what to look for, where to pay particular attention, and in the second reading I wanted to question whether I could document or justify my first impressions. In several cases I found that I could. In some I could not.[1] When I read through the second time, I also paid more careful attention to the differences among the three sites.

Perhaps the single most common method of research and evaluation in English is that which features a single reader working systematically through a corpus of texts (the novels of Charles Dickens, metaphysical poetry, American journalism from 1850 to 1900) and reporting on what she or he thinks and sees. This is not, however, a usual procedure in educational research. For many, it seems a bit suspect – impressionistic and unscientific. These concerns, I suspect, were behind the project directors' decision to couple my review with one by the Educational Testing Service (see Fowles, this volume).

The advantages of having a single reader working through the ENFI corpus are twofold. I worked with writing produced in the courses, not writing produced for examination. And my report is a description, delivered through examples I have selected as part of my ENFI-canon and justified through discussion. The examples and discussion will certainly reveal the limits and

---

[1] On a second reading, for example, I did not find evidence to support my initial sense that the ENFI papers were longer or more fully developed. Similarly, I could not support my sense that the ENFI essays showed more evidence of revision. I remain convinced that revision is different in the ENFI sections, but the sample is not reliable for this. I received more revisions from the ENFI sections, but this simply may be due to the fact that the revisions were easier to collect.

prejudices of the reader (my reliability, in a sense), but they will also give a more fine grained or thick description of the writing produced by the students than you can get from a numerical representation of writing quality. *Thick description* is an ethnographer's term. It was Clifford Geertz's (1973) way of explaining how ethnography could be useful if its data were filtered through an individual sensibility. The comparison is apt. One way of learning about literacy in a village would be to issue a survey, count the numbers of books and periodicals, administer a test. Another would be to live in the village and observe and record the practices of those who live there. One way to learn about the writing produced in the ENFI courses is to read it. That's what I've done, and in the rest of this chapter I describe what I found.

I should add that I found the reading more interesting than I thought I would, and I found the differences in the ENFI sample more strongly marked than I thought I would. I feel confident in saying that the ENFI sample was different; and it seems reasonable to conclude that the differences can be linked to writing on a network.

Let me also be quick to add that my job is not to idealize ENFI instruction. As you read through this chapter, please keep in mind that although I highlight differences, I am not arguing that every difference is a virtue. Nor am I willing to argue that a computer network is the only way to produce these differences. Nor, for that matter, would I be willing to argue that the network is the sole reason for the differences. I do believe, however, that the networks both created and supported certain specific ways of imagining and valuing writing that made a difference when students wrote.

The sample

We collected essays from the beginning, middle, and end of ENFI and non-ENFI courses at the three sites. We also collected drafts and, from the ENFI classes, transcripts of network conversations related to at least one of the essays. The total number of scripts (drafts and essays) we collected was 934, of which 482 were from ENFI courses. The average length was about 3.5 pages. The scripts were collected from 174 students, including 75 ENFI students. After the first reading, we decided to eliminate essays collected from one of the two ENFI classes at NYIT, because technical problems kept students from doing much of their work on the network. With those essays removed, the total number of scripts was 830; the total number of ENFI scripts, 469; the total number of students, 143; the total number of ENFI students, 62.

ENFI writing

The most notable differences I saw between the ENFI and non-ENFI essays can all be related to the ways in which work on the network invites students to imagine that writing is a form of speech. The ENFI essays were less formal, more colloquial, less predictable, more individualized, less likely to present themselves as texts, and more likely to imagine a direct form of address. The writers in the non-ENFI texts could be said to be working more a-rhetorically: They were producing a paper, worrying about whether there are four or five reasons for supporting the death penalty, fitting quotations from sources into paragraphs. The ENFI writers could be said to be thinking out loud, trying for effect, teasing or manipulating an auditor close to them and their situation, arguing with specific and unspecific interlocutors.

A brief and deliberately loaded example follows, but I use it to establish the ENFI/non-ENFI distinction in rough terms. (I am showing these examples to highlight the distinction I want to make. The essays do not generally fall into so neat a pattern.) What follows is the opening of a non-ENFI essay from the Minnesota sample. I compare it with the opening of a draft from an ENFI course at the same site.[2]

In both of these samples students are writing about current issues (child abuse and sexism). In both they are working from sources; that is, in both students have to find a place to "speak" within a conversation that has already begun. The problem each writer faces is how to enter the conversation. One speaks by reproducing the language of the textbook or term paper. The other speaks by reproducing talk – by patching together a hybrid discourse of classroom language, ENFI network talk, and conversation.

Child abuse is defined by the children have been deliberately inflicted with serious physical injury such as broken bones, burns, or internal injuries by their parents or caretakers. Child abuse has become one of our major social problems in the United States. It often occurs in the presence of three factors.

Here are the opening sentences of an essay from a student in the ENFI section of the same course:

I know this paper is going to be very negative towards the women studies course, but don't get me wrong. I feel the course does enlighten women and their views on the world today. First I would like to get my opinion of the Daily out of the way. This is because of the Daily's premature printing of Michael Olinecks article without a response to it. The paper and it's one sided view on alot of articles it writes is extremely bad, and the University should do something about it.

In the first sample the student is reproducing the language and rhetoric of the term paper – her representation of an academic text. The problem, as she imagines it, is presenting and organizing information on her subject, child abuse. The address outside the text – "child abuse has become one of *our* major social problems" – is a mechanical gesture. We, as readers, are not

---

[2] Here, and in the examples that follow, I reproduce the student prose exactly as it appeared in the essays.

really being addressed here. What the text is moving toward is the next step in its conceptual scheme, the "three factors" that will get "us" through the rest of the paragraph. One way of describing the problem facing the writer here is that she does not imagine herself, as a writer, speaking and needing to engage an audience. She does not imagine an interlocutor who might interrupt and ask, "Why only three?" or "Who says its our major problem?" Like many students in entry-level writing courses, she is writing writing. She is preoccupied with the problems of putting words together on the page and, as a consequence, not attentive to genre, audience, or subject. She does not think about a reader (Who might be interested in what I have to say? And why?) or a subject (What questions can I ask about child abuse? Why am I interested? How might I get information?) or the text as a text (the "term paper" as something other than a term paper; as, perhaps, an invitation to look at sources for style and method as well as for information). The second paragraph of this paper begins: "There are five needs parents must be able to meet for their children to develop and to be healthy."

In the second sample the student is extending the network conversation about an assigned article by Michael Olenick from the *Minnesota Daily* in which he speaks critically of a women's studies course. The students have read this article and a series of letters to the editor responding to Olenick. As a writer, the student begins by assuming an audience for whom this discussion has already begun (for whom the *Daily* is a meaningful reference; who knows what the article said and what the issues are; who shares a sense of the subject and its details) and uses the language and rhetoric of conversation. One way of describing the problem in this text is to say that the student does not imagine himself, as a speaker, working on a text or within a set of conventions answering to the habits and expectations of readers. He does not imagine a reader who needs to be introduced to this issue as an issue, or who needs to see reasons for his position, or for whom authority rests in example and demonstration, not in tone of voice: "The paper and it's one sided view on alot of articles it writes is extremely bad, and the University should do something about it." The second paragraph of this essay begins: "The women's studies course 1001 is just what the course is titled, a study of women in society, and for Michael Olineck to take that class was a big mistake. I really don't feel he had a positive attitude day one, giving a man's point of view in a course where it was not wanted."

Most teachers will recognize the first example. The second, however, is more surprising, particularly because of the degree of the writer's engagement with the issue. By engagement I mean not only the sense you get of a writer trying to think through a response to the material (rather than thinking about what to put next in a paragraph), but of a writer who needs to turn to his own resources in order to do so. The failure to account for the needs of an audience could be said to be common in the work of basic writers. What distinguishes the ENFI essays, however, is not only the ways in which they assume a listener rather than a reader, but also the form and degree of engagement with the material and the number and kinds of attempts to engage an audience, the presence of features that address the reader. These then are the areas of difference: voice/style, the address to a reader, the presence of a persona, the presence of linguistic features associated with speech, the dialogical engagement with a subject. I talk about these in more detail in the following sections. Because the distinctions were most clearly marked in the Minnesota texts, I will be using them for many of my preliminary examples.

Voice/style

The ENFI texts were, as a whole, more conversational and idiomatic. I was prompted to look for this in my conversations with people at the three sites, so I resisted this conclusion; but I think it is accurate to say that work on the network led students to reproduce and/or value conversational style.

In some cases I would say students reproduced this style by choice, as a strategy, but in some cases by default, without realizing what they were doing. This "style" is partly a matter of idiom, choosing the common rather than the formal or academic phrasing. It is also a matter of syntax, as in this construction: "I really don't feel he had a positive attitude day one."

The non-ENFI texts did more to reproduce not only the sound but also the methods of what I might loosely call "academic" discourse (the book report, the analysis of a poem, formal argument). I put academic in quotes because I want to be certain *not* to say that the non-ENFI students wrote like academics and the ENFI students wrote like students. The issue is more a question of motive, or of the discourse each took as a model or starting point. The non-ENFI students were more likely to write in the usual manner of freshmen trying to step outside of their usual language or habits of mind. The ENFI students were beginning with more familiar forms of language and seeing how they might be put to use in an academic setting. The ENFI students could more easily see or demonstrate the problematics of their relationship to the academy (its habitual ways of thinking and talking). To some teachers this is undesirable. To others it is one goal of instruction. (I would put myself in the latter camp and therefore find it easier to appreciate a quirky or unpredictable student essay.)

Address to the reader

Writing "speech" is partly a matter of idiom and syntax, but it is also a matter of rhetoric. When I read the middle and late ENFI texts, I found more frequent evidence of writers relying on the shared context a speaker has with

a listener – where much can be taken for granted and context does not have
to be stated or elaborated – and I found more frequent evidence of writing
to manipulate the audience's response – to create expectation, to provide
surprise, to joke or shock, to counter what was assumed to be a reader's
prejudice or assumptions. The non-ENFI essays were flat in comparison; that
is, they did not dramatize to the same extent an encounter between a reader
and a writer or a speaker and a listener.

I did not find that the ENFI texts incorporated different points of view into
the structure of an argument (e.g., seriously considering both pro and con in
a discussion of abortion), even though these were stated instructional goals
at one of the sites. I did, however, see writers imagining that their texts
existed in the context of prior discussion and prior beliefs, anticipating the
assumptions and prejudices of an audience. I saw this to a greater degree in
the ENFI than in the non-ENFI essays, and to a greater degree than I have
learned to expect generally in student writing.

The ENFI texts tended to be organized to establish authority by appeal or
by address – by insisting on or pleading for the authority of the speaker or
by manipulating the audience. They did this rather than use the forms of
appeal more common to academic texts, texts that deploy the more covert
rhetoric of dispassionate authority, the presentation of evidence, the citing
of proofs or master texts. Rather than appeal to conventional classroom
sources of authority, students in the ENFI class imagined a different context
and mode of address, one where the force of their own voice or eloquence
would create assent:

Should there be one person who sets the standard of they type of education
that we aquire in college? NO. . . . This is America (or at least it was the last
time I looked) and we have the right to choose the type of education we
receive.

Is this really the true western culture. Not hardly. It's just the opinion of a
small handful of men.

Personal/Point of View

In the previous example, the reader is asked to identify with a person speaking
rather than with a text (or a recognizable set of textual conventions) or with
the disembodied voice of reason that characterizes much student (and academic) writing – the voice you hear in "There are five causes of child abuse."
The ENFI essays more often included an "I" that functioned as a character,
as a dramatized speaker situated historically. A writer might write, "I think
that TV is designed to make us all consumers," or she might write, "When
I watch the Cosby show I feel differently about Blacks," or she might write,
"Gittings argues that the Cosby show is designed as a commercial; my sense

of the show, however, is different." The "I," stated or implied, functions differently in each case, largely by granting the writer (with her beliefs or her examples) equivalent status with either the experts in her texts (Gittings) or the unidentified sources of the general truths that provide topic sentences or points for argument. The student who says NO in capital letters insists on being present in the discourse. When a student has to say no to one of his sources, to talk back to Bloom, for example (Chapter 8), he needs to begin by creating in his writing the position from which he can speak his criticism – by speaking from experience, a "place" equivalent to the examples of students Bloom places in his argument, or by speaking in the name of some position outside of Bloom's, speaking for all students or for democracy or for reality in the samples I've cited.

I also found that students in the ENFI sections, when writing term papers or research papers, were similarly more likely than students in the non-ENFI sections (or students I have encountered before) to choose topics about which they had something first-hand to say. (I am thinking about a paper on teen-age suicide from a student whose brother had committed suicide; one on AIDS by a student whose uncle had AIDS; and one on gangs by a student who had contact with a gang.) Again, the writers were defining their position or presence as "speakers" in relation to their subjects.

Dialogue

I have been discussing the ways writers define a position that enables them to be present in their texts. In most cases they are present as a party of one. They speak in order to be heard. There is also a way of speaking that could be called *dialogical* – where a student is not simply summarizing Allan Bloom (or attesting to the truth of what Bloom says) or simply dismissing Bloom (with a loud NO), but engaging in a dialogue with Bloom. The politics of the classroom are such that it is hard for students to use the books and essays they read as anything other than the source of facts or "truth." But the ability to make use of a text as a text – that is, as one way of representing an issue or a position on an issue – is also something one learns as a writer, by learning other ways of positioning someone else's words in a discussion, where Bloom gets to speak and where the student gets to speak, too.

Here, for example, are two almost identical paragraphs from essays by two different students in one of the non-ENFI Minnesota courses:

Jonathan Kozol, who wrote "Illiterate America" quotes, to prevent other generations from having a not caring attitude toward school is to have higher standards at secondary and precollege levels." He also quotes, "we need a policy of tighter discipline and more emphatic focus on reading, writing and arithmetic." Kotka is the name of my 1988 Burnsville Senior High yearbook. It is a book that represents our high school. While looking through my senior year yearbook, I came to the conclusion that the yearbook reflects more emphasis on the fun and leisure of our school and less on the academics.

Nelson Burton Jr. writes about high school is in artical *Back to Jail,* "most students realize that school is not all it's cracked up to be. You will find no Mecca of knowledge and understanding in modern high schools." With headings such as, "Fasion: What's In," "Fun, Food and Football" or "Enthusiasm Creates a Super Fun Year!" This yearbook clearly shows that education is not the main topic.

In both cases the source essay, by Kozol or Burton, provides the context that makes the students' example meaningful. Because of the position occupied by Kozol or Burton the student need not (or cannot) say anything except to show how her experience fits the source. The personal example simply follows the master text as an illustration. Burton, for example, has the ideas; the student fits in her experience. This is similar to the standard ways students use master texts for proof (Kozol says . . .) or as the source of compelling or final examples (Burton shows . . .). The students in these examples could be said, as writers, to be unable to create a context where they are in conversation with Kozol or Burton's text, where Kozol or Burton provides a way of speaking within which, for or against, the student might speak as well.

As a counterexample, the following text is by a student from a Minnesota ENFI course. This student is trying to find a way of making use of a selection from Alan Bloom's *The Closing of the American Mind.* The opening paragraph of the student's essay is written from the student's point of view. He says that students are not fairly represented when adults speak of them. The second paragraph reads:

One way students are misrepresented is the way certain expectations are placed on students even before they enter the school system. High expectations by thinking that every student will have graduated with honors, or that students have studied chemistry and physics. An example of these false ideals is the description Allan Bloom makes concerning the good and bad students. He says, "the good ones studied their physics and then listened to classical music." Is this what students actual do or is it something that we would like them to do? This is what we would like them to do and its not reality if it were then the majority of students would be listening to classical music and studying physics. The truth is students will study the things they are interested in and that is what motivates them and makes them learn. Its one thing to say all students should do this but its another to have actual proof. The only proof Bloom has is the way education has affected him. He has his ideals but they only represent him and his belief's. It is his ideology and in no way does that mean it is the same for all students. Mostly because students are unique individuals with different interests and therefore cannot be grouped together.

It would be pushing the point to say that the ENFI example shows a dialogical relationship to Bloom. The writer falls back on statements that are

not open to question – "students are unique individuals" – with the goal
finally of showing Bloom to be wrong, not of working to some third position.
He is not moving back and forth from his position to Bloom's, aware of both
as positions. In the non-ENFI examples I opened with, however, the students
were unable to create *any* connection between their sources and their experience beyond the connection forced by the placement of sentences in the
paragraph. Here, however, the student has found a way of inserting himself
into a discourse initiated by the experts, by Bloom and others. This is partly
a matter of technique, of learning different ways of using quoted passages,
but it is also partly a matter of ideology, of learning different ways of imagining
writing and the position of the writer. There is a form of engagement in the
ENFI example that might be said to mark a fundamentally different understanding of how one works with sources.

Let me take this as the occasion for a quick note: I am not prepared to say
that students argued with their sources or found a place for themselves inside
their term papers *because* they worked on the network. The point of this
study is to describe differences. The network was certainly a contributing part
of both the developing methods and the developing ethos of the writing classes
in which it was used. But there are other ways of representing both speech
and dialogue as metaphors for writing, including classrooms where students
speak and discuss the material of a course.

There are clearly many influences at work in any classroom. And one of
the influences I don't want to ignore in this study of new technology is the
influence of a teacher. The teacher can produce effects independent of the
technology, of course, but a teacher can also make the technology work. As
Terry Collins, head of the Division of Arts, Communication, and Philosophy
at the University of Minnesota reminded me in a letter responding to an
earlier version of this chapter,

The ENFI classroom seems to provide a best-place situation for . . . very gifted
people to teach. I can imagine the same room being used by less skilled
teachers with negative outcomes – strong tools make good work better and
likely make bad work worse. The ENFI effects you see here may be Sirc/
Reynolds effects [Geoff Sirc and Tom Reynolds taught the ENFI sections I
reviewed], though I'd like to think that those fine teachers do what they do
in a rich context of program and support and curriculum.

As an example of how one teacher worked with the technology, let me
turn briefly to correspondence I had with Geoff Sirc after he had read a draft
of this chapter:

Let me start by saying that my whole experience with ENFI was shaped by
how it didn't work for me. I thought I would be able to use the network as
a peer-conference medium, one that would allow (encourage?) students to
articulate fully their comments on each other's drafts, save a transcript of

those comments, and then let them use the hard copy of that transcript to guide their revision. This plan devolved almost immediately. Students rarely wanted to stay fully on-task and discuss each other's writing, and they rarely used the commentary they got when (rather, *if*) they revised. But what they were doing turned out to be vastly more interesting to me than whether or not they completed the full cycle of what I felt should be the drafting process. And it was then that the true value of ENFI was made manifest – it showed me that there's more going on in a writing class than I could have ever dreamed. ENFI fractures open the class, allowing me to see deeper into my students and my curriculum, and makes it very difficult to go to business as usual. Additionally, for my students it offers a better heuristic representation (as well as actual medium) of the discursive flow, changing the conception of writing to, in your words, "a form of drafting that was almost an extension of the writing they were doing when they were 'talking' with the other students on the network."

Journal writing and drafting

As I said earlier, I don't feel I can make strong comparisons between revisions in the ENFI and non-ENFI sample. There were more revised drafts in the ENFI group of papers, but that may be an artifact of the network and the data collection. It may have been easier to collect or save drafts in the ENFI courses, or the ENFI teachers may have been more likely to ask students to save drafts from the beginning.

Even where there was evidence of multiple drafts, I found that students in both ENFI and non-ENFI classes did little real revision. In most cases the later drafts were simply new copies of old drafts with little beyond surface changes: Sometimes a handwritten copy was typed onto the computer; sometimes extra paragraphs were added at the end of an earlier draft (finishing a paper that was begun at an earlier sitting); sometimes corrections were made or sentences added. Students seldom used a new draft to reconceive or re-develop the ideas or their presentation.

I did, however, see something in the Minnesota sample worth commenting on. Many teachers feel that an important skill for students to learn is the ability to write quickly and freely as a way of beginning a first draft and generating ideas. Students are encouraged to write as though they were thinking out loud. This mode of writing is sometimes referred to as *free writing*. Free writing is not a term I like, because no writing is "free." There is, however, a form of writing where the writer turns off the editor, stops planning, and just writes, hoping that sentence will lead to sentence, working from inside the written language as it is produced on the page. Even though this is work with written language, it is often referred to as *thinking out loud* or *talking to oneself on the page*. Traditionally, teachers have tried this method to get students to imagine speech rather than the written text as the starting point, because speech seems easier, more intimate, more engaged. This is both a technique, something a writer learns to do, and a strategy, a way of getting words on the page, words a writer can go back to for revision. A writer is asked to pretend to be talking in order to reimagine the context and methods of written discourse. If writing is difficult, not only cognitively difficult, but culturally or politically difficult – how, for example, does a student get the authority to write like an expert about child abuse? – pretending that it is just a matter of speaking is a way of tricking oneself past the guards at the door to the essay one needs to produce by tomorrow morning.

It is easy to see how work on the ENFI network supports the pretense that writing is, or begins with, speech. ENFI provides the objective correlative for a metaphor common in writing classes – where writers "say" things and where writers are encouraged to turn to the tone, rhythm, and methods of conversation. The writers in the Minnesota ENFI sample seemed to have learned to use a form of drafting that was almost an extension of the writing they were doing when they were talking with other students on the network. I saw a surprising number of "think aloud" revisions, more than I would have expected to see. And, in the same set, I saw a surprising number of first drafts or journal entries that differed greatly from the later drafts, more than I would have expected even in a conventional course that encouraged revision.

The following paragraph is an example of the Minnesota-ENFI version of drafting. This sample from a student's journal shows a characteristic mix of bravado and reflection. The writer is trying to be present as a speaker but also to find some way of asserting his authority over the subject. Notice, for one thing, how the writer uses the strategies of conversation to keep the discourse moving forward, at some points as though he were in an argument about Bloom, at other points as though he were arguing with Bloom:

Mr. Bloom, is he man, myth, or legend. Is he really able to leap tall students with a single paragraph. That his classification of a good student is quote "The student that does his Physics homework then listens to classical music." Is this reality?. Not even close Mr. Bloom. I realize that the student of today is not as profound in the classical areas as he would like them to be, but not every student wants to be. I know that the classical era will not be my best subject, but that is because I'm not interested in that area of learning. Mr. Bloom wants to set the standard of what is taught. This is not right. What about freedom of choosing what you want to learn, and what you don't want to learn. Because we choose not to learn the Bible, or go indepth in arts this classifies us as savages. That we are closing our minds to the better way of life and prosperity. Highly unlikely Mr. Bloom. Not everyone was brought up with a classical education, and we all see things differently.

As a point of comparison, this writer's third and final draft begins:

The student, defined by the dictionary is "one who makes a study of something, to study, be diligent. Is this truely the proper definition of today's student or not. My definition of a student is, the person who puts fourth effort to learn and increase his or her knowledge in a certain area.

The fourth paragraph in the final draft seems to be the final version of the cited example of the opening section of the journal entry. It reads:

We cannot be and some don't want to be the students that some of the professers expect us to be. For instence, Mr. Bloom wants us to be the good student that he views as, the student that does his Physics homework then retires to his room to listen to classical music. This is not reality. The good student is the one that puts forth the effort to succeed and tries very hard to do so. For the modern student to do that today Bloom would categorize them as savages, closing their minds to the knowledge of books. It comes across to me as if he thinks that every book is gospel, and unless you have read the Bible or Shakespeare then you will acquire nothing of any meaning when it comes to knowledge.

The following is a quick sketch of the process of revision represented here. In the early network conversation about the assigned readings, a conversation that takes place before writing, the students begin by speaking against Allan Bloom: "I personally think he's a very frightened old man. Boring, long winded and classified all student in to one category that he saw fit 'The savage american student' get a grip bloom you can pass judgement like that on everyone." By comparison to the other groups, the Minnesota students seemed to have learned how to talk on the network—that is, they seemed to have learned how to talk with energy and style (like students) but at the same time to stay on-task.

The teacher periodically enters the conversation to direct students back to the text, as in this except from a Minnesota network transcript (the instructor's network name is JJJ):

MICHELLE: I hear that rock devilish music only affect's the weak minded kids, that have nothing better to believe in.

CHRIS: I don't have any negative feelings when I watch and if I did I am aware of it.

TRENT: These things were not met to be read into in the first place.

TRACY: What about subliminal messages in rock tht causes people to kill others or themselves thats satanic

CHRIS: I don't even know they did things like that is that really true.

MICHAEL: I feel that Bloom is a man set in his ways and it would probley take death to change his mine of something realy close to it

GERALDO: but I don't think is music who kill the people

TRACY: Yes there have been big controversies on the news and shows about it all the time

JJJ: On pp. 74–75 of Bloom, he gives us a picture which he thinks shows the horror of your generation – a boy doing his homework to MTV or some tape, listening to a heavily sexual beat or a message to kill his parents. Bloom thinks it's sad that people fought wars of freedom so this kid would have the right to listen to garbage music. Agree?

This passage from the assigned reading and others the teacher introduces become touchstones for the group, not only in the discussion but when they write. In a sense, the conversation provides a repertoire of examples the writers will turn to later. In the preceding drafts, you can see the student trying to find not only a strategy but a tone of voice to use in talking back to Bloom. He uses his definition and his experience as material for his counterargument, and he moves from being snide to a student's version of the detached indignation we often hear in letters to our journals.

Here, briefly, is a second example. This is the opening of another journal entry on Alan Bloom:

What a misconception this man has about writing. I am talking about Allen Bloom. Bloom has put a misconception on the American student like no one I have ever read before. Do we as students really listen to that old rock and roll that makes us want to kill our parents? Very unlikely, especially since we do not even have music that makes us what to kill our parents. Why don't we listen to classical music? Well I'm afraid to say that we do. At least many students that I know do. Sure we do not listen to it all the time but we do listen to it. We like to varietize what we listen to, sometimes we are in the mood for rock music, sometimes we are in the mood for quiet music and even classical.

This student's final draft begins,

In this paper the main emphasis is going to be on the education across America. Some of the things that we are going to look at, is the problems that the students face of people missrepresenting them. Some well known people will be written about to discuss some of these problems. Also we are going to take a look at some probable solutions to the student on enrollment into Universities. Finnaly we will close by taking a look the problems faced across America about illiteracy and what is being done to help those that need it.

And the "Bloom paragraph" reads like this:

This is not due to the society we live in either. Meaning the kind of society that Allen Bloom writes about. "A society that has no real culture because we don't read The Bible, or Shakespeare. The kind of society that makes our minds corrupt from listening to music that has satinism in it, and makes us want to kill our parents". Even if this was true, it is not what makes poor writers. The reason that many students are not good writers is because we are not getting enough help with writing. We are not shown a clear pattern of how to write. It is for us to come up with our own way of writing that everyone can understand, but first we have to learn these skills.

In many ways, this student's drafts can stand as an emblem for writing as it was represented in the Minnesota ENFI sample. In the journal the student announces (to whom?), "I am talking about Allen Bloom." And he *is* talking, or he is talking in a sense. It seems to me that *this* sense of what he is doing (talking rather than writing) enables him to write more and differently than if he had begun with the assumption that he had to *write*. The final draft announces itself clearly as a text: "In this paper the main emphasis is going to be on the education across America." It is a spatial object with parts. The reader is given a hint of its schematics. The writer speaks in the distant, authorial "we." Once the essay begins, its strategies of elaboration become a mix of textual conventions – quotation, transition from the prior discussion to the discussion of Allen Bloom, cohesive devices ("Even if this was true") – and conventions drawn from public address – for example, the rhetorical force of the closing sentences: "We are not shown a clear pattern of how to write. It is for us to come up with our own way of writing." The student is negotiating between his experience and his beliefs and the thematics of the Bloom debate, and he is negotiating between the language of conversation, even oratory, and the language of written academic discourse.

Local culture

The classes at each of the three sites used the ENFI network quite differently (as shown in the other chapters in this volume). When I was gathering material from each site, I asked for transcripts of network conversations related to at least one of the sets of student essays I would be reading. I have only a limited number of transcripts and cannot comment generally on how students used the network as part of their classwork. I can, however, comment on the relationship between talk on the network and final written essays.

The transcripts from all three sites showed students using the network to generate ideas or to talk through a subject or an assigned reading as a preparation for writing. The Minnesota transcripts also showed students commenting on each others' drafts. The NVCC transcript showed students writing collaboratively (two or three authors working on a single text). These uses of the network reflect the various goals of the project and the individual sites: to encourage collaboration, to improve the quality of the ideas students work with in their essays, to develop students' abilities to imagine other points of view through the exchange of ideas, to increase the range of examples students have at their disposal, to develop students' involvement with the methods and concerns of academic discourse, and to encourage a personal writing style.

If I were to judge the use of the network, as reflected in the transcripts, by the effects present in the writing, I would say that the Minnesota sample showed the highest frequency of transfer, NVCC the second, and NYIT the third. (Let me be quick to add that I am *not* saying that the Minnesota students were better writers. I am only saying that the effects of the network on the written texts seemed more pronounced at Minnesota.) I read the transcripts alongside the texts that followed, or in some cases that preceded, the network discussions. What I saw on paper was this.

When the written network "conversation" worked as conversation – that is, where it moved easily and developed from speaker to speaker and point to point; where students did more than goof around or announce positions; where there was give and take, and people acknowledged and responded to one another (this happened most at Minnesota) – there seemed to be a transfer of this mode to written work that was officially "writing." Students used the language and rhetoric of conversation when they wrote in their journals, wrote drafts, or prepared final copy. Their papers were less formal. They had a greater sense of audience, of their own point of view, and of their presence as a speaker.

Conversations on the network would establish for students a set of common examples, starting points, or conclusions about a work they had read or an issue they were to write about. At Minnesota, for example, students were writing in response to a series of articles that made reference to college students. At NVCC students had conversations about poems or stories they had read and about which they were to write. The conversation they had on the network, like a conversation in class, gave the group a common way of reading and referring to the material.

I have already given an example from the Minnesota transcripts. The following is an example from NVCC. In this case students are discussing the Tillie Olson story, "As I Stand Here Ironing."

The story seemed to show a mothers guilt toward her daughter. It told about the daughters early years and how her mother seemed to neglect her because of all the younger children that her mother had to take care of. Her mother felt alot of love for her daughter and always seemed to worry about her introverted personality. Finally at the end of the story her mother sees that her daughter has developed into a carefree, easygoing young woman and all of her worring was worth nothing.

The first thing to notice here is that the students don't sound like students. The Minnesota transcripts (like the essays) were characterized by a mix of discourses – students doing classroom talk and students talking as though they were not in class. At project meetings it became clear that there had been some prior concern at NVCC to maintain order and decorum in these discussions. They had had trouble with obscenity and rude aggression. Whatever the reason, you can see in these examples the way orderliness is translated into a particular way of speaking and thinking. The students here are *doing* English rather than struggling with or talking back to or having a dialogue with English (or with their representations of the conventional idiom of the English class). The pressure to maintain this decorum functions as a "corrective" even when one group challenges another. Here is an example from the same point in the semester, but at the other NVCC site (with a different teacher):

GONZO: the unknown citizen is depicting the life of an ordinary man. It is written in the states point of view. The state only sees the superficial evidence of a man's happiness and does not look on his trouble. It reveals the theme thru every aspect of society.

GROUP A: Gonzo, your explanation tells us nothing of the poem. What is the theme. We think it is about the average society man or everybody. It is asking us to reflect on our own life; our happiness our freedom.

GONZO: earthly greatness theme is that greatness comes to an end. The poem expresses this by giving examples of great people and things of long ago in comparison to what they are today.

These students are reproducing a way of speaking about the poem that is predictable in an essay but unpredictable in discussion. It is hard to imagine students talking this way about something they had read unless they were "doing English." They don't break out of this discourse, nor do they read out of its context to talk about impressions or associations when they read the poem, for example, or to comment on *what* they are doing, or to speak from a center of authority independent of their positions as students in a class. In a sense, you can see the instructors at NVCC working to counteract the effects of inviting students to "talk." It might be said, in fact, that the network seemed a threat – at least to the degree that it encouraged students to step outside of the more formal language of the classroom. If the collaboration on the network functioned, it functioned to counter the kind of underground, antithetical talk that went on at the other sites. That is, because students assumed an essaylike discourse in network talk, their writing was more seamlessly conventional, less unpredictable or individual, than I would have expected from any class, including those not working on a computer network.

The essays from this ENFI group are also, in this sense, relatively flat:

In the poem, *At the San Francisco Airport,* Yvor Winters uses words, images, and form to get the point across. The narrator is talking to his daughter, though she is not there. He remembers the past and is unsure of the future. He is at the airport; she just left. He is watching the planes take off.

This prose is neither voiced nor addressed to a reader. The writer is not establishing her presence and assumes that the point of the writing is to record information. The student is working from within a recognizable set of conventions – the dispassionate voice of the academic investigator and the text that tells the truth and does not rely on rhetorical appeal. The production of this kind of prose is often the goal of a composition course. The point I would make is that this prose is achieved in spite of, rather than in response to, the context of the network. The impression I have from reading the transcripts is that students and teachers have to work against ENFI to keep the prose this univocal and free of address.

The NYIT sample provides an interesting counterpoint. NYIT was also concerned with order and decorum when students were working on the network. This was made clear in the reports from that site, and after reviewing the transcripts in the sample it is easy to see why. The conversation was seldom on track, at least as the track is traditionally defined. Here is an example of a network conversation that is supposed to be about the relative benefits of writing in the computer lab (the participants are identified by number). The conversation opens like this:

9497: WHAT'S UP
0027: not bad
0027: you a sucka
5571: I'm so bored. I'm drinking bleach!
1109: what?
5571: In a world where migets murder Golf-pros.
0834: hey do
0027: hello
5571: Tacoland! It's a fantasy Yeah!
      Tacoland! I always wanna be there!
1935: More work gets done in a regular english class
1935: hi answer back
5571: The RED HOT CHILI PEPPERS Rule!
1935: new order rules

It is hard for an English teacher not to admire the wit and color of this prose, although the one sentence addressing the topic for discussion (and the ironic message of that sentence), "More work gets done in a regular English class," became lost in the flow. Here is a section from the middle of the transcript:

1935: You can write down your ideas rather than worring about the computer
1935: Is anyone alive out there
5571: Hangin' out in the camode. listenin' to Depeche Mode
      Why are you a MORON?
1935: Depeche Mode rules
1935: are you a MORON
1935: well?
5571: I'm still thinking.
1935: Who do ou like
1935: That word is suppose to be you
5571: Jane's Addiction

6142: When you are in the non-lab class you feel more relaxed and you don't have to sit in front of a computer. In the non-lab class, it's only for you and the instructor.

1935: Jane says don't wear . . .

5571: Discussion between the Prof. and the students is the best part of a classroom.

5571: Least likely to be distracted.

5571: Don't wear what 1935?

1935: You get to write down your ideas quicker rather then having to type them up.

1935: Don't wear Sergio . . .

1935: 5571, who else do you like?

In a sense, this reads like dialogue in an experimental novel. There are two discussions going on simultaneously – one about rock and roll, one directed at the assigned material. The official track (on writing in a computer lab) mixes with the unofficial track (talk about Jane's Addiction, a rock group); the official track drifts in and out, trying to find its place in this discursive world and learning that it has none, or only a provisional, ironic, or comic position. It is important to note that this is not a matter of a few students who want to stay on track struggling with those who want to goof around. Individual speakers (like 1935) produce both tracks simultaneously. Read with some detachment – as the Song of Schooling, for example – the transcript is a striking representation of the competing discourses that inhabit (or, according to some theorists, construct) the sensibility of late adolescence in the nineties.

There is, as others have noted, a postmodern quality to the text that is produced in network conversations. In correspondence over a draft of this chapter, Geoff Sirc described the carnival effect of writing on the network:

The ENFI-version of academic writing, then, is writing as carnival, the celebrants dressing in the drag of authority to mock it and affirm their own authority. . . . This might be, ultimately, the best function of ENFI, its ability to carnivalize a classroom, letting students put on the masks of pseudonyms and, amid lots of laughter, overturn official culture; by doing so they unmask official cultures. . . . My students' caricature of Allan Bloom is as much a carnival grotesque as the blusteringly pompous, ultimately laughable demon of *The Closing of the American Mind*. . . . It's no wonder you saw few traces of flat, sterile academese in the ENFI classes: the colloquia of carnival opposes itself to the authoritarian word, not accidently so but purposively so. But this means that there may be no question of the negotiation or reconciliation between ENFI-talk and academic discourse to which you point; it may always remain simple opposition. Maybe the reconciliation between the two worlds, academic/official and colloquial/quotidian will simply never take place except in High's appropriation of the Low (Lichtenstein, Brahms) or Low's of the High (carnival, my students' comic book battles with Bloom). Sontag said

the movement from Low to High resulted in a new, pluralistic form; I think
the movement from High to Low results in an equally new, equally pluralistic
form, but I also think (really, I know) that the history prof who heads the
writing standards committee thinks it's just shocking and degraded, "deval-
ued" as you term it.

Sirc is not alone in seeing the networks (and other forms of computer
technology) producing a postmodern text or literacy. For other discussions
of the new literacies produced by computer technology, see Myron Tuman
(1992a, 1992b) and Lester Faigley (1993).

In the transcript I have been summarizing, the teacher finally says,

XXXXX: Now, we have a half an hour. I want you to say something about
        that article I gave out on computers. Did anybody understand it?
        Please respond, or I'll have to turn this off and we'll talk about it
        off the computer.
1935:   Thanks 5571 me too
1109:   jimi hendrix
9445:   it was really good. channel 2 was dangerous, but it was good.
9497:   slow th !@#$ down
1109:   channel 8 right 0027

And, in the end, the network is turned off. I would not read this as one
teacher's failure to control a class, but as evidence of an understandable
despair over the possibilities of making productive use of the oppositional
energies in the students or the mixed language on the screen. Nor do I want
to idealize what the students wrote (or said). In many transcripts from this
site, the students' comments were rude, childish, and at one point threatening
to a teacher. Transgression is not necessarily criticism, and although I think
I would not be willing to call the mixed text of the transcript confusion, I
know I would not be willing to call it wisdom. The NYIT transcripts are
perhaps perfect for those tracking eruptions of postmodern writing. They
raise difficult questions about schooling. The Minnesota example by comparison is a model of a traditional form of schooling; that transcript shows
focused discussion marked by interventions from the professor – and, in
particular, interventions that moved students from conversation back to reading by referring them to specific pages.

Interestingly, the essay assignment at NYIT that followed the transcripts I
read was one where students were asked to write to other freshmen to advise
them whether to take their composition course in or out of the computer lab.
This was an assignment that prompted students to think about voice and
audience – how to be convincing, how to address another student. Many of
the essays in both the ENFI and non-ENFI sets from NYIT were flat (e.g.,
"Although there are some real benefits to the learning provided in the computer lab. The traditional classroom provides you with an environment and

a structure more conducive to learning."). They showed students working on sentences or paragraphs rather than thinking about how to write convincingly or effectively to other students about an issue on which they had some expertise.

In both sets, however, there *were* essays that addressed a "real" reader, that were more than classroom exercises. And between the groups I saw some interesting differences, although as I said earlier, the ENFI/non-ENFI distinction I have been tracking was not strongly marked in the sample from NYIT. Following are opening sections from both ENFI and non-ENFI essays to which I have assigned numbers. I will not identify them as ENFI or non-ENFI until later. I have chosen representative essays that demonstrate an attempt to address the student audience.

1: English 1010 is an English class which requires writing essays every week. The 1010 section would be better and easier if it was held in the lab. As in coming students you might ask what a computer lab looks like. A computer room looks just like a regular high school room, with an exception of computers. There is always a proctor available all the time, to help you get started with a load up disk to get you in the program.

2: Having class in the computer room stinks. I am sure that computers, in general, are an asset to the human race, but the computers at NYIT are not. I am sure that sitting down comfortably and typing in a computer room can be fun, but at NYIT it is not. To tell you the truth, there isn't one good thing I could tell you about the computer room at NYIT. This is why you should choose the conventional classroom over the computer room.

3: Computers are the way of the future. That was the famous line that our parents kept telling us all through high school. Well, the future is now! The best way to learn how to operate a computer is by working with one as often as you can. At New York Institute of Technology the best class to take in order to get hands on computer training is English 1010.

4: The computer room has its good points and its bad points and sometimes the bad points out number the good points. If the school officials would open their eyes and realize what is happening and actually attempted to do something about straightening things out, maybe the computers would be a help instead of a hinderance.

5: Did you ever have the urge to toss your typewriter through a window when you were typing a paper for school? If you have, you know that when you are use a typewriter, and you make a major mistake in typing you would properly have to retype the page you were working on. Now, lets consider the advantages of using a word processor. With a word processor your typing job will become a lot easier because you will have a chance to correct your mistakes before you hand in your work. At this point you may be ask yourself, Where would I go to learn how to use a word processor. Well, you are

in luck because NYIT is offering a 1010 English course in which they teach
you to write better essays as well as to teach you to use a word processor.
Therefore, if you would like to learn to use a word processor you should sign
up for a English class that is held in the computer lab.

6:    One of my classmates has already lost twenty minutes of class because
of a computer malfunction. One-third of the computers in the computer lab
are not working in today's English class. By the end of class student will be
lucky to get one hour out of the one hour and fifty minute class to concentrate
on the essay. Computers can be very helpful when it comes to writing almost
perfect sentences and to rewrite essays, but not for English class, especially
at NYIT computer lab where there's constant interruptions and an uncomfortable environment.

Essays 1, 3, and 5 were from the non-ENFI section; 2, 4, and 6 were from
the ENFI section. I see two differences between these sets of writing. The
first is that the opening position in the essays from the ENFI sections are all
negative. This does *not* suggest to me that the ENFI classes were a negative
experience (perhaps they were, perhaps they weren't). The network does,
however, allow for the creation of an alternative or counterclassroom discourse. Students use the network, in a sense, to step out of the roles and the
language required by the English class. In Minnesota, as I said earlier, this
produced an interesting tension or dialogue between classroom habits and
conventions and the habits and conventions of thinking, speaking, reading,
and writing outside the classroom. It also prompted students to talk back to
their texts. (Perhaps because the Minnesota class invited students to read
against the assigned material, criticism became an acknowledged rather than
an underground activity.)

My point is this. The ENFI students here did what I saw ENFI students
do at other sites and under other circumstances: They turned to their own
experience for material, and they seemed somehow authorized to break the
conventions of classroom or academic discussion. To put it simply, it is unusual
to see so many students write so defiantly. Among the traditional goals of
English instruction have been the fostering of critical and independent thinking. The difficulty, of course, is that students, because they are students,
imitate and respect authority – at least in their official student roles and acts
they do. And so teachers are left with the dilemma of modeling attitudes
meant to stand against imitation. The ENFI network seems to have enabled
students to step outside those usual roles and behaviors – with results that
can be both profitable and unprofitable, comfortable and uncomfortable.

The other difference I see in these two sets of essays lies in the nature of
the address to the reader. If you compare 2 ("Having class in the computer
room stinks.") and 6 ("One of my classmates has already lost 20 minutes of

class because of a computer malfunction.") with 3 ("The future is now.") and 5 ("Did you ever have the urge to toss your typewriter through a window when you were typing a paper for school?"), you can see the way the non-ENFI writers invite a comparison with advertising – both, in a sense, are writing ad copy – and the ENFI writers are inviting a comparison with oral language – both are making speeches, addressing an immediate audience. All these writers are writing – I don't want to say that ENFI writers are reproducing speech. I do want to say that all these writers draw upon prior texts – phrasings, rhythms, devices, tones of voice. The ENFI writers draw upon written representations of spoken forms.

It has become common to say that all writing begins with and alludes to other writing. If this is the case, student writers learn to consciously or unconsciously echo, imitate, or appropriate the forms and conventions of the discourse around them. To the degree that ENFI values and represents written representations of speech, the students work within that context. The effect of "The future is now" is derived from the way it echoes advertising, other texts that authorize this one. The effect of "Having a class in the computer room stinks" is derived from the way in which it reproduces the trope of the "real" – of a real person speaking real feelings without device or rhetorical intent. Both contexts are created; both are rhetorical; both writers are writing. The ENFI writer draws his or her stock from a different discourse and appeals to a different set of values.

Writer 4 is also speaking out loud, here making a speech ("If the school officials would open their eyes ... "), certainly less skillfully than writer 2, but he too draws his authority from the sound and structure of public address (the populist speaking out against the abuses of the bureaucracy). And writer 1 is writing less effective ad copy, inviting the reader into a less compelling scenario (" ... you might ask what a computer lab looks like.").

As I have said before, I do not believe that the ENFI writers write better than the non-ENFI writers. The important thing to point out is that ENFI creates a different instructional scenario for a teacher. Some may be interested in the way the network makes problematic the relationship between the student and authority or between speech and writing; some will be less interested, even offended, at the thought of a student saying officially that anything stinks.

Finally, as I reviewed the transcripts and the essays, I did not see any evidence that the collaborative writing changed the nature of the texts – either their quality or their forms of presentation. Nor would I say that the ENFI groups were smarter than the non-ENFI groups (that the ENFI essays had more or better ideas) because of the network discussion that preceded the writing. I would say, however, that the ENFI writers were more engaged with the ideas under discussion and they were more likely to turn to their own experience, opinions, or voices in presenting those ideas.

In the cited examples I think I have shown how the ENFI texts were different. In some cases they evolved differently through drafts. The ENFI writers were more likely to step outside of the conventions of classroom discourse. They addressed themselves to audience and subject differently. And they were more likely to reproduce the forms, language, and values of speech. As classroom documents, their texts were less predictable and less likely to reproduce the conventional forms of academic discourse than the non-ENFI essays.

Clearly, the project produced different effects at different sites. These differences should be understood as the product of different goals, different cultures, different resources (as discussed in Chapter 2). I would not make the case that some sites made better use of the networks than others: The situations and uses were different, both by design and by default; the students and faculty were different; students wrote differently; the writing was encouraged and evaluated by different measures. This should be obvious, but because educational researchers are so often looking for universals, standard treatments, and common results, the point is worth making.

Conclusions

I've described the differences I saw in the writing produced at three sites of the ENFI Consortium. I've interrupted the text several times to say that I am describing differences, not assigning value. It should be clear, however, that as I spent more time with the project, I became fascinated with what I saw at Minnesota. I liked the situations students and teachers found themselves in in the Minnesota ENFI course. I have spent many years teaching basic writers, and I was impressed by how much the students at Minnesota wrote, by how much they revised, and by the degree of their engagement with the material. Their essays were less predictable, but to my mind this is an advantage. Although they may not look as "finished" as essays from other sites, I think the students' work was more thoughtful and interesting, and opened up possibilities for learning and instruction that would not be possible with more finished writing. In the follow-up course at Minnesota (the second quarter course), the ENFI students produced more conventional forms of academic prose with equal if not greater fluency than writers in other courses.

I must also add that the network is not the only way to call into question the relationships between writing and speech or the student and the academy. One can also do this by reproducing students' writing and using it as a text in the class, by group work, by oral discussion. To this degree I do share Shirley Brice Heath's concern, expressed at one of the project meetings, that the network displaces real talk with written network talk and the talk on the network does not (will never) approach the level of spoken discussion in class.

Perhaps this is obvious. Some members of the project have argued that the network allows for a form of discussion not dominated by the figure of the professor, front and center. And yet for better or worse the figure of the professor was certainly evident in the network transcripts I read, even when the professor remained silent. The networks, however, allow students to experience writing as though it were not writing, as though it were speech. For some teachers this is an important reorientation for student writers.

I do not, however, completely share Shirley Brice Heath's concern that ENFI devalues speech or takes speech out of the classroom. If it devalues anything, it devalues writing, at least certain conventional forms of classroom writing, and it makes speech the dominant metaphor for the methods and aims of discourse. As I said, this will be troublesome to some teachers (as I think it was to the teachers at NVCC, whose stated goal was to prepare students for the formal demands of academic writing), and it will be intriguing to others. Many courses and textbooks argue that students must stop thinking of writing as the arrangement of words on the page and try to think of writing as spoken communication – as direct speech, as thinking out loud, as a form of public address. This is usually not the primary goal of a course of instruction, but it is often one of the key steps along the way.

The network encourages a conversational style, and it foregrounds the difficult and somewhat precarious relationship between a student and the habits, prejudices, and expectations represented by academic discourse. At sites where this was seen as an interesting educational moment (e.g., Minnesota), I think the network served their goals. The curriculum at Minnesota seemed particularly interested in raising questions about the academy and its ways of thinking and speaking and writing. At sites less interested in opening up the conventions of academic discourse for inquiry, what I have described as *ENFI-writing* presented itself more as a troubling side-effect. This was my impression about NVCC. The sample was harder to read at NYIT.

If I had to describe the idealized, pure instructional force of the network, some inevitable effect produced by the networks regardless of the goals and agendas at the individual sites, I would say that the network encourages a kind of counterwriting, driven partly by the conventions of speech and driven partly by the unspoken, often unacknowledged, desires of the students, represented here almost as the colonized, an underclass. The network became a place where students could write/say that which could not be written/said in any of the "official" channels provided by the institution. In this sense I think the networks both created and supported certain specific ways of imagining and valuing writing that made a difference when students wrote. For teachers who are eager for students to see the effects of a conversational style, for teachers who are eager for students to talk back to experts or break the format of the book report or the term paper, the networks could be seen as beneficial. The ENFI essays, drafts, and transcripts struck me as providing powerful resources and opportunities for examining and working on the kinds of issues of central concern to many teachers – including the possible relations between high and low and among the varieties of literacies that now make up American culture. At the same time, I must add that the writing, and the values, encouraged by the network could also be seen as a nuisance by some teachers, even as a threat to academic values.

14 Designing a writing assessment to support the goals of the project

Mary Fowles

When a group of educators decides to launch an innovative project or idea, questions about assessment soon surface. How should we assess the effects of what we are doing? Questionnaires? Interview? Review of classroom work samples or portfolios created by the students? Pre- and postessay tests? How do we decide what measures best serve our goals?

In order to develop a valid assessment plan, the project participants need to begin by asking *not* What kinds of measures should we use? but, rather, What, precisely, do we want to find out? and How will we use this information? Answers to these two questions set the course for planning and implementing a successful assessment.

For writing programs the first response tends to be enthusiastically vague: We want to know how well students write so that we can tell whether or not this new approach has improved their writing. But what do we mean by improved their writing? – something as focused and measurable as better sentence structure, or does it include more complex aspects of thinking and writing, such as development of ideas? Does *writing* mean paragraphs or reports, summaries or argumentative essays, a timed writing test or a collection of writings that result from classroom assignments, peer review, and extensive revision?

Does a formative assessment make sense for this project? – that is, can we provide useful, ongoing results that will help teachers adjust their instruction? If so, are the faculty members themselves prepared to commit the time and effort necessary to help critique and refine the assignments they give, to reflect on the learning processes they set in motion, and to examine the ways in which they respond to their students' writing? Or should the assessment be summative, providing consistent snapshots of the students' writing and reporting the results systematically at the end of the study? The teacher's role in a summative assessment may be less intensive than in formative assessment, but it is no less important, for the teachers themselves need to confirm that the writing assignments, process, content, and criteria for evaluation are appropriate for their students.

The questions continue. Which students should be assessed? All? Some, selected randomly or chosen to meet certain instructional, ethnic, regional, or other specifications? What do we need to know about the students' previous experiences or writing instruction that might affect the way they respond to the innovation? If the assessment includes students in various classes, what goals and instructional approaches do the teachers share, and how do they differ? What do we need to know about the larger social and pedagogical context in which the innovation occurs?

In the process of considering such questions, faculty and administrators soon realize that they are not only defining the writing assessment but also arriving at a better understanding of the way they and their colleagues are using the innovation in the classroom. Additionally, when the assessment brings teachers together to read and discuss their students' writing, this process of review and reflection is one of the most instructionally valuable experiences writing teachers can have, even if they are teaching different kinds of students and have different instructional goals.

The more diverse the curricula, the students, and the instructional settings, the greater the challenge of setting common goals for assessment. Such was the case for the ENFI Project. What the members of the ENFI Consortium had in common was that they all were using the innovation, a local-area computer network for interactive writing, and they were all committed to improving students' writing. Their differences, on the other hand, were considerable. The consortium sites varied greatly in size and location, ranging from a community college with an open-door admissions policy to a selective four-year university. The academic and writing ability of the students varied greatly from site to site and, consequently, so did the writing curricula. Some classes focused on personal narratives and paragraphs, whereas others assigned expository essays requiring critical analysis of a subject. Students at one site were deaf, and students at at least one of the other sites were considered "at risk," for this was their last chance to pass the college's required writing course. Faculty members had been experimenting with a variety of strategies for using this new technology in the classroom. Finally, within each class and across all sites, students varied in their ability to compose on computers and to use computer networks. These differences raised the important question of the extent to which the sites were in fact using the same innovation (cf. Chapter 2).

Because of these important differences, the faculty members and the project officer from Annenberg/CPB, the consortium's funder, decided initially that the project evaluation would consist entirely of separate studies; each site would develop its own plan to demonstrate the effects of the interactive network on the students' writing. When I first met with the ENFI Advisory Board, these studies were underway and site representatives had been submitting progress reports. However, because the studies had little in common, they provided no systematic information to demonstrate the effects of ENFI on students' writing. As the project officer explained,

I feel as if I am moving through a large, dark house with a flashlight. I shine the light on one spot and see something interesting. Then I shine it on another spot and learn something else, but I don't have a sense of the whole house – how these various studies connect or what they mean for the project as a whole.

At the request of the project officer and advisory board, the consortium members agreed to participate in a single unified writing assessment across all sites that would assess the effects of ENFI on the students' writing. In contrast to the site-based studies, this one would need to give systematic information about the students' writing before and after ENFI instruction; it would also need to compare any progress made by ENFI students to that made by similar students in non-ENFI classes. Finally, the progress of both groups would need to be interpreted in the larger context of well-established writing assessment methods and standards – a well-lighted house inside and out.

Planning the writing assessment of ENFI: Issues and questions

I met with ENFI faculty members, the ENFI Advisory Board, and the project officer to review writing assessment issues and determine the kind of assignments, scoring method, and scoring criteria most appropriate for their students. What follows is a summary of the assessment questions we considered, the final decisions that arose from our discussions, and the rationale behind each decision.

What is the purpose of the writing assessment?

For this project the purpose of the assessment was twofold:

- To assess, by campus, the change in writing ability of students enrolled in ENFI computer writing classes compared to that of students in non-ENFI classes
- To learn how students were using computers for composing

What is meant by writing?

Although the types of writing done in class varied considerably from site to site, the faculty agreed that a valid common assignment would be to ask students to write essays in which they reflect on a personal experience. The teachers reviewed sets of disclosed essay prompts and approved the kind used in the Pre-Professional Skills Test (PPST), a national basic skills test for students, primarily college sophomores, who are entering educational or training programs, such as teacher education. Following are the two prompts used in the ENFI study.

Prompt A   Which of the things you own would be the most difficult for you to give up or lose? Discuss why.

Prompt B   Describe one of your most memorable school experiences. Explain why it is so memorable.

Under what conditions should the students write?

Although the PPST-based prompts were acceptable for this project, the standardized PPST testing conditions were not. The PPST allows examinees 30 minutes to write an essay. The ENFI faculty members felt that because their students were used to drafting and revising, the testing time should be increased to two 40-minute class periods. Students would write first drafts one day and final drafts the next. Both drafts would be submitted, but only the final one would be judged. This 2-day sequence would be repeated at the end of the semester for the posttest.

Students in the ENFI classes were also used to interacting as they developed their responses to class assignments, but the ENFI faculty decided that for the purposes of this study, only the students' independent writing would be assessed. Students would write under standardized conditions, separate from each other and separate from ENFI. If ENFI instruction did improve the students' writing, those effects would have to be transferrable to nonnetwork writing conditions.

Should the essays count toward class grades?

It was agreed that individual teachers should decide whether or not to grade their students' test essays, depending on how relevant the test was to their own teaching. To what extent did these decisions affect student performance on the writing test? Motivation, or taking the test seriously, is an important factor in all assessments and a variable that is difficult to control, especially in research studies in which students think they have little to gain by performing well. In this study we cannot be sure to what extent having the essays count or not count toward a course grade affected the students' writing performance.

What writing features will be assessed?

Across sites faculty members shared the goal of trying to improve students' general writing ability. Consortium members therefore agreed that the students' essays should be judged holistically, for the overall quality of the writing. Holistic scoring acknowledges the diversity of good writing; success or effectiveness does not depend on a particular strategy or way of writing. Organization and development of ideas, sentence control, appropriate word choice, and the correct use of grammar and mechanics all contribute to the students' ability to express their ideas effectively, and these features are integrated in the single holistic score.

The faculty reviewed several scoring guides and found the 6-point PPST holistic scoring guide appropriate for this assessment, with its score categories ranging from a low of 1 (Demonstrates fundamental deficiencies in writing skills) to a high score of 6 (Demonstrates a high degree of competence in response to the assignment). The guide is shown in Appendix A at the end of this chapter.

How many writing samples should be assessed?

Although multiple writing samples would have increased test reliability, it was unrealistic for teachers to devote more than four class periods (two for the pretest and two for the posttest) for this study. Therefore, it was decided that each student would write on one prompt at the beginning of the semester and another prompt at the end. Using two different prompts would prevent what is known as the *practice effect* (I can do better because I've seen the prompt before) and its alter ego, a kind of *weariness effect* (Oh, no, not that topic again! I have nothing new to say). We decided that by using the two prompts in a counterbalanced design in each ENFI and non-ENFI class, we could eliminate the effects of prompt variability. In each ENFI class and non-ENFI class, a random half of the students would be assigned Prompt A and the other half Prompt B at the beginning of the semester. At the end of the semester the students' assignments were reversed, as shown in Table 14–1.

Should students compose on the computer or with paper and pencil?

The consortium members wanted students to have a choice of writing their essays either on the computer or with paper and pencil but questioned the effects of these two versions on readers. Might not handwritten essays receive lower scores than essays composed on the computer? Could the two kinds of essays be intermingled for scoring? These questions were, in fact, being explored at ETS.

Table 14-1. *Plan for administering the writing assignments*

Students	Pretest	Posttest
ENFI	1/2 class writes on Prompt A 1/2 writes on Prompt B	Same group writes on Prompt B Same group writes on Prompt A
Non-ENFI	1/2 class writes on Prompt A 1/2 writes on Prompt B	Same group writes on Prompt B Same group writes on Prompt A

Preliminary research on another ETS project indicated that handwritten essays did not receive lower scores than word-processed versions of the same essays. On the contrary, readers reported being much more aware of mechanical errors and lack of development in word-processed essays. Readers expect typed text to be carefully edited, and when it is not they notice errors that might not stand out in handwritten text.

In a subsequent study, Powers, Fowles, Farnum, and Ramsey (1992) examined the effects of intermingling handwritten and word-processed essays in the scoring process. The study involved having college students compose essays on the word processor and with paper and pencil and then selecting a subset of 60 essays to be converted. The word-processed essays were rewritten by hand; the handwritten essays were word processed. The original set of essays was selected to represent a wide range of writing ability and a mix of essay topics or prompts. The original and converted sets of essays were each scored by two pairs of readers who did not know the previous scores, nor did they know whether the essay was originally handwritten or word processed. Again, the word-processed essays generally received lower scores than the handwritten essays. This effect was noted mainly with essays in the lower score range. Scorers attributed the differences to their increased awareness of surface errors and limited development of ideas when they read word-processed essays.

Because of these findings, and because the ENFI students would have ample time to revise their essays and use the computer's spell-check functions, it was decided that the two kinds of essays would be intermingled at the ENFI scoring session. However, in future studies, project directors should be aware of this phenomenon and consider the effects of intermingling essays composed on the computer and with paper and pencil.

How many and which students should participate in the evaluation?

For comparison purposes the evaluation design needed to have carefully matched groups of students from each site, and the numbers needed to be large enough to report meaningful mean scores. It was decided that 50

ENFI and 50 non-ENFI students at each site would participate in the study and that classes at each site would be matched – that is, ENFI and non-ENFI classes would be different sections of the same writing course. To the extent possible, classes would also be matched by teacher, for some faculty members were teaching both the ENFI and non-ENFI sections in this study. Class and teacher differences were one variable that we wanted to control so that the results could be attributed as clearly as possible to the influence of ENFI.

Who should score the essays?

Continuing with the decision to apply PPST standards, the consortium agreed that highly experienced readers for the PPST should score the students' essays, led by an experienced chief reader. To strengthen the validity of the scoring process and to help ENFI teachers understand the scoring process, an ENFI teacher from each project site participated in the ETS scoring session as well.

What scoring procedures should be used?

Validity and reliability refer not only to essay tests but also to the ways in which their responses are scored. Procedures have been developed to bring validity and reliability to the scoring process, and these are outlined in the booklet entitled *ETS Quality Assurance Guidelines for Developing and Scoring Free-Response Tests*. The ENFI project followed these procedures, which included the following: Names of students and schools are concealed from the readers, as are dates and pre- and posttest information; readers must first demonstrate scoring accuracy in a training session before they begin actually scoring the tests; pre- and postessays are intermingled for scoring; each essay is scored by two different readers; the second reader does not know the first reader's score; essays with discrepant scores (scores more than a point apart) are rejudged; statistics are collected for interreader reliability.

What additional information about the students is needed?

Students in ENFI and non-ENFI sections of writing courses filled out questionnaires at the beginning and end of the semester. This survey helped determine the comparability of the two groups in terms of their general characteristics (year in school, age, ethnicity, first language) and the ways they had been using computers to write before this semester and in these ENFI/non-ENFI classes. The questionnaire that was distributed to the ENFI students at the beginning of the semester is shown in Appendix B at the end of this chapter.

Data collection and analysis

The student population

Readers evaluated the writing of 458 students, most of whom were in matched classes of developmental and regular freshman English at the five participating sites (four consortium sites and one additional school for the deaf, National Technical Institute for the Deaf, NTID). One school, North Virginia Community College, included an honors class in its non-ENFI group. Although the number of students varied by campus, each site had fairly well matched groups of ENFI and non-ENFI students. The total population from whom we received both pre- and postessays was ENFI, 228 students; non-ENFI, 230 students.

From the results of the questionnaire survey it is clear that not only were the numbers of students comparable, but also the ENFI and non-ENFI groups were remarkably similar in age, year in school, gender, ethnicity, and language. Student characteristics are summarized here and shown in more detail in Appendix C at the end of this chapter.

The majority of ENFI and non-ENFI students were freshmen (83% and 91%, respectively), but other school years were represented in both groups. Gender differences between the ENFI and non-ENFI groups were minimal; both had a slight majority of male students (59% and 55%, respectively). Most of the students in both groups were white (84% ENFI and 82% non-ENFI). The majority of students in each group (72% ENFI and 77% non-ENFI) were between 17 and 19 years old. Although the overwhelming majority of ENFI and non-ENFI students reported speaking English at home (82% and 83%, respectively), quite a few reported using American Sign Language or speaking other languages such as Italian, Greek, and Spanish. Slightly more ENFI than non-ENFI students (8% compared to 4%) reported using sign language in their homes. Most students reported having had no previous experience with ENFI (94% ENFI and 88% non-ENFI).

Administering the test

The teachers administered the questionnaires and essay tests in their own classrooms, according to plan. Many more students wrote with paper and pencil at the beginning of the semester than at the end.

Students were permitted to compose on the computer or with paper and pencil. They were also free to use a variety of traditional and on-line writing aids such as thesauruses and spelling checkers. Each pre- and postessay test was administered during two 40-minute class periods, allowing students time to review and revise first drafts. Only final drafts were evaluated.

Scoring the essays

The essays were scored at ETS by a team of nine readers: three ENFI instructors participating in this study (one each from Minnesota, Northern Virginia Community College (NVCC), and New York Institute of Technology (NYIT)); the project evaluation coordinator (from Gallaudet); and five experienced readers for PPST and other national essay testing programs. A member of the English department at Rutgers University and a highly experienced scoring leader for many ETS essay programs served as chief reader.

The procedures followed the ETS Guidelines for Free-Response Scoring. The interreader discrepancy rate for the total group was a respectable 3.45%. Discrepancy rates, before resolution, typically vary from 1% to 8%, depending on the experience and expertise of the readers, the complexity of the prompt, and the complexity of the scoring guide.

Handwritten and typed essays were intermingled at the reading so that criteria could be systematically applied to all essays together. Mixing the two types of essays posed no apparent problems for the readers.

Results

Pretest and posttest comparisons

Both the ENFI and the non-ENFI groups improved slightly their ability to write an essay under the conditions set forth in this study, as shown in Table 14–2. Since gains were nearly the same for both groups, the use of the ENFI network did not appear to contribute significantly to student writing ability, at least not as writing ability was measured in this study. At the same time, considering that ENFI is still in its early stages, it is reassuring that ENFI classes performed as well as students receiving more traditional instruction.

The greatest gains tended to be made at sites where students began the semester with relatively high scores; the highest gains were made by a non-ENFI group that included an honors section of a freshman English class. Conversely, the deaf population, whose essay pretest mean scores were about a whole point below those of all other groups, made minuscule gains. These disappointing results confirm what we often hear from teachers of the deaf – that change comes very slowly indeed.

In addition to reviewing group data, we analyzed the essays of individual

Table 14-2. *Comparison of pre- and posttest essay score means, ENFI and non-ENFI classes, by school*

School	ENFI classes			Non-ENFI classes		
	Pretest	Posttest	Change	Pretest	Posttest	Change
Gallaudet/NTID	N = 54			N = 29		
Mean score:	2.78	2.84	+ .06	2.79	2.88	+ .09
SD:	.97	.82		.94	.85	
Minnesota	N = 49			N = 46		
Mean score:	3.91	4.19	+ .28	3.75	3.97	+ .22
SD:	.83	.75		.84	.82	
NVCC	N = 46			N = 77		
Mean score:	3.69	3.89	+ .20	3.84	4.23	+ .39
SD:	.73	1.02		.88	1.06	
NYIT	N = 79			N = 78		
Mean score:	3.86	4.23	+ .37	3.84	4.03	+ .19
SD:	.78	1.01		.84	.82	
Total group:	N = 228			N = 230		
Mean score:	3.58	3.82	+ .24	3.69	3.94	+ .25
SD:	.89	1.05		.90	1.07	

students whose scores increased significantly, with gains of one or more points on the 6-point scale. The kinds of improvements they made were highly individualistic. Some used brighter language, others provided more effective beginnings, some explained their ideas more fully, and some had more control of complex sentence structure. Within classes and within the ENFI population, no single feature accounted for the improved quality of writing. If students did develop certain styles or writing strategies as a result of ENFI-based instruction, they did not clearly demonstrate those writing features in the essays they wrote for this study. Whereas David Bartholomae (this volume) noted a more conversational style in the teacher-assigned writing at Minnesota and attributed that characteristic to the use of ENFI, no such features were evident in the Minnesota posttest essays scored at ETS.

Effects of ENFI on the students' word-processing capabilities and uses

Both ENFI and non-ENFI students reported making progress in their ability to use word processors during the semester they participated in this study. One way in which the two groups differed was that ENFI students were much more likely to compose essays directly at the word processor than were non-ENFI students.

Analysis of the deaf students' writing

The smallest increases in writing ability were made by deaf students, who had the most to gain. The low scores were probably influenced by the writers' frequent errors in word endings ("order" for "ordered"), missing articles ("It was good party"), and word use and structural problems ("I always love to tackle someone however my freshman year I haven't tackle anyone which miss me a lot"). In addition, essays with the lowest scores tended to have undeveloped ideas, repetitive comments, and short choppy sentences, as in this first half of an essay on the importance of the writer's credit card.

The most difficult for me to lose is my credit card! I can't afford to lose my credit card because it is so important and very valuable.
    If I lose my credit card and someone has found it and they will use it! It is to risky for me to lose my credit card. I must have my credit card with me and cary my cards with me all the time.

Several deaf students *did* appear to make real progress, however. For example, compare the quality of writing in the two excerpts that follow. The writer, in an ENFI class at Gallaudet, wrote essays of similar length but not quality. His pretest scores were 3 and 2; his posttest scores were 4 and 3. This increase of 1 point on a 6-point scale is significant.

In these closing lines from the student's pretest essay, the ideas are expressed clearly but not well. Sentences are choppy, awkwardly structured, and limited in thought.

We manage to win. When the game was over. Everyone included the stands ran to the team. We were so happy. This is the best memory I ever had about my school.

In closing lines of the student's posttest essay the errors are still obvious, but the sentences are more complex, the use of language is more effective, and the writing is more interesting to read because the student is trying to express more complex ideas:

Because I can't imagine how a human beings could think of something like that which amazed me and I end up laughing when it happens. If I don't have that kind of expiences and memories, I guaranteed that I will be a totally different person that I am now. It's part of my personality.

Analysis of essays written by other students

What kinds of differences were apparent between the pre- and postessays of the hearing population? In an effort to identify the kinds of changes in students' writing that developed throughout the semester of instruction, I paired pre- and postessays from several sites and read them impressionistically, looking for differences. I was especially looking for evidence that ENFI students, more than non-ENFI students, wrote in the manner described by David Bartholomae, who noted that many of the students "turned to their own experience for material" or broke "the conventions" of academic discussion and wrote "defiantly." In the pre- and posttest essay pairs from the University of Minnesota, I was on the lookout for the changes that Bartholomae observed in the classroom work, writing that he described as "more aggressively conversational, open-ended, and informal."

On the basis of this review, I detected no patterns within a class, a site, or an ENFI population. The reason seems obvious. The writing prompts used in this study asked students to draw from personal experience. Personal writing tends to be informal, and the writing we evaluated was indeed informal, though not especially conversational. The classroom pieces that Dr. Bartholomae reviewed were written for very different, more academic purposes. Neither the academic writing he found in non-ENFI classes nor the more conversational styles he observed in the ENFI classes appeared to transfer to the essay-writing situation established for this study.

Excerpts from two Minnesota essays illustrate what I found. An ENFI student at the beginning of English Composition 1421, recounting a varsity baseball experience, wrote these lines in the early, middle, and final parts of his essay. Note their lively, informal style.

At the beginning of the season I wasn't really sure what position I wanted to play. My answer came to me about the third day of practice. Out of nowhere, CATCHER jumped out at my head. . . .

There were two other guys going out for the position. The first game finally came along, and when the coach gave the starting line-up, I wasn't on it. I was *furious*. . . .

Along with this success came a *hot* senior girlfriend, but I wont get into that. (Student 1, pretest essay)

This student's pretest essay received scores of 4 from each reader, as did his posttest essay. Compared to his writing in the pretest, his posttest writing is no more expressive or conversational. It is, however, more fully developed and more ambitious in its use of language and reasoning, even though these efforts are not always successful. Notice the sometimes rambling lack of clarity in the opening lines.

Which of the things that I own would I have the greatest discomfort separating with?

I have thought of this before and I came to the conclusion that I wouldn't feel too great if my home stereo was taken away without my consent (or even with my concent). I have been working ever since I was fourteen years old and I really don't have anything to show for it in my banking account for all these years of dedicated work, but I do have my stereo, and all the music that goes with it. I safely say that out of the five years that I have been employed, one of them is spent entirely on stereo equiptment. It's like an addiction, as soon as I get enough money to buy something that I think that will improve the sound of my stereo, I do it. I think it has a lot to do with the people at the place at which I buy my stuff at. (Student 1, posttest essay)

The more pairs of pre- and posttest essays I read within each class, the clearer it became that no patterns or common features emerged. The influence of ENFI was not apparent. What *was* apparent was that individual students differed greatly in their writing styles and strategies and that, in many cases, these individual characteristics were just as strong at the beginning of the semester as at the end. For example, a Minnesota ENFI student who organized her pretest essay with an introductory statement, followed by three paragraphs beginning with the words *first, second,* and *third,* and then a summative statement employed the same organizational strategy in her posttest essay. Another Minnesota ENFI student who wrote a highly descriptive but elusive essay at the beginning of the semester produced a posttest essay that was just as descriptive and elusive in thought.

If students were writing one way in their classrooms and another in the project assessment, how can we demonstrate the effects of ENFI? The next step for the consortium might be to develop a writing assessment based on writing assignments that are part of classroom instruction and use the ENFI network. The assignments would necessarily vary from school to school, and the scoring criteria might need to vary as well, but the assessment would be more integrated into the ENFI curriculum.

Comparison with other groups

Can we compare the performance of these students to the performance of national populations taking the PPST? Yes and no. The writing assignments were similar and the scoring guide the same, but the differences were significant. The standards for the ENFI scoring session were based on ENFI essays. The PPST standards are based on essays written by a different population who were permitted only one 30-minute session for writing instead of the two 40-minute class periods used in the ENFI Project. Further, the PPST essay is combined with a multiple-choice test on sentence skills; the ENFI study was based on a single essay at each administration.

However, given these differences, and given the lack of other available populations, the PPST examinees can serve as a convenient reference group to provide a context for this study. Table 14–3 compares PPST and ENFI/non-ENFI mean essay scores.

From 1988 to January, 1990, PPST essay raw score means ranged from

Table 14-3. *Comparison of PPST scores to ENFI and non-ENFI scores*

Source	Mean essay score	Population
PPST (30 minutes)	4.07–4.30	Primarily candidates for teacher-education programs
ENFI pretest	3.58	Primarily freshmen assigned to developmental or regular composition classes
Non-ENFI pretest	3.69	"
ENFI posttest	3.82	"
Non-ENFI posttest	3.94	"

4.07 to 4.30, with standard deviations ranging from 1.23 to 1.39. None of the ENFI or non-ENFI groups performed within that range at the pretest stage. However, by the end of the semester, students at several ENFI and non-ENFI sites were writing at least as well as the average person taking the PPST essay, disregarding differences in topics and timing.

Interpreting the relatively small gains made by ENFI and non-ENFI students at Gallaudet and NTID, where students are deaf, is difficult because we have little information about the kinds of gains that are possible for this population in similar conditions. One reference group for whom we do have information of writing ability on a standardized essay test comes from a study conducted by Traxler (1990).

Traxler administered a Test of Written English (TWE) prompt to 36 freshmen, 40 juniors, and 22 seniors, all of whom were deaf students at Gallaudet. Although the essays were scored at ETS by readers using a 6-point scale, differences between the two groups are considerable. (See Table 14–4.)

Unlike the students in the ENFI study, those in Traxler's study were a self-selected population, having volunteered to participate in her research. Students had 30 minutes to write on the essay portion of the Test of English as a Foreign Language (TOEFL), which is developed by ETS and administered internationally to assess the English language ability of students for whom English is a second language.

The test questions, student attitudes, times allowed for writing, and the scoring criteria differed. However, given these differences, Traxler's findings may serve as a useful reference for the Gallaudet and NTID students in the ENFI study.

The students' use of word processing

Questions about the students' experiences with word processing were asked on the survey questionnaires at the beginning and end of the semester.

Table 14-4. *Comparison of deaf students' holistic scores in the Traxler study and the ENFI study*

Source	Mean essay score	Student sample
Gallaudet/NTID Precollege ENFI pretest essay means	2.78	$N = 54$, nonvoluntary
Gallaudet/NTID Precollege ENFI posttest essay means	2.84	$N = 54$, nonvoluntary
Gallaudet freshmen essay means Traxler's TWE study	3.8	$N = 36$, voluntary
Gallaudet junior essay means Traxler's TWE study	4.0	$N = 40$, voluntary
Gallaudet senior essay means Traxler's TWE study	4.6	$N = 22$, voluntary

Table 14-5. *Students' responses to presemester and postsemester questions about their use of word processing*

	ENFI		Non-ENFI	
Question and response	Pre	Post	Pre	Post
1. Do you know how to use a word processor?				
Yes, fairly well	30%	59%	31%	55%
Yes, a little	40%	37%	44%	39%
No	30%	4%	25%	6%
2. How would you rate your typing ability?				
Not at all	10%	1%	7%	2%
Minimal (-30 wpm)	40%	42%	48%	41%
Average (30–60 wpm)	49%	51%	41%	51%
Proficient (60+ wpm)	1%	6%	4%	6%
3. When writing for your classes (in the past/in this course), do you compose your essays directly at the word processor?				
Always	6%	18%	5%	9%
Sometimes	47%	49%	40%	42%
Never	47%	33%	55%	49%

From the data in Table 14–5, it is clear that the majority of students in both groups think they greatly improved in typing ability and in their knowledge of how to use word processors. One of the most significant ways in which the two groups differed is that the ENFI students reported being more likely to compose essays directly at the computer, no doubt a direct result of using the ENFI system to discuss and explore topics before writing essays about them.

Conclusions: What did we learn? What might we have done differently?

The ENFI Consortium can take considerable satisfaction in knowing that, in one semester, the general writing ability of the students in the study improved. It is probably unrealistic to expect greater gains on a holistic scale after only one college semester. The skill being assessed is a complex one, and change comes slowly. Had an overriding goal of this project been to report dramatic results, the consortium could have narrowed its instructional focus to more teachable points and assessed only those features in the students' writing. Obviously, the importance of developing the students' general writing skills and the need for experimentation with the interactive network precluded such a narrow approach.

The fact, too, that the ENFI students had to transfer their writing skills to a non-ENFI situation for the test might have put them at a disadvantage. That they "held their own" against students in non-ENFI classes was a positive result.

Finally, the consortium can also take pleasure in knowing that not only did general writing ability improve for all students, but the ENFI students had the advantage of learning how to use the interactive network and gaining more experience in composing on computers.

For this kind of summative study, there is little we would have changed. The control and experimental groups were remarkably well matched; the writing performances of these two groups can therefore be compared with confidence. The results can be interpreted fairly cleanly. If we were to design another, complementary study, what might it look like? What might it tell us?

One approach is portfolio assessment. In a writing portfolio assessment, students review the writings they have done throughout the course and select several to put into a portfolio. They make their selections according to certain category requirements, or portfolio specifications, and they are aware of the standards by which people outside the classroom will judge their work. Preparing the portfolio for assessment can, in itself, be an effective learning experience for the students.

In order for such an assessment to work, consortium members would need to agree on how the portfolio would be integrated into the learning process of the classroom and what pieces the students would submit for evaluation. Given the need for diversity across classrooms, would projectwide consensus be possible? Probably, so long as the categories are not so narrow that they constrict effective teaching practices. Also, the faculty should have had time to experiment with the interactive network system and should be in a good position to define what is working well and what is not. The portfolio could be designed not only to evaluate writing but also to highlight the way the network activities contributed to the students' writing.

What kinds of portfolios might suit this project? The categories would probably need to reflect the shared goals and experiences of the ENFI classes – but they would *not* necessarily require students to write on the same writing assignments. For example, if the faculty all agreed that "improved writing" was an important objective for their students, one portfolio category could ask students to review the pieces they have written throughout the course and select two that illustrate improvement in their writing. If the class focused on paragraph writing, each student in the class could select a paragraph written early in the semester and one written later in the year and write a covering note comparing the qualities of writing evidenced in the two pieces. In another class, one that emphasized persuasive writing, for example, the students could select an early and late persuasive piece and explain how these two pieces illustrate the improvements the student has made in the course. Scoring criteria might focus on the degree of change, the kinds of change, and the student's ability to analyze the change. This category can be effective instructionally, especially for students who have had little experience in critiquing and analyzing their own writing.

Another category that all faculty members might value is "writing process;" students would prepare a portfolio entry illustrating the steps they took to create a final product. This entry could include the final piece of writing plus any notes, discussion summaries, computer network transcripts, rough drafts, or peer review comments that illustrate the writing process that led to the final piece. Again, specifications for this entry might require the student to describe the process. The scoring guide for this entry might focus on the quality of the final product, the effectiveness of the process, and the ability of the student to describe that process clearly and well.

Expository writing might be another category, or creative pieces, or any other kind of thinking and writing that the teachers find instructionally valid. Because the ENFI Project was based on technology, the portfolio design for this project might also ask students to reflect on the importance of technology in communicating ideas and to provide supporting evidence from their own writings.

One advantage of trying to define the categories for a portfolio is that the process asks teachers to review what they are teaching and why. Faculty often find that they need to change their instruction for a portfolio assessment, but that the change is a positive one.

What are the advantages and disadvantages of this kind of portfolio assessment compared to a pre- and postresearch study like the one conducted for the ENFI Project? First of all, the two complement each other. The pre- and postessay or a similar assignment could, in fact, be one entry in the portfolio. It would be the one entry that was written independently, under standardized conditions. The other entries would round out the picture of how the student writes in other, more interactive, situations.

The following list points out possible advantages of a writing portfolio assessment:

- It is student centered – students select pieces, critique their own writing, and prepare the portfolios for evaluation.
- It is a valid way to assess the effects of classroom instruction, for the entries are actual responses to classroom assignments.
- It can demonstrate the process used to create a piece.
- It increases test reliability because it includes multiple and very diverse examples of students' work.
- It encourages careful revision and reflection, for students have time to review and discuss their writing before entering it into the portfolio.
- If the portfolio is judged by faculty outside the classroom, the student's teacher can serve as a mentor or coach rather than a judge.
- The assessment can be formative as well as summative. When students select pieces and have them reviewed in the classroom before sending the portfolio to an evaluation team, the feedback from the teachers and other students can be "formative" for the student. If students build their portfolios and update them throughout the semester, teachers can review them at any time for a quick survey of what the students still need to work on. Then, when the portfolios go outside the classroom for evaluation, they serve as the basis for summative assessment.

Still, many project directors would agree that despite the advantages of a portfolio assessment for instruction and evaluation, there are advantages to a systematic pre- and postassessment in which all students write on the same assignment and under the same conditions. Comparisons are easier, because all students "ran the same race." The quality of the scoring process can be controlled, because the writings are usually scored at a centralized group session. Also, project activities, standards, and results can be linked to other studies and projects – although as portfolio assessment becomes more popular in the United States, outside models, standards, and research studies of this approach may become readily available, too.

The two approaches are complementary, and this kind of two-pronged assessment can serve multiple purposes. Will it provide a better assessment process for students, teachers, and project directors? The promise is in, but the jury is still out.

Appendix A: PPST scoring guide

Scores

6 A 6 essay demonstrates a high degree of competence in response to the assignment but may have a few minor errors.
An essay in this category
   • is well organized and coherently developed
   • clearly explains or illustrates key ideas
   • demonstrates syntactic variety
   • clearly displays facility in the use of language
   • is generally free from errors in mechanics, usage, and sentence structure

5 A 5 essay demonstrates clear competence in response to the assignment but may have minor errors.
An essay in this category
   • is generally well organized and coherently developed
   • explains or illustrates key ideas
   • displays facility in the use of language
   • is generally free from errors in mechanics, usage, and sentence structure

4 A 4 essay demonstrates competence in response to the assignment.
An essay in this category
   • is adequately organized and developed
   • explains or illustrates some of the key ideas
   • demonstrates adequate facility with language
   • may display some errors in mechanics, usage, or sentence structure, but not a consistent pattern of such errors

3 A 3 essay demonstrates some degree of competence in response to the assignment but is clearly flawed.
An essay in this category reveals one or more of the following weaknesses:
   • inadequate organization or development
   • inadequate explanation or illustration of key ideas
   • a pattern or accumulation of errors in mechanics, usage, or sentence structure
   • limited or inappropriate word choice

2 A 2 essay demonstrates only limited competence and is seriously flawed.
An essay in this category reveals one or more of the following weaknesses:
   • weak organization or very little development
   • little or no relevant detail
   • serious errors in mechanics, usage, sentence structure, or word choice

1 A 1 essay demonstrates fundamental deficiencies in writing skills.
An essay in this category contains serious and persistent writing errors or is incoherent or is undeveloped.

Appendix B: Student information sheet for beginning of semester ENFI students

Please provide the following information. All of this information will remain confidential and be used for group data only. No student will be singled out by name or ID number. We are asking for your name ONLY so we can locate you again at the end of the semester.

1. Date _____
2. Name _____
3. Student ID _____
4. Class (e.g., English 50, Freshman Comp. 103, etc.) _____
5. Teacher of this class _____
6. Year in school
    _____ Freshman
    _____ Sophomore
    _____ Junior
    _____ Senior
    _____ Other (please specify)
7. Age (optional)
    _____ 17–19
    _____ 20–21
    _____ 22–30
    _____ 31–40
    _____ 40 +
8. Gender
    _____ Male
    _____ Female
9. Ethnicity (optional)
    _____ White
    _____ Black
    _____ Native American
    _____ Hispanic
    _____ Asian American
10. Language spoken in the home
    _____ (please specify)
11. Language you feel most comfortable with
    _____ (please specify)
12. What kinds of writing aids did you use when you wrote this paper?
    _____ none
    _____ on-line dictionaries
    _____ in-class dictionaries
    _____ on-line thesauruses
    _____ in-class thesauruses
    _____ on-line spelling checkers
    _____ other (please specify) _____

13. Please indicate your experience with ENFI (using a computer network to communicate with the teacher and other students)

    _____ This is my first semester/quarter in an ENFI class

    _____ This is my second semester/quarter in an ENFI class

    _____ I have had two ENFI classes before

    _____ I have had three or more ENFI classes before

14. Do you know how to use a word processor?

    _____ yes, fairly well

    _____ yes, a little

    _____ no

15. Do you use a word processor for your writing classes?

    _____ always

    _____ sometimes

    _____ never

16. When writing for your classes, do you compose with pencil and paper before entering your text into the word processor?

    _____ always

    _____ sometimes

    _____ never

17. When writing for your classes, do you compose your essays directly at the word processor?

    _____ always

    _____ sometimes

    _____ never

18. How would you rate your typing ability?

    _____ I do not type at all

    _____ minimal (under 30 wpm)

    _____ average (30–60 wpm)

    _____ proficient (60+ wpm)

Appendix C:
Students' responses to questionnaires

The students' responses to demographic questions are presented as percentages. Because of rounding, the percentages for some columns may not always add up to 100%.

1. The majority of ENFI and non-ENFI students were freshmen although other school years were represented in both populations.

Year in School	ENFI	Non-ENFI
Freshman	83%	91%
Sophomore	0%	1%
Junior	3%	2%
Senior	13%	6%

2. Gender differences between the ENFI and non-ENFI groups were minimal, with a majority of male students in both groups.

Gender	ENFI	Non-ENFI
Male	59%	55%
Female	41%	45%

3. Ethnicity characteristics were similar for ENFI and non-ENFI, with a preponderance of white students.

Ethnicity	ENFI	Non-ENFI
White	84%	82%
Black	9%	9%
Native American	2%	0%
Hispanic	4%	4%
Asian-American	2%	6%

4. ENFI and non-ENFI students were similar in age. The majority of students in each group were between 17 and 19 years old.

Age	ENFI	Non-ENFI
17–19	72%	77%
20–21	17%	12%
22–30	10%	9%
31–40	1%	0%
40+	1%	2%

5. Although the overwhelming majority of ENFI and non-ENFI students reported speaking English at home, quite a few students reported using American Sign Language or speaking other languages such as Italian, Greek, and Spanish. Slightly more ENFI than non-ENFI students reported using sign language in their homes.

Language spoken at home	ENFI	Non-ENFI
English	82%	83%
American Sign	8%	4%
Other	10%	13%

6. Although most students answered "English" when asked to specify the "language you feel most comfortable with," it is interesting to compare the "American Sign" and "Other" responses in the two tables pertaining to language. Many more students report feeling "most comfortable" with American Sign Language than say they use it at home, and most of the students who reported speaking a foreign language at home still reported that English is their "most comfortable" language.

Most comfortable language	ENFI	Non-ENFI
English	86%	88%
American Sign	12%	9%
Other	2%	3%

Previous experience with ENFI	ENFI	Non-ENFI
None	94%	88%
One class	5%	7%
Two classes	1%	3%
Three or more	1%	1%

References

Akrich, M. (1987). *The de-scription of technical objects.* In W. E. Bijker & J. Law (Eds.), *Shaping technology/Building society: Studies in sociotechnical change* (pp. 205–224). Cambridge: MIT Press.

Allen, T. (1986). Patterns of academic achievement among hearing impaired students: 1974–1983. In A. N. Shildroth & M. A. Karchmer (Eds.), *Deaf children in America* (pp. 161–206). San Diego: College-Hill Press.

Apple, M. (1986). *Teachers and texts: A political economy of class and gender relations in education.* New York: Routledge & Kegan Paul.

Balester, V., & Halasek, K. (1989). Sharing authority: Collaborative teaching in a computer-based writing course. In T. Batson, G. Sirc, & W. Wright (Eds.), *Proposal abstracts from the Fifth Computers and Writing Conference* (pp. 4–6). Washington, DC: Gallaudet University.

Balestri, D. (1988). *Ivory towers, silicon basements.* Paper presented at EDUCOM88 conference, Washington, DC.

Barthes, R. (1985). *From speech to writing. The grain of the voice.* New York: Hill and Wang.

Bartholomae, D. (1985). Inventing the university. In M. Rose (Ed.), *When a writer can't write* (pp. 134–165). New York: Guilford.

Bartholomae, D. (1987). Writing on the margins: The concept of literacy in higher education. *A sourcebook for basic writing teachers* (pp. 66–83). New York: Random House.

Bartlett, F. C. (1932). *Remembering.* Englewood Cliffs, NJ: Regents/Prentice-Hall.

Batson, T. (1987, January). *The ENFI project: Computer networks in the writing classroom.* Project proposal to the Annenberg/CPB Project. Washington, DC: Gallaudet University.

Batson, T. (1988a). The ENFI Project: A networked classroom approach to writing instruction. *Academic Computing, 2,* 32–33, 55–56.

Batson, T. (1988b). *A study of conversation as a heuristic in face-to-face and computer network interaction.* Paper presented at the Conference on College Composition and Communication, St. Louis.

Batson, T. (1990). *Network-based classrooms: Fond memories and ripe possibilities.* Paper presented at the Maine Conference on Classroom Applications for Computer-Assisted Composition Instruction, Orono.

Baudrillard, J. (1983). *In the shadow of the silent majorities, or the end of the social and other essays.* New York: Semiotext(e).

Baudrillard, J. (1990). *Seduction.* New York: St. Martin's.

Beach, R. (1979). The effects of between-draft teacher evaluation versus student self-evaluation on high school students' revising of rough drafts. *Research in the Teaching of English, 13,* 111–119.

Beil, D. (Ed.). (1989). *Teacher's guide to using computer networks for written interaction.* Washington, DC: Realtime Learning Systems.

Bereiter, C., & Scardamalia, M. (1987). The role of production factors in writing ability. In Bereiter & Scardamalia (Eds.), *The psychology of written composition* (pp. 97–132). Hillsdale, NJ: Erlbaum.

Berlin, J. (1982). Contemporary composition: The major pedagogical theories. *College English, 44,* 765–777.

Berman, P., & McLaughlin, M. (1975). *Federal programs supporting educational change: Vol. 4. The findings in review.* Santa Monica: Rand Corporation.

Bernard, H. R., & Pelto, P. (1987). *Technology and social change* (2nd ed.). Prospect Heights, IL: Waveland Press.

286

Bijker, W. E., Hughes, T. P., & Pinch, T. (1987). *The social construction of technological systems.* Cambridge: MIT Press.

Bishop, W. (1988, May). Helping peer writing groups succeed. *Teaching English in the Two-Year College, 15,* 120–125.

Bizzell, P. (1982). Cognition, convention, and certainty: What we need to know about writing. *Pre/Text, 3,* 213–243.

Bjerknes, G., Ehn, P., & Kyng, M. (Eds.). (1987). *Computers and democracy: A Scandinavian challenge.* Brookfield, VT: Gower Press.

Bloom, A. (1987). *The closing of the American mind.* New York: Simon & Schuster.

Boggs, S. T. (1985). *Speaking, relating and learning: A study of Hawaiian children at home and at school.* Norwood, NJ. Ablex.

Borich, G. D. (1990). Decision-oriented evaluation. In H. J. Walberg & G. D. Haertel (Eds.), *The international encyclopedia of educational evaluation* (pp. 31–35). Oxford: Pergamon Press.

Boruta, M., Carpenter, C., Harvey, M., Keyser, T., LaBonte, J., Mehan, H., & Rodriguez, D. (1983). Computers in the schools: Stratifier or equalizer? *The Quarterly Newsletter of the Laboratory of Comparative Human Cognition, 5,* 51–55.

Bowles, S., & Gintis, H. (1976). *Schooling in capitalist America: Educational reform and the contradictions of economic life.* New York: Basic Books.

Britton, J. M., Burgess, T., Martin, N., McLeod, A., & Rosen, H. (1975). *The development of writing abilities (11–18).* Urbana, IL: National Council of Teachers of English.

Brown, J. S., Collins, A., & Duguid, P. (1989). Situated cognition and the culture of learning. *Educational Researcher, 18,* 32–42.

Bruce, B. (1991). Roles for computers in teaching the English language arts. In J. Jensen, J. Flood, D. Lapp, & J. Squire (Eds.), *Handbook of research on teaching the English language arts* (pp. 536–541). New York: Macmillan.

Bruce, B., Michaels, S., & Watson-Gegeo, K. (1985). How computers can change the writing process. *Language Arts, 62,* 143–149.

Bruce, B., & Peyton, J. K. (1990). A new writing environment and an old culture: A situated evaluation of computer networking to teach writing. *Interactive Learning Environments, 1*(2), 171–191.

Bruce, B., & Rubin, A. (1993). *Electronic Quills: A situated evaluation of using computers for teaching writing in classrooms.* Hillsdale, NJ: Erlbaum.

Bruffee, K. (1983). Writing and reading as collaborative or social acts. In J. Hayes, P. Roth, J. Ramsey, & R. Foulke (Eds.), *The writer's mind: Writing as a mode of thinking* (pp. 159–170). Urbana, IL: National Council of Teachers of English.

Bruffee, K. A. (1984). Collaborative learning and the "conversation of mankind." *College English, 46* (7), 635–652.

Bruffee, K. A. (1985). *A short course in writing: Practical rhetoric for teaching composition through collaborative learning.* Boston: Little, Brown.

Brunswik, E. (1956). *Perception and the representative design of psychological experiments.* Berkeley: University of California Press.

Bump, J. (1990). Radical changes in class discussion using networked computers. *Computers and the Humanities, 24,* 49–65.

Burke, J. (1978). *Connections.* Boston: Little, Brown.

Burns, H. (1979). *Stimulating rhetorical invention through computer-assisted instruction.* Doctoral dissertation, University of Texas at Austin. (ERIC Document Reproduction Service No. ED 188 245)

Bussis, A. M., Chittenden, E. A., & Amarel, M. (1976). *Beyond surface curriculum.* Boulder, CO: Westview Press.

Butler, W. (1991, March 21). *Building an electronic discourse curriculum.* Paper presented at the Conference on College Composition and Communication, Boston.

Carter, L. (1989, March 17). *Telecommunications and networked personal computers: Opening up the classroom.* Paper presented at the Conference on College Composition and Communication, Seattle.

Caswell, S. (1988). *E-mail.* Boston: Artech.

Chandler, M. J. (1973). Egocentrism and anti-social behavior: The assessment and training of social perspective-taking skills. *Developmental Psychology, 9,* 326–332.

Charrow, V. (1974). *Deaf English: An investigation of the written English competence of deaf adolescents* (Tech. Rep. No. 236). Stanford University, Institute for Mathematical Studies in the Social Sciences.

Charrow, V. R. (1981). The written English of deaf adolescents. In M. F. Whiteman (Ed.), *Writing: The nature, development, and teaching of written communication* (pp. 179–187). Hillsdale, NJ: Erlbaum.

Clifford, J. (1986). On ethnographic allegory. In J. Clifford & G. E. Marcus (Eds.), *Writing culture: The poetics and politics of ethnography* (pp. 98–121). Berkeley: University of California Press.

Clyne, S. (1990). Adversary evaluation. In H. J. Walberg & G. D. Haertel (Eds.), *The international encyclopedia of educational evaluation* (pp. 77–79). Oxford: Pergamon Press.

Cohen, D. K. (1988). Educational technology and school organization. In R. Nickerson & P. P. Zodhiates (Eds.), *Technology in education: Looking toward 2020* (pp. 231–265). Hillsdale, NJ: Erlbaum.

Collins, T. (1989). Some possible limits to the system. In D. H. Bell (Ed.), *Teacher's guide to using computer networks for written interaction* (pp. 53–57). Washington, DC: Realtime Learning Systems.

Cronbach, L. J. (1982). *Designing evaluations of educational and social programs.* San Francisco: Jossey-Bass.

Cuban, L. (1986). *Teachers and machines: The classroom use of technology since 1920.* New York: Teachers College Press.

Cummings, T. G. (1981). Designing effective work groups. In P. C. Nystrom & W. H. Starbuck (Eds.), *Handbook of organizational design* (pp. 250–271). Oxford: Oxford University Press.

Dewey, J., & Bentley, A. F. (1949). *The knowing and the known.* Boston: Beacon Press.

Dexter, L. A. (1970). *Elite and specialized interviewing.* Evanston, IL: Northwestern University Press.

DiMatteo, A. (1990). Under erasure: A theory for interactive writing in real time. *Computers and Composition, 7* (special issue), 71–84.

Dorr-Bremme, D. W. (1990). Naturalistic evaluation. In H. J. Walberg & G. D. Haertel (Eds.), *The international encyclopedia of educational evaluation* (pp. 66–68). Oxford: Pergamon Press.

Dukes, W. F. (1965). *N1. Psychological Bulletin, 64,* 74–79.

Elbaz, F. (1981). The teacher's "practical knowledge": Report of a case study. *Curriculum Inquiry, 11*(1), 43–71.

Elbow, P. (1973). *Writing without teachers.* New York: Oxford University Press.

Elbow, P. (1981). *Writing with power.* New York: Oxford University Press.

Elbow, P., & Benaloff, P. (1989). *A community of writers: A workshop course in writing.* New York: Random House.

Emig, J. (1971). *The composing processes of twelfth graders.* Urbana, IL: National Council of Teachers of English.

ENFILog (1985 to present). Washington, DC: Gallaudet University, ENFI Project.

Evans, M., & Bernard, H. R. (1987). Word processing, office drudgery, and the microcomputer revolution. In H. Bernard & P. Pelto (Eds.), *Technology and social change* (2nd ed., pp. 329–358). Prospect Heights, IL: Waveland Press.

Faigley, L. (1989). Judging writing, judging selves. *College Composition and Communication, 40,* 395–412.

Faigley, L. (1990). Subverting the electronic workbook: Teaching writing using networked computers. In D. Daiker & M. Morenberg (Eds.), *The writing teacher as researcher: Essays in the theory and practice of class-based research* (pp. 290–311). Portsmouth, NH: Boynton/ Cook, Heinemann.

Faigley, L. (1993). *Fragments of rationality: Postmodernity and the subject of composition.* Pittsburgh: University of Pittsburgh Press.

Flower, L. S. (1979). Writer-based prose: A cognitive basis for problems in writing. *College English, 41,* 19–37.

Flower, L. S. (1981). *Problem-solving strategies for writing.* San Diego: Harcourt Brace Jovanovich.

Flower, L. (1985). *Problem-solving strategies for writing* (2nd ed.). New York: Harcourt Brace Jovanovich.

Flower, L., & Hayes, J. R. (1981). A cognitive process theory of writing. *College Composition and Communication, 32,* 365–387.

Fondacaro, R., & Higgins, E. T. (1985). Cognitive consequences of communication mode. In D. R. Olson, N. Torrance, & A. Hildyard (Eds.), *Literacy, language, and learning: The nature and consequences of reading and writing* (pp. 73–101). Cambridge: Cambridge University Press.

Foucault, M. (1972). The discourse on language. In *The archaeology of knowledge and the discourse on language* (A. M. Sheridan Smith, Trans.) (pp. 215–237). New York: Pantheon.

Freedman, S. W. (1987). *Response to student writing.* Urbana, IL: National Council of Teachers of English.

Fulkerson, R. (1979). Four philosophies of composition. *College Composition and Communication, 30,* 343–348.

Fullon, M. (1982). *The meaning of educational change.* New York: Teachers College Press.

Gann, K. (1990, May 1). Plundering for art. *The Village Voice,* p. 102.

Gee, J. (1990). *Social linguistics and literacy.* Philadelphia: Taylor & Francis.

Geertz, C. (1973). Thick description: Toward an interpretive theory of culture. In C. Geertz (Ed.), *The interpretation of cultures: Selected essays by Clifford Geertz* (pp. 3–33). New York: Basic Books.

George, E. L. (1990). Taking women professors seriously: Female authority in the computerized classroom. *Computers and Composition, 7* (special issue), 45–52.

Gergen, K. J. (1985). The social constructionist movement in modern psychology. *American Psychologist, 40,* 266–275.

Ginzberg, E. (1982). The mechanization of work. *Scientific American, 247,* 66–75.

Goetz, J. P., & LeCompte, M. D. (1984). *Ethnography and qualitative design in educational research.* Orlando: Academic Press.

Goffman, E. (1981). *Forms of talk.* Philadelphia: University of Pennsylvania Press.

Goody, J., & Watt, J. (1963). The consequences of literacy. *Comparative Studies in Society and History, 5,* 304–345.

Hairston, M. (1982). The winds of change: Thomas Kuhn and the revolution in the teaching of writing. *College Composition and Communication, 33,* 76–88.

Hamilton, E., & Cairns, H. (1961). *The collected dialogues of Plato including the letters.* New York: Pantheon Books.

Harste, J. C., & Burke, C. L. (1977). A new hypothesis for reading teacher research: Both teaching and learning of reading are theoretically based. In P. D. Pearson (Ed.), *Reading: Theory, research, and practice* (pp. 32–40). Chicago: National Reading Conference.

Hartman, K., Neuwirth, C. M., Kiesler, S., Sproull, L., Cochran, C., Palmquist, M., & Zubrow, D. (1991). Patterns of social interaction and learning to write: Some effects of network technologies. *Written Communication, 8,* 79–113.

Havelock, E. (1976). *Origins of Western literacy.* Toronto: Ontario Institute for Studies in Education Press.

Hawisher, G., & Selfe, C. (1990). Letter from the editors. *Computers and Composition, 7* (special issue), 5–14.

Hawkins, J. (1987a). The interpretation of Logo in practice. In R. Pea & K. Sheingold (Eds.),

Mirrors of minds: Patterns of experience in educational computing (pp. 3–34). Norwood, NJ: Ablex.

Hawkins, J. (1987b). Computers and girls: Rethinking the issues. In R. Pea & K. Sheingold (Eds.), *Mirrors of minds: Patterns of experience in educational computing* (pp. 242–257). Norwood, NJ: Ablex.

Hayes, J. R., & Flower, L. S. (1980). Identifying the organization of writing processes. In L. W. Gregg & E. R. Steinberg (Eds.), *Cognitive processes in writing* (pp. 3–30). Hillsdale, NJ: Erlbaum.

Hebdige, D. (1988). *Hiding in the light.* London: Routledge.

Higgins, E. T., McCann, C. D., & Fondacaro, R. (1982). The "communication game": Goal-directed encoding and cognitive consequences. *Social Cognition, 1,* 21–37.

Hord, S. M., Rutherford, W. L., Huling-Austin, L., & Hall, G. (1987). *Taking charge of change.* Alexandria, VA: Association for Supervision and Curriculum Development.

Horowitz, D., & Peyton, J. K. (1988a, December). *The ENFI Consortium: Report of work conducted during spring, 1988.* Washington, DC: Gallaudet University ENFI Project.

Horowitz, D., & Peyton, J. K. (1988b). *The ENFI Consortium: Research report submitted to the Annenberg/CPB Project.* Washington, DC: Gallaudet University.

Huyssen, A. (1989). The cultural politics of pop. In P. Taylor (Ed.), *Post–pop art* (pp. 45–77). Cambridge: MIT Press.

Johnson, R., Liddell, S., & Erting, C. (1989). *Unlocking the curriculum: Principles for achieving access in deaf education* (Working paper, pp. 89–93). Washington, DC: Gallaudet University, Gallaudet Research Institute.

Kaufer, D., Geisler, C., & Neuwirth, C. (1989). *Arguing from sources: Exploring issues through reading and writing.* New York: Harcourt Brace Jovanovich.

Kiesler, C. A. (1971). *The psychology of commitment.* New York: Academic Press.

Kiesler, S., Siegel, J., & McGuire, T. W. (1984). Social psychological aspects of computer-mediated communication. *American Psychologist, 39*(10), 1123–1134.

Kiesler, S., Zubrow, D., Moses, A. M., & Geller, V. (1985). Affect in computer-mediated communication: An experiment in synchronous terminal-to-terminal discussion. *Human–Computer Interaction, 1,* 77–104.

Klima, E., & Bellugi, U. (1979). *The signs of language.* Cambridge: Harvard University Press.

Kling, R. (1980). Social analyses of computing: Theoretical perspectives in recent empirical research. *Computing Surveys, 12,* 61–110.

Kling, R., & Scacchi, W. (1982). The web of computing: Computing technology as social organization. *Advances in Computers, 21,* 3–78.

Kraut, R. E., & Lewis, S. H. (1984). Feedback and the coordination of conversation. In H. Sypher & J. Applegate (Eds.), *Cognition and communication.* Hillsdale, NJ: Erlbaum.

Kraut, R. E., Lewis, S. H., & Swezey, L. W. (1982). Listener responsiveness and the coordination of conversation. *Journal of Personality and Social Psychology, 43,* 718–731.

Kremers, M. (1988). Adams Sherman Hill meets ENFI: An inquiry and a retrospective. *Computers and Composition, 5*(3), 69–77.

Kremers, M. (1990). Sharing authority on a synchronous network: The case for riding the beast. *Computers and Composition, 7* (special issue), 33–44.

Langston, M. D., & Batson, T. (1990). The social shifts invited by working collaboratively on computer networks: The ENFI Project. In C. Handa (Ed.), *Computers and community: Teaching composition in the twenty-first century* (pp. 141–159). Portsmouth, NH: Boynton/Cook, Heinemann.

Latour, B. (1986). Visualization and cognition: Thinking with eyes and hands. *Knowledge and society: Studies in the sociology of culture, past and present, 6,* 1–40.

LeFevre, K. (1987). *Invention as a social act.* Carbondale: Southern Illinois University Press.

Lepper, M. R., & Gurtner, J. L. (1989). Children and computers: Approaching the twenty-first century. *American Psychologist, 44*(2), 170–178.

Lofland, J. (1984). *Analyzing social settings.* Belmont, CA: Wadsworth.

Lou, M. (1988). The history of the education of the deaf in the United States. In M. Strong (Ed.), *Language, learning and deafness* (pp. 75–112). New York: Cambridge University Press.

Lucas, C. K. (1988a). Toward ecological evaluation. *The Quarterly of the National Writing Project and the Center for the Study of Writing, 10*(1), 1–3, 12–17.

Lucas, C. K. (1988b). Toward ecological evaluation: Part 2. Recontextualizing literacy assessment. *The Quarterly of the National Writing Project and the Center for the Study of Writing, 10*(2), 4–10.

Lunsford, A. A. (1979). Cognitive development and the basic writer. *College English, 41*, 38–46.

Lunsford, E., Lunsford, L., & Lunsford, A. (1984). Audience addressed/audience invoked: The role of audience in composition theory and pedagogy. *College Composition and Communication, 35*, 155–171.

Macrorie, K. (1970). *Uptaught*. Rochelle Park, NJ: Hayden Book Company.

Macrorie, K. (1980). *Searching writing: A contextbook*. Rochelle Park, NJ: Hayden Book Company.

MacKenzie, D., & Wajcman, J. (Eds.). (1985). *The social shaping of technology: How the refrigerator got its hum*. Milton Keynes, UK: Open University Press.

Malone, T. W., & Rockart, J. F. (1991). Computers, networks, and the corporation. *Scientific American, 265*(3), 128–136.

Mander, J. (1978). *Four arguments for the elimination of television*. New York: Quill.

Marcus, G. (1989). *Lipstick traces: A secret history of the twentieth century*. Cambridge: Harvard University Press.

Michaels, S., Cazden, C., & Bruce, B. (1985). Whose computer is it anyway? *Science for the People, 17*(36), 43–44.

Miles, M. B., & Huberman, A. M. (1984). *Qualitative data analysis: A sourcebook of new methods*. Beverly Hills: Sage Publications.

Moffett, J. (1968). *Teaching the universe of discourse*. Boston: Houghton-Mifflin.

Morris, J., Satyanarayanan, M., Conner, M., Howard, J. H., Rosenthal, D. S. H., & Smith, F. D. (1986). Andrew: A distributed personal computing environment. *Communications of the ACM, 29*, 184–201.

Neuwirth, C. M., Gillespie, T., & Palmquist, M. (1988). *A student's guide to collaborative writing with CECE Talk: A computer network tool*. Pittsburgh: Carnegie Mellon University, Center for Educational Computing in English and Annenberg/CPB.

Neuwirth, C. M., Kaufer, D. S., Keim, G., & Gillespie, T. (1988, Jan.). *The Comments program: Computer support for response to writing* (Tech. Rep. No. CMU-CECE-TR-2). Pittsburgh: Carnegie Mellon University, Department of English, Center for Educational Computing in English.

Neuwirth, C., Palmquist, M., & Cochran, C. (1989, April). *Computer-mediated collaborative planning: Some affective and cognitive dimensions*. Paper presented at the 1989 AERA Annual Meeting, San Francisco.

Neuwirth, C. M., Palmquist, M., & Gillespie, T. (1988). *An instructor's guide to collaborative writing with CECE Talk: A computer network tool*. Pittsburgh: Carnegie Mellon University, Center for Educational Computing in English and Annenberg/CPB.

Neuwirth, C., Palmquist, M., & Hajduk, T. J. (1990, April). *Collaborative writing and the role of external representations*. Paper presented at the 1990 AERA Annual Meeting, Boston.

Noble, D. F. (1984). *Forces of production: A social history of industrial automation*. New York: Knopf.

Palinscar, A. S., & Brown, A. L. (1984). Reciprocal teaching of comprehension-fostering and monitoring activities. *Cognition and Instruction, 1*, 117–175.

Papanek, V. (1973). *Design for the real world*. New York: Bantam Books.

Papert, S. (1980). *Mindstorms*. New York: Basic Books.

Papert, S. (1987, January–February). Computer criticism vs. technocentric thinking. *Educational Researcher, 16*, 22–30.

Parlett, M. R. (1990). Illuminative evaluation. In H. J. Walberg & G. D. Haertel (Eds.), *The international encyclopedia of educational evaluation* (pp. 68–73). Oxford: Pergamon Press.

Peyton, J. K. (1989a). Computer networks in the writing classroom: An annotated bibliography. *Computers and Composition, 6*(3), 105–122.

Peyton, J. K. (1989b). Cross-age tutoring on a local area computer network: Moving from informal interaction to formal academic writing. *The Writing Instructor, 8*(2), 57–67.

Peyton, J. K. (1990). Technological innovation meets institution: Birth of creativity or murder of a great idea? *Computers and Composition, 7* (special issue), 15–32.

Peyton, J. K., & Batson, T. (1986). Computer networking: Making connections between speech and writing. *ERIC/CLL News Bulletin, 10*(1), 1–7.

Peyton, J. K., & Mackinson, J. (1989). Writing and talking about writing: Computer networking with elementary students. In D. M. Johnson & D. H. Roen (Eds.), *Richness in writing: Empowering ESL students* (pp. 100–119). New York: Longman.

Peyton, J. K., Michaelson, S., & Batson, T. (1988, February). *The ENFI Consortium: Report of work conducted during fall, 1987.* Washington, DC: Gallaudet University.

Peyton, J. K., & Miller, J. D. (1989). Dramatic interaction on a computer network: Creating worlds with words and ideas. In D. Beil (Ed.), *Teacher's guide to using computer networks for written interaction* (pp. 101–110). Washington, DC: Realtime Learning Systems.

Powers, D. E., Fowles, M. E., Farnum, M., Ramsey, P. (1992). *Will they think less of my handwritten essay if others word process theirs? Effects on essay scores of intermingling handwritten and word-processed essays* (Research Report No. RR 92–45). Princeton, NJ: Educational Testing Service.

Pre-Professional Skills Test (PPST). Princeton, NJ: Educational Testing Service.

Quigley, S. P., & Paul, P. (1984). *Language and deafness.* San Diego: College Hill Press.

Rafoth, B. (1988). Discourse community: Where writers, readers, and texts come together. In B. Rafoth & D. Rubin (Eds.), *The social construction of written communication* (pp. 131–146). Norwood, NJ: Ablex.

Rice, R. E., & Love, G. (1987). Electronic emotion: Socio-emotional content in a computer-mediated communication network. *Communication Research, 14*(1), 85–105.

Richardson, V., Anders, P., Tidwell, D., & Lloyd, C. (1991). The relationship between teachers' beliefs and practices in reading comprehension instruction. *American Educational Research Journal, 28,* 559–586.

Rodrigues, R., & Rodrigues, D. (1984). Computer-based invention: Its place and potential. *College Composition and Communication, 35,* 78–87.

Rohman, D. G. (1965). Pre-writing: The stage of discovery in the writing process. *College Composition and Communication, 35,* 106–112.

Rosaldo, M. (1980). *Knowledge and passion.* New York: Cambridge University Press.

Rose, M. (1983). Remedial writing courses: A critique and a proposal. *College English, 45,* 109–128.

Rosenblatt, L. M. (1978). *The reader, the text, the poem: The transactional theory of the literary work.* Carbondale: Southern Illinois University Press.

Rubin, A., & Bruce, B. (1990). Alternate realizations of purpose in computer-supported writing. *Theory into Practice, 29,* 256–263.

Rubin, D. L., & Dodd, W. M. (1987). *Talking into writing.* Urbana, IL: NCTE and ERIC Clearinghouse on Reading and Communication Skills.

Rubin, D. L., & Rafoth, B. A. (1986). Social cognitive ability as a predictor of the quality of expository and persuasive writing among college freshmen. *Research in the Teaching of English, 20,* 9–21.

Ruggles-Gere, A. (1987). *Writing groups: History, theory, and implications.* Carbondale: Southern Illinois University Press.

Russell, S. J., Mokros, J. R., & Foster, J. C. (1984). *Ten years and counting: Who will use computers?* Unpublished manuscript. Cambridge, MA: Technical Education Research Centers.

Safire, W. (1990, July 15). Empowerment and denouncement. *New York Times Magazine,* p. 12.

Scardamalia, M., & Bereiter, C. (1985). Fostering the development of self-regulation in children's knowledge processing. In S. S. Chipman, J. W. Segal, & R. Glaser (Eds.), *Thinking and learning skills: Current research and open questions* (Vol. 2, pp. 563–577). Hillsdale, NJ: Erlbaum.

Scardamalia, M., Bereiter, C., & Steinbach, R. (1984). Teachability of reflective processes in written composition. *Cognitive Science, 8,* 173–190.

Scollon, R., & Scollon, S. B. K. (1981). *Narrative, literacy and face in interethnic communication.* Norwood, NJ: Ablex.

Scott, J. W. (1982). The mechanization of women's work. *Scientific American, 247,* 166–187.

Selfe, C. (1988, July). *Computers as tools of literacy reform: Using feminist theory to inform our use of technology.* Paper presented at the Penn State Conference on Rhetoric and Composition, State College.

Sharp, L. (1952). Steel axes for stone age Australians. In E. Spicer (Ed.), *Human problems in technical change. A casebook* (pp. 69–92). New York: Russell Sage Foundation.

Shavelson, R. J., Winkler, J. D., Stasz, C., Feibel, W., Robyn, A. E., & Shaha, S. (1984, March). *"Successful" teachers' patterns of microcomputer-based mathematics and science instruction* (Report No. N–217–NIE/RC). Santa Monica, CA: Rand.

Siegel, J., Dubrovsky, V., Kiesler, S., & McGuire, T. W. (1986). Group processes in computer-mediated communication. *Organizational behavior and human decision processes, 37,* 157–187.

Sirc, G. (1990, March). *What basic writers talk about when they('re supposed to be) talk(ing) about writing.* Paper presented at the Conference on College Composition and Communication, Chicago.

Sirc, G., & Reynolds, T. (1990). The face of collaboration in the networked writing classroom. *Computers and Composition, 7* (special issue), 53–70.

Slavin, R. E. (1980). Cooperative learning. *Review of Educational Research, 50*(2), 315–342.

Solis, E. G., & Peyton, J. K. (1989, October). *The ENFI Consortium: Report of work conducted during the 1988–1989 school year.* Washington, DC: Gallaudet University ENFI Project.

Sproull, L., & Kiesler, S. (1991). *Connections: New ways of working in the networked organization.* Cambridge: MIT Press.

Stake, R. E. (1990). Responsive evaluation. In H. J. Walberg & G. D. Haertel (Eds.), *The international encyclopedia of educational evaluation* (pp. 75–77). Oxford: Pergamon Press.

Stake, R. E., & Easley, J. (1978). *Case studies in science education.* Urbana: University of Illinois, CIRCE.

Staton, J., Shuy, R., Peyton, J. K., & Reed, L. (1988). *Dialogue journal communication: Classroom, linguistic, social, and cognitive views.* Norwood, NJ: Ablex.

Staudenmaier, S. J. (1985). *Technology's storytellers: Reweaving the human fabric.* Cambridge: The Society for the History of Technology and The MIT Press.

Stecher, B. (1990). Goal-free evaluation. In H. J. Walberg & G. D. Haertel (Eds.), *The international encyclopedia of educational evaluation* (pp. 41–42). Oxford: Pergamon Press.

Stein, M. I. (1974). *Stimulating creativity.* New York: Academic Press.

Stenhouse, L. (1990). Case study methods. In H. J. Walberg & G. D. Haertel (Eds.), *The international encyclopedia of educational evaluation* (pp. 644–649). Oxford: Pergamon Press.

Stewart, D. (1986). *The versatile writer.* Lexington, MA: D.C. Heath.

Suchman, L. (1988). Designing with the user [Review of *Computers and democracy: A Scandinavian challenge* by G. Bjerknes, P. Ehn, and M. Kyng, Eds.]. *ACM Transactions on Office Information Systems, 6*(2), 173–183.

Tannen, D. (1985). Relative focus on involvement in oral and written discourse. In D. R. Olson, N. Torrance, & A. Hildyard (Eds.), *Literacy, language, and learning: The nature and consequences of reading and writing* (pp. 124–147). Cambridge: Cambridge University Press.

Tate, G. (1990). *Teaching writing in 1990.* Paper presented at the Maine Conference on Classroom Applications for Computer-Assisted Composition Instruction, Orono.

Taylor, P. (1989). Computer networks, discourse communities, and chaos. In T. Batson, G. Sirc, & W. Wright (Eds.), *Proposal abstracts from the Fifth Computers and Writing Conference* (pp. 91–92). Washington, DC: Gallaudet University.

Thompson, D. P. (1988a, July). *Comparison of networked and non networked composition classes.* Paper presented at the Penn State Conference on Rhetoric and Composition, State College.

Thompson, D. P. (1988b). Conversational networking: Why the teacher gets most of the lines. *Collegiate Microcomputers, 6*(3), 193–201.

Thompson, D. P. (1989a). Using the ENFI network to distribute text for discussion. In D. Beil (Ed.), *Teacher's guide to using computer networks for written interaction* (pp. 119–122). Washington, DC: Realtime Learning Systems.

Thompson, D. P. (1989b). Using a local area network to teach computer revision skills. *Journal of Teaching Writing, 8*(2), 77–85.

Thompson, D. P. (1990a). Electronic bulletin boards: A timeless place for collaborative writing projects. *Computers and Composition, 7*(3), 43–53.

Thompson, D. P. (1990b). Network capabilities and academic realities: Implementing interactive networking in a community college environment. *Journal of Computer-Based Instruction, 17*(1), 17–22.

Traxler, C. B. (1990, April). *Assessing the writing competence of deaf college students: A new use for the TOEFL TWE.* Paper presented at the Annual Meeting of the American Educational Research Association, Boston.

Tuman, M. (1992a). *Literacy online: The promise (and peril) of reading and writing with computers.* Pittsburgh: University of Pittsburgh Press.

Tuman, M. (1992b). *Word perfect: Literacy in the computer age.* Pittsburgh: University of Pittsburgh Press.

Wagner, B. J. (1987). *The effects of role playing on written persuasion: An age and channel comparison of fourth and eighth graders.* Unpublished doctoral dissertation, University of Illinois at Chicago.

Walberg, H. J., & Haertel, G. D. (Eds.). (1990). *The international encyclopedia of educational evaluation.* Oxford: Pergamon Press.

Wiener, H. (1986). Collaborative learning in the classroom: A guide to evaluation. *College English, 48,* 52–61.

Wittgenstein, L. (1953). *Philosophical investigations* (G. E. M. Anscombe, trans.). New York: Macmillan.

Wolf, R. L. (1990). Judicial evaluation. In H. J. Walberg & G. D. Haertel (Eds.), *The international encyclopedia of educational evaluation* (pp. 79–81). Oxford: Pergamon Press.

Wolf, R. M. (1990). The nature of educational evaluation. In H. J. Walberg & G. D. Haertel (Eds.), *The international encyclopedia of educational evaluation* (pp. 8–15). Oxford: Pergamon Press.

Further reading

The interested reader might wish to consult the following articles written by members of the ENFI Consortium, but not included in the reference list.

Barker, T. T., & Kemp, F. O. (1990). Network theory: A post-modern pedagogy for the writing classroom. In C. Handa (Ed.), *Computers and community: Teaching composition in the twenty-first century* (pp. 1–27). Portsmouth, NH: Boynton/Cook.

Batson, T. (1988). The ENFI Project: An update. *Teaching English to Deaf and Second-Language Students, 6*(2), 5–8.

Batson, T. (1989, March). *A selective national survey of ENFI real-time conferencing in the composition classroom.* Paper presented at the Annual Meeting of the Conference on College

Composition and Communication, Seattle. (ERIC Document Reproduction Service No. ED 303 827)

Batson, T. (1989). Teaching in networked classrooms. In C. L. Selfe, D. Rodrigues, & W. R. Oates (Eds.), *Computers in English and language arts: The challenge of teacher education* (pp. 247–255). Urbana, IL: National Council of Teachers of English.

Batson, T., & Peyton, J. K. (1986). The computer as fifth sense: Networking with deaf students to simulate natural language acquisition. *Teaching English to Deaf and Second-Language Students, 4*(2), 12–18.

Erhmann, S. C. (1988). Assessing the open end of learning: Roles for new technologies. *Liberal Education, 74*(3), 5–11.

Miller, J. D. (1989, March). *Script writing on the ENFI computer system.* Paper presented at the 23rd Annual TESOL Convention, San Antonio.

O'Connor, D., Peyton, J. K., & Solis, E. (1989). Performance of ENFI and non-ENFI students on Gallaudet University's English Placement Test: 1988–89 school year. *Teaching English to Deaf and Second-Language Students, 7*(2), 15–18.

O'Connor, D., Peyton, J. K., & Traxler, C. (1990). Performance of ENFI and non-ENFI students on Gallaudet University's English Placement Test: 1989–90 school year. *Teaching English to Deaf and Second-Language Students, 8*(2), 10–17.

Peyton, J. K. (1988). Computer networking: Providing a context for deaf students to write collaboratively. *Teaching English to Deaf and Second-Language Students, 6*(2), 19–24.

Peyton, J. K. (1988). Local area networks with deaf students: Some benefits and some considerations. *Teaching English to Deaf and Second-Language Students, 6*(2), 10–15.

Peyton, J. K., & Mackinson, J. (in press). Studying the power and possibilities of interactive writing on a computer network: A teacher-researcher collaboration. In S. Hudelson & J. Lindfors (Eds.), *Working together: Collaborative research in language education.* Urbana, IL: National Council of Teachers of English.

Peyton, J. K., & Michaelson, S. (1987). *The ENFI Project at Gallaudet University: Focus on teacher approaches and reactions.* Unpublished manuscript, Gallaudet University, Washington, DC.

Sirc, G. (1988). Learning to write on a LAN. *T.H.E. Journal, 15*(8), 100–104.

Thompson, D. P. (1987). Teaching on a local area network. *T.H.E. Journal, 15*(2), 92–97.

Thompson, D. P. (1988). Interactive networking: Creating bridges between speech, writing, and composition. *Computers and Composition, 5*(3), 2–27.

Index